THE SCHOOL LIBRARIAN'S SOURCEBOOK

The
School Librarian's
Sourcebook™

CLAIRE RUDIN

R. R. BOWKER
New York

Published by R. R. Bowker Company
a division of Reed Publishing (USA) Inc.
Copyright © 1990 by Reed Publishing (USA) Inc.
All rights reserved
Printed and bound in the United States of America

Library of Congress Cataloging-in-Publication Data
Rudin, Claire, 1929–
The school librarian's sourcebook / Claire Rudin.
p.   cm.
Includes bibliographical references.
ISBN 0-8352-2711-1
1. School libraries—Bibliography.   2. Media programs (Education)—
Bibliography.   I. Title.
Z675.S3R79   1990
016.0278'223—dc20   89-25274
                                                              CIP

ISBN 0-8352-2711-1

9 780835 227117

For Leo Rudin, encouraging husband, faithful friend,
who makes all adventures joyful

For Eliza and Rachel, our joy and pride and future

For those school library media specialists whose
dedication to their profession remains constant through
adversity and good fortune alike, and brings
enrichment to young people's lives

Contents

CONTENTS

Preface

When the twin technologies for preserving knowledge and information, papyrus scrolls and the alphabet, were transported to ancient Greece from the Middle East, Plato and his contemporary philosophers were alarmed. What would happen to the human faculty of memory when it fell into disuse as written words displaced it? How could the fragile papyrus be depended on as the repository of human thought and memory? They need not have worried, as human ingenuity invented first the book, and then the library, and librarians emerged as the guardians of the books.

Now the library's mission has been changed by time and technology. Knowledge and the information that precedes and inspires it is no longer confined to books chained to tables. Civilization's memory has expanded beyond the printed page and technology has provided bits and bytes and disks and tapes for holding it. The librarian's function has changed from guardian of the written word to facilitator of its dissemination, to make information as accessible as possible in whatever form it is stored.

The mission of school librarians is to help children learn how to access and use that information. Their goal is to awaken a spirit of inquiry in the young people they work with and to foster an ability to learn independently, which will remain with them throughout their lives. To that end, school library media specialists study selection guides, search data bases, plan instruction, and consult with teachers. Yet these very librarians, who endeavor to foster the pursuit of lifelong learning in others, have lacked a convenient guide to further their own independent learning. This book was conceived as a means of filling that void.

That the gatekeepers of information need to keep themselves

informed about the new developments that impinge on their professional lives should go without saying. On the brink of the final decade of the twentieth century, changes and challenges in school librarianship continue to accelerate. Automation looms, to some as a promise, and to others, a threat. Literacy has declined while information proliferates. AIDS and drugs continue to destroy. New immigrants are changing the nature of our school populations. Programs for the disabled, mainstreaming, new emphases in curriculum, and a new vision of the school library media specialist's role in education all require a reassessment of their mission and, therefore, of school library media programs and services.

As managers and dispensers of information, librarians understand its importance as the foundation of policy and the root of decision. The purpose of this book is to provide current sources of information, of knowledge, and of controversy as well, to help librarians as they shape policies, programs, and services, and make the daily decisions that determine how effective the school media program will be. Relying on the nearest professional journal article for information, or the textbooks saved from graduate library school courses, or a colleague in a nearby school library, will not always provide the needed answers.

Because school library media specialists function not only as librarians, but also as teachers, they require a knowledge of the craft and the philosophy of both worlds. In addition to knowing how to automate library media centers and develop collections, school librarians need to know about special education programs and planning and implementing curriculum, particularly in areas of current concern in education. This book will guide users to the information sources they need about these and other topics.

In *Information Power* (ALA, 1988) the challenges to school library media specialists in a changing world are laid down and the goals that must be achieved in order to fulfill their mission are described. The challenge: to assume leadership in planning for the utilization of information in the education of children and young adults. Among the goals: to provide physical and intellectual access to information, to act as consultants and instructional leaders in the use of information and technology, and to maintain the library as the information center of the school. Accomplishing these goals requires planning and leadership, and success in these areas is based on knowledge of current professional trends.

Written for school library media specialists who are ready to take charge of their own learning, this book will also serve many of the information needs of public and academic librarians, as well as students preparing for library careers. *The School Librarian's Sourcebook* consists of five parts, each of which is further subdivided. The first part, The School Library Enterprise, presents books about managing the school library media center. "Enterprise" is a term that was deliberately chosen to emphasize the analogy to business management so frequently found in the current literature. Chapter 1 includes general works about library management, while the next four chapters are concerned with specific management functions: technical services, facilities design, publicity and public relations, and evaluation.

The second part, The School Library Media Collection, focuses on that all-important phase of library work—building and maintaining the collection. Books about collection management are discussed in Chapter 6, the selection and development of nonbook materials are the subject of Chapter 7, and book selection tools are covered in Chapter 8.

The third part centers on services to students. Serving student needs includes such topics as library media programs and activities (Chapter 9), and reference services and materials (Chapter 10), which also includes books on on-line searching. Despite the inroads on the school media specialist's time and attention made by technology and other functions, fostering reading and a love of literature is still a major focus of library service in schools. Chapter 11, "Reading Guidance and Motivation," reflects that emphasis by its sheer size and the variety of its offerings. It is divided into five sections: general works, children's literature, young adult literature, storytelling, and booktalking. Chapter 12 includes books that inform about various disabilities and library services to disabled learners, and also presents books about gifted learners and some curriculum and library programs that serve their needs.

The fourth part is devoted to educating the library user. Chapter 13 explores the library media center's curriculum support role, Chapter 14 examines teaching library and information skills, and Chapter 15 considers the principles of curriculum development.

The final part focuses on the current issues and concerns of librarianship and education not fully covered in earlier chapters. These include technology and automation and its various uses (Chapter 16), and concludes with Chapter 17, devoted to such issues as censorship, copyright, education reform, and various current problems in education.

Individual entries include a description of the book's purpose, a summary of its contents, information about the author(s) or editor(s), and a final comment. Authority statements are based largely on information found in the book itself or publishers' catalogs, and reflect the author(s) status at the time of publication. Where this information was not available reference sources were searched. In spite of every effort to track down some facts about every author and editor, there were some whose background simply could not be found and an authority statement was omitted for those entries. Also, where International Standard Book Numbers (ISBNs) are lacking, this was because they could not be located. While the comments vary in enthusiasm, all of the books included here are recommended for use, and those books that are not recommended, or that duplicated coverage in the books that are included, were omitted.

This book was not designed as a comprehensive bibliography, but rather as a compendium of sources that school librarians could refer to for the best titles to fill their information needs. An effort was made to mix some time-tested titles that have become standards in the field with publications of the most recent vintage. The reader will find added references in almost every book that has been cited here, and books with particularly good bibliographies are noted in the comments. Books that are outdated in some respects are included because they fill a void that has not been filled by a more recent publication. Many Bowker titles have been included because they remain unique and useful, in spite of the older dates of some of them.

Among the types of books that were omitted are familiar, comprehensive bibliographic tools such as *Books in Print;* indexes to poetry, plays, and the like; and cataloging tools such as Dewey and Sears. Since these are basic to many introductory library science courses it seemed superfluous to include them here.

Arranging the entries in chapters according to their subject is a challenging exercise in classification. The effort of finding the one right place for each entry has been eased by the use of cross-references in each chapter in which an entry might have been placed, but was not. Author, title, and subject indexes can also be used to locate particular titles. To extend the usefulness of this book without adding greatly to its size some briefly annotated Additional Readings are found at the end of selected chapters, and Chapter 16, "Technology and Automation," provides directories of selected on-line data base vendors and producers of library automation products. A list of professional periodicals and a directory of the publishers whose books are represented in *The School Librarian's Sourcebook* precede the indexes.

ACKNOWLEDGMENTS

The completion of this book was helped by a number of people, and my gratitude to them is boundless. Family, friends, and colleagues saw me through trying times with encouragement, support, and understanding, and a never failing confidence that the end of the journey was in sight, and the trip worth taking.

Some very special New York City school librarians took time from their busy after-school lives to provide information, advice, and title suggestions. They were never too busy to answer a question and responded to calls for help in countless ways. They are, alphabetically: Priscilla Balch, Midwood High School; Suzanne Burach, Edward R. Murrow High School; Naomi Feller, Seward Park High School; Susan Hess, Juan Morel Campos Intermediate School; Susan Rosenblum, Port Richmond High School; Sara Sloan, Maggie L. Walker Intermediate School; Eileen Weinstein, formerly of Roy H. Mann Intermediate School and now a valued colleague at the New York City School Library System; and Carolyn Weiss, High School of Telecommunication Arts and Technology.

Eileen Rogot, Bay Terrace branch librarian, kept me supplied with books through the Queens Borough Public Library's interlibrary loan system. The libraries at Queens College, St. John's University, and C. W. Post Center of Long Island University all provided access to their graduate library school collections. Professor David Cohen of the Queens College Library and Information Science faculty graciously advised about and shared the resources of the Ethnic Materials Information Exchange (EMIE) at the college, which is under his direction.

Publishers of books for and about library service responded graciously and generously to requests for review copies of their books. I am grateful to ALA Publications, ABC-CLIO, Ablex, R. R. Bowker, Libraries Unlimited, Library Professional Publications, McFarland, Neal-Schuman, Oryx, Prentice-Hall, and Scarecrow for their unstinting cooperation.

My thanks are also due to Marion Sader, Publisher, whose encouragement saw me through the earliest stages of this book's preparation. Her vision of what the book should be carried me beyond what I thought possible.

Final and exuberant gratitude belongs to Iris Topel, avowed perfectionist and most competent editor, who saw me through the final stages of authorship, with patience, unfailing good humor, and expertise.

CLAIRE RUDIN
New York City School Library System
School Library Services Unit
New York City Board of Education

The School Library Enterprise

1
Library Management

Efficient management of the school library media center and its programs and services is the first essential in effective school librarianship. Twenty years ago the introduction of nonprint media in school libraries heralded a major change in the services they offered. School librarians became school library media specialists, and it was not only the name that changed, as the evaluation and use of audiovisual materials became an everyday part of the job.

Today it is the microcomputer that is causing a reexamination of the media center's function in the school and a reevaluation of how the media center can best meet the needs of the community it serves. While some see it as just another audiovisual aid, and others as an administrative tool, still others consider it a revolutionary force to be reckoned with in the education of young people. Varying degrees of emphasis on this technology are to be found in the literature on library management, often depending on when the publication was written.

Included in this chapter are general introductions to school media center management and some provocative looks at political realities. Case studies, such as those offered by Mary Biagini in *A Model for Problem Solving and Decision Making* and Daniel Callison and Jacqueline Morris in *Case Studies in Managing School Library Media Centers,* help unearth the political realities of media center management. William Schmid offers some sound political advice in *Media Center Management: A Practical Guide,* and Eleanor Kulleseid offers a survival tool and some lessons on empowerment in *Beyond Survival to Power for School Library Media Professionals.* Addressing inadequate funding for school media programs, Emmett Corry provides direction in the pursuit of grants in his *Grants for Libraries.* Other helpful sources for the library manager are found in Ruth Toor and Hilda Weisburg's book of library forms. Lois Kershner carries the process one step further by producing forms for managing automated libraries, and May Ho teaches the use of AppleWorks in library management.

"Management" itself is a term that has only recently been applied to what librarians do to keep things going smoothly, and it is derived from a businesslike approach to running a library. Management theory is used by Blanche Woolls and Emanuel and Joyce Prostano to provide a structure for efficient functioning—all of which is why this part has been entitled "The School Library Enterprise." Whereas this first chapter focuses on management in general, the succeeding ones in this part deal with such particular aspects of management as technical services, standards and facilities, publicity and public relations, and evaluating the school library media program. A supplementary list of briefly annotated sources appears at the end of this chapter.

Adams, Helen R. *School Media Policy Development: A Practical Process for Small Districts.* **Libraries Unlimited, 1986. 174 pp. ISBN 0-87287-450-8.**

PURPOSE

This handbook describes the process of policy development, implementation, and revision for school library media specialists and district supervisors.

CONTENTS

A rationale for developing policies is provided in the first chapter, which also details the advantages of having them. Principles of policy development and an overview of the process are presented in the second chapter, and succeeding chapters flesh out the preliminary synopsis. Determining what the policy should be and writing it are just part of policy development, and political considerations are discussed as well.

A step-by-step prescription for accomplishing the process is covered in the next five chapters, which include information on how to prepare a draft statement; how to work effectively with consultants; steps in involving the school staff, students, and parents; obtaining the support of school and district administrators; and securing the cooperation of the board of education. Effective implementation of policies, a case study based on the author's own school and district, and strategies for coping with a determined lack of support from the board of education and administrators are the subjects of the concluding chapters.

4

Sample policy statements are provided in an appendix; they include access to the school media center, guidelines for dealing with copyright issues, sharing of resources and interlibrary loan, providing for the security of audiovisual equipment, and selection policy and reconsideration procedures. Job descriptions and evaluation procedures and methods for evaluation of the district school media director, school media specialist, audiovisual director, and media center aide are also provided. Directories of state school library media agencies, national and state media associations, and school board associations round out the handbook.

AUTHORITY

The author is district librarian/audiovisual director for Rosholt Public Schools, Wisconsin.

COMMENT

Often school library media specialists who understand the need for a policy or policies related to their responsibilities plunge right into the preparation process, overlooking the political context in which educational systems function, however large or small they may be. This book will guide the user through the practical realities of the total process, from initial planning to final adoption and implementation.

American Association of School Librarians and Association for Educational Communications and Technology. *Information Power: Guidelines for School Library Media Programs.* SEE Chapter 5, Evaluating the School Library Media Program.

Asp, William G., et al. *Continuing Education for the Library Information Professions.* **Library Professional, 1985. 348 pp. ISBN 0-208-01897-2.**

PURPOSE

Continuing education is a necessity in every professional enterprise, if standards of quality in the services provided are to be maintained. This need, however, also requires the establishment of standards of excellence in the delivery of continuing education programs themselves. This book explores the continuing education needs of the library profession and how they are to be met.

CONTENTS

School library media specialists have, perhaps, a larger stake and a wider scope to deal with than other library professionals in their search for opportunities to pursue continuing education. Their professional concerns involve not only staying abreast of library developments and practices but those in education as well. This book is concerned primarily with library education, but it is not simply a list of places or programs that provide opportunities for extending knowledge. Rather, each of its four sections considers a different aspect of the subject.

After an examination of early thought and practice in providing continuing education, Asp and his coauthors explore, in Section I, the mission and goals of continuing education on the current national scene, noting the gaps that exist between available knowledge and its application on the job. They discuss the need for planning on a nationwide scale to reduce those gaps. Many terms have been used to describe different aspects of continuing education, and the authors describe and define them: lifelong learning, self-directed learning, continuing competence, technological obsolescence, professionalization, and, of course, continuing education itself. Problems of funding, development of criteria, and methods of evaluation and assessment are also discussed.

The responsibility for providing continuing education programs is recognized and shared by schools of library service, professional associations, governing agencies, and employing institutions, all of which exist on national, regional, state, and local levels. How each of these types of institutions meets this responsibility is explored, and the need for standards and coordination of efforts is established. Section II deals with library associations' efforts in continuing education, and Section III with those of state and regional agencies. Section III also includes a separate chapter on school library media personnel, both as providers of education for teachers, aides, and other members of the instructional team and as consumers of continuing education themselves. A combination of district, regional, and state professional associations and governing agencies is supposed to meet these continuing education needs, but success in doing so has been somewhat less than overwhelming. The authors provide suggestions for improving the outlook.

The text is supplemented with three appendixes: A provides outlines of five quality programs, B presents the ALISE (Association for Library and Information Science Education) Policy Statement on Continuing Library and Information Science Education, and C describes the interrelated roles of the Continuing Library Education Network and Exchange (CLENE), the National Commission on Libraries and Information Science (NCLIS), and the National Council on Quality Continuing Library and Information Science Education. A statement on "The Principles of Good Practice in Continuing Education" is also part of Appendix C. Notes, a bibliography, and an index conclude the book.

AUTHORITY

Asp and his four coauthors—Suzanne H. Mahmoodi, Marilyn L. Miller, Peggy O'Donnell, and Elizabeth W. Stone—combine experience in state library development, consulting in education and planning, and continuing education. William G. Asp is director of the Office of Library Development and Service, Minnesota Department of Education. Suzanne H. Mahmoodi specializes in continuing education at the Office of Library Development and Service of the Minnesota Department of Education. Marilyn L. Miller is an associate professor of library science at the University of North Carolina at Chapel Hill. Peggy O'Donnell is a consultant in education and planning for library agencies, schools, and associations. Elizabeth W. Stone, past president of ALA and founder of CLENE (Continuing Library Education Network and Exchange), is a well-known advocate of continuing education for librarians.

COMMENT

Continuing education is a common interest of all library professionals and certainly of school library media specialists. Concerned with the state of the art, this book offers guidelines for providers rather than practical assistance on what is available and where to turn for programs that meet specific needs. In raising issues and establishing criteria, however, it supplies the foundation for program development and assessment and provides an important perspective on problems and opportunities.

Aversa, Elizabeth S., and Jacqueline C. Mancall. *Management of Online Search Services in Schools.* SEE Chapter 16, Technology and Automation.

Biagini, Mary K. *A Model for Problem Solving and Decision Making: Managing School Library Media Programs.* **Libraries Unlimited, 1988. 164 pp. ISBN 0-87287-589-X.**

PURPOSE

The author has created practice and role-playing exercises for developing skills in solving problems and making decisions, important to acquiring expertise in management. The book is appropriate for use in preservice and in-service courses and workshops offered to students and practicing librarians alike.

CONTENTS

The library media specialists in the schools of Trent, an imaginary suburban town somewhere in America, are in for a bumpy year. Budget problems are causing district administrators to take a close look at school programs, and the library media specialists will have to justify their programs' continuing existence. How can they demonstrate their programs' relevance to the instructional programs in the Trent schools? This is the central theme, as users of this book will go through all the ensuing problems and make decisions that will determine the fate of the school library media centers and their programs. Along the way, they will become efficient and effective media center managers.

Part I describes the town in detail, with particular attention to the Trent Public Library, and provides equally detailed information about its schools, their central administrative structure, and their library media centers and staffs. Each school is profiled individually, as are the school media centers.

Twenty-seven case studies are presented in seven sections in Part II, each section dealing with an issue in school library media center management. These include planning and evaluation, defining and communicating the center's mission, working with teachers, providing services to students, collection building and evaluation, gaining support from the community, and evaluating the performance of school library media specialists. Each case presents a new situation, a scenario, and some probing questions for participants to wrestle with, either alone or in group situations.

Part III presents an additional 27 cases, designed to provide experience in solving problems, making decisions, and assessing and dealing with political issues. Each case has three parts, a problem requiring an analysis or a product of some kind, a simulation that arises out of the problem, and some questions for the supervisor (an imagined district coordinator of the school media centers) to deal with. Many of these simulations are based on events and situations described in Part II. Participants/readers identify with the characters, gain insight into the situations through role playing, and practice problem solving.

Appendixes provide information to supplement the beginning descriptions and data. Documents, statistics, goal statements, biographies of the cast of characters, and so on are included here. In addition, indexes of cases and character names are provided.

After all their travails, Trent's library media specialists cope with the school year's most pressing problem, burn-out, discussed in the final case study. The solutions may be less effective than a well-deserved summer vacation and the satisfaction derived from their newly acquired management skills.

AUTHORITY

Biagini is an associate professor in the department of library science at the University of Pittsburgh, with added experience in providing continuing education programs for practicing school librarians.

COMMENT

Workshop leaders and other providers of staff development and continuing education programs will find plenty here for many productive sessions. School library media specialists can use the contents as a workbook for examining and working through problems that reflect their own situations, either alone or in peer groups.

Callison, Daniel, and Jacqueline Morris. *Case Studies in Managing School Library Media Centers.* **Oryx, 1989. 194 pp. ISBN 0-89774-441-1 (pap.).**

PURPOSE

This publication presents library school students and library media center managers practice and guidance in solving simulated library management problems.

CONTENTS

Based on their experience that previously published case studies have been outdated by the passage of time and the arrival of new problems, Callison and Morris have culled these case studies from suggestions offered in their library management courses. The selected cases have been validated by working school library media specialists, and possible responses were gathered from the field.

In the introduction, the authors describe new developments in school library media management, stressing the emphasis on interactive management and media program integration with school curriculum and mentioning some of the writers whose work described and influenced these trends. Many of the case studies reinforce these concepts.

The cases are grouped in three sections. The first section deals with people problems, that is, human relations and personnel management issues. Among the problems are typical evaluation methods used by a principal, a censorship attempt by a volunteer helper

9

in the library, use of the library media specialist to provide planning periods for teachers, and scheduling of a Bible study group in the library outside of school hours. The second section is concerned with resource management and access to information. Among the cases considered are copyright issues, a principal's decision against weeding outdated material, ill-conceived purchasing procedures for software, censorship as part of the selection process, and a student aide's injury when moving equipment. Budgeting and facilities management are discussed in the third section. Among the topics considered are the need for statistics, how a facility plan went awry, selling the concept of interlibrary loans, and aiding the disabled.

Each case study in the book includes a description of the situation, some questions that point to possible solutions, responses from the field, and a brief annotated bibliography of sources dealing with aspects of the problem. A detailed index concludes the book.

AUTHORITY
Callison is assistant professor and associate dean of the School of Library and Information Science, Indiana University, Bloomington, and has served as director for media programs at Topeka High School in Kansas. Morris is manager of the Learning Resources Unit, Indiana Department of Education, and has been a building level school library media specialist in Georgia, North Carolina, and Indiana. She served (1988–1989) as president of the American Association of School Librarians. Contributors of responses include library media specialists and district directors, library educators, state department consultants, and graduate students.

COMMENT
There is no denying the applicability of these case studies to situations that occur frequently in the professional lives of school library media specialists. Some represent dilemmas that defy resolution, and the responses reflect that. Sample policies, guidelines, and other helpful materials are provided along with the responses, and the citations in the bibliographies invite further research. This is a highly recommended approach to problem solving in school library media centers.

Caputo, Janette S. *The Assertive Librarian.* Oryx, 1984. 256 pp. ISBN 0-89774-085-8 (pap.).

PURPOSE
Librarians and other library employees seeking to develop patterns of assertive behavior will find guidance in this handbook. It pro-

vides a practical approach to behavioral change and emphasizes the greater effectiveness of assertive behavior over other ways of handling problem situations.

CONTENTS

Assertiveness and a positive self-image are the keys to the satisfactory resolution of conflict situations, according to Caputo, and she sets about demonstrating her point in a variety of ways. She uses charts to compare characteristics of different behavior types and dialogues to illustrate possible reactions to confrontational situations. She also examines the risks involved in being assertive. The stereotype of the nonassertive librarian is analyzed and found to have some basis in actual behavior.

An introductory chapter provides some background on behavior management and notes that electing assertiveness over other types of behavior is a matter of conscious choice. Assertive behavior is defined and distinguished from other forms, such as nonassertive and aggressive behavior.

Assertive behavior is a way of protecting one's rights in interaction with others, but it also includes responsibility for other people's rights as well. These rights and their relevance in library situations are described in the second chapter. Setting goals for establishing assertive behavior is the subject of Chapter 3. Inventories and charts are provided for determining one's current level of assertiveness and "discomfort," as a means of deciding what goals to begin with.

Having established a foundation for initiating behavioral changes, the author then demonstrates how the desired changes may be instituted. Some principles of psychology and techniques of exploring human interaction are discussed. Exercises are presented for determining one's level of self-esteem and methods identified for increasing it. The elements of verbal and nonverbal assertion are examined and techniques and practice exercises offered. Assertive statements are analyzed and examples provided of various types. Games, traps, and pitfalls are described, and the importance of listening is emphasized. Since facial expression, gesture, posture, voice, and other nonverbal cues can support or conflict with what one says, a chart is employed to indicate how to use body language that is congruent with verbal behavior. Irrational beliefs and fears often interfere with the attainment of assertive behavior, and the reader is advised how to build and substitute a more rational belief structure. The stress that results from feelings of guilt, anger, and other emotions can be relieved by learning how to deal with criticism and avoid guilt feelings. Techniques and coping mechanisms, including deep breathing and other relaxation methods, are provided in Chapter 8.

In the final two chapters the author demonstrates how the application of assertiveness skills can increase effectiveness and improve interpersonal relations, and brings the reader back to the importance of both asserting one's own rights and recognizing the rights of others. A model for developing skills in assertive behavior is presented and the need for continuing practice and self-analysis described. An appended response key to the assertiveness inventory, a bibliography, and an index complete the work.

AUTHORITY
The author characterizes herself as an assertive librarian, and has led assertiveness workshops for librarians.

COMMENT
Successful leaders rarely lack assertive skills, and school library media specialists who feel the need to learn how to be more assertive will find this author to be a willing guide. Assertiveness occupies a middle zone between passivity and aggression, and rests on improved communication as well as a healthy dose of self-esteem. When practiced with respect for the rights of others as well as one's own rights, it can eliminate the harmful effects of bottled up or boiling up anger. This book not only develops an awareness of what constitutes appropriate assertive behavior but provides practical help in attaining it as well.

Corry, Emmett, O.S.F. *Grants for Libraries: A Guide to Public and Private Funding Programs and Proposal Writing Techniques,* **2nd ed. Libraries Unlimited, 1986. 341 pp. ISBN 0-872-534-2.**

PURPOSE
Lack of funds has sunk many a library program. Librarians and district directors who wish to seek financial support outside the school district or school will find practical assistance in this book.

CONTENTS
Having witnessed the decline of elementary school library services in the New York City public schools, Brother Corry begins with a study of the impact of revisions of education legislation on urban schools. The Education Consolidation and Improvement Act of 1981 (ECIA), Chapter 2, not only eliminated categorical funding for libraries but also shifted its funding priorities from urban to rural schools. Assistance for desegregation also decreased, causing cities to use ECIA monies to advance their desegregation plans. As a

result, maintaining library standards became a matter of local effort in many urban school systems, where other priorities intervened, including massive purchasing of microcomputers.

Other federal funding sources do remain, however, and although not directly aimed at school libraries, they might be tapped for projects that demonstrably require library support. Among such sources are those that support bilingual education, Indian education, the National Diffusion Network, law-related education, and Excellence in Education. Information on such sources can be obtained from the *Catalog of Federal Domestic Assistance*, which the author calls the grant seekers' bible.

The importance of citizens' groups who come to the aid of library programs was demonstrated in New York City by the wide publicity given to the city's failure to support its school libraries. After the Education Priorities Panel, a coalition of influential New Yorkers, issued a report deploring the condition of the city's elementary school libraries, the City Council and the state legislature provided supplementary funding for building library collections in the city's schools. The author uses this instance to urge librarians to develop joint lobbying efforts with citizens' groups to secure adequate financial support and suggests ways to accomplish this.

Private foundations are another important source of funds, and several chapters are devoted to effective methods of securing their financial assistance. Lists of foundations are provided in chapters that consider funding sources, both governmental and private, for all types of libraries. Determining eligibility is an important step in the process, and the author is firm in his insistence that libraries should refrain from applying for funds indiscriminately. The Foundation Center and its regional and cooperating libraries offer essential sources and services for identifying potential funding sources among private foundations and for preparing proposals. The author provides a list of libraries in the Foundation Center network, explains how to use its publications, and shows how to write an effective grant proposal.

A number of appendixes provide helpful supplementary information for fund-raisers, including, among others, lists of state supervisors of school library media services and coordinators of ECIA, Chapter 2; a list of potential federal support sources for school library media programs; programs for academic and public library support; and a directory of state councils on the humanities. A bibliography and an index complete the book.

AUTHORITY

The author, a member of the Franciscan Order, is an associate pro-fessor and dean of the School of Library and Information Science at St. John's University, New York. He has written and spoken about grantsmanship in many library settings.

COMMENT

The damage done to library programs in urban centers by the with-drawal of federal categorical support and simultaneous shifting of available monies to rural areas is clearly depicted here. Its efforts to help librarians substitute other available funding sources will pro-vide effective assistance to those seeking to finance special projects.

Davies, Ruth Ann. *The School Library Media Program: Instructional Force for Excellence,* **3rd ed.** SEE Chapter 13, The Library Media Center and the Curriculum.

Gillespie, John T., and Diana L. Spirt. *Administering the School Library Media Center.* **Bowker, 1983. 381 pp. ISBN 0-8352-1514-8.**

PURPOSE

This comprehensive guide to school media center management is directed at students in preservice courses, librarians just entering the profession, and practicing librarians who wish to revitalize their professional skills.

CONTENTS

From the introductory chapter on the history of school library devel-opment to the concluding discussion of major library associations and agencies, Gillespie and Spirt focus on the individual school library media center, placing it in the wider context of the evolution of the profession and the current state of its support systems. They guide the reader through the basics of school library media center management, including the functions of school media centers in terms of user activities and resources; the school library media cen-ter program and its components, developing policies, publicity and public relations activities, and evaluating its services and effective-ness; budgeting procedures and systems; staffing patterns, job de-scriptions, recruitment, selection, and supervision; and facilities planning, space, and furnishings.

After describing the human and physical resources that support the school library media program, the authors turn to the intellectual contents of the center, that is, the print, nonprint, and software materials that constitute the collection and the equipment necessary for their use and retrieval.

Gillespie and Spirt outline and describe media selection policies, procedures, and criteria and list selection aids for print and nonprint media and equipment. They emphasize the importance of preparing a selection policy statement, and suggest steps in composing one. Problems and policies regarding censorship also receive careful attention. The nuts and bolts of media center management—acquisition and organization of media, circulation, inventory and weeding, collection maintenance and processing, records and reports—are also covered in thorough detail.

Final chapters deal with computer technology, providing a prescient look at the future, and offer an introduction to the concepts of networks and networking.

Each chapter concludes with a generous bibliography for further study, and an index is also provided. The appendixes provide directories of library associations and agencies, including names and addresses of chief officers, and a directory of library furniture and supply houses. The texts of key library documents—The Library Bill of Rights, ALA and AECT codes of ethics, and the ALA Freedom to Read Statement—end the book.

AUTHORITY
The authors have written, both together and separately, many books for school librarians. Both have been on the faculty of the C. W. Post graduate program in library and information science for a number of years.

COMMENT
Managing a school library media center is a complex task, and describing how to do it requires careful organization and attention to detail. The authors have done just that, presenting a sound foundation of knowledge for the successful administration of a school media center. A second copy should be in the hands of every school principal.

Hart, Thomas L., ed. *Behavior Management in the School Library Media Center.* **ALA, 1985. 166 pp. ISBN 0-8389-0429-7 (pap.).**

PURPOSE

Positive solutions are provided to problems in behavior that arise in school media centers. Whatever their school level, whatever their experience level, library media specialists will find ways here to improve the quality of life in their media centers.

CONTENTS

Although school librarians prefer a warm and comfortable atmosphere in the media center, some unique qualities of such an environment are an invitation to discipline problems. Children seated around tables act differently from children seated at individual desks. Freestanding bookstacks and separately enclosed areas are a barrier to visual control. A class of children using various sources for research at the same time is different from the same group working at a single task in the classroom.

Effective answers to these problems are offered by the authors of this collection of articles, whose manner of solving them rests on the application of behavioral modification techniques. Those who are disinclined to accept such an approach might want to give some thought to what teaching is all about. When school library media specialists give a booktalk, is it not to modify children's reading behavior? When they teach children how to research a topic, is it not to modify their behavior so that they will seek and use information independently? When they establish fines for not returning books on time, is that not a behavior modification technique?

The point made so frequently, in both the general, introductory articles about behavior modification and in the articles specific to the library media center, is that rewarding the child who exhibits desired behavior is far more effective than punishing the child who does not. Ways of putting this precept into action are the subjects of the articles. Most of them suggest strategies that help build students' self-esteem and many rely on peer reinforcement. Adult modeling of the desired behavior is another approach, though not startlingly innovative. Although the suggestions are applied to particular school levels, many are relevant, with some modifications, to older or younger groups than those for which they have been proposed.

For further reading, a bibliography is provided, and some nonprint materials are also suggested.

AUTHORITY

Thomas L. Hart is a professor at the School of Library and Information Studies, Florida State University, and the contributors are experienced school library media specialists, educators, and psychologists.

COMMENT
The use of behavior modification techniques has raised cries of
alarm among humanists, and librarianship is a notably humane profession. As used in this collection, the term simply describes some
systematic ways of encouraging the repetition of desirable behavior
in school libraries by providing suitable rewards. The applications
described offer, for the most part, positive approaches to common
problems, and the book is therefore recommended.

Ho, May Lein. *AppleWorks for School Librarians.* **Hi Willow
Research, 1985. 129 pp. ISBN 0-931510-17-1 (pap.).**

PURPOSE
This introduction to the use of AppleWorks, an integrated program
that combines applications for spreadsheet, data base management,
and word processing, will prepare any librarian for the accomplishment of management tasks that utilize Apple capabilities.

CONTENTS
Beginning in Section 1 with instructions for booting (starting up)
the computer, Ho takes her readers on a step-by-step tour of Apple
applications to library management tasks. Each command is explained and practice exercises ensure against error, thus providing
the user with a thorough familiarity with Apple computers and
AppleWorks. A disk with additional lessons and templates for specific library applications of the program accompanies the book.

Instructions for using the word processor are provided in Section
2, which also offers detailed instructions for each operation and
explains how to use the printer. Creating, manipulating, and printing data bases are the subject of Section 3, which also explains how
to use Boolean search procedures for locating specific information
in the data base file. Section 4 provides instructions for using the
spreadsheet application of AppleWorks, and discusses planning the
spreadsheet, creating a budget template, and following the other
steps that are involved.

"Cutting and pasting" allows the user to move data and files from
one application to another and within applications, the subject of
Section 5. A chart of possible applications of AppleWorks to library
management functions is presented in Section 6. Some 140 are
listed, along with the software function used to produce it (data
base, spreadsheet, or word processor) and its use in library management. Collection and curriculum mapping are introduced in Sections 6 and 7, and an index completes the book.

17

Each chapter begins with instructions for getting started, and concludes with a summary of the commands used and several exercises for practicing what has been learned. Examples of sample products resulting from the combination of AppleWorks with the template disks are printed with the relevant instructions, and a list of files on the template disk can be found with the introductory material.

For more information on collection mapping and curriculum mapping, see the comments on David Loertscher and May Lein Ho's *Computerized Collection Development for School Library Media Centers* and Michael Eisenberg and Robert Berkowitz's *Curriculum Initiative*, both in Chapter 13, "The Library Media Center and the Curriculum."

AUTHORITY

May Lein Ho is director of the Learning Resource Center at the University of Arkansas, Fayetteville.

COMMENT

There is no doubt that the combination of the ease of use built into the Apple computer, with the applicability of AppleWorks for library management tasks, and the easy-to-follow instructions presented in this book and its accompanying templates, will enable school librarians to improve their management efficiency.

Intner, Sheila S., and Jane Ann Hannigan, eds. *The Library Microcomputer Environment: Management Issues.* SEE Chapter 7, Nonprint Media and Computer Software.

Katz, Bill, ed. *The How-to-Do-It Manual for Small Libraries.* **Neal-Schuman, 1988. 387 pp. ISBN 1-55570-016-0 (pap.).**

PURPOSE

Written for librarians in all types of small libraries, some of whom responded to an informal poll and questionnaires about what should be included, this book provides articles about those aspects of library management librarians preferred to read about.

CONTENTS

The 35 chapters in this book are divided into five sections, each of which covers a major aspect of librarians' professional responsibilities. Although the focus is largely on public libraries, most of the material applies to other types of libraries as well. The contributions were written specifically for this book, largely by librarians in small libraries, rather than assembled from those published in professional journals.

Section 1 introduces a general overview of life and its problems and rewards in each of five specific settings from librarians who work in them. Included are a public library, a school library, four- and two-year college libraries, and a special library. For library school students and practicing librarians considering a change, these snapshots of the scene may help them decide what to do next.

Section 2 discusses some of the problems of small library management and suggests practical solutions. Among the problems identified in the first article are professional isolation, inadequate budgets for salaries, collection, and training opportunities, and lack of guidance and supervison. Workable solutions are proposed. Other chapters in this section discuss personnel policies and practices and provide sample evaluation forms; the budgeting process and accounting; physical facilities standards, policies, and maintenance; library boards and managers and how to work with them effectively; planning and its implementation; manuals of procedures and how to create them; and standards and evaluation.

Collection development and maintenance are the subjects of Section 3, which includes articles about censorship, principles of collection development and selection tools, donations, vertical file maintenance, nonprint materials, weeding, cataloging and use of bibliographic utilities, and circulation policies and procedures.

Public services are what libraries exist for, and Section 4 covers services to different age groups and various types of service, including readers' advisory, reference, and instruction. Such allied subjects as promotion, user and community studies, and friends of the library are considered as well. Friends groups can be a blessing or otherwise, and school librarians who are entertaining the idea of developing such a group might want to read this material beforehand.

The final section offers an introduction to automation and microcomputer technology by an author somewhat less committed to its adoption than many other writers. His commendably cautious approach gives way, finally, to a modest enthusiasm, but with warnings about the inevitable workings of Murphy's law. A second article deals with laser technology with considerably more enthusiasm, and in its few pages presents a good deal of information about compact disks, videodisks, CD-ROM, and the like. Both of these articles include resources that will be of interest and use to the reader.

Several of the chapters provide reference sources and footnotes. Bibliographies and an index complete the book.

The articles are written primarily by librarians and directors of small public, school, and other libraries. The editor is known for his prolific output, particularly in the areas of reference services and magazines for libraries.

COMMENT
The aura of warmth and friendliness that one expects to find in small libraries has been captured in this informative book. The feelings of isolation that beset school librarians in their one-person media centers are shared by their public library counterparts, and other problems cross type-of-library boundaries as well. While school media specialists in need of specific information about their own domain will prefer to have books about school media center management at hand, this book is also a likable companion.

Kershner, Lois M. *Forms for Automated Library Systems: An Illustrated Guide for Selection, Design & Use.* **Neal-Schuman, 1988. 307 pp. ISBN 1-55570-026-8 (loose-leaf with binder).**

PURPOSE
The forms used in manual library systems are no longer applicable in those libraries that have converted to automated systems. This collection of hundreds of forms offers the day-to-day work tools for automated libraries that are a necessary part of library management.

CONTENTS
The forms have been divided into nine categories and a section is devoted to each; comments on the procedures and the workflow that the forms are designed to assist accompany them. In some cases more than one sample form for a particular purpose is presented, providing a basis for comparison and permitting selection of the one most appropriate.

Among the forms provided for the first topic, acquisition control, are purchase orders, a patron request form, and a form to enclose with orders for vendor cancellations. Bibliographic data base maintenance and conversion, Section 2, provides worksheets for cataloging, bar-coding, correcting the data base, and adding or deleting items. Forms relating to patrons are provided in Section 3, which includes a wide variety of application forms and sample library cards, as well as a form for teachers requesting public library support.

For circulation control, in Section 4, are date due slips, manual transaction forms, payment and refund slips, requests for payments, bills, and others. Patron forms, in Section 5, include reserve request forms, interlibrary loan requests, and the like. On-line searching is substantially assisted with the use of the forms in Section 6. Boolean searching is explained, and samples of searches are provided. Some of the forms lend themselves to use by high school students (others can be adapted for their use) and will help patrons and librarians define and plan projected searches. To assist public use of microcomputers, Section 7 provides forms for in-house use or borrowing. Among the forms for automated system operations in Section 8 are logs for recording activities, downtime, tape backups, and job requests. Report forms for administration and management, in Section 9, include records of bar coding, titles cataloged, and equipment maintenance. There are 31 forms in this section, including even certificates of achievement, one of which is owed to the helpful author, whose achievement in increasing the efficiency of automated libraries should not go unnoticed.

AUTHORITY

Kershner has been implementing automated systems in libraries for more than 20 years. Her work has included analysis, design, preparation, and management of systems, as well as planning and provision of training programs.

COMMENT

This informative guide is a useful addition to the collections of school library media centers that use computers for administrative tasks, reference, or instruction. School librarians who use computers for any library task will find forms that will simplify their work and enable them to discover other uses for their computers.

Kulleseid, Eleanor R. *Beyond Survival to Power for School Library Media Professionals.* **Library Professional, 1985. 173 pp. ISBN 0-208-02031-4.**

PURPOSE

Addressed to all school library media specialists, this book examines the political, economic, and social realities that affect not only the success but the continuing existence of library media centers in elementary schools. The means of developing and exercising power in their roles is explored through case studies of several school library professionals in the New York City public schools who have survived successfully in their professional roles.

THE SCHOOL LIBRARY ENTERPRISE

CONTENTS

In her 1982 doctoral study, Kulleseid investigated elementary school library programs in the New York City public schools to determine what enabled them to survive in a city where such programs lacked financial, political, and any other kind of support. This book, based on and extending that study, is concerned with the nature of power in the context of schools and school systems—that is, the kind of power that school library media specialists need to exert if their programs are not only to survive but to flourish. Its conclusions are applicable to school library programs at all school levels.

Power can be examined in many contexts. Nationally, school library programs were given financial power by Title II of the Elementary and Secondary Education Act (ESEA) of 1965. As this funding declined, so also did elementary school libraries, especially in New York City, where the level of financial support in many schools was reduced to zero when the city's 1974 financial crisis struck. According to Kulleseid, those programs that survived were able to do so because of the attitudes, behaviors, and competencies of their library media professionals.

The author suggests that those competencies that will permit survival include an understanding of the political structure of the school and its district, an ability and willingness to communicate with the formal and informal wielders of power, flexibility in dealing with authority and with change, and professional competency as a manager, a leader, and a teacher. The only power school library media specialists can exert, she suggests, is the informal one of personal and professional influence. To attain this influence, Kulleseid recommends principles of survival power and presents some checklists that provide further guidance. She points out that librarians who know themselves and their constituents and the setting in which they come together, and who can change and communicate their mission, strengthen their cause. The reader will find the author's elaborations of these principles a concrete summing up of the behaviors that constitute the ability not only to survive but to prevail.

The book concludes with notes, an index, and the following appendixes: a list of pedagogical competencies, a list of library media competencies, an activities checkoff list, and a professional communications profile.

AUTHORITY

Eleanor R. Kulleseid is director of the Learning Resource Center of the Bank Street College of Education, New York, and earned her doctorate at Columbia University.

22

COMMENT

Lack of power, the ability to influence the decisions and actions of others, has plagued the librarian professional in recent years. What can be done about the diminution of financial power caused by the demise of federal funding sources? How can school library media specialists exercise some control over their professional lives? How can they influence their colleagues and supervisors to view them in a more favorable light? Some thoughtful and provocative answers are provided in this text.

Lindsey, Jonathan A., ed. *Performance Evaluation: A Management Basic for Libraries.* SEE Chapter 5, Evaluating the School Library Media Program.

Loertscher, David V., ed. *School Library Media File.* **Libraries Unlimited, 1989. Unp. and unbound. ISBN 0-87287-685-3.**

PURPOSE

This collection of ideas, hints, suggestions, and resources presents an assortment of tips for the school media specialist's professional vertical file and use on the job.

CONTENTS

The first edition of a publication that has been promised on an annual basis, this product is not a book, but a package consisting of single or folded double sheets designed to be filed by subject in a vertical file or kept in a loose-leaf binder. The information sheets cover five main topics: Management, Collection Development, Curriculum, Public Relations, and Technology. The physical layout is well-designed, making for easy filing and finding: Reading across the right-hand margin is an indication of grade level range, the main subject and specific subject, and a blank line to enable users to enter an alternate subject heading. A brief introduction in a box across the top credits the presenter of the idea and summarizes the content.

Typical examples of the content found under Management are:

"Effectively Preparing for Questions about Materials in School Library Media Centers." A list of questions to help the school media specialist to determine his or her preparedness for possible censorship attempts.

"Unique Ways to Raise Funds." A list of suggested fund-raising events.

"Personal Opinion Survey." Questionnaires, one sample each for teachers and parents.

Examples under Technology include:

"The Novice User and CD-ROM Database Services." An ERIC Clearinghouse digest of information on CD-ROM, with bibliography.

"Equipment Inventory." A format for entering inventory records on a data base.

"Networking Update." Using local area networks (LANs) to connect computers and software; includes a bibliography.

Some examples under Collection Development follow:

"Elementary Periodical Survey." Frequency of use information on children's use of periodicals.

"Developing a Cooperative Collection Development Plan for School Libraries." A statement on various aspects of the subject; includes bibliography.

"Sample Selection Policy." A model for comparing, repairing, or preparing one.

Curriculum examples are:

"Primary Sources for Secondary Students." A lesson plan and sample assignment sheet.

"Creating a Travel Brochure: Research Presentation with Appeal." A unit plan for geography and foreign-language teaching using library media skills and resources.

"Abilities Students Must Have to Be Effective Users of Information." A model outline of information skills.

Finally, Public Relations examples are:

"Ideas for Public Relations." Suggestions for promoting the library media center and publicizing its services and resources.

"Making It with Media: Hints for Preparing a Media Newsletter." Advice and subject matter for keeping the newsletter professional and informative but not dull.

"Tried but True Ways to Make Teachers Happy." A list of suggestions whose use will make librarians happy, too, and on the verso, "Nonprint Bibliographies" and "Fall Materials Preview." A paragraph on each suggests ways of keeping teachers informed.

The package includes an introduction, list of contents, index to contributors, and fill-in form for potential contributors.

AUTHORITY

Loertscher is senior acquisitions·editor for Libraries Unlimited, and is a former professor at the University of Oklahoma Graduate School of Library and Information Studies, Norman, as well as at the University of Arkansas, Fayetteville, and Purdue University, West Lafayette, Indiana. Suggestions from all parts of the country were selected and edited by Loertscher and associate editors Elizabeth Bankhead, Mary Alice Hunt, Retta Ball Patrick, and Joanne Troutner, all school library media specialists. Professional publications, associations, and school districts also provided some material.

COMMENT

These materials for the professional vertical file include something for everyone. Ideas are presented in clear and readable format, and many will inspire replication. Information is clearly written and the bibliographies are useful. The package arrived at this reviewer's office in no particular order, possibly in an effort to help meet a close deadline with a publication just off the press. The set ought to be in the same order as the contents list. However, this is a minor flaw in an otherwise eminently useful compilation.

Loertscher, David V. *Taxonomies of the School Library Media Program.* SEE Chapter 13, The Library Media Center and the Curriculum.

McDonald, Frances Beck. *The Emerging School Library Media Program: Readings.* **Libraries Unlimited, 1988. 328 pp. ISBN 0-87287-660-8.**

PURPOSE

A revolution in school library media programs is an event waiting to happen, and its major proponents are represented in this anthology of current thought about what school library media professionals do, or should be gearing up to do. Compiled for student and practicing professional alike, this collection urges a transformation of the school library media specialist's role.

CONTENTS

A change from passive to active is at the center of the revolutionary changes proposed, in one way or another, in the articles collected in this book. They are revolutionary because they shift the focus of school library media programs from a quiet place for reading and borrowing books to a dynamic center for learning, where the person in charge is a leader and consultant in instructional planning as well as a provider of resources for teaching and learning.

Assume this active role, and the misperceptions of teachers and administrators concerning the true function of school library media centers will turn to understanding. Undertake the transformation in small steps. Stop teaching library skills in isolated lessons. Integrate skills of inquiry with classroom instruction. Integrate the collection with the curriculum of the school. Integrate automation technology with library management, instruction, and reference services. Increase visibility to staff and students. Promote. Proselytize. These are the imperatives embedded in the articles selected for this book.

The articles are arranged in six parts, each depicting a different aspect of the school library media program. Part 1 considers the school library media center in its educational setting, presenting research on its impact, a discussion of its genesis, reflections on its changing role, and descriptions of exemplary programs. Part 2 sets forth the impetus for change, offering models, taxonomies, and descriptions of the school library media specialist's role and providing approaches and rationales. The process of instructional design is presented in the context of school library media center realities; partnerships with teachers are advocated, and media resources become integrated into the instructional pattern.

Part 3 is a "how-to" section, demonstrating how many school library media specialists have transformed their role from passive provider of resources on the run to dynamic and indispensable instructional design consultant and planning partner with teachers. While the school library media specialist–teacher partnership develops strategies that include student use of media resources, the effectiveness of these strategies will be determined by students' ability to use the resources. They must be taught not only how to locate what they need but also, and primarily, how to evaluate, analyze, and synthesize the information they find. These thinking skills are the essence of the library media center instructional program. Part 4 presents various approaches to teaching information skills.

The impact of technology, resource sharing, library networks, and on-line searching on school library media services is considered in Part 5. Two articles also describe how elementary school library media services promote independence and lifelong learning skills and attitudes in those early years of schooling. The final part consists of two articles. The first considers the accomplishment of change, with the school library media specialist in a staff development role as an initiator of change. The second treats the concepts of leadership and the exercise of power by school library media specialists, thus helping to complete the shift from passivity to more active control of the professional environment.

Most of the 29 articles are footnoted, and bibliographies of recommended additional readings conclude each part. An index is also provided.

AUTHORITY

Contributors include library media specialists, district program administrators, and faculty members of library schools and schools of education, most of whose names will be familiar to readers of professional journals. McDonald is associate professor of library media education, Mankato State University, Minnesota.

COMMENT

The spirit of innovation and reform that energized school library media professionals toward innovation in the 1960s rises again. Then, the catalyst was audiovisual technology; today, it is the advent of computer technology combined with an innovative approach to education, instructional design, that promises a new dawn for information centers. In Milton's epic *Paradise Lost,* after Adam and Eve have been banished from Eden, they are admonished to "awake, arise, or be forever fallen." That still sounds like good advice, and this book, therefore, merits attention.

Naumer, Janet Noll. *Media Center Management with an Apple II*. Libraries Unlimited, 1984. 223 pp. ISBN 0-87287-392-7 (pap.).

PURPOSE

Shortcuts and management tips for using Apple II computers and related software are presented in this book designed to assist librarians in performing necessary library media center administrative and clerical tasks.

CONTENTS

Focusing on the use of Apple II–compatible software in library media center management, this book walks the reader through the processes each step of the way, with minimal technical jargon. It offers the reader case studies and notes, provides an overview of the hardware and its function within the basic structure of the Apple computer, and explains the commands and what they accomplish.

The introduction offers a description of the hardware and advises the reader about the proper care of disks and software programs. Chapter 1 introduces management software programs and discusses planning methods for designing a system of management. Chapter 2 describes how to use such data base management programs as DB Master, PFS: File, and PFS: Report, and provides templates for data base management programs. Chapter 3 discusses the utilization of VisiCalc and VisiPlot in the maintenance of statistical records and reporting, and is followed, in the next chapter, with an investigation of the uses of word processing programs, presenting the Bank Street Writer and Screen Writer II as models. Brief bibliographies offer sources of further information and appear at the end of Chapters 2, 3, and 4.

An appended bibliography contains descriptions of software designed for specific library tasks such as bibliographic management, cataloging, circulation, and so forth. An index concludes the book.

AUTHORITY
Naumer is director of the Library Media Center, Porterville College, California.

COMMENT
The presence of Apple II microcomputers in so many schools has made them a natural candidate for use in managing school media centers. This guide offers library media specialists guidance in their use in a manner that is easy to follow. Those librarians who have mastered the basics and are ready for AppleWorks will find step-by-step instruction in *AppleWorks for School Librarians* by May Lein Ho (reviewed in this chapter).

Nickel, Mildred L. *Steps to Service: A Handbook of Procedures for the School Library Media Center.* **Rev. ed. ALA, 1984. 129 pp. ISBN 0-8389-0387-8 (pap.).**

PURPOSE
Now in its fourth printing (1988), this handbook identifies the major areas of concern for inexperienced library media specialists and those in need of review. It offers the information and practical suggestions needed to get a unified media program under way and reminders for those who need help in getting over the rough spots.

CONTENTS
The first two chapters deal with functions and standards for school library media centers. The standards are based on ALA's 1969 publication on standards, although readers are advised to keep up to date, as new standards are introduced. Administration is the next topic, and the aspects discussed include budget, automation, collection development, organization, circulation and maintenance of materials, and reports. Sample forms, cards, and records are reproduced, and various lists are provided: vendors, sources, supplies, and so on.

Activities of the school media center are described in Chapter 4, which also includes some good advice about the pursuit of professional growth, staff relationships, and volunteer student assistance. The chapter on facilities describes pertinent aspects of functional design, outlines the elements for which space should be provided, and suggests guidelines for space allocation. A checklist of furniture and equipment is provided, and sources of library furniture and audiovisual storage cabinets are also supplied.

Each chapter has a bibliography, and the book concludes with a glossary, a directory of publishers, producers, and suppliers, and an index.

AUTHORITY

The author has been an administrator of school library programs in city and state systems and for the U.S. Air Force in Europe. Active in ALA and state library media associations, Nickel has been published in professional journals.

COMMENT

This invaluable compilation of information and sources for media center management is highly recommended.

Prostano, Emanuel T., and Joyce S. Prostano. *The School Library Media Center,* **4th ed. Libraries Unlimited, 1987. 257 pp. ISBN 0-87287-568-7.**

PURPOSE

This consideration of the role of the school library media center as part of the educational enterprise focuses on practices and practicalities of media center management. Written for students, teachers, administrators, and practitioners, it examines the elements of the media center, which it treats as a system, and describes its potential for achievement.

CONTENTS

Setting the school library media center squarely in the context of educational reform, the Prostanos describe the responses to *A Nation at Risk* (National Commission on Excellence in Education, 1983) made by the library community and the role of libraries in improving education. Recommendations for reform in library media centers are listed in the first chapter. The second chapter describes research in library media center effectiveness, adds information on standards and guidelines that have influenced their development, and sets forth a guiding philosophy, including checklists of the needs of teachers and students that school media centers are meant to fulfill. The school library media center is defined as a system "designed for the improvement of teaching and learning" (p. 33) that functions within a macrosystem—the school. The components of the system are interrelated and consist of such resources as the staff, facilities, collection, and budget and the activities provided by management, that is, the program and services.

Each of the system elements is taken up in succeeding chapters. Chapter 3 provides a discussion of management theory and analyzes its various aspects in the school library media center setting: planning, organizing, staffing, leading, and controlling (monitoring might be a less disquieting word). Some effective systems for controlling such management processes as budgeting and evaluation are explained, and organizational relationships are explored through organization charts. Next, school library services and programs are discussed in terms of "achievements." These include guidance and consultation, in-service programs and instruction of teachers and students, media production and design, and curriculum design and implementation. Models, charts, guidesheets, and other figures expand the concepts on in-service and instruction, and library and information skills and activities are outlined.

Chapter 5 returns to the first element of the system, its "assets," and considers personnel and staffing. It provides job descriptions and responsibilities and lists competencies and functions of professional and support staff members. Assets of the system are further defined in the following two chapters, which deal with facilities, furniture, and equipment. Factors in the planning and design of space utilization and facilities are considered, as are aspects of furniture and storage. A chart indicates quantitative standards for media and equipment, and drawings illustrate various types of equipment. The components of media collections are listed and explained, and collection building, resource sharing, selection principles, and technical services are explored.

More thorough attention to the budget is offered in the final chapter, which analyzes and explains such systems for preparing budgets as line item budgets, PPBS (Planning, Programming Budgeting System), and ZBB (Zero Base Budgeting). The characteristics and procedures of each are outlined.

Each chapter is introduced with a set of three or four objectives, and concludes with a summary, learning activities, footnotes, and a bibliography. Charts, models, diagrams, and other figures are used to illustrate many of the concepts. Appendixes include a scope and sequence for library skills, a chart showing computer uses in education, a job description for the LMC director, appraisal and evaluation forms, and ALA statements on the School Library Bill of Rights and on copyright as it applies to videotapes and computer software use in the classroom and library. An index completes the work.

Emanuel T. Prostano is dean and professor of library science and instructional technology at Southern Connecticut State University. Joyce S. Prostano is director of the division of library media services at South Central Community College in Connecticut.

One of a series of library science texts, this book offers a different perspective on library media center administration, one that analyzes management tasks by means of a systems approach. It sheds new light on how the school library media center functions, enabling it to be seen as an organic part of a larger organism, the school. While less comprehensive than John Gillespie and Diana Spirt's *Administering the School Library Media Center* (also reviewed in this chapter), its approach merits the attention not only of school library media specialists but also of school administrators and supervisors and library school students.

Rowley, Jennifer. *Computers for Libraries*, **2nd ed.** SEE Chapter 16, Technology and Automation.

Schmid, William T. *Media Center Management: A Practical Guide.* **Hastings House, 1980. 232 pp. ISBN 0-8038-473-0.**

Directed at students, this text will serve as a brushup source for practicing school library media specialists as well. It provides practical techniques for managing media programs and discusses concepts relevant to a wide variety of media services.

The book is divided into ten chapters. Chapter 1, on media center organization, looks at various factors that influence the organization of a media center. The advantages and disadvantages of different organizations and structures are discussed. In Chapter 2, personnel practices are examined. Selection of personnel, orientation and training, reviewing and evaluating performance, and termination procedures are among the management concerns that are analyzed. Chapter 3 is devoted to forms for reporting services. Documenting the value of the services provided by a media center is an important survival technique, and the tips on designing effective service forms are helpful.

Data on the utilization of the center and its services are the most important part of the reporting process, and methods for obtaining and using such data are described in Chapter 4. Constructive use of this information will help to confirm a program's success and provide a rationale for requests for additional funding. Chapter 5 deals with cost accounting and discusses procedures for determining cost-effectiveness, an important concern when questions arise about monetary support of the program.

In Chapter 6, the procedures for selecting and purchasing media are discussed, and Chapter 7 presents a step-by-step approach to selecting and purchasing the equipment necessary for media utilization. Techniques for effective public relations are presented in Chapter 8, and Chapter 9 suggests ways for media professionals to work together with patrons to improve the effectiveness of the media program and the materials it provides. Methods for effective handling of complaints are discussed in Chapter 10, which also offers some useful tips.

A summary of each chapter's contents is provided. Appended are two resource sections: One provides service forms that can be used as is or adapted to specific needs, and a second provides an annotated bibliography of additional information sources on media center management. An index completes the work.

AUTHORITY

The author is director of media services at Illinois State University, and has a degree in communications from Ohio State University.

COMMENT

The realities of media center management are emphasized in this book, which recognizes the political elements in management success as well as the professional ones. Schmid's perspective and advice and their practical applications will serve all people working in media programs.

Thomason, Nevada Wallis. *Circulation Systems for School Library Media Centers: Manual to Microcomputers.* Libraries Unlimited, 1985. 250 pp. ISBN 0-87287-370-6.

PURPOSE

This guide to circulation systems offers a fresh look at the need to impose order on the comings and goings of library materials and patrons, and the records they engender.

CONTENTS

Circulation systems are almost as old as libraries, and in a brief overview, beginning in the late nineteenth century, Thomason describes the aim then, as now, for simplicity and efficiency. Descriptions of manual and semiautomatic systems (charging machines) commonly in use are discussed in the first half of the book. They will be familiar to all librarians who have struggled with book cards, filing systems, circulation records, and overdues, usually attended to by student volunteers. Beginning librarians will find some helpful hints.

With the introduction of automated systems, a new struggle awaits those librarians who have not yet ventured into computer territory. To ease the way, the author introduces computers, explaining how they operate and defining the all-important role of software in creating a system that is appropriate for a given library's needs.

The various kinds of systems are described in general terms, and factors that should be taken into account in making purchasing decisions are considered—such as whether hardware is already at hand, budget, size of the school population, and possible future needs. Criteria for selecting both software and hardware are also provided.

Circulation policies and procedures are just as important in library management as are those for selection, and some samples are provided in considerable detail in Appendix A, along with sample forms and records. Appendix B describes the software available at the time of writing (1985). Each description includes producer name and address and indicates what hardware is needed, then explains what the system will do. Appendix C lists review sources, hardware manufacturers, and software suppliers, including sources of free software. A bibliography and index complete the book.

AUTHORITY

The author has been associate professor of library media education in the College of Education, University of New Mexico.

COMMENT

School library media specialists seeking assistance in upgrading circulation systems, whether manual or automated, will find it in this book. As noted in its foreword, although books have been written about circulation, about media center management, and about computers, this is the first work that has combined all three subjects in a single book.

Toor, Ruth, and Hilda K. Weisburg. *The Complete Book of Forms for Managing the School Library Media Center.* **Center for Applied Research in Education, 1982. 256 pp. ISBN 0-87628-229-X (pap.).**

PURPOSE

Forms for conducting the business of school library media center management are provided in abundance in this publication.

CONTENTS

This aid to school library management offers some uniquely useful features. Particularly relevant is the fact that many of the forms are unavailable from commercial vendors; other considerations are savings in time and money, ease in duplication assisted by the spiral binding, help in organizing, scheduling, and monitoring library activities, and help in communicating with parents and the community outside the library and school.

The book follows the school calendar, with forms appropriate for the opening days at the beginning and closing tasks at the end. The physical facilities and collections are the immediate concern when the school year begins, and forms include a grid for creating a floor plan, checklists for supplies, surveys of the print and nonprint collections, and a hardware inventory.

Developing relationships with and organizing personnel are the subject of the next group of forms, which includes job descriptions, interview schedules, an applicant evaluation form, volunteer recruitment letter and volunteer schedule, training checklist, task assignment sheet, student sign-up sheet, and more. Circulation control forms are next: sign-in sheets for students, sign-out cards and sheets, hardware distribution records, overdue and reserve forms, circulation statistics, records of additions to the collection, and discards.

A section on technical services offers forms for cataloging, processing, evaluation of hardware, and the like, and management of programs is included in the next section. Provided are file cards for bibliographies and reference questions, various record and report forms for library skills teaching, storytelling programs, and book fairs. Teacher-related forms include film and librarian's schedules and request forms for various purposes.

Forms for working with district and school administrators include

34

planning guides, monthly and annual report outlines, and even a five-year plan, all with samples. Correspondence forms are provided with sample letters of request, complaint, thanks, and many others. Having almost reached the end of the school year, exhausted no doubt from filling out all those forms and mailing all those letters, the school librarian is now ready to complete preparations for closing shop, and the necessary forms are here, including an inventory schedule, a thank-you for volunteering, summary forms for inventory results, service certificates and awards, and a form for teacher evaluation of the media center.

In case things didn't go too well in spite of all those forms, there are a sample résumé, letter of application, and thank-you for the interview; some other forms are included as well. Also provided by the thoughtful authors are a directory of commercial suppliers of library forms and an index.

AUTHORITY

Ruth Toor is a library media specialist at Southern Boulevard School in Chatham Township, New Jersey, and Hilda K. Weisburg is a library media specialist at the Harry S. Truman and Dwight D. Eisenhower schools in Sayreville, New Jersey.

COMMENT

The thoroughness with which library media specialists' needs have been met in this book is truly impressive. The forms are well done, eminently usable, and a boon for the busy librarian. More importantly, implicit in all those thank-yous, forms, and reports is a message about the importance of positive communication with members of the school and outside communities, thorough and accurate record keeping, and information flow to administrators, to let them know what the school library media center is achieving.

Woolls, Blanche. *Managing School Library Media Programs.* Libraries Unlimited, 1988. 181 pp. ISBN 0-87287-590-3.

PURPOSE

As the twenty-first century approaches, school library media specialists need to take a fresh look at how they manage the school library media center. This book, the first in a series of manuals planned to assist specialists in their management function, is primarily an overview for beginners and workshop leaders, but it also offers new patterns of thought and action for more experienced professionals as well.

CONTENTS

Beginning with a brief overview of school library media center history, Woolls looks at the current scene, describing a day in the life of a high school media specialist, and cites some changes in direction offered by automation, on-line information services, and integrated instruction. Professional preparation, certification requirements, how to find and interview for a job, and how to select a job and get started in it constitute the subject matter of the next two chapters. Factors to consider—facilities, staff, administration, teachers, and students—are discussed, with some good political advice imparted along the way.

Modeling the management of the school library media center on business practices, Woolls consistently draws parallels, not only in the vocabulary she uses but also in the concepts she introduces. A suggested advisory committee is akin to a board of directors. Planning, facilities, and staff management and evaluation follow efficient business practices.

Materials selection is now an aspect of the more generalized process, collection management, and is discussed here. Decisions about automating circulation systems are based on business principles. Equipment and materials selection and acquisition methods are topics of discussion, along with methods of defending the collection or items in it should the need arise. "Deselection," or weeding, is also given attention. A list of criteria for deciding what to discard presents invaluable guidelines for each Dewey class number. The essential functions of budgeting and budget preparation are considered. Given the state of school library media center budgets in many schools, proposal writing is placed in inevitable juxtaposition with media center budgets, with directions for preparing each part of the proposal thoughtfully discussed.

School library media services are at the heart of the center's reason for being, and the author is concerned with their management. In the absence of sufficient staff and other resources, setting priorities becomes a major necessity, and, Woolls advises, clerical tasks should be secondary to service. That this choice must be made is an absurdity that many school library media specialists contend with constantly; that services can be offered without attention to clerical necessities is a problem still open to discussion. Woolls relates marketing as used in a business setting to the school library media center, and methods and measures for appraising services, collection, and staff are discussed.

The next chapters carry the reader out of the school library media center and into the larger contexts of interlibrary cooperation and networking, and into the exercise of leadership in professional associations of educators, as well as membership in library professional associations. The final chapter looks to the future and exhorts library media specialists to focus on curriculum, responsibilities to students, and technological progress as a means of changing the continuing misperceptions of their role.

Each chapter concludes with practice exercises and footnotes. Appendixes include competencies and professional preparation requirements for Pennsylvania and Ohio, course offerings at Pittsburgh and Kent State universities, a media center evaluation checklist, a five-year plan for media center development to meet ALA standards, and various policy statements and forms. An index concludes the book.

AUTHORITY

Blanche Woolls is chairperson and professor of library science at the University of Pittsburgh.

COMMENT

An excellent introduction to a challenging profession, this book also challenges experienced practitioners to think about their responsibilities from a new perspective, that of a business entrepreneur. Adapting business management procedures to library management in an educational setting has promise. Moving necessary clerical tasks to the end of a priorities list fails to solve the dilemma posed by lack of clerical support staff.

Woolls, E. Blanche, and David V. Loertscher, eds. *The Microcomputer Facility and the School Library Media Specialist.* SEE Chapter 16, Technology and Automation.

ADDITIONAL READINGS

Cheever, Daniel S., Jr., et al. *School Administrator's Guide to Computers in Education.* Addison-Wesley, 1986. 356 pp. ISBN 0-201-10564-0. This practical planning guide for administrators also includes chapters of special interest to school library media specialists—"Politics and Funding" (Chapter 3) and "Staff Development" (Chapter 5)—and offers useful appendixes with forms for budgeting, comparing, and evaluating. A glossary, annotated reference list, and index are also provided.

Greenfield, Jane. *Books: Their Care and Repair.* H. W. Wilson, 1984. 204 pp. ISBN 0-8242-069509. An illustrated manual on book maintenance that explains the causes of book deterioration and provides repair instructions for undoing the damage.

Morrow, Carolyn Clark, and Carole Dyal. *Conservation Treatment Procedures: A Manual of Step-by-Step Procedures for the Maintenance and Repair of Library Materials,* 2nd ed. Libraries Unlimited, 1986. 225 pp. ISBN 0-87287-437-0. Illustrated and comprehensive, this handbook offers instructions for repairing and maintaining library materials.

Ramsey, Jackson E., and Inez L. Ramsey. *Library Planning and Budgeting.* Franklin Watts, 1986. 217 pp. ISBN 0-531-15506-4. This overview of principles and practices of planning and budgeting for libraries includes applications to school library media centers, describes and illustrates the preparation of a school library budget request, and explains the use of computers and spreadsheets in the process. Sample forms are included.

Townley, Charles T. *Human Relations in Library Network Management.* Library Professional Publications, 1988. 161 pp. ISBN 0-208-02086-1. A thoughtful and practical guide to developing effective relations among library network members, this book applies human relations theory and techniques to situations in library network management. Case studies are used to illustrate organizational behavior and conflict resolution.

2
Technical Services

In today's school library media center, usually a one-person operation, many of the technical aspects of the job have necessarily given way to the time required by more pressing endeavors. Since cataloging and processing are now available from book jobbers, and catalog cards accompany many audiovisual materials, a major technical service function has been eliminated, or certainly diminished considerably, as a source of concern to school library media specialists.

Because acquisitions and circulation are now considered to be an aspect of collection management, books on those subjects are reviewed in Chapter 6, "Collection Management." See a review of David Loertscher and May Lein Ho's *Computerized Collection Development for School Library Media Centers* in Chapter 13, "The Library Media Center and the Curriculum," placed there because of its relationship to that subject. Additional material on both of these subjects is also found in books about library management in Chapter 1. What remains, therefore, is this small chapter, with some useful books that offer guidance in technical services. An overview of the entire topic is provided in Irene Godden's *Library Technical Services,* and a beginner's introduction to cataloging is supplied by Herbert Hoffman in *Small Library Cataloging.* Sheila Intner, in *Access to Media,* suggests computer cataloging of media to improve access and integrate nonprint media with the rest of the collection, and Virginia Boucher provides a handbook on interlibrary loan. Forms that are helpful in conducting various technical service activities are discussed in *Forms for Automated Library Systems* by Lois Kershner and *The Complete Book of Forms for Managing the School Library Media Center* by Ruth Toor and Hilda Weisburg. Both books are reviewed in Chapter 1, "Library Management." A supplementary list of briefly annotated sources appears at the end of this chapter.

Boucher, Virginia. *Interlibrary Loan Practices Handbook.* **ALA, 1984. 195 pp. ISBN 0-8389-3298-3 (pap.).**

PURPOSE

As library networks and resource sharing have increased the number of interlibrary loan requests and fulfillments, a need has arisen to provide the information that librarians require in order to handle such requests expeditiously. This manual fills that need for librarians without previous experience in the area.

CONTENTS

Chapter 1 provides instructions for libraries that need to borrow materials. It defines interlibrary loan, explains the need for it, and gives the codes that govern its operation. (The two basic codes are reprinted in Appendix A.) To clarify borrowing policies, a statement should be prepared, and suggestions for format and contents are provided. Recommended supplies are listed. Borrowing procedures include an interview with the requesting patron, an application for borrowing, and verification of the request. The importance of confirming an item's existence, describing it accurately, and using the correct main entry is emphasized. Verification sources are presented at the end of the chapter and at the end of the book. Preparing, sending, following up, problem solving, and reporting are also considered here.

Information for the lending library is provided in Chapter 2. Sample report forms are reprinted, and such matters as which libraries will be served, what will be loaned, and in what way service will be provided are discussed. Recommended supplies are listed, as in Chapter 1, and lending procedures enumerated. These include locating material and photocopying where necessary, shipping, following up, and reporting transactions.

Chapter 3 explains reproduction rights under photocopy law and the need to keep up with the changes that result from case law and further interpretations. Relevant excerpts from the law are reprinted with brief commentary. A bibliography is provided at the end of the chapter. (For further information on copyright requirements, see R. S. Talab, *Commonsense Copyright,* reviewed in Chapter 17, "Issues in School Library Media Services.") Chapter 4 deals with dissertations and master's theses, related bibliographic sources, verification methods, and sources for obtaining them.

Chapter 5 presents a case study of interlibrary cooperation, based on the Colorado State network and its regional systems, which offer cooperative interlibrary loan services. In Chapter 6 international developments in interlibrary loan are discussed, request forms are provided, and instructions presented for receiving and responding to requests.

Managing interlibrary loan services is the subject of Chapter 7. As with every other library function, careful planning is a necessity if mere coping is to be avoided. Fitting this service area into the library's mission, goals, and objectives is an important component of planning and evaluation as well. Organization and operations, necessary files that are to be maintained, staffing, training, and supervision are also discussed here, in the context of larger libraries. Small libraries will adapt the suggestions to their own operational scale.

Nineteen appendixes provide model codes and policies, forms, and guidelines. An index completes the work.

AUTHORITY

Virginia Boucher is head of interlibrary cooperation for the University of Colorado libraries. She has conducted workshops on interlibrary loan, has lectured on the subject at professional association meetings, and has been active in ALA's Reference and Adult Services Division (RASD).

COMMENT

Once again, the importance of planning and information has been established, this time in the case of interlibrary loan. This manual provides invaluable assistance to librarians involved in or planning to initiate interlibrary loan services.

Ellison, John W., and Patricia Ann Coty, eds. *Nonbook Media: Collection Management and User Services.* SEE Chapter 7, Nonprint Media and Computer Software.

Godden, Irene P., ed. *Library Technical Services: Operation and Management.* **Academic Press, 1984. 272 pp. ISBN 0-12-287040-9.**

PURPOSE

Librarians who need to update their knowledge and students of library science will find thorough coverage of the major aspects of technical services here.

CONTENTS

While the technical services function assumes a more structured form in academic and research libraries, whose operations are the primary focus of this book, than in school library media centers, it is an aspect of library management that can neither be ignored nor taken for granted. Circulation must be maintained, and materials must be acquired, cataloged, processed, inventoried, and weeded—and school librarians are often the sole administrators of those tasks in their libraries. Books may be ordered with complete processing and cataloging, but the other technical functions must still be performed. The contributors of articles in this book describe these tasks and how to do them efficiently.

The introduction presents an overview, describing their development and examining the future role of technical services. Their administration is the subject of Chapter 2, which discusses management in general and personnel management and evaluation in particular. The advent of automation has affected the delivery of technical services, and some of the changes are detailed in Chapter 3. Considered here are changing concepts of technical services, training and standards, networks, commercial services, resource sharing, applications of automation to various operations, potential improvements in service, and future prospects.

Chapter 4 deals with acquisitions, examining such matters as relationships with vendors, maintenance of records and files, and ordering procedures. Bibliographic control is the subject of Chapter 5. Among the topics treated are the management of cataloging activities, cataloging and classification, various kinds of catalogs and their maintenance, and retrospective conversion of automated catalogs. Processing, preservation of materials, and weeding are considered in Chapter 6, and circulation functions and management are discussed in the seventh and final chapter, along with a historical overview.

Each chapter provides advice on keeping up with trends, references, and a bibliography. An index concludes the presentation.

COMMENT

Traditional practices and new developments are combined in this treatment of technical services. It provides a review of the subject, pays attention to future trends, and offers suggestions for keeping up with a changing facet of library management.

Hoffman, Herbert H. *Small Library Cataloging*, 2nd ed. Scarecrow, 1986. 216 pp. ISBN 0-8108-1910-4.

PURPOSE

Written for nonprofessional library workers who have not had instruction in library cataloging, this book offers some simplifications as well as explanations of cataloging rules. More experienced library media specialists will find this a useful source for review.

CONTENTS

At the outset, Hoffman posits a realistic view of what a person newly assigned to a small library will encounter. In some school systems, elementary school libraries may have been closed for some years. Now revived, with, perhaps, a teacher or an inexperienced librarian in charge, the library awaits organization and bibliographic control. Hoffman's advice is well conceived: Clean up and weed, organize and arrange, then start cataloging. Begin, he advises, by discarding, or packing up and storing all materials not relevant to the library's purposes and clientele. Discard everything that is outdated, and carefully evaluate duplicates. Put aside incomplete sets of books so that if missing volumes reappear the set can be cataloged later.

The first section of the book explains the shelf arrangement of the library's collection. A chapter is devoted to each of the following: "Structure of Publications," "Files, Shelf Arrangement, and Classification," and call numbers. When the organizational tasks are completed, the cataloging may begin.

The second section discusses principles of cataloging and includes principles of description, main entry and information in title main entries, added entries, author and title added entries, categorical added entries, analytics, shelf list, and cross references, and instructions for filing. Helping the reader are a number of worked-out examples, illustrations, and sample cards, some in the text and others in an appendix. Other appendixes include explanations of how to use other libraries' cataloging, in which Library of Congress cards are compared with others. Typical examples of cataloging in publication are shown, as well as on-line aids and the MARC format. Appendixes also provide instructions for preparing cards on a word processor and lists of library supplies and equipment. An index completes the work.

AUTHORITY

Hoffman is a librarian at Rancho Santiago Community College, Santa Ana, California.

COMMENT

Cataloging practice in a simplified form is effectively explained in this book, which offers well-organized guidance to the uninitiated in the systematic organization of a library collection.

Intner, Sheila S. *Access to Media: A Guide to Integrating and Computerizing Catalogs.* **Neal-Schuman, 1984. 301 pp. ISBN 0-918212-88-X (pap.).**

PURPOSE

School library media specialists, public and academic librarians, students of library and information services, and district media supervisors will find enough thought and information here to move them toward automated systems of bibliographic access.

CONTENTS

Divided into two sections, the book examines problems and prevailing practices in providing access to media in libraries (first section) and suggests that all types of libraries may give access by integrating the media in an automated catalog (second section).

The problems of dealing with media begin in Section 1 with an attempt to define the term, an elusive task because of its different connotations. As used in this work, the term encompasses everything in a library collection that is not a book, including materials that are usually characterized as nonbook, nonprint, and audiovisual. In the first chapter, Intner provides an overview of the acceptance of media in libraries and the problems of display, availability, and cataloging.

Attempts to establish cataloging rules for media have included those provided by the Library of Congress, the Anglo-American Cataloging Rules (AACR or AACR1), those promulgated by the Association for Educational Communications and Technology (AECT), the Canadian Library Association (CLA), and the British Library Association and National Council for Educational Technology (LANCET) rules. None proved satisfactory because of inconsistency, flaws in terminology, disagreement about main entry, and other problems. The second edition of AACR, referred to as AACR2, solved most of the problems, and has become the standard.

Equivalent in its complexity is physical access to the media themselves. Cost and the potential for damage are much greater; equipment for their use must be available; and shelf arrangement and classification are some of the difficulties that make media considerably less accessible than books. Maintaining adequate bibliographic records is thus all the more important. With the advent of Machine Readable Cataloging (MARC) and the development of regional networks—Online Computer Library Center (OCLC), Southeastern Library Network (SOLINET), Illinois Library Network (ILLINET), southwestern network (AMIGOS), and others—

librarians now have access to uniform bibliographic data for media provided by these bibliographic utilities, either by computer or by purchasing computer-generated catalog cards.

A thorough grounding in the problems and practices of integrating media with books in library collections has set the stage for a rationale for changing to computerized systems, the subject of Section 2. Here the author describes the bibliographic utilities (e.g., OCLC), vendor-generated acquisition systems, such as Baker and Taylor's LIBRIS II, and turnkey systems that provide the software and hardware in a convenient and ready-to-use package. She also describes the characteristics a computerized system should have.

The skills required for planning and implementing automated catalogs that integrate all media are described, and ways of attaining or providing them are outlined. Standards and the organizations that make them are described, and the organizational implications are explored. The considerations that will affect catalog integration, the advantages that will accrue, and the results of providing computerized access systems are discussed in the final chapters.

Appendixes include highlights of media acquisition history, a list of cataloging codes, a questionnaire used for one of the surveys cited, a list of acronyms, and a glossary. An index is also provided.

AUTHORITY

Intner is an associate professor in the Graduate School of Library and Information Science at Simmons College, Boston.

COMMENT

Intner has provided some powerful arguments for offering library patrons access to media through the use of automated catalogs. Although the cost of automating has prevented many school librarians from embarking on such a course, and lack of familiarity with its potential may be another factor, increasing numbers of school libraries are becoming involved in this undertaking. The information in this book will help to understand what such an enterprise entails.

Kemp, Betty, ed. *School Library and Media Center Acquisitions Policies and Procedures,* **2nd ed. Oryx, 1986. 274 pp. ISBN 0-89774-160-9.**

PURPOSE

An update of a 1981 publication, this edition has a chapter on computer software. It also features a collection of current (as of 1985) selection and acquisition policies and other data from libraries, districts, and state education agencies that can serve as models for revising policies or creating new ones.

CONTENTS

Selecting, acquiring, and maintaining the library collection is a primary responsibility of the school library media specialist. Establishing the policies and procedures that determine how this will be done is the precursor to a systematic approach to carrying out this responsibility. A random national survey disclosed that 30 percent of the reporting libraries were without policy and procedures statements, causing such problems as vulnerability to censorship pressures. Several states require such statements; some recommend them; only ten states leave it to the individual school districts to decide.

The questions and results of the national survey have been tabulated and reproduced in the book. They provide information about district and school population, budget and size, and state budgeting requirements or recommendations. They also cite figures about computer and software budgets, locations, and quantities, and how they and other materials are selected, acquired, processed, and otherwise handled.

Of the selection policies and procedures that were submitted, 15 were chosen for inclusion in their entirety. These constitute Part I of the book. The statements included present positions on philosophy, objectives, purposes, responsibility, procedures, scope, and selection criteria. The manner of handling controversial subjects, gifts, and challenged materials is described, and forms for handling complaints are provided. Supplementing these full statements are parts of other statements. Presented in Part II, they include the policy elements listed above and additional material on selection principles, selection aids, special criteria, computer software, weeding, duplication and replacement, interlibrary loan, and free or sponsored materials. Part III presents procedures statements and forms. Included are materials requests, media and software evaluation forms, forms for requesting reconsideration of materials, and forms for reporting on the collection as a whole and in part.

Appendixes include a list of selection tools, computer review sources, jobbers, subscription agencies, and a directory of state education agencies. Statements on intellectual freedom are also provided, and an index concludes the book.

AUTHORITY

Betty Kemp is a library media specialist at Hillcrest Elementary School, Lake Stevens, Washington.

This compilation of policy and procedures statements offers library media specialists a selection of models on which to base their own statements, and they make good subjects for analysis.

Thomason, Nevada Wallis. *Circulation Systems for School Library Media Centers: Manual to Microcomputers.* SEE Chapter 1, Library Management.

Van Orden, Phyllis J. *The Collection Program in Elementary and Middle Schools: Concepts, Practices, and Information Sources.* SEE Chapter 6, Collection Management.

Van Orden, Phyllis J. *The Collection Program in High Schools: Concepts, Practices, and Information Sources.* SEE Chapter 6, Collection Management.

ADDITIONAL READINGS

Carothers, Diane Foxhill. *Self-Instruction Manual for Filing Catalog Cards.* ALA, 1981. 120 pp. ISBN 0-8389-0326-6. The principles underlying the 1980 changes in ALA filing rules are explained and illustrated with practice exercises.

Curley, Arthur, and Jana Varlejs. *Akers' Simple Library Cataloging,* 7th ed. Scarecrow, 1984. ISBN 0-8108-1649-0. Combining theory and practicality, this revision of the venerable "Akers" reflects the AACR2 rules and the 11th editions of *Sears List of Subject Headings* and the *Abridged Dewey Decimal System,* to guide librarians in small libraries and school library media centers.

Rogers, JoAnn B., and Jerry D. Saye. *Nonprint Cataloging for Multimedia Collections,* 2nd ed. Libraries Unlimited, 1987. ISBN 0-87287-523-7. Methods of cataloging nonprint materials incorporating AACR2 and MARC formats with examples that illustrate the discussion are presented in this updated edition. Also included is a chapter on cataloging computer software and the use of on-line bibliographic utilities.

Wynar, Bohdan S. *Introduction to Cataloging and Classification,* 7th ed. by Arlene G. Taylor. Libraries Unlimited, 1985. 641 pp. ISBN 0-87287-512-1. Covering cataloging and classification with Dewey and LC classification systems and Sears and LC subject headings, processing, filing, and catalog maintenance, this book also considers trends and influences of on-line systems and networking.

3

Facilities Design

The design of library facilities can be either a hindrance or a positive factor in effective media center management. The scarcity of material on this subject is most likely due to the general retrenchment that has occurred in education over the last few years. The wholesale building of schools resulting from the post–World War II baby boom is long since over, and the interest in school media centers that developed during the 1960s as a result of federal incentives for school library program development has waned.

The need at that time for rethinking the design of school media centers to accommodate individualized study programs was responded to by the Educational Facilities Laboratories with *The School Library* (reviewed in this chapter). Some of the books on administering school media programs that were published in the 1970s gave some attention to facilities, but much of what was said was based on or quite similar to the EFL book.

Now, again, many library facilities are being squeezed for space because of changing needs occasioned by the acquisition and new patterns of use of microcomputers. Of the more recent treatments of space planning and library interior design that are discussed here, Ruth Fraley and Carol Lee Anderson's *Library Space Planning* is the latest (published in 1985), and its realistic advice is to meet space shortages by redesigning available space. *Designing and Space Planning for Libraries,* Aaron Cohen and Elaine Cohen's book, offers a comprehensive discussion of planning for change and emphasizes various behavioral aspects of the process. In the other books included here, emphasis may vary, but the overall coverage is fairly similar.

ALA's *Information Power: Guidelines for School Library Media Programs* (see Chapter 5, "Evaluating the School Library Media Program") includes a chapter on facilities and another on resources and equipment; an appendix provides guidelines on library media facilities.

Cohen, Aaron, and Elaine Cohen. *Designing and Space Planning for Libraries: A Behavorial Guide.* **Bowker, 1979. 250 pp. ISBN 0-8352-1150-9.**

PURPOSE

This survey of the planning and interior design elements that must be considered in the design of a library facility has been written for librarians, design professionals, and school administrators as an aid in the planning process.

CONTENTS

Of all aspects of library management, the one least considered in professional preparation courses has been facilities planning and design. Yet the design elements that are put in place will surely influence the effectiveness of library programs and services. This book presents the design elements that planners work with: space, color, light, furniture, and equipment, and shows how aesthetic, functional, and behavioral considerations will influence the planning process. Special attention is given to the psychological and behavioral implications of change resulting from a renovation, as well as to minor alterations that may make an existing facility work better.

The Cohens present detailed planning outlines, from program requirements to cost and feasibility studies, and descriptions of various kinds of consultants. The roles of architects, engineers, interior designers, space and facilities planners, manufacturers, and vendors are also described. Using text and charts, diagrams, and other visuals, the authors proceed to the nuts and bolts: how to plan and arrange library space, how to select and place furniture and equipment, how to use and select lighting and provide for power and energy sources, effects of and provisions for color, signs, and acoustics, and what to do about moving. (Vacations, resignations, and leaves of absence are not considered options.) All of these aspects of planning are presented with clear examples and with emphasis on their psychological and behavioral effects on patrons and staff. The principles that the authors have established can be applied to any size library, and a plan for change can be as simple as moving some furniture or providing space for new equipment or as complex as designing an entire building.

A bibliography and an index are included.

AUTHORITY

Aaron Cohen, an architect, and Elaine Cohen, a behaviorist, have combined their specialties in a series of seminars on space planning and practical design that they conducted at universities across the country. Those seminars were the springboard for this book.

COMMENT

That librarians are often the last people to be consulted when alterations or a new facility are being planned is an ironic truism. That they are often ill prepared to deal with such change when it is in the planning stages may also be true. This book will fill the knowledge gaps at both ends of the process of library design or redesign. The authors are well versed not only in the physical problems that may arise but also in the human element, from the comfort of users and staff to the politics and protocols of bureaucratic behavior in decision making. This work merits careful study.

Draper, James, and James Brooks. *Interior Design for Libraries.* **ALA, 1979. 152 pp. ISBN 0-8389-0287-0 (pap.).**

PURPOSE

This book, prepared for the use of librarians in all types of libraries, discusses the principles and elements of interior design and offers tips on improving the library's appearance and efficiency.

CONTENTS

Guiding the librarian step by step, Draper and Brooks apply the fundamentals of interior design to their specific uses in libraries to create a lively interior that will reflect the functions of each element in the library. They begin with seeking professional help and advise consulting an interior designer, suggesting ways of locating, hiring, and working with one. Having gotten this out of the way, however, the rest of the book describes how librarians can actually do it themselves.

Preparing the floor plan is the first step, with the authors providing a list of needed supplies and walking the reader through the stages of rough sketch, measurement, scale drawing, identifying symbols for lighting and outlets, the use of furniture templates, and the like. Understanding, observing, and marking traffic patterns are the next steps, followed by provisions for space utilization and furniture and shelving arrangements in the patrons' area and in the workroom.

The effects and uses of color and fabric come next, and various dos and don'ts of painting and other wall treatments are discussed. Window treatments, floor coverings, and solutions to storage problems follow. A chapter on display offers suggestions on promoting new books and parts of the collection, promoting programs, and providing signs, and explains how to set up display areas and plan displays. Finishing touches such as plants, pictures, and landscaping complete the design features; budgeting, cost estimates, and billing are discussed last.

A final word from the authors emphasizes the importance of interior design and educating oneself about interior design, and admonishes the reader not to be intimidated by the designer or the process. A glossary of design terms and an index complete the work. Photographs illustrate many of the design ideas that have been discussed.

AUTHORITY
James Draper is a former interior designer who became a librarian, and James Brooks is a writer on libraries and library services.

COMMENT
The simple step-by-step approach that the authors have used provides what appear to be quick and easy solutions to the problems of library redecoration. Aaron and Elaine Cohen's *Designing and Space Planning for Libraries* offers a behavioral approach and more detail overall; *Library Space Planning* by Ruth Fraley and Carol Lee Anderson offers particular help in redesign that makes better use of space. Both are reviewed in this chapter.

Educational Facilities Laboratories. *The School Library*. Educational Facilities Laboratories, 1963. 143 pp.

PURPOSE
Written for educators, architects, and library personnel, this book presents a variety of ideas and specifications for school libraries that encourage individual use and independent study.

CONTENTS
Although published in 1963, this book is still available in libraries and for purchase. It was farsighted enough to be applicable to to-

day's school library media center. The only necessary addition would be some space and other related necessities for accommodating computers appropriate to an individual school's requirements.

The concepts that are most relevant to libraries today, and that have influenced library design since the book's publication, are the care with which library "keys" are located, and the provision for carrels and other accoutrements of individualized study. Furniture is chosen and arranged to suit that need, but is flexible enough to accommodate a number of uses, from individual study to small- and large-group instruction. Floor plans, photographs, and sketches present the user with a clear picture of furniture arrangement, as well as the dimensions of individual components of the design.

The text is brief. The introductory chapter discusses the changing nature of the school library, with the then new concepts of individualized study and the use of nonprint media. Succeeding chapters compare school libraries with those in colleges, and explain the relevance of college librarianship to that in the schools. The new school library concept is that of a teaching laboratory, with a carefully planned relationship of keys (catalog and indexes), learning materials, and staff.

Layouts are provided for the physical contents of each area of the library, and space needs for furniture, shelving and audiovisual equipment, materials, and storage are all provided, as well as requirements for the library media staff and teacher preparation and consultation areas. The environmental elements—shape, lighting, color, temperature, and sound levels—are considered in the planning.

A separate section presents prototype architectural designs; a bibliography and notes are also included.

AUTHORITY

The Educational Facilities Laboratories (EFL) was affiliated with the Ford Foundation, and consulting architects worked on the plans. EFL is now a division of the Academy for Educational Development based in Washington, D.C.

COMMENT

The design prototypes presented in this book, along with the specifications of space needs, make it a useful tool for librarians planning new arrangements of space.

Fraley, Ruth A., and Carol Lee Anderson. *Library Space Planning.* **Neal-Schuman, 1985. 158 pp. ISBN 0-918212-44-8 (pap.).**

3: FACILITIES DESIGN

PURPOSE

A practical guide for altering space arrangements in all types of libraries, this book provides systematic planning methods for reallocating space and/or adding to it, as well as possible alternative solutions to insufficient space.

CONTENTS

When library space is inadequate, patrons, programs, and staff suffer. In this period of retrenchment, in spite of all the public arousal about the inadequacy of schools, few outcries are heard about the deficiencies of school buildings, let alone the need to increase school library space. This book suggests some answers to space shortages, ranging from "zero-growth" collection planning and in-depth weeding to redesign of available space.

Once the redesign option is selected, careful planning is required, and Fraley and Anderson guide the space planner through the process. They begin, as all planners must, with the parent organization's and the library's goals and objectives, from which the space plan will emerge. This is followed by advice on how to collect the data on the collection and its housing that will precede a decision on how best to deal with the space shortage. Assessing the building (wiring, placement of windows and doors, and other structural elements) and counting furniture and equipment are also included in the planning process. Next come the budget and other financial considerations, then the new design plan, and some public relations activities to make the inevitable disruptions less painful.

Now the project can begin. Layouts are made, work teams organized, and a sequence of events for moving is developed. How the moving will be done and whether library services will continue during the move and to what extent are important considerations that will influence planning. The final chapters discuss the moving process and the inevitable evaluation that will follow, along with the data gathering that will be useful the next time around.

The appendix provides sample bids, specifications, a sample bid sheet, and an inventory list. A bibliography and index are also included.

AUTHORITY

Ruth Fraley is presently chief librarian of the New York Unified Court System, Office of Court Administration. She was head of the graduate library at the State University of New York at Albany. Carol Lee Anderson is assistant director of Access Services, State University of New York at Albany, and was access services librarian at the University of Oklahoma.

COMMENT

What to do when there isn't enough room in the library is rarely a preoccupation of school administrators, but often concerns the school librarian, particularly when plans for automation rest on finding or rearranging space for the new equipment. The costs of not changing, in productivity and morale, can be convincing factors when put to an administrator in dollars and cents terms. This is only one of the points that add to the value of this book. A shortcoming is that it omits some of the factors to be considered in preparing a new layout, such as traffic and other use patterns. Overall, however, it offers practical guidance in what can be a hazardous undertaking.

Pierce, William S. *Furnishing the Library Interior.* Marcel Dekker, 1980. 288 pp. ISBN 0-8247-6900-7.

PURPOSE

Although librarians in public, academic, and special libraries are the suggested audience for this book, school library media specialists and district directors of media programs should be involved in planning renovations or new facilities for school library media centers as well. Here they are told what to look for in the selection of library furniture and equipment and other design elements of library interiors.

CONTENTS

The overall arrangement of library interiors is the key to how efficiently the library can be used and how pleasing its aspect will be to the user. Building flexibility into the plan will ensure its ability to continue to adapt to changing conditions. This is a major consideration for the planning team, and is discussed in Chapter 1.

Comfort, efficiency, and convenience are the major concerns in planning for users and staff and service areas; and space allocations and furniture are considered with respect to these concerns in Chapters 2 and 3. Chairs, tables, carrels, lounge seating, and group study facilities are discussed in Chapter 2, which also covers space allocations, table size and shape, and other relevant dimensions. The "keys" areas, catalog and reference, and various service functions and their furniture and equipment needs are considered in Chapter 3, and Chapter 4 deals with additional service and staff areas, such as document, map, and other special collections.

Chapters 5 and 6 consider housing the collection—how the collection is organized, floor loads, special-purpose shelving, various types of shelves and their evaluation, and so on. Special requirements for housing and using nonprint media include such considerations as electrical needs, storage requirements, accommodating listening and viewing hardware, and the like.

Of major concern in planning new facilities or renovations is the selection of furniture and equipment, the subject of Chapter 7. The selection team should include the librarian, purchasing agent, and designer. Visits to other libraries, examination of descriptive literature, preparation of specifications, and contact with sales representatives are all part of the selection process—all of which is detailed in this chapter, along with standards and evaluation criteria.

The concluding chapters provide some background information on the library furniture industry and marketing practices, new developments in materials for interiors, and other considerations in interior design, such as security and communications systems and devices.

A selected bibliography, two appendixes, and an index complete the book. Particularly noteworthy is Appendix A, which provides specifications for wood library furniture, including seating and shelving, and steel bookstacks, and comments on the importance of some of the requirements specified. Appendix B lists library buildings visited by the author between 1960 and 1976.

AUTHORITY

Pierce is a librarian as well as a library planner and has been facilities planning officer for the Pennsylvania State University Libraries for a number of years.

COMMENT

This comprehensive survey of furniture and equipment needs and their evaluation, selection, and purchase answers most of the questions librarians have when planning library design or redesign. Although published some years ago, it has not lost any relevance (automation requirements might require some additional investigation). It is certainly a book to consult before purchasing decisions are made.

4
Publicity and Public Relations

The importance of publicizing the school library media center is emphasized in many books concerned with their management. Some have likened public relations activities to marketing strategies, in keeping with the analogy to business management currently in vogue. Whatever one prefers to call it, assuring a public conscious- ness that the school library media center is an important site of learning in the school is an essential management activity.

Like any other library management effort, publicity and public relations require careful planning before execution and evaluation after their implementation. The involvement of teachers and stu- dents is not only essential to success but also provides an opportu- nity for developing harmonious relationships that have a lasting impact not only on the school media program but throughout the school.

The library media center creates a public effect by providing a visually attractive background for its activities—and that is where lively and engaging bulletin boards and displays enter the picture. They proclaim to anyone entering the library the librarian's enthusi- asm for what occurs within its walls, whether for the books displayed on its shelves, the information it dispenses, or the learning that it fosters. Books on bulletin board and display ideas of library service publishers are not always among their proudest offerings, but some are serviceable, and they are included in this chapter. *Off the Wall* by Alan Heath and *The Creative Copycat* series by Marian Canoles are perhaps the most effective. The most imaginative (and extravagant) approach to library special events is Louise Liebold's *Fireworks, Brass Bands, and Elephants,* which offers enthusiasm and planning exper- tise. All these books are helpful in making the library, a vital center of the school, known for what it contributes to the education of children.

Canoles, Marian L. *The Creative Copycat, The Creative Copycat II, The Creative Copycat III*. Libraries Unlimited, 1982, 1985, and 1988 respectively. 265 pp., 202 pp., 200 pp. respectively. ISBN 0-87287-340-4, ISBN 0-87287-436-2, ISBN 0-87287-576-8.

PURPOSE

Canoles's series of books meets the needs of librarians and teachers for unique bulletin board ideas for the library and classroom, from primary grades through high school.

CONTENTS

Well over 200 ideas for bulletin boards based on events for every month of the year are presented in *The Creative Copycat*. With simple illustrations, Canoles captures such themes as holidays and seasons and subjects like music careers, exercise, and literature. Many of the ideas can serve double duty. For example, the Fourth of July firecracker can illustrate a bulletin board on the "big bang" theory of the origin of the universe or ignite some interest in the creation versus evolution controversy. Halloween masks can enliven a display on psychology, and a pulpit in the January mounting in honor of Dr. Martin Luther King, Jr., can become the base of a gazebo in February's "The Game of Hearts." The possibilities for adaptation are limited only by the imagination.

The Creative Copycat II has a somewhat narrower scope. It concentrates on American holidays, 26 federal holidays in all, and includes such minor ones as Arbor Day, Groundhog Day, and Grandparents' Day. The seasons, as well as weekly and monthly observances like Black History Month, Children's Book Week, and National Library Week, are also the subjects of displays. Again, many of the ideas can be used in other contexts.

The Creative Copycat III is based on literature. Here the purpose is to motivate reading and to arouse young readers' interest in finding out more about the incidents depicted in the displays. A variety of genres are represented, among them fantasy, historical fiction, realism, mystery, adventure, animals, and romance.

Instructions for each display include suggestions for background, color, type of lettering, method of construction, and materials needed. All bulletin boards are composed of readily available inexpensive materials, the most important of which is paper.

AUTHORITY

The author is a former librarian at Booker T. Washington High School in Norfolk, Virginia.

COMMENT

School library media specialists who have run out of ideas for bulletin boards will find a great deal of help in these books.

Edsall, Marian S. *Practical PR for School Library Media Centers.* **Neal-Schuman, 1984. 165 pp. ISBN 0-918212-77-4 (pap.).**

PURPOSE

Communication with the world outside the school library media center is necessary if the center is to function as an effective force within the school. A practical approach to communicating with the various publics—students, faculty, administration, parents, and other citizens of the community—will enable school library media specialists to keep them informed and gain their support.

CONTENTS

However exemplary a school library media center's collection, budget, physical design, and staff may be, if the school community and the community outside the school are unaware of its program, lack understanding of its philosophy, and are ignorant of its role in education, the center will be unable to fulfill its mission effectively. A dynamic public relations and publicity program keeps youngsters coming to the library, develops a collegial and cooperative attitude among teachers and administrators, and creates a support base within the community. The keys to a successful public relations program are planning, setting goals and objectives, taking action, and evaluating results. Using such a planned system rather than a scattershot approach enables the media center manager to keep control of the public relations program and monitor its effectiveness.

The first section states that successful public relations begins with its initiator, the school library media specialist. Self-examination is prescribed, and suggestions are provided for evaluating the image that one projects and for changing the attitudes behind the less than positive likenesses the public might perceive. Smiling though one's feet hurt and a sense of humor are important prerequisites.

In the second section students are the main target; and questionnaires, surveys, and comment boxes will elicit their attitudes and needs. A variety of activities and special events are described, many of them punctuated with a certain admirable lightheartedness. Among them are Melvil Dewey Day; a Medieval Fair, including a skit entitled "Hastle in the Castle"; book days; author festivals; and an overnight sleep-in (only for the very brave). Such activities must be duly reported to the local press and should involve other members of the school staff.

The contents of the next section can perhaps be best summed up by one of the suggested steps in promoting the school library media center among teachers, administrators, and district staff: "Never Let Them Forget You." Recommended ways of maintaining a high awareness level are simple but effective if practiced regularly.

Reaching parents and relating to the public outside the school community are the subjects of succeeding chapters in which methods and attitudes are discussed. Press and media coverage, preparing displays and exhibits, and methods of developing cooperative relationships with public library peers are the subjects of additional chapters. A useful lesson in effective public speaking is also provided. The book concludes with a chapter on planning and evaluating the public relations program. A bibliography and an index round out the presentation.

AUTHORITY

Edsall has gathered examples and ideas from her own experience and a variety of reports on ideas that have worked for school library media specialists throughout the country.

COMMENT

A light but persuasive touch, careful organization, and a firm footing in the realities of school library media center operation inform this book, and make it the first step on the journey to successful relations with the public both inside and outside the school.

Franklin, Linda Campbell. *Publicity and Display Ideas for Libraries.* **McFarland, 1985. 264 pp. ISBN 0-89950-168-0 (pap.).**

PURPOSE

Written primarily for public libraries, this book can serve the display needs of school libraries as well. It suggests a variety of ways to get youngsters into the library and how to market the riches that are there for them.

CONTENTS

An earlier book by Franklin (*Library Display Ideas,* McFarland, 1980) presents ideas geared for school libraries with information on lettering techniques, making papier-mâché objects, and using other crafts, but was unavailable for review here. This companion piece presents a variety of marketing tools for promotion and display and offers suggestions for posters, brochures, and newsletters.

Among the display elements are easy-to-make hand cutouts for holding signs, a giraffe book display rack, and small dummy figures for display windows. Using and combining clip art figures is another ingenious source for pictorial displays. Display designs and bulletin boards are illustrated, and materials needed and instructions for using them are provided. Ideas for inviting and encouraging patron participation in library activities are also presented.

Developing a character to represent a particular library is another good suggestion, which is followed by ways of using the character in publicizing the library. A few quotations to use in the publicity are provided, and some additional ideas are briefly described with suggestions for using them. A calendar lists momentous events, birthdays, and other causes for celebration of every day of the year.

Bibliographies, a list of materials and supplies and their sources, and an index complete the book.

AUTHORITY
Linda Campbell Franklin, a writer-artist, has been a librarian, bookstore manager, and display artist.

COMMENT
The gift of creativity has clearly been bestowed on this writer-artist. Her ideas will suggest many ways to publicize and promote library media centers and their activities.

Heath, Alan. *Off the Wall: The Art of Book Display*. Libraries Unlimited, 1987. 153 pp. ISBN 0-87287-578-4 (pap.).

PURPOSE
Attractive displays help get the books "off the wall" and into readers' hands, and Heath offers ideas and techniques for displays, decorating walls, and enlivening other areas in the library with color and images.

CONTENTS
Heath starts off with some idea sources and basic concepts, reminding the reader that inspiration can be found in department stores, museums, films and magazines, among other places, and that keeping ideas on file holds them ready for future use. He demonstrates the use of various design shapes and describes and illustrates lettering techniques and offers some rules to follow. He shows how to use paper towel tubes and similar castoffs, and suggests that photo-

graphs of readers will promote reading. How to make puppets and mobiles is also illustrated and described.

Specific display themes addressed include a treasure chest, Valentine's Day, Christmas and other holidays, sailing and the sea, fishing, and folklore. The author has also concocted an enchanted forest setting using silhouettes that makes a perfect border for folktales and other themes of fantasy and mystery. Children can participate in this sort of display, and Heath describes how to involve them and use the display as a learning center. There are ideas for science fiction, all-season displays, and creating stock characters.

Illustrations are in generous abundance; with these and some imagination and paper and scissors, the reader is invited to create some equally effective displays. A bibliography and an index complete the book.

AUTHORITY

Heath teaches at the American School in London, and has been chairman of the Media Services Committee of the European Council of International Schools.

COMMENT

While the bibliography includes several English sources, there are many American ones as well. The author presents many good ideas and offers helpful information and techniques, but their execution will require time, patience, and some degree of native skill. Some fine displays can result from the use of this book.

Kohn, Rita, and Krysta A. Tepper. *Have You Got What They Want? Public Relations Strategies for the School Librarian/ Media Specialist: A Workbook.* **Scarecrow, 1982. 222 pp. ISBN 0-8108-1481-1 (pap.).**

PURPOSE

An effective public relations program for a school library media center will promote understanding of its functions and enthusiasm for its goals. Kohn and Tepper offer some strategies for relating school library services to the public that it serves.

CONTENTS

The best plans for providing excellence in school library programs and services are doomed unless the school community is aware of them. A planned public relations program will put the school library in the school's consciousness as an indispensable partner in the teaching-learning process. Communication is essential to that awareness, and involves the giving and receiving of messages on both sides of the communication equation. The process, according to Kohn and Tepper, involves, first, deciding what the library media specialist wants to provide and, second, determining what all members of the school community—administration, faculty, students, and parents—want of the media center. They suggest an open-ended survey.

The danger is, however, that sometimes the public may want something other than what the school library media specialist may have in mind. The administration, for example, may envision a media center with a rigid schedule of 20 periods a week of language arts classes. The students may want a place to hang out when class gets boring or the lunchroom too noisy. The faculty may want a subscription to the *Wall Street Journal,* and an occasional class visit to learn about the card catalog. And some parents may want a collection devoid of controversial materials.

Consider, then, a safer approach, a structured survey, in which the librarian suggests the alternatives and the school community chooses from a menu of possibilities. Room for additional suggestions can always be provided. The book provides a wealth of strategies to employ once a clear direction has been determined: Find a business sponsor, work with the Chamber of Commerce and other community organizations, develop a library booster club. These are just a few of the suggestions offered. The authors also provide ideas for bulletin boards, posters, and fliers to announce special activities and various other ways of reminding the audience that someone is there and willing.

The importance of securing and maintaining administrative support is emphasized, and ways of assuring it are described. Methods of fund-raising for special projects are also suggested. Appendixes provide forms that may be used or adapted, as well as a planning outline. A bibliography and an index conclude the book.

AUTHORITY

The authors have visited many media centers in their search for successful ideas, and their research and forethought are evident.

COMMENT

The many sketches, layouts, and verbal suggestions in this handbook suggest a variety of ways to stimulate awareness of the school media center, what it does, and what it can do.

Liebold, Louise Condak. *Fireworks, Brass Bands, and Elephants: Promotional Events with Flair for Libraries and Other Nonprofit Organizations.* **Oryx, 1986. 135 pp. ISBN 0-89774-249-4 (pap.).**

PURPOSE

In this how-to book of ideas for special events, Liebold shares her know-how and experiences in devising and organizing many successful public happenings on behalf of libraries and other institutions. Although public librarians are the intended audience, creative school librarians can make their own adaptations, mostly on a smaller scale.

CONTENTS

The color and enthusiasm that Liebold brings to her work are captured in the lively prose and perky layouts that are characteristic of this book. Beginning with "Guidelines for Success" and concluding with "Over 100 Exciting Ideas," many of them appropriate for school libraries, Liebold lays the groundwork for some exciting and effective public events. All of them exemplify the advice she offers her readers.

A chapter is devoted to each of several kinds of special events: celebrations of birthdays, anniversaries, building dedications, and various other themes; ventures cosponsored with other community groups; fund-raising events; games and contests; and festivals and fairs. Whatever the program, the same ingredients are required: freeing one's creative impulses, careful planning, seeking the cooperation of others, effective publicizing and promoting, anticipating the unexpected, recording the event, and finding a gimmick—not necessarily in that order.

As the hows and whys of publicity are explored, some valuable suggestions are made on the design and use of graphics, the preparation of newsletters, the selection of type, the preparation of news releases, and other elements of effective publicity activities. Each chapter provides a list of resources, including books, periodicals, organizations, and people. An index is also included.

Perhaps the most important advice to program planners is to seek and use the help of others. Experience in preparing conferences, festivals, and other special events has taught that most people will happily contribute their ideas during the planning process, others are pleased to share their expertise and enthusiasm in carrying out the event, and a well-prepared audience will flock to and participate in a well-conceived and well-publicized program. The bonus is the enthusiasm and interest generated among those who were involved in some way in developing the program, as well as those who participated in the event itself.

AUTHORITY

A total of 25 years' experience in the creation and promotion of special events, some of these in the service of the East Meadow Public Library, New York, provided the background for Liebold's book.

COMMENT

While some of the events described here are of the blockbuster variety—the Bronx Zoo's celebration of Astor the baby elephant's first birthday, R. H. Macy's tap dancing extravaganza (3,450 dancers tapping to "Give My Regards to Broadway" on that very thoroughfare in New York City)—most can be adapted to any setting. The trick is to exercise creativity, get lots of help, and begin in a small way.

Mallett, Jerry J. *Library Bulletin Boards and Displays Kit.* Center for Applied Research in Education, 1984. 295 pp. ISBN 0-87628-533-7 (pap.).

PURPOSE

Prepared for the use of elementary and middle school library media specialists and reading teachers, this book offers display ideas to motivate children to read and help them learn library skills.

CONTENTS

The book is divided into two sections: "Circulation Motivators" and "Skills Builders." In the first section are 27 ideas for bulletin boards and displays that are designed to catch the children's eyes and encourage them to read. Many of them involve participation as well. The idea is to create the bulletin board using the patterns in the book, the materials that are listed, and the instructions that are provided, and then complete it with book titles and jackets from books that are in the library. The author suggests titles as well. Many of the patterns are large enough to use as they are; others can be enlarged through the use of an overhead or opaque projector.

The second section provides aids for teaching library skills. Skills building display ideas are grouped together in ten sections among which are alphabetizing, card catalog, table of contents, and guide words. Each group includes an introductory lesson followed by the display ideas and patterns. The 49 bulletin boards and displays can be used to reinforce skills that have already been taught in a curriculum integrated fashion.

Mallett is a professor of education at Findlay College, Ohio, and has been a teacher, reading specialist, and school principal.

This large format book (8½ × 11 inches) allows most patterns to be easily duplicated and used as they are, although some require enlargement. They will not win any prizes for aesthetics, but they will help the busy librarian keep bulletin boards filled with pleasant and mildly amusing displays that will attract children and reinforce reading habits and skill instruction.

Matthews, Judy Gay, et al. *ClipArt & Dynamic Designs for Libraries and Media Centers: Books and Basics*, Vol. 1. Libraries Unlimited, 1988. 193 pp. ISBN 0-87287-636-5.

A lack of clip art prepared specifically for books has prompted Matthews and her coauthors (Michael Mancarella and Shirley Lambert) to provide librarians, teachers, and others interested in books and libraries not only book-related art but also instructions and suggestions for designing their own graphics and printed items.

Those who have ever tried to prepare a brochure, poster, or other graphic product know how difficult it can be to turn out a professional-looking job without the proper tools or training. Part 1 of this book offers advice on planning the product and lists and describes the tools that are needed. It explains terms used in describing type and type design, and demonstrates or describes the results of using various kinds of type and leading, as well as placement of copy. Commercial lettering, page decorating devices, and techniques of handlettering are also described and illustrated.

The elements of preparing layouts are discussed and illustrated, as are various ways of folding paper. The uses and reproduction of color are explained, and information is provided about paper size, weight, texture, finish, and other qualities. Instructions are provided for sizing illustrations, along with helpful information about the use of photographs.

Printing the product brings another set of concerns: Assembling, pasting up, and otherwise readying the mechanical, providing instructions for the printer, determining costs and specifications, checking page proofs, and deciding on bindings are all part of the process of working with the printer. For simpler projects, a photocopier may suffice, and its use is also described. A final, brief chapter focuses on the uses and design of posters, followed by some poster layouts and other simple projects that begin Part 2.

Some 130 pages are devoted to clip art of various kinds: line drawings, cartoonlike characters, a few photographs, and some printed material. Although the text is copyrighted, the art may be reproduced for other than commercial use. A brief bibliography identifies other clip art sources, a glossary explains graphics and printing terms, and an index helps locate specific art or information.

AUTHORITY
Judy Gay Matthews is production manager and Shirley Lambert is marketing director, both at Libraries Unlimited; Michael Mancarella is a free-lance graphic artist.

COMMENT
Achieving that professional look in newsletters, handouts, posters, signs, and the like can be a difficult task. This guidebook and art source provides the wherewithal for eye-catching and effective graphic communication. Another valuable source is Dover Publications, whose catalog lists its books of uncopyrighted clip art.

Tuggle, Ann Montgomery, and Dawn Hansen Heller. *Grand Schemes and Nitty-Gritty Details: Library PR That Works.* **Libraries Unlimited, 1987. 237 pp. ISBN 0-82787-565-2 (pap.).**

PURPOSE
Informing the community about its programs and services is an often neglected part of a library's management scheme. This book describes award-winning models of successful public relations programs.

CONTENTS
Based on their examination of award-winning programs (the John Cotton Dana Public Relations Award), Tuggle and Heller have developed some recommendations for successful public relations programs. Included among their approaches are partnering with other groups, offering strong programs, demonstrating a caring atmosphere in the library, and highlighting special events.

The book is divided into two sections, the first of which offers nine principles for successful programs of public relations. Each of these ideas is elaborated in one of the chapters, and the exemplary programs are described. The second section provides the nitty-gritty details, and offers practical advice for carrying them out. Illustrations provide visual examples of effective graphics and other eye-catching features, and the authors analyze those qualities of the models that led to their success.

An appendix lists the award-winning libraries, and an index completes the book.

AUTHORITY

Tuggle is chairperson of the Library Media Services Department of Glenbard East High School, Lombard, Illinois. Heller is media coordinator at Riverside-Brookfield District 208, Riverside, Illinois.

COMMENT

While some of the winning projects described are for libraries other than school library media centers, all have features that may be adapted for use in school media centers. This book helps identify those factors that make for success not only in public relations and publicity but also in school library media programs and management.

Volz, Carol Brandenburg, and Mari Tru. *Keep It Simple— Bulletin Board Ideas for Grades 7–12.* **Scarecrow, 1987. 133 pp. ISBN 0-8108-1969-4 (pap.).**

PURPOSE

Ideas for bulletin boards and patterns for constructing them are presented for the use of secondary school teachers; they can be suitably used by school media specialists as well.

CONTENTS

Nineteen ideas for bulletin board displays are presented, with titles, designs, and patterns for their various parts. While the ideas are classroom-oriented, they are readily adaptable for displaying book jackets, presenting book lists, and other library display purposes. Volz and Tru describe how the patterns can be enlarged with the use of an overhead projector. They also list materials needed, suggest alternative titles and themes, and offer instructions.

AUTHORITY

Carol Brandenburg Volz has been a teacher of business subjects at Lloyd Memorial High School, Kentucky, and Mari Tru is an art teacher in the same school.

COMMENT

These ideas are not exactly inspired, and might better serve upper elementary and junior high school librarians and teachers rather than those in high schools, for whom the book was prepared. A forthcoming book from the publisher might better serve display needs: Nancy Everhart, et al., *Library Displays* (Scarecrow, 1989. 124 pp.).

Wilson Patricia, and Ann C. Kimzey. *Happenings: Developing Successful Programs for School Libraries.* SEE Chapter 9, The School Library Media Program.

5
Evaluating the School Library Media Program

When evaluation was set up as one of the chapters in this book, it was with the supposition that the importance of evaluation would have prompted the recent appearance of a number of books on the subject. That supposition seems to be incorrect. Instead, while chapters on evaluation appear in books on other aspects of library service or in books about library management in general, there is a scarcity of books devoted just to evaluating the total school library media center in all its diverse functions.

Fortunately, those few books that are available are good ones, as has been noted in the reviews. Of particular importance is ALA's recently published *Information Power.* Among the books that include material about evaluation, in addition to those reviewed here, are David Loertscher, *Taxonomies of the School Library Media Program* and Ruth Ann Davies, *The School Library Media Program,* both discussed in Chapter 13, "The Library Media Center and the Curriculum." The evaluation of school library standards and guidelines is traced in the additional readings at the end of this chapter.

American Association of School Librarians and Association for Educational Communications and Technology. *Information Power: Guidelines for School Library Media Programs.* **ALA, 1988. 171 pp. ISBN 0-8389-3352-1 (pap.).**

PURPOSE

Defining the mission of the school library media center and what is needed to accomplish its goals, the ALA and AECT writing committee sets forth guidelines for library media professionals toward the achievement of programs that meet the needs of students, teachers, and parents in the twenty-first century.

CONTENTS

Responding to the changing nature of educational programs in the nation's schools and the new demands of information technology, this publication is a comprehensive guide to new standards for school media programs. While avoiding stating quantitative standards in absolute terms, the book offers guidelines based on "high service programs" that were identified in a national survey conducted by the Center for Educational Statistics, U.S. Department of Education.

From the mission statement in the opening chapter to the final chapter on district, regional, and state services, emphasis is on the vital instructional role of media centers in individual schools. The importance of qualified, trained media personnel is discussed, and guidelines are established for preparation programs and continuing education, as well as the personal and professional competencies required. In focusing on the media professional's role in the school media program, the authors stress the importance of confident and enthusiastic leadership, planning, and management as the basic requirements for accomplishing the mission, goals, and objectives of the building level program. Underlying the focus of this landmark publication is the vision of dynamism in the school library media program, and the importance of interaction among the school library media specialist, faculty, administration, and students.

For those who doubt the imminence of change, these guidelines provide a rational, needs-based imperative for change and the suggested means by which it may be accomplished—leadership, planning, and example. The example is provided in the appended "Survey of School Library Media Centers" which describes numerically the staffing, collections, facilities, and budgets of schools in the 75th, 90th, and 95th percentiles of schools covered in the survey. Those who have had to make do with a good deal less can read it and weep, or exercise the leadership and planning required for moving forward.

Appendixes on the results of the Center for Educational Statistics survey include statistics on staff, collections, facilities and equipment, and budget; formulas for determining budget allocations in various circumstances; facilities guidelines; policies and statements (e.g., Library Bill of Rights); a bibliography; and a list of contributors.

AUTHORITY

The writing committee, consultants, and editorial committee constitute the leadership of the school library and educational communications world and include a range of competencies and experience, from school and district library media specialists to graduate library school and academic library personnel.

Written with clarity and conviction, this book presents a philosophical and practical framework for the future of school library media programs. Those in need of renewal of their sense of mission will find it here; those in need of support for fulfilling the mission will find that also. After reading the book, present a copy to your school administrator. Then find the opportunity to talk about it and get her or his support in implementing its recommendations.

Blazek, Ron, ed. *Achieving Accountability: Readings on the Evaluation of Media Centers.* **ALA, 1981. 266 pp. ISBN 0-8389-0349-5 (pap.).**

PURPOSE

As funding for school library media programs began to dwindle in the 1970s, a wave of self-examination broke upon the profession, and "accountability" became the watchword in education. The articles selected for this book, written during this period, provide tools for evaluation and change.

CONTENTS

Blazek notes in his introduction the adaptation of business management techniques to educational settings. The managment process continues to influence educational planning, and evaluation is an important part of this process, since it may lead to revisions of other phases of the planning and implementation strategies. Evaluation of school media programs can no longer rest on such data as circulation, size of the collection, budget, and the like, but seeks also to determine the program's impact on learners.

"Understanding Accountability" is the subject of the first of five parts. Blanche Woolls examines the purpose and methods of evaluation and urges that evaluation results be reported, however they turn out. A look at the evaluation models depicted in the second article is enough to reveal the complexities inherent in the process. Or is it a process? A semantic analysis of "evaluation" suggests that it also means a product, and in either case, the emotional baggage it carries is threatening. Absent a better descriptor, however, evaluation is still the management tool that is needed to determine any program's effectiveness. Evaluation is subject to limitations and abuses, and such barriers as the threat it poses and its sometimes contradictory purposes are analyzed in the third article. Jane Anne Hannigan is concerned that accountability to the institution will replace the true and essential object, the child. The affective results of the media program should not be overlooked, she asserts.

Part 2, "Preparing for Accountability," focuses on setting goals and objectives as a next step toward program evaluation. Four articles describe media program management, state objectives and standards, and offer an overview of the process of determining goals and objectives.

Part 3, "Selecting a Course of Action," discusses various methods for determining accountability, including planning, programming, budgeting system (PPBS), management by objectives (MBO), and program evaluation review technique (PERT). Rosalind Miller's article offers a checklist of criteria to replace the approach that had favored counting the collection, and Janet Stroud suggests tools for evaluating the program for use by practitioners.

In "Measuring Service," Part 4, the articles suggest ways of appraising services of the school library media center as a preliminary to improving its program. Some studies and research on aspects of media center programs are presented here, and the roles and functions of school library media specialists are examined.

Part 5 discusses "Evaluating Impact." The impact of school library media services in particular settings is studied in two evaluation projects, and reports on evaluations of Elementary and Secondary Education Act (ESEA) Title II programs are discussed in an article by Mary Helen Mahar.

In an epilogue, Shirley L. Aaron comments on evaluation of media programs for the 1980s, noting the importance of focusing on learner outcomes. Positive evaluation results will influence the attitudes of school decision makers only when they are informed of the effectiveness of the school media program. School media specialists must learn how to present the persuasive information in an effective way.

AUTHORITY

Ron Blazek is a member of the faculty of the School of Library Science, Florida State University. The contributions were written by leaders in school library media services.

COMMENT

Readers looking for specific evaluative criteria will find some in a few of the articles presented here. The book's primary importance, however, is in the philosophical framework it has built and in its assurance that evaluating media programs is an important step toward their high consideration among educational priorities.

Lindsey, Jonathan A., ed. *Performance Evaluation: A Management Basic for Libraries.* Oryx, 1986. 222 pp. ISBN 0-89774-313-X.

PURPOSE

This collection of articles about performance appraisal describes the process and its components and offers advice and analysis of its elements. Its insights and arguments are directed at administrators of larger libraries, and may prove useful to district media supervisors and school principals. The objects of appraisal, school library media specialists, may find comfort (or frustration) in these examinations of what ought to be.

CONTENTS

School library media specialists who are faced with a yearly evaluation of their performance and competence may wonder at appraisal forms that include such teacher-directed items as wise use of classroom time, fairness in evaluating pupil progress, and other classroom-oriented criteria. Two of the articles included here deal with this anomaly, and suggest other methods of determining the effectiveness of school library media specialists. Successful evaluation methods not only examine past performance but can contribute to current and future improvements in performance.

Some of the factors that contribute to the inadequacy of performance appraisal as applied to school librarians are enumerated in "A Practical Model for a Developmental Appraisal Program for School Library Media Specialists" by Fred C. Pfister and Nelson Towle. The article describes the development of a performance appraisal model and its positive effects not only on performance but also on communication and understanding of the school library media specialist's role. Clearly, school library media specialists should not be evaluated by performance measures that are based on other job requirements than the ones they perform, yet in most cases they are, and the time for change has long since arrived.

The remainder of the articles deal with various other aspects of performance appraisal but outside of the context of the school library media specialist's role. They are applicable to academic and public librarians primarily, and examine the process from the viewpoint of managers rather than practitioners. Among the concerns considered are how to conduct appraisal interviews, the importance of effective communication, issues raised by considerations of law and ethics, different methods of appraising performance, evaluating the appraisers, and problems of appraisal.

AUTHORITY

Jonathan A. Lindsey is coordinator of library affairs at Baylor University, Waco, Texas, and the co-author of *Professional Ethics and Librarians* (Oryx, 1985). The articles were written by management experts, consultants, college faculty members, and librarians.

COMMENT

Those looking for concrete standards by which school library media specialists may be evaluated will not find them in this book. Instead, this is a collection of useful comments on the evaluation process and its principles and practices, with two articles that deal specifically with evaluating school library media specialists. As a useful tool for those who have appraisal responsibilities, school and district level supervisors, and a key to understanding their problems and methods, it is recommended reading for school library media specialists, as well as those who evaluate their performance.

Loertscher, David V., ed. *Measures of Excellence for School Library Media Centers*. Libraries Unlimited, 1989. 148 pp. ISBN 0-87287-652-7.

PURPOSE

This collection of articles that first appeared in the *Drexel Library Quarterly* (vol. 21, no. 2) presents new ways of measuring the effectiveness of school library media programs.

CONTENTS

If a new conceptual framework is emerging concerning the management of school library services, then new ways of evaluating them become an important element not only in examining management practices, but also in revising them. The basic precepts on which these new measures are based appear to be, first, that the school library media center's primary function is inseparable from the school's instructional purpose, and, second, that evaluating the effectiveness of the program is basic to its successful management. The old quantitative measures of school library programs no longer satisfy the imperatives of school library media center management. Meaningful indicators of quality programs are those that reveal their effects on schools' instructional programs.

The new concept suggests that the school library media specialist is an essential partner in the instructional program, providing the materials of instruction and participating in curriculum planning and implementation as a bona fide member of the instructional team. This role takes precedence over all other activities, and therein lies the difference. If this model is valid, then it is important to evaluate how well the collection meets curriculum needs, how effectively the school library media specialist participates in planning with teachers, and what results of sample teaching activities in the school library media center can be observed.

The articles in *Measures of Excellence for School Library Media Centers* describe some of the research and various evaluation strategies that measure potential and actual performance of school library media specialists in the areas of instructional teamwork, personality, and ability to communicate; effects of media production in the library media center; methods of media utilization in the classroom; use of periodicals on microfiche; and effectiveness of 16mm film libraries.

Most attention is given to collection development, and collection mapping is the subject of three articles. The first describes it as a means of evaluating a collection in terms of the school's curriculum, the second summarizes research on collection mapping, and the third suggests its usefulness as a planning tool in collection development. Techniques for performing these analyses rely on the use of computers, and a detailed procedure for collection mapping is the substance of David Loertscher and May Lein Ho's subsequent publication, *Computerized Collection Development for School Library Media Centers* (reviewed in Chapter 13, "The Library Media Center and the Curriculum"). Each of the other articles treats one of the performance or program areas.

AUTHORITY

Loertscher is senior acquisitions editor for Libraries Unlimited, and is a former professor at the University of Oklahoma Graduate School of Library and Information Studies, Norman, as well as at the University of Arkansas, Fayetteville, and Purdue University, West Lafayette, Indiana. Contributors are school media specialists, district supervisors of media services, and present or former members of library school faculties.

COMMENT

Evaluation is an essential element in effective management, whether of a business or an educational enterprise, simply because it enables the manager to judge the success of a plan and to correct its deficiencies. The "measures of excellence" described in these articles are, at the very least, provocative and may spark a change of course in some school library media programs. They merit study.

Needham, William L., and Gerald Jahoda. *Improving Library Service to Physically Disabled Persons.* SEE Chapter 12, Serving Special Learners.

Yesner, Bernice L., and Hilda L. Jay. *The School Administrator's Guide to Evaluating Library Media Programs.* **Library Professional, 1987. 236 pp. ISBN 0-208-02147-7.**

PURPOSE

Prepared for school administrators' use in evaluating the school library media program, this guide also provides material for school media specialists to use in self-evaluation. The suggested evaluation modules can be effective reminders to teachers of what the media program is all about and what it can do for them.

CONTENTS

Evaluating school library media specialists and the programs they offer has been at best a spotty proposition and at worst a totally inappropriate procedure. Many administrators still use the same irrelevant (as applied to school library media specialists) instruments that are used for teacher evaluations, and some still lack a clear concept of what they should be evaluating. This book applies the evaluation process to the aspects of the media center program and its goals and objectives that need improvement or merit approval.

Sixty evaluation modules are presented on topics that range from access to weeding and include collection development, integrated print and nonprint collections, faculty use of the school library media center program, inventory and follow-up, networking, management of computers for educational use, leadership role of the school library media center, facilities, controversial topics and censorship, and displays and exhibits. Accompanying the modules are checklists for determining positives and negatives, and sample questionnaires.

Appendixes provide sample evaluation forms used in the Montgomery County public schools: a comparison of criteria used to evaluate library media specialists and classroom teachers, evaluation of media specialists' services, and performance criteria for media specialists and for teachers. Questionnaires for student evaluation of the elementary and secondary school media programs; job description, functions, and procedures for the circulation desk aide; and an interpretation of the Library Bill of Rights are also included. Notes, a glossary, a bibliography, and an index complete the book.

Bernice Yesner has been a school librarian, consultant, and library school teacher. Hilda Jay has written many professional books for school library media specialists and was director of a high school library media program.

Those school administrators who know exactly what they want from the school library media program and establish a suitable climate for getting it are rare indeed, and should be given every encouragement. Some tend to ignore the program entirely; others make unreasonable and unknowing demands; and still others are content to leave things to their capable media specialists. All will find this book a useful tool for assuring optimum school library media services, programs, and performance. It can also be used by media specialists for help in establishing policy guidelines.

ADDITIONAL READINGS

School library media specialists interested in the evolution of school library standards will find some key documents listed chronologically below.

NEA and North Central Association of Colleges and Secondary Schools, Committee on Library Organization and Equipment. *Standard Library Organization and Equipment for Secondary Schools of Different Sizes.* C. C. Certain, Chairman, ALA, 1920.

ALA, Committee on Postwar Planning. *School Libraries for Today and Tomorrow: Functions and Standards.* ALA, 1945.

AASL. *Standards for School Library Programs.* ALA, 1960.

NEA, Dept. of Audiovisual Instruction. *Quantitative Standards for Audiovisual Personnel, Equipment and Materials in Elementary, Secondary, and Higher Education.* Developed by Gene Faris and Mendel Sherman. NEA, Dept. of Audiovisual Instruction, January 1966.

AASL and NEA, Dept. of Audiovisual Instruction. *Standards for School Media Programs.* ALA and NEA, 1969.

AASL and AECT. *Media Programs: District and School.* ALA and AECT, 1975.

The School Library
Media Collection

6
Collection Management

Changes in nomenclature usually signal changes in the underlying concept of the process being named. "Collection management" in school library media centers underwent a change in focus as non-print media entered the picture, and the advent of computer software adds another change. "Book selection" no longer fits the process. Beyond the recognition of the diversity of the collection's components is the acknowledgment that the collection can no longer be considered a simple assemblage of books but a dynamic and changing entity that reflects the specific and general needs and purposes of the population that the library serves.

Because of this, selection has become a more complex task, one no longer satisfied by choosing new materials individually because of favorable recommendations to add to an already established core collection. Selection must take into account new instructional programs in the school, perhaps a changing population, and imperatives arising from the curriculum and other changes. The development of cooperative collection development in library networks will also influence the selection process, as school libraries are linked to each other and other types of libraries in regional systems. Periodical holdings may be altered by the introduction of on-line searching, and the reference collection may be altered by it as well.

Managing the collection requires a host of new skills, from the use of automated acquisition methods and bibliographic utilities to the political savvy required to fend off censorship attempts or shepherd a selection policy through the education hierarchy. Fortunately, a number of publications are at hand that offer guidance in all of these complexities. The most recent and comprehensive work is Phyllis Van Orden's *The Collection Program in Schools*. Betty Kemp offers a more limited scope for librarians interested in policies and procedures (see Chapter 2, "Technical Services"), and Alan Scham, in *Managing Special Collections,* deals with special collections, not ordinarily a consideration in most school media programs, but relevant for those participating in cooperative collection development or seeking ways of preserving school archives.

The curriculum/collection relationship is explored by David Loertscher and May Lein Ho in *Computerized Collection Development for School Library Media Centers.* This entry is part of Chapter 13, "The Library Media Center and the Curriculum," despite its title, because of its emphasis on curriculum as the decisive factor in collection decisions, as well as its relationship to Loertscher's *Taxonomies of the School Library Media Program,* also in Chapter 13. *Human (and Antihuman) Values in Children's Books,* from the Council on Interracial Books for Children, is included here because of its influence on collection policies. Reviews of the other books indicate their relevance and contribution to knowledge of the subject.

Broadus, Robert N. *Selecting Materials for Libraries.* **Wilson, 1973. 342 pp. ISBN 0-8242-0659-2.**

PURPOSE

Writing for students of library science as well as practicing librarians, Broadus offers approaches to selection that encompass an understanding of the general principles involved, as well as the problems inherent in particular fields in which selections will be made.

CONTENTS

Beginning with an introduction to the basic problem, the sheer quantity of materials that exists, Broadus proceeds to establish the general selection principles that must be considered, relating them to the various kinds of libraries. He follows this with a description of the publishing world and presents some book trade tools, such as *Books in Print* (Bowker) and other comprehensive bibliographies. From here, Broadus proceeds to a discussion of selection criteria and such general aids and guides to selection as the Wilson catalogs and various readers' guides and advisers. He describes various reviewing media and such print materials as government publications, periodicals, and free and inexpensive materials. Chapters on nonprint materials and principles for selecting them conclude this section of the book.

To his discussions of selection in the various fields of human knowledge, Broadus brings a uniquely perceptive and often witty point of view. He defines each field and takes its measure, surveying its values and structure and mentioning seminal publications in the subject, selection criteria and aids, notable periodicals, and special principles and problems in selection that are particular to a given field. The subjects covered are biography, literature and fiction, history, geography, and the social sciences in general, and in particular (included here are psychology, education, economics, political science, sociology and anthropology), the humanities, religion, philosophy and the arts, science and technology.

Appended to each chapter are notes that refer to major works in the field discussed. An index completes the book.

AUTHORITY

Broadus is a professor in the School of Library Service, University of North Carolina at Chapel Hill.

COMMENT

The final sentence of the book indicates Broadus's premise that people who have both a knowledge of information management and an understanding of people will be able to bring the two together and thereby retain a place for themselves. To serve a library's clientele, it is important to understand them and their needs and aspirations and to know how to select those materials that will best suit them. Although Broadus has not considered children's books in this work, his comments have valid applications in that area as well. And certainly high school librarians will find his observations both helpful and enlightening.

Council on Interracial Books for Children, Racism and Sexism Resource Center for Educators. *Human (and Anti-human) Values in Children's Books: A Content Rating Instrument for Educators and Concerned Parents.* **CIBC, 1976. 279 pp.**

PURPOSE

The Council on Interracial Books for Children (CIBC) has long been in the forefront of organizations that are striving to raise consciousness about racism, sexism, and a good many other isms as depicted in children's books. In its effort to promote books that avoid these isms, CIBC has developed a checklist for rating books according to the absence or presence of the characteristics it deplores. This book was written to present and justify that rating system and to demonstrate its application.

CONTENT

The books analyzed in this publication were selected from those submitted by publishers in response to the Council's request for books published in 1975 that had minority, feminist, and social issue themes. From these, 235 books were selected for analysis and review. (The criteria used for their selection were not stated in the introductory text.) The reviewers were matched racially or ethnically with the books they reviewed; blacks reviewed books about blacks, Chicanos reviewed books about Chicanos, and so forth. Reviewers were asked to watch for sexism, elitism, and other anti-human values. Some of the reviewers, however, were not sensitive to all the areas of concern, and so their reviews were rejected.

Each review is followed by a reproduction of the checklist, with the reviewer's checks. The checklist consists of a column of words such as anti-racist, anti-ageist, anti-individualist, and so on, followed by a space for a check for art and another for words. A second column substitutes the prefix non- for anti-, and a third eliminates the prefixes. Thus a book can be rated anti-sexist, non-sexist or sexist, and there are seven such terms. At the bottom of the checklist is a place for checking excellent, good, fair, or poor for literary quality and art quality. Reviewers are also asked to rate the book's treatment of females and minorities. Does it inspire the reader to act against oppression? Is it culturally authentic? A place for check marks is again provided. The first appearance of the checklist in the book is accompanied by definitions of the terms used.

The books that are analyzed range in age level from preschool to teenage, and the subject matter includes various contemporary problems, among them divorce, substance abuse, and adoption.

AUTHORITY

The introduction was written by Beryle Banfield and Bradford Chambers, president and vice president, respectively, of the Council. The reviewers were not identified.

COMMENT

One can applaud the wish to eliminate all the isms and stereotypes deplored by the Council without agreeing with its methods or its premise that by reading books that are tainted with what the Council considers sexism or racism or ageism children will be corrupted by them. This approach is no more valid than any other that judges books from a political rather than a literary and artistic perspective. While a critic may reject a book because its characters are presented as stereotypes, that is a literary rather than a political distinction. In selecting books librarians must be sensitive to the values inherent in a book's treatment of its theme, but checklists are not necessarily an

84

index to them. Their use smacks uncomfortably of censorship, and librarians should be wary of them, however much they may agree with the goals of the group that urges it.

Curley, Arthur, and Dorothy Broderick. *Building Library Collections.* **6th ed. Scarecrow, 1985. 339 pp. ISBN 0-8108-1776-4.**

PURPOSE

Writing on collection development for students as well as practitioners, the authors go beyond book selection to consider the theoretical framework upon which collections are built and the practices that result from putting the theories into action.

CONTENTS

Although earlier editions were concerned primarily with the functions and collection practices of public libraries, the current one covers other types of libraries as well. School library media centers are part of this picture, both as themselves and also because many basic principles of collection development are applicable to all kinds of libraries.

A brief discussion of libraries' *raison d'etre* leads to the first principles: that a written collection development policy should exist, and that it should be based on a thorough awareness of the community that a particular library serves. Note the phrase "collection development" as opposed to "book selection." The broader "collection development" implies a more inclusive scope not only in the variety of communications media but also in the selector's breadth of outlook. In addition to the quality of a particular item, selection will also depend on its place as part of a larger entity, the total collection.

The principles of selection lend themselves to all kinds of debate, and some of the knotty questions evoked by traditional principles are asked, even if they cannot be answered definitively. For example, "See to it that no race, nationality, profession, trade, religion, school of thought, or local custom is overlooked." What of the constraints imposed by budget, space, the need for balance, and concern for the social good? And, of course, the opposing pulls of demand versus quality are always with selectors, to say nothing of the diversity of the clientele that schools, particularly, must serve.

The chapter on censorship and selection places the librarian's role in a historical context and demonstrates a notable change in perspective, from an earlier censorial approach to its current antithesis, opposing censorship. While the issues are stated and defined, they are not resolved, particularly in the case of school libraries, as a familiarity with U.S. Supreme Court decisions will confirm.

Other chapters deal with selection aids for print and nonprint materials, the structure and problems of the publishing industry, resource sharing, national and trade bibliography, acquisitions, collection evaluation, and weeding, storage, and preservation.

Each chapter has a lengthy bibliography; and appendixes reproduce the Library Bill of Rights and Freedom to Read and Freedom to View statements. An index concludes the book.

AUTHORITY
Arthur Curley has been director and librarian at the Boston Public Library since 1985. Before that he was deputy director of the New York Public Library and the Detroit Public Library. Dorothy Broderick is editor of *Voice of Youth Advocates* (*VOYA*), published by Scarecrow.

COMMENT
Collection building is so central to library work that it is inconceivable that a single book might satisfy the need for exploring varying points of view. While school librarians might naturally turn to Phyllis Van Orden's work, they would be well advised to examine the subject from the wider perspective offered by Curley and Broderick, as well as Robert Broadus's *Selecting Materials for Libraries*. Curley and Broderick have expanded the concepts involved in selecting materials for libraries in ways that merit attention, at least, and study, at best.

Ellison, John W., and Patricia Ann Coty, eds. *Nonbook Media: Collection Management and User Services.* SEE Chapter 7, Nonprint Media and Computer Software.

Intner, Sheila S. *Access to Media: A Guide to Integrating and Computerizing Catalogs.* SEE Chapter 2, Technical Services.

Katz, William A. *Collection Development: The Selection of Materials for Libraries.* **Holt, 1980. 352 pp. ISBN 0-03-050266-7.**

PURPOSE
The principles and practices of selection are the main emphasis of this book, designed to introduce librarians in all types of libraries and library science students not only to materials selection but also to the development and analysis of the library collection as a whole.

For all libraries, selection is a major concern. For the school library media center particularly, the combination of diminishing budgets, an increasing amount of materials in many formats, and the influence of on-line searching and membership in library networks makes selection increasingly complex. Katz tackles these complexities in three separate sections, the first of which is an introduction.

Beginning with a discussion of selection philosophy, he examines particular concerns by type of library and discusses goals and objectives, issues in developing a philosophy from different points of view, and policy formulation and preparation. The public that the library serves is obviously an important factor in policy decisions, and an analysis of the library's community, with data gathered from observations and questionnaires, provides direction for policy design. Other factors that influence selection are recommended standards and guidelines, the collection's overall size, and goals of level and depth that have been set for parts of the collection. The budget and how it is allocated among various collection areas is clearly a major factor, and decisions must be made that will determine budget allocation not only by subject but also by type of material.

An ongoing analysis and evaluation of the collection will take into account such events in its maintenance as the receipt of gifts, disappearances due to theft, and the effects of weeding. Periodic inventories, user evaluations, and consultants all contribute to the analysis and evaluation of the collection. Katz offers rules for weeding, suggestions on security systems, and some useful comments on gifts. In the fifth and final chapter in the first section, Katz discusses the process of selection, covering evaluation and guidelines and elaborating on aspects of fiction selection. He examines the demand versus quality arguments, and considers the roles of librarian and selection committees and the influence of patrons.

Aids to the selection of print materials are the subject of the second section. Katz identifies and analyzes a wide variety of bibliographies, reviews, review sources, and retrospective lists, covering the gamut of selection tools for books, periodicals, microforms, and pamphlets. He discusses ways of keeping informed on new titles and considers out-of-print materials as well.

The same thoughtful and systematic coverage is applied to nonprint materials in Section 3, which covers selection tools and other considerations in selecting films, recordings, video, filmstrips, pictures, slides, and other nonprint media. This final section offers a discussion of censorship, considering the distinctions between selection and censorship, the cases for and against censorship, identifying the censors and their targets, and discussing steps that can be taken to avoid and combat censorship.

AUTHORITY

Bill Katz is a professor at the School of Library and Information Science, State University of New York at Albany, editor of *The Reference Librarian,* and a columnist in *Library Journal.* He has authored a number of books for the use of librarians, primarily about magazines and reference service.

COMMENTS

While this book ranges widely among the issues, principles, and practicalities of collection development, it does not cover the entire spectrum, omitting such areas as government documents, reference materials, and specific subject fields, and touches only briefly on acquisitions and ordering. The selection tools published since 1980 necessarily have not been included either. Despite these lacks, Katz's book is a useful and practical introduction to collection development.

Kemp, Betty, ed. *School Library and Media Center Acquisitions Policies and Procedures,* **2nd ed.** SEE Chapter 2, Technical Services.

Loertscher, David V., and May Lein Ho. *Computerized Collection Development for School Library Media Centers.* SEE Chapter 13, The Library Media Center and the Curriculum.

Scham, Alan M. *Managing Special Collections.* **Neal-Schuman, 1987. 201 pp. ISBN 0-918212-98-7 (pap.).**

PURPOSE

This guide to managing special collections is designed not only for curators of rare books but also for librarians with single author and genre collections or who are involved in cooperative collection development programs.

CONTENTS

Special collections have unique qualities that frequently require different management policies from those used for the rest of the collection. Besides preserving and protecting these collections, particularly if they contain rare and valuable books, librarians have an obligation to inform others of those works so that they may use them. Scham provides guidance in effective management and development, as well as illustrations of budget forms, cataloging examples, and a variety of forms, charts, and tables.

The first of the book's ten chapters describes the importance of a specific development policy, which should contain a mission statement, goals and objectives, and a statement of priorities. The author emphasizes the importance of avoiding generalities and stating the obvious, and suggests instead a focus on such specifics as encouraging donations, establishing endowment funds, listing collection parameters, producing publications and exhibits, and the like. Chapter 2 discusses budgets, including examples and descriptions of line item and five- and ten-year priority budgets. Priorities should be flexibly enforced within the framework of the overall acquisition policy.

Descriptive cataloging and classification are the subjects of Chapter 3, which includes examples of rare book cataloging in antiquarian as well as machine-readable form. Formats are explained and examples provided. Conservation and preservation are discussed in Chapter 4, which also provides some cautionary notes about deterioration of book paper from a former chief of preservation of the Library of Congress, suggesting that everyone may soon be in the book preservation business.

Forms and sources for obtaining insurance and appraisals are included in Chapter 5, which also discusses security and offers some brief but fascinating accounts of several infamous biblioklepts. The contents of statistical and descriptive annual reports are discussed in Chapter 8, with some good advice about contents from the author. Chapters 9 and 10 provide lists of professional organizations, national libraries, and networks and bibliographies about incunabula, bookbinding, printing, and others.

COMMENT

This informative book offers practical advice not only for librarians with special collections but also for any librarian who selects, budgets, deals with administrators, works with the public, and has received gifts of books.

Thomason, Nevada Wallis. *Circulation Systems for School Library Media Centers: Manual to Microcomputers.* SEE Chapter 1, Library Management.

Van Orden, Phyllis J. *The Collection Program in Elementary and Middle Schools: Concepts, Practices, and Information Sources.* **Libraries Unlimited, 1982. 301 pp. ISBN 0-87287-335-8.**

PURPOSE

In this introductory text, Van Orden considers the school library media collection in its relationship to the school environment and education theory. Writing for elementary and middle school library media specialists and those preparing for careers in that profession, she explores the principles, practices, and issues that guide and influence the development, maintenance, and evaluation of library collections.

CONTENTS

The book's 18 chapters are grouped into three parts. Part 1 discusses the setting in which the collection exists, both as part of the school media program and in relation to the school as a whole. Collection development principles are enumerated and discussed, and practical applications and actual situations are presented. The role of the media program in the school, the school library media specialist's role, and the interaction of various elements of the program with the school community and the external community are examined. The collection, the activities that revolve around it, the issues that influence decisions about it, and the policies and procedures that direct its development and maintenance are all discussed in Part 1.

Part 2 is devoted to materials selection, considering procedures, criteria, and the various needs that determine the choices that are made. Van Orden first discusses general selection criteria, then the criteria for the formats in which information and knowledge are presented, including print, visual, aural, and multisensory materials. Beyond evaluating the intrinsic merits of individual materials, however, the librarian must also consider whether an item being considered will meet instructional needs, the general needs of students, and the special needs of various individuals and groups (reluctant readers, exceptional children, students with limited proficiency in English).

The administrative aspects of collection management are the subject of Part 3, which includes discussions of the processes used in acquiring materials, the relationship between acquisitions policies and procedures, and some good advice on planning and organization, paying vendors on time, and the overall development of business acumen. Maintenance policies and procedures and methods for measuring and evaluating the collection are discussed, and a final chapter on initial collections and closing a collection completes the text.

Each chapter ends with a summary, notes, and a bibliography. Two appendixes, associations and agencies, and bibliographic and selection tools, and an index complete the book.

AUTHORITY

Van Orden is associate dean of the School of Library and Information Studies, Florida State University in Tallahassee.

COMMENT

This well-organized introduction to the principles and practices of collection management in school library media centers provides an excellent, clearly written overview of the subject, and is amplified by helpful lists of selection tools and organizations related to library work and education. It won the Blackwell North America Scholarship Award in 1983. While retaining its utility, this book has been superseded by *The Collection Program in Schools: Concepts, Practices, and Information Sources* (reviewed in this chapter).

Van Orden, Phyllis J. *The Collection Program in High Schools: Concepts, Practices, and Information Sources.* **Libraries Unlimited, 1985. 288 pp. ISBN 0-87287-483-4.**

PURPOSE

Van Orden presents the principles and practices of school media collection development. With an eye on education theory, she examines the educational setting within which the collection functions, to present a view of collection development in the high school environment.

CONTENTS

To meet the changing needs of the school with an appropriate collection development program requires zest, knowledge, and an armament of policies, flexibly applied. This text offers an organized approach to the principles that form the base of collection development and the practices that evolve from them. Its three major focal points are the school setting, materials selection, and administrative matters.

Replete with models, charts, and other visual representations of processes and relationships, each chapter presents the theoretical underpinnings and problems of a particular aspect of collection development and concludes with notes and a bibliography. Subjects covered in the first section include the school, physical, and external environments of the collection; issues, policies, and procedures; and methods of developing policy statements.

The materials selection portion, the second section, deals with procedures, criteria, the high school and its purposes and demands, and the media specialist's role in meeting curricular, instructional, and individual needs. The final section covers the management aspects: policies and procedures of acquisition, collection maintenance and evaluation, and starting and closing collections.

There are two appendixes. The first appendix lists associations and agencies and the second provides a comprehensive list of bibliographic and selection tools. A detailed index concludes the book.

AUTHORITY

Van Orden is associate dean of the School of Library and Information Studies, Florida State University in Tallahassee. She is also the Blackwell North America Scholarship Award winner (1983) for her earlier *The Collection Program in Elementary and Middle Schools* (reviewed in this chapter). Van Orden has written extensively on collection development.

COMMENT

Few librarians would dispute the view that the collection is the basic element of the school library media program. It follows, then, that a thorough familiarity with and continuing review of the principles and practices of collection development are essential to maintaining professional competence in this area. This book is an important tool for beginning high school librarians and those who wish to maintain their skill in this vital enterprise. The use of anecdotes, case studies, samples, and questions keeps the text lively and provocative, and its detailed coverage is commendable.

Van Orden, Phyllis J. *The Collection Program in Schools: Concepts, Practices, and Information Sources.* **Libraries Unlimited, 1988. 347 pp. ISBN 0-87287-572-5.**

PURPOSE

Addressing the concerns of all school library media professionals and library school students, this book discusses the essential principles, practices, and issues of collection development, management, and maintenance.

Building on the format and content of her earlier works, one each for high schools and for elementary and middle schools, Van Orden brings a practical approach to collection management. She has considered not only general principles but also their application in the school setting.

The book is divided into three sections, the first of which is devoted to the educational environment and purposes that the media center serves. Integration of the collection with the total school program is a collaborative effort, and is the basis for all that follows. The collection is described as a physical entity that is purposeful and accessible, each item of which relates to the whole. It must satisfy the informational, instructional, and personal needs of users. In order to accomplish this, the media specialist must develop policies and procedures for acquisition and maintenance, taking into consideration all the factors that govern these activities. Among the issues considered are the usefulness of quantitative standards, selection according to demand as opposed to quality, creating a balanced collection, and intellectual freedom and censorship.

Materials selection is the subject of the second section. It begins with a description of selection procedures, and is followed by a discussion of selection tools, publishers' catalogs, personal examination of materials, and involvement of teachers and students in the selection process. General selection criteria are enumerated, followed by criteria according to format. Three separate chapters discuss approaches to meeting needs created by curriculum and instruction and by the range of subjects taught in the school, as well as the needs of individuals, including those with disabilities.

The last section is devoted to administration of the collection. Among the concerns discussed are inventory and weeding. Charts indicate such specifics as replacement rates for books and nonprint media and guidelines (listed by Dewey category) for withdrawing materials from circulation according to age and circulation data. Techniques for measuring and evaluating a collection are presented, along with lists of sources for standards and guidelines and for evaluation instruments. The final chapter deals with special situations, how to cope with having to create an initial collection, and shifting and closing collections.

Each chapter concludes with a summary, footnotes, and a bibliography. Appendix 1 lists associations and agencies and their publications that relate to the particular concerns of collection development; Appendix 2 provides bibliographic information on publications mentioned in the text and lists additional selection tools; and Appendix 3 reprints the Library Bill of Rights and other statements on intellectual freedom. An index concludes the book.

AUTHORITY

Van Orden is associate dean of the School of Library and Information Studies, Florida State University in Tallahassee, and the Blackwell North America Scholarship Award winner in 1983 for her earlier *The Collection Program in Elementary and Middle Schools* (reviewed in this chapter).

COMMENT

This update of Van Orden's two earlier works synthesizes material from both and adds more recent information on networks and resource sharing and their implications in collection development, on evaluating collections, and on selection aids. This book can be highly recommended for all school librarians regardless of school level and experience level. Although it incorporates the latest thought on collection management, there is not enough new substance to merit replacing one of the earlier books if it is already owned, and the budget is limited.

7

Nonprint Media and Computer Software

Nonprint media offer a variety of problems in selection and management. While many school library media specialists have adapted to the hanging plastic bags and unattractive binders needed for the physical integration of media with books, some still opt for the use of storage cabinets that unite these materials with each other but separate them from books. Neither is a particularly happy alternative, but either will suffice.

Computer software poses entirely different problems and provides some wonderful exercises in decision-making skills. Among these are determining who will use the software, whether they should circulate, what kinds to collect, and whether to integrate them or keep them separately in cataloging and physical location— and other questions abound. Librarians who are starting computer software collections will find a good exploration of problems and practices in Sheila S. Intner and Jane A. Hannigan's well-organized and comprehensive *The Library Microcomputer Environment,* and guidance in evaluating and selecting software in Carol Doll's *Evaluating Educational Software.*

Audiovisual materials are not especially new to school library media specialists, but videotapes are a recent enough arrival to warrant further study. James Scholtz's *Developing and Maintaining Video Collections in Libraries* is an excellent guide in this area. Some interesting selection aids and directories of audiovisual equipment and materials are also included. A supplementary list of briefly annotated sources appears at the end of this chapter.

AV Market Place 1989: The Complete Business Directory of Audio, Audio Visual, Film, Video, Programming. Bowker, 1989. 802 pp. ISBN 0-8352-2392-2 (pap.).

PURPOSE

This comprehensive guide to the audiovisual industry lists products, producers, services, and other related information, primarily for the use of industry affiliates. School library media specialists will find it useful for locating information about producers, audiovisual events and organizations, periodicals, and reference materials.

CONTENTS

An alphabetical list of companies constitutes the main body of this publication, and provides address, telephone numbers, contact persons, branch offices, and catalog information in each entry. Indexes and other aids make up the rest of the book. Included are a Products and Services Index with 1,200 classifications with page references; a classified products, services, and companies index organized by six major segments of the industry (audio, audiovisual, film, video, programming, and miscellaneous); a Company Directory; a directory of audiovisual trade and related associations, with address, purpose, publication, and membership data; a directory of state and local agencies providing information and services to film, television, and commercial producers; a listing of awards and festivals with relevant information; a calendar of association meetings and conventions; a list of periodicals about or related to media production, utilization, and evaluation; and a selected bibliography of reference materials on audiovisual production and techniques, hardware and software review sources, and multimedia education.

A final section, "Industry Yellow Pages," lists company, personnel, and organization names in a single alphabetical index. Front matter includes an explanation of how to use *AVMP* and a list of acronyms and initialisms.

AUTHORITY

AV Market Place 1989 was prepared by R. R. Bowker's Database Publishing Group in collaboration with the Publication Systems Department.

COMMENT

While this directory can be highly recommended for its comprehensiveness, and school library media specialists should be aware of its existence, its cost and limited usefulness in individual school libraries preclude purchase. It should, however, be available in district media centers.

Doll, Carol A. *Evaluating Educational Software.* **ALA, 1987. 78 pp. ISBN 0-8389-0474-2 (pap.).**

PURPOSE

Software as tools for learning in the library and classroom is the subject of this handbook on software evaluation and selection, prepared for the guidance of school library media specialists and teachers.

CONTENTS

This book describes and categorizes the various types of educational software now on the market and suggests ways of determining which ones to purchase. Not considered here are products that are used as management tools in libraries or classrooms, such as software for circulation or for calculating and recording student grades.

Among the main factors to consider in evaluating software are their content, their educational quality, the quality of the documentation and other support material, and the computer and user interaction provided by the program. Each of these factors is examined in a separate chapter.

Software should take advantage of the unique advantages offered by computers, such as the speed with which they handle data and their ability to provide immediate feedback, to use branching, and to present problems randomly or in response to teacher input. Their use in managing instruction by recording student scores, distinguishing first-try correct answers from those answered correctly after more than one try, ease of use, and provisions for protecting the security of student information are also important considerations.

Categories of educational software include tutorials, drill and practice programs, problem solving, and simulations. Shell programs enable teachers and/or library media specialists to specify content within a predesigned format, permitting variations in the level of difficulty or curriculum emphasis. Each of these types is discussed in the book.

Procedures for identifying, locating, and obtaining software for preview are suggested, and a method for evaluating the computer programs is presented, along with specific recommendations about when not to purchase.

An evaluation checklist form, glossary, bibliography, and index complete the book.

AUTHORITY

Doll is an associate professor in the College of Library and Information Science at the University of South Carolina. An active member of ALA, she has been a teacher and school librarian.

COMMENT

Its freedom from computer jargon, straightforward clarity, and careful organization make this book an excellent introduction to evaluating computer software.

Ellison, John W., and Patricia Ann Coty, eds. *Nonbook Media: Collection Management and User Services*. ALA, 1987. 388 pp. ISBN 0-8389-0479-3 (pap.).

PURPOSE

This guide for librarians and library science students gathers together information about 22 nonbook media.

CONTENTS

While most of the media formats discussed are familiar to school library media specialists, a few may be new. In any case, this guide provides comprehensive information, and discussions of the special characteristics and advantages and disadvantages of the various media formats present useful summaries.

A chapter is devoted to each type of format, and the chapters are alphabetically arranged. Among the visual media covered are original art and reproductions, holographs, flat pictures and study prints, maps, models, overhead transparencies, photographs, realia, and slides. Sound media include tapes and records, and visuals with sound include films and filmstrips, videodisks, and videotapes. Nonbook print media include microforms, music scores, pamphlets, programmed materials, simulations, and machine-readable data files.

Contributors of articles were asked to follow an outline provided by the editors; results vary in covering the items requested, but some information is provided for each item. Each medium is defined, a brief history provided, and its unique characteristics and advantages and disadvantages presented. Information on selection follows, with special criteria and sources of reviews, both evaluative and non-evaluative. Aspects of maintaining and managing each medium are discussed, among them storage and care, as well as any special problems, with suggested solutions, the medium may present.

A bibliography of the cited periodicals and a list of the editors and contributors conclude the book.

Ellison is an associate professor at the School of Information and Library Studies at the State University of New York at Buffalo. Patricia Ann Coty is an information specialist in the Information Services, Science and Engineering Library, State University of New York at Buffalo. Previously she was administrator of special projects, Western New York Library Resources Council. The contributors are experienced practitioners with particularly extensive experience in the formats they have written about.

While variations in coverage exist, each writer covers the medium thoroughly. Although many of the sources may not be found on school library media center shelves, they should be available in district media managers' offices or college and university libraries. Many of the media are regularly reviewed in professional journals, many of which are cited in the bibliography. This comprehensive guide provides excellent coverage of a variety of formats and is highly recommended for all school library media specialists who need updating on the subject.

Gaffney, Maureen. *Using Media to Make Kids Feel Good.* **Oryx, 1988. 253 pp. ISBN 0-89774-345-8 (pap.).**

Although primarily to help therapists in hospitals plan film programs for pediatric patients, this book is also a guide to some excellent short films for children that can be used by elementary school librarians as a purchasing or programming aid.

Individual films and videos, as well as programs in which some are shown together and combined with related activities, are the basic subject of this book. Gaffney notes that the films and programs may be used for preschool and primary grades in school settings and that many of the films are particularly suitable for children with limited English proficiency and learning disabled children. The book is divided into sections that include an introduction, annotations of films and videotapes, program descriptions and evaluations, and appendixes, resources, and indexes.

The introduction describes the project from which the book has grown, and provides recommendations and guidelines for programming and criteria used for evaluating films. The frame of reference is therapy in a hospital setting, and school librarians using this book will need to take that into account as they read this section.

The 62 annotated films are art films for children. Annotations are extremely detailed, providing a description of the narrative, the visual and sound attributes, clarity of image and sound, and pace and structure. Descriptive information includes distributor, price for film and videotape versions, length, type (for example, live action, animation, nonverbal), and age level. The next section offers programs and accompanying activities, which include making collages, drawing, mask making, sculpture, and making shadow puppets. Directions, needed materials, illustrations, and patterns are provided.

The appendixes are primarily of interest to hospital personnel. Resource lists include related children's books and recordings and a directory of film and videotape distributors. Indexes include films and videotapes by age, theme, and other categories.

AUTHORITY

Gaffney is founder and director of the Media Center for Children, New York City, an information resource on educational media, and author of *More Films Kids Like* (ALA, 1977). She has a wide and varied background in children's media and teaching.

COMMENT

In spite of its title, which suggests a general applicability to school library service to children, this book is aimed at programmers for children in hospital settings. It is included here because of its good suggestions for film programs and related activities that can be used in elementary school, and for the excellence of its selections and detail of its annotations.

Hunt, Mary Alice, ed. *A Multimedia Approach to Children's Literature: A Selective List of Films (and Videocassettes), Filmstrips, and Recordings Based on Children's Books,* **3rd ed. ALA, 1983. 182 pp. ISBN 0-8389-3289-4 (pap.).**

PURPOSE

Written for the use of teachers and librarians who work with children from preschool to sixth grade, this book is a purchasing guide for audiovisual materials based on children's books.

CONTENTS

Versions of children's books that can be viewed and/or listened to are a favored way of presenting children's literature to large groups and to those who have disabilities that interfere with their reading. They also help introduce variety to programming for children. The interest in locating and adding such materials to library collections is evident in the fact that this book is now in its third edition.

This annotated list, which was compiled by a committee of the Association for Library Service to Children (ALSC), a division of the American Library Association, includes 568 books, 153 16mm films (with video versions noted, where available), 385 sound and silent filmstrips, and 348 recordings on disk and cassette. Editor Hunt notes in the preface that included in the list are picture books, traditional and folk literature, literary fairy tales, fiction, drama, and poetry and song. Material about authors and illustrators is also provided. Selections derive from the knowledge and experience of committee members, and while the books may be anything from excellent to merely acceptable, they have all been enjoyed by children. The list is arranged alphabetically by book title, with its nonprint versions immediately following, permitting the user to locate all materials pertinent to a particular book at the same time. The entries are numbered consecutively, making them easy to locate from the author and subject indexes or the indexes for film, filmstrip, and record titles.

Ellin Green's foreword introduces the advantages of using audiovisual materials and describes how to plan multimedia programs, presenting 13 examples to start the user off. Included are a birthday story hour honoring Hans Christian Andersen's birthday and a program of tall tales focused on John Henry. Other added features are a list of resources and program aids for professionals, a section on realia suggesting types that might be added to the collection and their sources, a key to abbreviations, and annotated sample entries as an aid to use of the bibliography. In addition to the indexes, a directory of distributors is provided.

AUTHORITY

Hunt is a professor in the School of Library and Information Studies at Florida State University.

COMMENT

A real timesaver for librarians and teachers seeking audiovisual versions of children's books, this guide presents the best available versions. The selections are varied and popular, ranging from Beatrix Potter's *The Tale of Peter Rabbit* (Warne, 1904) to Harry Mazer's

Snowbound (Delacorte, 1973) with accompanying audiovisual materials. Users are bound to value this book.

Intner, Sheila S. *Access to Media: A Guide to Integrating and Computerizing Catalogs.* SEE Chapter 2, Technical Services.

Intner, Sheila S., and Jane A. Hannigan, eds. *The Library Microcomputer Environment: Management Issues.* **Oryx, 1988. 258 pp. ISBN 0-89774-229-X (pap.).**

PURPOSE

The introduction of microcomputers and their attendant software into libraries raises many issues related to their management. This book was written for the guidance of librarians and library administrators in purchasing, utilizing, and managing computers in the library environment, and for library school students and faculty seeking enlightenment on the roles of microcomputers within the library's structure and functions.

CONTENTS

The book is divided into three parts, each of which is further subdivided into chapters. The focus of Part I is on the traditional aspects of software as a new format of library material. Many questions arise concerning applications and operating system disks, and their selection, acquisition, use, and organization into or apart from the library collection. Among these considerations, whose determinations underlie any systematic collection development plan, are identifying users and resources, determining the relationship of the software to the rest of the collection, and their potential contribution to the library's goals. These collection development issues are discussed in Chapter 1, which also provides a list of software categories, an outline of planning steps, and some additional words of advice.

A history of patterns for organizing software, and a description of the current state of the art of cataloging, storing, and providing subject access, are the substance of Chapters 2 and 3.

Reference work with computers is the subject of Chapter 4. Searching on-line data bases and CD-ROM disks, networking with other libraries, using bibliographic utilities, and bibliographic instruction are among the topics considered here. Among the reference-related issues discussed are the protection of patrons' privacy, computer use in promoting literacy, and determining information format (for example, whether to provide a source in print form, or CD-ROM, or both). The chapter concludes with a look at the future of information dissemination, document delivery, and the role of the reference librarian.

Looking at software as a nontraditional entity in library collections is the substance of Part II. Chapter 5 offers an analysis of the special factors to consider in selecting software and surveys a variety of review sources: popular magazines and directories, professional journals and periodicals, evaluation and review centers, on-line data bases, commercial review services, and user group newsletters. Chapter 6 offers guidelines for selecting hardware and a step-by-step thought process that will help narrow the choice. Chapter 7 considers the issues of copyright and its specific application to computer software and offers recommendations for handling problems that are posed by the peculiar nature of the product. Chapters 8 and 9 have a more technical bent, the first describing UNIX, an operating system developed by AT&T Bell Laboratories, and the second discussing IOTA, an instructional program in the design of data bases.

Part III deals with the potential for enhancing library services provided by newly developing technologies and introduces some of the terminology that will help in understanding them. An example is what Roger B. Wyatt, author of Chapter 10, calls the "New Medium," a merged and interactive combination of video, telecommunications (by satellite), mass storage devices (CD-ROM), and computers, which opens up new areas of capability. Chapter 11 deals with the management concerns of local area networks (LANs), a technology that permits the interconnection of computers, peripherals, and software in a building or on a campus. Extending the network outward via telephone lines or cables permits LAN users to link up with a wide area network, or WAN, increasing communication possibilities among library systems. Chapter 12 examines the managerial role in overseeing the "microcomputer environment" and details the tasks of planning, implementing, maintaining, and evaluating an ongoing system. Chapter 13 considers aspects of computer training and the documentation and tutorials that play a part in that preparation.

An afterword looks to the future, considering trends in technology, in society, and in libraries. Footnotes and bibliographies at the end of each chapter point the way to further reading and additional resources. A detailed index concludes the book.

AUTHORITY

Intner and Hannigan are both leaders in the field of library applications of microcomputer technology. Sheila S. Intner is an associate professor in the Graduate School of Library and Information Science at Simmons College, Boston. Jane Anne Hannigan is Professor Emerita, Columbia University School of Library Service, and author of many books and professional journal articles.

COMMENT

The thoughtful and authoritative studies that comprise this book will guide its readers past the pitfalls and onward to confidence and competence in the management of computers in their libraries.

Jones, Dolores Blythe, ed. *Children's Media Market Place*, 3rd ed. Neal-Schuman, 1988. 387 pp. ISBN 1-55570-007-1.

PURPOSE

Designed for the use of all people who work with children, this directory includes audiovisual, print, computer software, and other media for children, giving their creators, sources, and producers.

CONTENTS

The major portion of this publication consists of directories of publishers, software producers and distributors, audiovisual producers and distributors, and periodicals. Each listing in the publishers' section describes types of books and audience, subjects, special interests, discounts, and information services (such as catalogs and exhibits). The publishers are listed by format, subject, and special interest following the alphabetical directory. The software producers' directory indicates format and type (for example, whether for education or administration), hardware required, audience, subjects, how available, and preview policy. It is followed by lists classified by format and subject. The audiovisual producers' directory describes format and audience, subjects, special interest, and services, followed by classified lists by format, subject, and special interest.

The periodicals directory has three separate lists: children's, professionals' and parents' periodicals, and review journals, services, and indexes. Listings indicate audience, focus, contents, reviews, and availability of back issues and reprints.

Entries in other directories, accompanied by relevant information, include wholesalers, bookstores, antiquarian booksellers, and book clubs, agents for children's materials, children's museums, television and radio program sources, distributors, and broadcasters. Organizations, associations, and professionals concerned with children and young adult services and media in public libraries and state agencies are listed as well. Examination centers, sources for federal grants supporting children's programs, an events and conferences calendar, a list of children's media awards, and a briefly annotated bibliography of selection aids complete the main section of the work.

A brief introduction to each listing in the directory offers information relevant to that section, and each main entry provides an address, telephone number, and contact person as well as the information described above. A quick-reference index indicates where the main entry can be found, and also provides an address and telephone number.

AUTHORITY

The listings were compiled from responses to questionnaires, telephone calls, and research.

COMMENT

A comparable product is Bowker's *AV Market Place 1989* (reviewed in this chapter), which is more exhaustive in its coverage of the audiovisual world. It is not limited to products for children and young adults, however, and does not include sources of print materials such as books and periodicals for children, or computer software sources. School library media specialists are most likely to prefer *CMMP* because of its specificity for children.

Mason, Sally, and James C. Scholtz, eds. *Video for Libraries: Special Interest Video for Small and Medium-Sized Public Libraries*. ALA, 1988. 163 pp. ISBN 0-8389-0498-X (pap.).

PURPOSE

Although this core list was developed for the use of public librarians, it includes a number of videos that are recommended for young adults and children, making it a useful selection guide also for school libraries at all levels.

CONTENTS

Approximately 1,000 programs are included in this list of highly recommended videos, which were culled from those recommended by several contributing editors, each of whom had submitted a list of 150 recommended titles. Selection was based on *Booklist*'s criteria for films and videos, among which are currency and freedom from bias, usefulness and appropriateness for the intended audience, well-organized and well-written content, and satisfactory technical qualities, including sound, visuals, editing, acting, and narration.

Feature films are not included in the main list, although the book does include a chapter by James Limbacher on feature films, which offers purchasing guidelines. The value of video as a resource for pursuing special interests in public libraries has been stressed in the selection process.

To simplify access, the videos are arranged in Dewey Decimal order, and the liberal use of cross-references assists in location of titles. Children's titles are arranged alphabetically, and titles for young adults in the main list are identified with a YA symbol. Included in the collection are programs from such television series as "Nova" and "National Geographic"; other titles include tapes from educational producers as well as inexpensive tapes made for home use.

The entries include information on producer, distributor, running time, price, and availability of rights for public performance, followed by a brief evaluative annotation. Among the subjects relevant to school libraries are world issues, social issues in the United States, languages, nuclear issues, drugs and alcohol, animals, the human body, health, hobbies, music, dance, crafts, sports, and history. Appendixes include "Professional Library Viewing," a directory of producers and distributors, and another of video wholesalers and retailers. An index completes the book.

AUTHORITY

Sally Mason is coordinator of the ALA-Carnegie Video Project and director of video and special projects for ALA. James Scholtz is the consultant for audiovisual services for the Northern Illinois Library System and reviews home videos for *Booklist*.

COMMENT

School library media specialists seeking guidance in selecting videos for their libraries from among the 50,000-odd titles available will find many appropriate choices in this handy and helpful book.

Neill, Shirley Boes, and George W. Neill. *Only the Best, 1990: The Annual Guide to the Highest-Rated Educational Software Preschool–Grade 12.* **Bowker, 1989. 136 pp. ISBN 0-8352-2766-9 (pap.).**

PURPOSE

Prepared for school personnel who select or use educational microcomputer software, as well as students and parents, this annual guide identifies the highest-rated products available.

Using authoritative evaluations from education agencies, evaluation services, and professional journals in the United States and Canada, the editors chose only those programs that received excellent or good ratings, and no negative ones. The rating system is explained in the book's introduction, which also describes the evaluation methods of many of the agencies whose reviews form the basis of the selection process. The 185 programs included in Part 1 were selected after 6,000 evaluations were consulted. Part 2 lists 46 programs produced in 1988 and 1989 that are promising but haven't yet collected enough favorable reviews to be placed among the highest rated. The choices from *Only the Best, 1989* are briefly cited in Part 3.

Following a page of suggestions to users of the book (read the original reviews; try the program; verify the format and hardware requirements, and so on), the programs are listed alphabetically in chart form, and producer, curriculum area and computer are identified. The citations in Part 1 are then presented, grouped by curriculum area: Arts, College Entrance Exams, Early Childhood Education, Foreign Language, Health Education, Language Arts, Mathematics, Problem Solving, Science, Social Studies, Student Helpers, Tool Programs, and Typing. Each entry includes producer, copyright date, grade level, subject, hardware requirements, cost of program with network version and site license information if available, and a brief description. Evaluation sources and rating and locations of magazine reviews are also provided.

Parts 2 and 3, the 46 "Alert" programs and the 1989 programs, respectively, provide brief citations, and are arranged by subject. Part 4 is a directory of software producers whose programs are included in the book.

Shirley Boes Neill is former editor of *Critical Issues Reports,* a publication of the American Association of School Administrators. George W. Neill was an assistant state superintendent of schools in California, where he was responsible for public information, publications, and program dissemination.

This gathering of highly rated educational programs for microcomputers can be used as part of the process of selecting software. While the entries do not provide evaluations, most do refer the user to reviews in other sources. School library media specialists will want to consult reviews before purchases are made.

Also available from Bowker is *Only the Best, 1985–89 Cumulative Edition,* which cites 550 highest-rated programs.

Scholtz, James C. *Developing and Maintaining Video Collections in Libraries.* **ABC-Clio, 1988. 196 pp. ISBN 0-87436-497-3.**

PURPOSE

Although written principally for public librarians, this book's contents reflect most of the information needs, problems, and issues that concern school library media specialists and academic librarians as well.

CONTENTS

Many of the practical aspects of managing video collections are virtually identical with those concerning other nonprint and even book collections. School library media specialists, having pioneered the acquisition and use of audiovisual materials in their collections, have grappled with the problems of providing descriptive cataloging, storage and access, and suitable equipment for films, filmstrips, recordings, and the like for a number of years. With the emergence of business management techniques applied to library management, more formal and precise planning and implementation measures are now recommended, and they are described in this book, along with the special problems posed by video.

Planning for video collections begins with an analysis of community needs, requirements of budget, space, storage, security, and ease of access. Acquisition, circulation, and maintenance policies and procedures must be developed. Collection goals must be determined and a collection development policy prepared. Methods for accomplishing these tasks are described, and issues involved in the process are discussed.

Scholtz presents evaluation and selection criteria, and offers review sources, aids, and reference guides in annotated, descriptive lists. A chapter on the selection and maintenance of video equipment describes the technology, and compares Beta and VHS recorders. What to consider in selecting equipment, trends in equipment design, methods of repair and maintenance, and typical problems are among the topics covered. Repair and maintenance of videotape cassettes are also described.

Among the problems specific to video collections, copyright is major. The revised Copyright Act of 1976 took effect in January 1978, and some of its provisions have been, and continue to be contested. The issues that affect libraries and schools are discussed, among them fair use and off-air recording, and some of the relevant court decisions are briefly described. Sample guidelines on the use of copyrighted video programs are provided.

A variety of optional purchase plans enable public library systems to rotate packets of videos among branch or member libraries, a chapter that school library media specialists can probably skip. A final chapter looks to the future and predicts growth in the output of educational titles, video magazines, and music video. Advances in technology will increase format options; changes in licensing procedures will improve availability.

The Freedom to View Statement of ALA is appended, and an index concludes the book.

AUTHORITY

Scholtz is general consultant/A-V Services, Northern Illinois Library System. He is a frequent contributor to *Booklist* and *Advend Video Newsletter*.

COMMENT

Video use in schools is primarily educational in nature, while public libraries are concerned largely with entertainment videos. This major difference in collection development focus should be taken into account in considering this book. On the other hand, the general management considerations and their treatment are of considerable interest to school media specialists, and the technical chapters provide helpful information. Educational videos are supplanting films and sound filmstrips in many school library media centers. Feature length and shorter videos for children and young adults are encroaching on books as recreational sources, raising questions concerning their inclusion in school library media collections. The issues raised by these trends will have to be addressed by school library media specialists.

Software for Schools 1987–88: A Comprehensive Directory of Educational Software, Grades Pre-K through 12. SEE Chapter 8, Selection Guides and Resources.

Tenopir, Carol, and Gerald Lundeen. *Managing Your Information: How to Design and Create a Textual Database on Your Microcomputer.* SEE Chapter 16, Technology and Automation.

Williams, Kim, ed. *The Equipment Directory of Audio-Visual, Computer, and Video Products,* **34th ed.** SEE Chapter 16, Technology and Automation.

ADDITIONAL READINGS

Ellison, John W., ed. *Media Librarianship.* Neal-Schuman, 1985. 449 pp. ISBN 0-918212-81-2. Problems and practices of developing and maintaining the nonbook media collection are examined in 30 articles that describe history, organization, storage, production, copyright, and other topics.

Green, Lee. *Creative Slide/Tape Programs.* Libraries Unlimited, 1986. 141 pp. ISBN 0-87287-444-3. A practical guide to producing programs combining slides and tapes, this handbook offers directions and illustrations of planning, design, and production.

Heinich, Robert, et al. *Instructional Media and the New Technologies of Instruction,* 2nd ed. Wiley, 1985. ISBN 0-4718-7835-9. Covers the selection and use of nonbook media.

Perritt, Patsy H., and Jean T. Kreamer, comps. *Selected Video and Films for Young Adults.* ALA, 1986. ISBN 0-8389-3327-0. Selections from the annual lists prepared by the Young Adult Services Division of ALA.

Senf, Gerald M., ed. *Microcomputers in the Classroom: Courseware Reviews.* Professional Press, n.d. 156 pp. Originally published in the *Journal of Learning Disabilities,* the reviews cover 140 courseware programs suitable for use with learning disabled children and young adults in grades pre-K to 12.

Sive, Mary Robinson. *Media Selection Handbook.* Libraries Unlimited, 1983. 171 pp. ISBN 0-87287-342-0. How to use and select media, and develop strategies and use tools for retrospective and current searching are explained in this convenient and practical guidebook.

————. *Selecting Instructional Media: A Guide to Audiovisual and Other Instructional Media Lists,* 3rd ed. Libraries Unlimited, 1983. 330 pp. ISBN 0-87287-342-0. Some 400 lists for guiding the selection of a wide variety of media for grades K–12 are annotated and organized by subject and media type, and a list of comprehensive selection tools is also included.

8
Selection Guides and Resources

This collection of selection guides attempts to provide access to materials of different kinds and various subject matter. Some of the guides are comprehensive, whereas others are selective. All have some special merit, either in the comprehensiveness of their coverage, the appeal or current relevance of their subject, the quality of their contents, or the uniqueness of their topic. An example of the latter is Patricia Havlice's *Oral History: A Reference Guide and Annotated Bibliography*. Recency of publication was also an important consideration. Almost all of the guides included here were published in the last five years. Notable exceptions are Selma Richardson's *Magazines for Young Adults*, since most of the selections there are in continuous publication, and Eileen Tway's *Reading Ladders for Human Relations*, because its unique approach is unduplicated in any other publication. Additional selection guides are reviewed in those chapters that deal with their subject matter, especially in Chapters 10, 11, and 12. A supplementary list of briefly annotated sources appears at the end of this chapter.

Abrahamson, Richard F., and Betty Carter, eds. *Books for You: A Booklist for Senior High Students*, 10th ed. SEE Chapter 11, Reading Guidance and Motivation—Young Adult Literature.

ALA, Reference Books Bulletin Editorial Board. *Purchasing an Encyclopedia: 12 Points to Consider*, 2nd ed. SEE Chapter 10, Reference Services.

Allen, Adela Artola, ed. *Library Services for Hispanic Children: A Guide for Public and School Librarians*. SEE Chapter 13, The Library Media Center and the Curriculum.

American Foundation for AIDS Research (AmFAR). *Learning AIDS: An Information Resource Directory,* **2nd ed. Bowker, 1989. 270 pp. ISBN 0-9620363-1-5 (pap.).**

PURPOSE

This collection of information sources on AIDS is directed at educators and other professionals interested in identifying educational materials about AIDS appropriate to the people they work with.

CONTENTS

Over 12,000 organizations were surveyed for their recommendations on information sources to be included in this directory, and over 900 items were submitted in response. These items were screened and grouped into three chapters. Chapter 1 presents educational tools for use in instructional settings, which are reviewed, and also includes materials for public information such as public service announcements and posters. Chapter 2 includes materials for reference and resources, which were not reviewed; and Chapter 3 provides producer and distributor information.

Three experts reviewed each of the items in Chapter 1, and the reviews include a description of contents, evaluative comments, and a symbol for recommended or not recommended status. A list of criteria used in evaluation is provided, and includes content, design of the instructional package, technical quality, methods, support materials, and administrative details.

The reviewed materials are grouped according to the audience for whom they are intended, such as age group, ethnic group, gender, professional interest, sexual preference, drug users, whether AIDS-infected or at-risk, and so on. Among the types of materials included are audio- and videotapes, courses of study, curriculum guides, posters, and a variety of print materials.

The wide range of topics covered varies according to the intended audience. For children and adolescents the topics include general information about AIDS, methods of prevention, and the connection with drug abuse. For the general community there is also material about the legal aspects of discrimination against people with AIDS, testing for AIDS, symptoms of the disease, safe sex, and the like. Many Spanish and other non-English-language materials are also included. The source of each item is identified in the review, and a reference to Chapter 3, "Producer and Distributor Information," enables the user to locate ordering information.

Chapter 2, "A Collection of References and Resources," includes a variety of print materials, including bibliographies and conference papers, on-line data bases, and directories, as well as films and tape recordings. Names and addresses of federal and state agencies and the World Health Organization are also included.

There are three indexes: Titles Listed with Product Type Identification, Titles Sorted by Product Type, and Titles Available in Languages Other Than English.

AUTHORITY

The editors are Trish Halleron, AmFAR's Director of Education; Janet Pisaneschi, Program Consultant; and Margi Trapani, Project Director. The large panel of reviewers includes medical and health experts in AIDS and related disciplines.

COMMENT

The resource information has been well organized and assembled with care, and the indexes and other user aids provide for convenient access. Where reviews have been included they are clearly written and nontechnical, and added comments describe why a product was recommended and what flaws exist. Those that were rated below average were simply listed without a review.

Andrews, Theodora. *Substance Abuse Materials for School Libraries: An Annotated Bibliography.* **Libraries Unlimited, 1985. 215 pp. ISBN 0-87287-476-1.**

PURPOSE

School librarians, health professionals, and parents will find materials about drug and alcohol abuse and tobacco to share with young people in this helpfully annotated source.

CONTENTS

Close to 500 annotated entries introduce materials published within the last 15 years. Some of the entries were carried over from earlier works of this author (*A Bibliography of Drug Abuse, Including Alcohol and Tobacco,* 1977, and *Bibliography of Drug Abuse: Supplement 1977– 1980,* 1981), but 235 new titles have been added. Listed are reference materials (close to 90 in all) such as bibliographies, indexes and abstracts, pamphlets and periodicals, as well as trade books. The latter are arranged by subject category and include such materials as personal stories, prevention, community programs, self-help, and fiction.

The descriptive and evaluative annotations give an overview of the work and comment thoughtfully on its suitability for the young reader. Andrews notes in the preface the importance of careful

113

screening of material before its inclusion in the school library collection, and she helps to implement this caution by providing the information needed to guide the prospective purchaser, warning about books that might encourage experimentation and alerting users elsewhere where necessary, as well as commenting on the quality of the writing. Author/title and subject indexes complete the work.

AUTHORITY
Andrews is pharmacy, nursing, and health science librarian and professor of library science at Purdue University.

COMMENT
Thoughtful appraisal, careful selection, and a quantity of useful titles characterize this guide to literature on substance abuse.

Barstow, Barbara, and Judith Riggle. *Beyond Picture Books: A Guide to First Readers.* **Bowker, 1989. 336 pp. ISBN 0-8352-2515-1.**

PURPOSE
This selective, annotated bibliography was prepared for the use of children's librarians and elementary school library media specialists in selecting books for beginning readers.

CONTENTS
The authors selected some 1,600 titles for inclusion in this annotated, alphabetical list, and analyzed them for readability. Entries are numbered sequentially and arranged by author. Each entry includes title, illustrator, publisher, date, ISBN or out-of-print status, series title, subjects, reading level, and a brief (25–50 words) critical annotation. Subject headings are based on *Sears List of Subject Headings,* Library of Congress headings from cataloging in publication data, and the authors' experience. Readability levels were determined by computer applications of the Spache formula.

The annotated bibliography is preceded by a list of 200 outstanding first readers currently in print, and is followed by subject, title, illustrator, readability and series indexes.

AUTHORITY
The authors are children's librarians with the Cuyahoga County Public Library in Ohio.

COMMENT
Plugging the gap between selection aids for picture books and books for experienced readers, this guide fills a need that has long existed.

The subject index reveals an astounding range of subject matter for beginning readers, and the author index includes some surprisingly familiar names associated with fine books for older children. The titles are well selected, and the annotations are clear and succinct.

Baskin, Barbara H., and Karen H. Harris. *More Notes from a Different Drummer: A Guide to Juvenile Fiction Portraying the Disabled.* **Bowker, 1984. 495 pp. ISBN 0-8352-1871-6.**

PURPOSE

As the title indicates, this book is a follow-up to *Notes from a Different Drummer.* Both present lists of critically analyzed and annotated juvenile fiction that deals with physical and emotional disabilities. *Notes* covers the period from 1940 to 1975, and *More Notes* continues with books published from 1976 to 1981.

CONTENTS

Two introductory chapters set the annotated list into a contemporary social context. Chapter 1 considers the change in attitudes toward and treatment of the disabled in recent years, but reminds the reader that there is much progress still to be made. Chapter 2 deals with the literary treatment of disabled people in recent juvenile titles. While the quantity of books dealing with impairments has increased, and books of quality and sensitivity have appeared, there are still mixed messages, misinformation, and some latent hostility observable in some writers' attitudes toward their disabled characters. Illustrations also vary, from the sensitive and accurate to the shallow and deficient.

Declaring that "books are among the most potent tools available for promoting attitudinal change," the authors proceed to introduce the 348 books that have been selected for inclusion and to describe and analyze them. The books are arranged alphabetically by author, and indexes provide access by subject and title. Reading level codes and disability designations are provided for each book cited. The critical analyses of the titles are carefully considered and blunt, making for a list that is not necessarily restricted to recommended books. The thoughtful user of this book will find provocative material for book discussions.

AUTHORITY

Baskin has done extensive consultant work in service to special children; Harris is associate professor of library science at the University of New Orleans. An earlier publication, *The Special Child in the Library* (1976), was co-edited by these authors.

COMMENT

Eight years after the publication date of the most recent title in this book, it has lost some of its value as an up-to-date selection tool, but retains its usefulness for retrospective purchasing and for its critical point of view. It can be supplemented with more recent titles in reviewing journals.

Beilke, Patricia F., and Frank J. Sciara. *Selecting Materials for and about Hispanic and East Asian Children and Young People.* **Library Professional, 1986. 178 pp. ISBN 0-208-01993-6.**

PURPOSE

Written for school and public librarians, this book provides powerful arguments, and guidelines, for selecting and introducing books about the cultural backgrounds of the ethnic minorities named in the title.

CONTENTS

Among the many challenges that face our schools today is that presented by the influx of recent immigrants to the United States. Meeting their educational needs with sensitivity and competence requires an understanding of the cultural heritage they have brought with them and the problems they face in a land that is new to them and not always accepting of diversity. The place of school librarians in this picture is clear: to find and present the materials that will lead to understanding, acceptance, and self-knowledge.

Beilke and Sciara present background material on these groups, with suggested reading for further understanding of their cultural and historical experience in America. They emphasize the diversity and number of subgroups within both the Hispanic and Asian communities. They describe how to assess community needs, and present some outreach programs that were developed in response to these. Underlining the need for in-service study and staff development programs, they also present bibliographic material for self-directed learning.

Helping young Americans learn "to value the cultural pluralism of our society—their own cultural heritages as well as that of others" (p. 85) is a major goal in selecting books for school and public libraries. Selection criteria are discussed by the authors. The need to avoid stereotyping in content, language, and illustration is stressed, and sources for criteria and recommended reading lists are offered. These include "Ten Quick Ways to Analyze Books for Racism and

Sexism" by the Council on Interracial Books for Children and Eileen Tway's *Reading Ladders for Human Relations* (reviewed in this chapter).

Guidelines for selecting materials and designing programs, and human and organizational resources for planning and information are provided in the final chapter. An extensive index, notes, and a bibliography conclude the book.

AUTHORITY

Beilke is associate professor of library science and Sciara is professor of elementary education at Ball State University. They have acknowledged the assistance and contributions of many colleagues in the preparation of the book.

COMMENT

The immigrant experience is fraught with uncertainty and hope and conflict of many kinds. The first generation contends with poverty, prejudice, a new language, and a new culture. Then the second generation struggles with the first generation. These burdens, anxieties, and triumphs, too, have been captured in the words of books that ought to be available to the youngsters involved in the struggle and those who witness it from outside. School librarians need to make that special effort to provide them, and this book will help them do it.

Bernstein, Joanne E., and Masha Kabakow Rudman. *Books to Help Children Cope with Separation and Loss: An Annotated Bibliography*, Vol. 3. Bowker, 1989. 532 pp. ISBN 0-8352-2510-0.

PURPOSE

Prepared for the use of teachers, librarians, parents, and counselors, this book is a guide to current (1983–1988) fiction and nonfiction books that deal with the stresses and traumas in the lives of young people.

CONTENTS

Proceeding from their conviction that bibliotherapy is a sound measure for helping children cope with sorrow, Bernstein and Rudman present 606 annotated titles that range in interest and reading level from early childhood to young adulthood. The book is divided into three parts: Part I, "Using Books to Help Children Cope with Separation and Loss"; Part II, "Reading about Separation and Loss: An

Annotated Bibliography"; and Part III, "Selected Reading for Adult Guides." There is also an appendix: "Directory of Organizations."

Part I expands the authors' statement of purpose and establishes their orientation. They begin with a description of their criteria and other considerations in selection and in determining reading and interest levels. They define and explain with great sensitivity the effects of separation and loss on children at different ages and the emotions that accompany these events. That reading can bring catharsis, insight, and a kind of companionship to the bereaved is the basis for the authors' bibliotherapeutic approach to books; and the successes, limitations, and cautions in using this approach are noted. Classroom strategies and applications of bibliotherapy are discussed at some length, and the section concludes with a discussion of how some particularly notable authors approach their work, and a list of their books.

Part II presents the annotated books. Each annotation includes a description of plot and characters, an analysis of the book's literary value, and its potential in helping the reader resolve a similar conflict or problem. The bibliography is arranged alphabetically by author, within the type of separation or loss that the protagonists are faced with. This includes, but is not limited to, the appearance of a new sibling, entering a new school or neighborhood, losing a friend, experiencing a parent's loss of employment, growing up, leaving home, old age, serious illness, death, divorce, abuse, war, foster care, and homelessness. Indexes by author, title, subject, reading level, and interest level guide the user to the titles sought.

Selections for parents and professionals who work with children are listed in Part III. They include such titles as *Drug Addiction: Learn about It before Your Kids Do; Divorced Families: A Multidisciplinary Developmental View; We, the Homeless: Portraits of America's Displaced People; Preventing Teenage Suicide: The Living Alternative Handbook;* and more—a truly diverse, comprehensive, and valuable compendium.

A second bibliography, Chapter 10, "Bibliotherapy," provides sources of additional information. The Directory of Organizations includes addresses and telephone numbers of self-help groups and professional and voluntary organizations.

AUTHORITY

Joanne E. Bernstein is a professor at the School of Education, Brooklyn College at The City University of New York. Bernstein is also a speaker and consultant to school systems, industry, and other organizations. Masha Kabakow Rudman is a professor at the School of Education at the University of Massachusetts at Amherst.

COMMENT

The experience of separation and loss begins at the moment of birth and reappears in many circumstances throughout the life of every person. Identifying with others, such as characters in books, as they undergo emotional pain and crisis and search for ways to deal with their difficulties often provides consolation and insight. This book will help librarians find that right book for a time of need.

Bernstein and Rudman demonstrate a winning combination of authority over subject matter and sensitivity to the emotional needs of children. The annotations, which are both critical and descriptive, can form the basis of booktalks and suggest topics for discussion.

Dewey, Patrick R. *101 Software Packages to Use in Your Library: Descriptions, Evaluations, and Practical Advice.* **ALA, 1987. 160 pp. ISBN 0-8389-0455-6 (pap.).**

PURPOSE

This directory of recommended library-related software offers guidance in microcomputer software selection, along with specifics about the software included, to librarians in all types of libraries.

CONTENTS

An introduction includes selection criteria for software and hardware, and particular attention is given to printers. Recommendations about caring for disks and computers are also provided. Book and article references are included here for further information, as well as in subsequent chapters.

The remainder of the book consists of descriptive and evaluative reviews of software and sources of further information. They provide all necessary information for ordering, including name, type of program, vendor, and cost; hardware compatibility, including memory capacity required; and separate descriptions of the program and its documentation with evaluative comments about both. The reviews probably presuppose the presence of a color monitor. Librarians using monochrome monitors will need to ascertain whether a desired program will function in a monochrome environment, particularly in the case of graphics and children's programs (for example, library skills and puzzle makers).

Reviews are arranged by the tasks programs are designed to perform, and vary from one for interlibrary loan to fourteen for word processing. The tasks include, in addition to the two mentioned, acquisitions, bibliography, cataloging, children's services and library skills, circulation, communications and on-line data base access systems, data base management, integrated software, public relations, serials control, spreadsheets, training programs, a miscellaneous group, and utilities.

Appendixes provide a directory of library user groups, a vendor list, and a hardware-software cross-reference that lists hardware and the recommended programs with which it is compatible. A glossary and indexes of applications and of software are also included.

AUTHORITY

Patrick R. Dewey is administrative librarian of the Maywood, Illinois, Public Library and also served in the Chicago Public Library System. He has published articles in many computer and library professional journals and has edited a software reviewing column in *Wilson Library Bulletin*.

COMMENT

This book has been written with a minimum of computerese and a maximum of comprehension of librarians' needs in library-related computer software. It is what the author intended, easy to use and low in cost. Library applications software, however, have continued to increase in number and in the complexity of the tasks that they can perform, and many versions of the software reviewed have been revised and updated. As an introductory guide it can be highly recommended, but it should be supplemented with more current reviews in the professional literature and preview of the software before purchasing decisions are made.

Dreyer, Sharon Spredemann, ed. *The Bookfinder, Vol. 2: A Guide to Children's Literature about the Needs and Problems of Youth Aged 2–15.* SEE Chapter 11, Reading Guidance and Motivation—General Works.

EPIE Institute. *T.E.S.S.: The Educational Software Selector.* SEE Chapter 16, Technology and Automation.

Felsted, Carla Martindell, ed. *Youth and Alcohol Abuse: Readings and Resources.* SEE Chapter 13, The Library Media Center and the Curriculum.

Field, Carolyn W., and Jacqueline Shachter Weiss. *Values in Selected Children's Books of Fiction and Fantasy.* SEE Chapter 11, Reading Guidance and Motivation—Children's Literature.

Friedberg, Joan Brest, et al. *Accept Me as I Am: Best Books of Juvenile Nonfiction on Impairments and Disabilities.* SEE Chapter 12, Serving Special Learners.

Gaffney, Maureen. *Using Media to Make Kids Feel Good.* SEE Chapter 7, Nonprint Media and Computer Software.

Giese, James R., and Laurel R. Singleton. *U.S. History: A Resource Book for Secondary Schools, Volume 1, 1450–1865; U.S. History: A Resource Book for Secondary Schools, Volume 2, 1865–Present.* ABC-Clio, 1989. 347 pp., 340 pp. ISBN 0-87436-505-8, ISBN 0-87436-506-6.

PURPOSE

This two-volume set provides a variety of resources for secondary schools for teaching and learning about U.S. history from 1450 to the Civil War (Volume 1) and from the post–Civil War period to the present (Volume 2).

CONTENTS

The first chapter in Volume 1 provides an introduction to the discipline, examining historians' approach to learning about the past and how different schools of thought and varying interpretations may arise. A detailed chronology is presented in the next chapter, beginning with 10,000 B.C., an approximate date for the crossing of the land bridge between Asia and America, and concluding with the abolition of slavery and other events of 1865. Consistent with the book's emphasis on historiography, the following chapter provides an alphabetical list of important American historians and biographical information about them. To encourage students to use primary sources, Chapter 3 offers 15 different types of primary sources with a brief explanation of how they may be interpreted and a citation of the source document. The rest of the book consists of information sources. Examples are as follows: a directory of agencies, associations, societies, and other groups of interest to students of American history; a list of reference works about American history, including atlases and early maps, bibliographies and indexes, biographical and subject dictionaries, almanacs, general and history encyclopedias, chronologies, and handbooks; on-line data bases and vendors, periodicals and resources for teachers; classroom materials, including computer and audiovisual software and such visual aids as posters and study prints; supplementary print materials and textbooks; and videocassettes and films. All materials listed are annotated; and a glossary and detailed index complete the book.

Using a format that is identical to Volume 1 (and some text that has been revised to suit a later period in U.S. history), Volume 2 carries the user almost to the present day. Chapter 1 is a slightly revised version of the one in Volume 1. Chapter 2 offers a chronology consistent with the later historical period. The list of historians in Chapter 3 offers some different names and Chapter 4 provides primary source material appropriate to a study of post-Civil War U.S. history. The resources included in Chapters 5 through 7 are of the same type as in Volume 1, and there is some duplication of directory entries and reference titles, but most items reflect the different subject matter.

AUTHORITY

James Giese is executive director of the Social Science Education Consortium, Inc., and adjunct assistant professor of history at the University of Colorado, Boulder. Laurel Singleton is director of editorial production for Graphic Learning Corporation, Boulder.

COMMENT

The wealth of material presented in this two-volume work will enhance the American history collections of secondary school library media centers.

Additional resource books available, or soon to be available, from ABC-Clio are *Geography: A Resource Book for Secondary Schools; U.S. Government: A Resource Book for Secondary Schools; Global/International Issues and Problems: A Resource Book for Secondary Schools;* and *Economics: A Resource Book for Secondary Schools.*

Gillespie, John T., and Corinne J. Naden, eds. *Best Books for Children: Preschool through Grade 6*, 4th ed. Bowker, 1990. 608 pp. ISBN 0-8352-2668-9.

PURPOSE

Now in its fourth edition, *Best Books for Children* has served as a selection tool for many years, with continuing updating. A list, by subject, of recommended books for preschool to sixth-grade children, for which the authors suggest the following uses: to evaluate existing collections, to assist in book selection for starting or expanding collections, to help in reading guidance, and to aid in the preparation of bibliographies and reading lists.

CONTENTS

Starting with books for younger children (alphabet, counting and concept books, nursery rhymes, picture books, beginner books), the authors proceed to fiction, listed by subject (family stories, adventure and mystery, science fiction, and so on), and then on to other favorite subjects of young readers (mythology, holidays, sports and games, and so forth). These are followed by the arts and language, music, performing arts, poetry, and folklore. Other subjects taught in the elementary grades—such as history and geography, religion, careers, health, and the sciences—are covered, as are biography, personal development, and pets.

Criteria for listing include recommendations from multiple reviewing sources, availability, currency, accuracy, usefulness, and relevance. Sources that were consulted include *Children's Catalog, The Elementary School Library Collection,* and such current tools as book-reviewing periodicals and annual bibliographies. Entries provide the following information, when applicable: author, title, suitable grade levels, adaptor or translator, indication of illustrations or illustrator's name, date of publication, publisher, price, binding(s), ISBN(s), a brief annotation, and review citations. Approximately 11,000 titles are listed, over half of which are new to this edition. Out-of-print titles have been eliminated. Four indexes complete the work: author, illustrator, title, and subject/reading level.

AUTHORITY
Gillespie is a longtime member of the faculty of the School of Library and Information Science, C. W. Post Center, Long Island University. Naden is a free-lance editor and children's book author.

COMMENT
The listings provide an almost current guide to the best in children's books as reviewed and described in authoritative sources. Annotations are descriptive and patterns of coverage in some areas have been dictated by trade publishers' output. Where new titles are plentiful, as in computers and automation, the listings are generous.

Hauser, Paula, and Gail A. Nelson. *Books for the Gifted Child,* Vol. 2. Bowker, 1988. 244 pp. ISBN 0-8352-2467-8.

PURPOSE
Modeled after Barbara H. Baskin and Karen A. Harris's *Books for the Gifted* (1980), this second volume describes appropriate books published from 1980 to 1987. Prepared for the use of parents, teachers, librarians, and others who work with gifted children from preschool to sixth grade, it offers fare to challenge the intellect and understanding of these youngsters.

CONTENTS

An introductory chapter entitled "Reading and the Gifted Child" provides a definition and characteristics of gifted children, explains their needs for special guidance, and depicts their reading interests and attitudes. The interplay of various genres with gifted children's abilities and developmental needs is also described. While selection criteria are not clearly specified, they are implicit in the authors' understanding of these children's inclinations and aptitudes.

With only 195 entries, Hauser and Nelson have been extremely selective and abundantly descriptive. Not only is content summarized and evaluated, but illustrations are carefully described and the book's particular suitability for gifted children is analyzed. With some simplification of language, the annotations can form the basis for booktalks.

The organization is alphabetical by author. There is no suggestion of age level; only a parenthetical indication of suitability for beginning, intermediate, or advanced readers is provided after the entry. This requires the user to consult a "Level Index" to determine which books are recommended for each category. A title index is also included.

AUTHORITY

Paula Hauser is Facilitator of Elementary Gifted Students in the Shawnee Mission School District, Kansas. Gail A. Nelson is Facilitator, Elementary Gifted Education, QUEST Gifted Education Program in Olathe, Kansas.

COMMENT

Careful selection and descriptive annotations mark this book, but some forethought about organization would have made it easier to use. There is no distinction by subject or type of book, nor by age range. Perhaps these limitations will be dealt with in a subsequent edition. Meanwhile it does provide guidance in selecting books for a very special clientele.

Havlice, Patricia Pate. *Oral History: A Reference Guide and Annotated Bibliography.* **McFarland, 1985. 140 pp. ISBN 0-89950-138-9 (pap.).**

PURPOSE

Oral history has sparked the interest of teachers and school library media specialists in recent years. Its use for primary sources in social studies and in language arts and history projects may be widened and extended through the sources offered in this book.

CONTENTS

Alex Haley's *Roots* (Doubleday, 1976), followed by Eliot Wigginton's "Foxfire" project kindled a genealogy and family culture interest that has yet to abate. Young people, armed with tape recorders, microphones, and some prepared questions, prowl corridors, streets, and shopping malls, pursuing that right someone with a story to tell, emulating historians and social scientists who seek to record the past and present for the enlightenment of the future.

Those with a serious interest in this pursuit will find a treasury of information and resources in Havlice's book. It covers some three decades of material in the form of articles, books, and dissertations, all of them annotated descriptively. The reference sources—bibliographies, journals, and colloquia—used to find the material are also described, and the subject headings used have been listed. The results of this searching are 773 citations, all carefully indexed by subject and title. Several of the entries describe school and library projects in oral history, some providing a rationale and others offering some how-to advice. Minority groups, immigrants, women, war, and frontier experiences are favored subjects.

AUTHORITY

Havlice is a reference librarian at the University of Houston—Clear Lake in Texas.

COMMENT

There may be better ways than oral history of getting youngsters involved in biography, history, sociology, and folklore, but it is doubtful that any could be as soul-satisfying. This book suggests resources for getting started and then for moving forward.

Hunt, Mary Alice, ed. *A Multimedia Approach to Children's Literature: A Selective List of Films (and Videocassettes), Filmstrips, and Recordings Based on Children's Books,* **3rd ed.** SEE Chapter 7, Nonprint Media and Computer Software.

Jenkins, Esther C., and Mary C. Austin. *Literature for Children about Asians and Asian Americans: Analysis and Annotated Bibliography, with Additional Readings for Adults.* **Greenwood, 1987. 303 pp. ISBN 0-313-25970-4.**

PURPOSE

This selection guide for elementary and secondary librarians suggests books to help readers learn more about the people of Asia, those who are still living on that continent and those who have immigrated to the United States.

CONTENTS

The Asian and Asian-American peoples discussed in this book are Chinese, Japanese, Koreans, and those from various cultures of Southeast Asia: Vietnam, Burma, Cambodia, Indonesia, Malaysia, Thailand, and the Philippines. The types of literature devoted to each group include folk literature, with subtopics such as myths and hero tales, and contemporary literature, grouped as picture books and picture storybooks, general fiction, historical fiction, and nonfiction, with such subgroups as geography, poetry, and songs.

In their introduction Jenkins and Austin discuss the importance of literature as a help to understanding other cultures. They also present an overview of the criteria to be used in selecting books, and continue and expand the discussion in chapter notes at the end of the book, where content and story elements are considered (plot, characterization, point of view, and so on). Additional text material includes introductions to the literature of each country or cultural group. Outstanding books are singled out for discussion, which tends to follow the arrangement described above. The number of books included in each section varies, with the largest number being devoted to the Japanese and Japanese Americans and the second largest to the Chinese and Chinese Americans.

The annotations are brief, but many include evaluative comments on the illustrations as well as the content of the book, and a grade level is suggested in addition to the bibliographic information. Entries are alphabetically arranged by author within each section. A sequential numbering system is used to facilitate finding entries from the indexes, which are by author, translator and illustrator, title, and subject. In addition, a glossary of Asian terms is appended.

AUTHORITY

Each author is professor emeritus at the University of Hawaii and they coauthored *Promoting World Understanding through Literature, K–8* (Libraries Unlimited, 1983).

COMMENT

As the world shrinks and emigrants from far and wide find their way to American cities and towns, it has become increasingly important for children to understand other world cultures and the cultural backgrounds of their classmates and friends. The textual material will enrich school professionals' understanding of Asian and Asian-American cultures, and the books described in this guide will help support multiethnic curricula and can be used also in the absence of a formal curriculum. The sections on folklore will assist librarians in expanding the folk literature section and provide additional sources for storytelling.

Katz, Bill, ed. *Magazines for School Libraries: For Elementary, Junior High School, and High School Libraries.* Bowker, 1987. 238 pp. ISBN 0-8352-2316-7.

PURPOSE

This selection guide for magazines includes titles for children and young adults, as well as professional periodicals for librarians, teachers, administrators, and other school personnel.

CONTENTS

Some 1,300 titles have been selected from the 6,500 titles in *Magazines for Libraries* (Bowker, 5th ed., 1986) for inclusion in *Magazines for School Libraries*. Selection for students was based on quality, the likelihood that they will be read, either for recreation or curriculum needs, and their suitability for the age and reading ability of their intended audience. Those for school professionals were listed if they met the curriculum interests of teachers, librarians, or administrators and provided the "educational assistance" that is required by that audience. Also considered were format, quantity of advertising, and bias. While indexing was a factor, it was not the major consideration for inclusion, since useful titles may not be indexed and some that are indexed were not included for other reasons. Some consideration was given to what is actually purchased by school libraries and what other experts recommend.

In addition, Katz supplies in his introduction some general recommendations for librarians to consider as they decide on what to select. Also provided are reviewing sources of current magazines in professional periodicals. He notes that grade and interest levels are approximate, and that adult magazines are recommended for high school students where they meet curriculum needs and reading interests and abilities.

Over 70 subject areas are covered; introductions describe the topic and list some basic titles and indexes. The topics are subdivided by audience, and titles are listed alphabetically in these subgroups. Information provided under each title includes year of origin, frequency, cost, address, presence of illustrations, index and advertising, circulation, and availability in other formats. A description follows, along with an indication of the political point of view where relevant, and the particular strengths and shortcomings of the title.

Indexes provided include one for titles and sections and another of titles by audience.

AUTHORITY

Bill Katz is a professor at the School of Library and Information Science, State University of New York at Albany, editor of *The Reference Librarian,* and a columnist in *Library Journal.* Katz has authored a number of books for the use of librarians, primarily about magazines and reference service.

COMMENT

While many more magazines are indexed here than in Selma Richardson's *Magazines for Children* (ALA, 1983) and *Magazines for Young Adults* (reviewed in this chapter), Richardson's annotations are considerably more detailed and the evaluations more thorough. In addition these ALA publications are more affordable and less cumbersome. Budget considerations, the number of titles covered, and depth of coverage of individual titles will be the deciding factors for prospective purchasers.

Kister, Kenneth F. *Best Encyclopedias: A Guide to General and Specialized Encyclopedias.* **Oryx, 1986. 386 pp. ISBN 0-89774-171-4.**

PURPOSE

To provide a buyer's guide particularly for general encyclopedias, but also for specialized works, Kister has provided both factual and evaluative information for the potential purchaser.

CONTENTS

From the *Academic American Encyclopedia* to *The Young Students' Encyclopedia,* Kister reviews 51 general encyclopedias at length and 450 special encyclopedias briefly. Each general encyclopedia review contains a detailed analysis, discussing length and breadth of coverage, indexing, language, cross-referencing, format, and so on. Also provided are purchasing information, comparisons with other works for a similar audience, and citations of reviews. A separate chapter discusses considerations in encyclopedia selection.

Appendix A is a comparison chart of general encyclopedias, allowing the user to compare number of volumes, pages, words, articles, and illustrations and maps and also providing retail and school/ library prices. Appendix B provides a briefly annotated list of special encyclopedias on 30 subjects ranging alphabetically from architecture to transportation. Many of the subjects have 20 to 30 entries, depending on the subject. Appendix C includes a number of foreign-language encyclopedias. Appendix D is an annotated list of books and articles dealing with encyclopedia evaluation and the making and using of encyclopedias. Appendix E lists publishers and distributors. A title-subject index completes the coverage.

AUTHORITY

Kister teaches at the School of Library and Information Science at the University of South Flordia, and has written widely about encyclopedias and other reference works.

COMMENT

Current as of March 1, 1986, this book is a good quick-reference source for making purchasing decisions and refreshing one's familiarity with a wide range of general and special encyclopedias. For further study of reference books, the appended bibliography is useful. *Reference Books for Young Readers* by Marion Sader (reviewed in this chapter) is more recent. It includes coverage of dictionaries, wordbooks, and atlases but lacks information on special encyclopedias. Both publications are helpful for guiding parents who seek recommendations on encyclopedia purchases.

Kohn, Rita. *Once Upon . . . a Time for Young People and Their Books: An Annotated Resource Guide.* SEE Chapter 11, Reading Guidance and Motivation—Children's Literature.

LiBretto, Ellen V. *High/Low Handbook: Books, Materials, and Services for the Problem Reader,* **2nd ed.** SEE Chapter 12, Serving Special Learners.

Lynn, Ruth Nadelman. *Fantasy Literature for Children and Young Adults: An Annotated Bibliography,* **3rd ed. Bowker, 1989. 771 pp. ISBN 0-8352-2347-7.**

PURPOSE

Primarily a guide to selection, this book also provides a wealth of critical and research sources for further investigation of the genre.

CONTENTS

What is fantasy for children and young adults? What is its appeal? What is its value? Ruth Lynn considers these questions and others in her introductory chapter, whose brief comments on such topics as definition, purpose and imagery of fantasy, children's versus adults' fantasy, responses to and appeal of fantasy, mythic elements, criticism and history of fantasy, and contemporary fantasy can only touch the surface of this vastly fascinating subject. She finds definitions in dictionaries and some apt quotations in the writings of critics of children's literature and authors of fantasy fiction, and expresses some sound thoughts of her own, concluding that fantasy written for children can be enjoyed in all its richness and variety by people of all ages.

Those who wish to pursue further study of the subject will find a rich selection of research sources ranging from reference works (bibliographies and indexes to fantasy criticism) to historical and critical works, as well as studies of individual authors. But the basic purpose of the book is realized in its annotated lists of fantasy literature. The titles are subdivided into the following categories, with further subdivision in some of these: Allegorical Fantasy and Literary Fairy Tales; Animal Fantasy; Fantasy Collections; Ghost Fantasy; High Fantasy; Humorous Fantasy; Magic Adventure Fantasy; Time Travel Fantasy; Toy Fantasy; and Witchcraft and Sorcery Fantasy. In all, some 3,300 titles are listed, representing novels and story collections published between 1900 and 1988. Each main entry provides complete bibliographic information, review citations, and grade level symbols. Symbols also indicate whether a book is of outstanding quality, recommended, or acceptable; the annotations are brief, usually consisting of two or three sentences. Author, illustrator, subject, and title indexes conclude this presentation.

AUTHORITY

Ruth Nadelman Lynn has been a children's librarian and supervisor of children's services in public libraries in Massachusetts.

COMMENT

Of use not only for selection but also for the preparation of reading lists and building of special collections, this book also supplies reading guidance for librarians who wish to extend their knowledge of fantasy literature for children. A chapter entitled "Teaching Resources" lists articles and studies on the educational and psychological uses of fantasy.

Mahoney, Ellen, and Leah Wilcox. *Ready, Set, Read: Best Books to Prepare Preschoolers.* **Scarecrow, 1985. 348 pp. ISBN 0-8108-1684-9.**

PURPOSE

This guide to books for preschool children begins with books, rhymes, and songs that will delight infants, and continues to the day before kindergarten. Thus it is of great value as a selection tool in schools that offer preschool programs. Although written primarily for parents, it can be used in high school programs that introduce young adults to the concerns and practice of good parenting.

CONTENTS

Mahoney and Wilcox carry the reader lovingly through the early childhood years, describing in each of five chapters the characteristics of children at each developmental stage and suggesting the best books for appealing to that age's interest and fancy. Each chapter begins with text material that is based on theories of early childhood development and offers advice on how to engage preschoolers in language play, an important precursor to reading readiness. Mahoney and Wilcox include rhymes, songs, games, and other activities for fostering children's interest in books, and suggest ways of developing listening and looking skills, notably storytelling.

In each chapter, the selected books and their annotations are part of the textual material and are used to exemplify the authors' suggestions on how they may be introduced and used with children. Bibliographic information about the cited books is provided at the end of each chapter, where additional books are also presented, and a supplemental list suggests further reading for parents. Author, subject, and title indexes conclude the book.

AUTHORITY

Ellen Mahoney is a children's librarian at San Francisco Public Library and has taught children's literature at various universities. Leah Wilcox is a member of the English department at Illinois State University, teaching courses in children's literature, storytelling, and literature for preschool children.

COMMENT

This authoritative source not only provides an abundance of well-annotated entries in each chapter but also offers a wealth of background information on children's developmental stages from infancy to early childhood. Supplementary bibliographies offer many additional books.

Malinowsky, H. Robert, and Gerald J. Perry, eds. *AIDS Information Sourcebook,* **2nd ed. Oryx, 1989. 215 pp. ISBN 0-89774-544-2 (pap.).**

PURPOSE

In his foreword to this resource guide, James L. Holm, acting executive director of the National AIDS Network, notes that information is the only vaccine available today to stop the spread of AIDS. This book was prepared to help information professionals in their efforts to provide sources of information to their patrons.

CONTENTS

The book is organized into three parts. The first is a sequentially numbered chronology of the spread of AIDS and other events in its history, beginning with the cases that first led to identification of its characteristic syndrome in 1981 and covering events up to April 1989. The dates and events included represent research milestones, shifts in public reactions, funding changes, news events about public personalities, and the like. A subject index follows the chronology to help in the location of specific topics.

The second part is a directory of more than 800 organizations and facilities. It is arranged alphabetically by state and then by organization name within each state. Entries include address, telephone and hot-line numbers, key personnel, organizational affiliation and type, sources of funding support, outreach/educational services, publications and other materials provided, non—English languages spoken, and other descriptive information. An index follows, which provides access by type of facility; an alphabetical listing of facilities is also included.

Publications pertaining to AIDS that have appeared over the last six years are included in the third part. Categorized by type of publication, this section includes periodical articles, brochures and pamphlets, bibliographies, fiction and nonfiction books, audiovisual resources, and on-line data bases. Spanish-language materials are also included. Entries are briefly annotated and include all bibliographic information. Much of the literature is devoted to safe sex practices, and the dangers of intravenous drug use and sharing of needles. The items included are numbered, and a subject index is provided.

Appendixes include statistics and comments from the United States Centers for Disease Control, and a status report on products being developed for control of AIDS and its manifestations, compiled by the Pharmaceutical Manufacturers Association.

AUTHORITY

Malinowsky is professor and bibliographer of science and technology at the library of the University of Illinois. Perry is reference librarian and user education coordinator at the library of Rush University, Chicago.

COMMENT

This comprehensive sourcebook is the most up-to-date reference for information about AIDS, and offers a number of materials that will support educational programs in schools.

Mason, Sally, and James C. Scholtz, eds. *Video for Libraries: Special Interest Video for Small and Medium-Sized Public Libraries.* SEE Chapter 7, Nonprint Media and Computer Software.

Matthews, Dorothy, ed. *High Interest-Easy Reading for Junior and Senior High School Students,* **5th ed.** SEE Chapter 11, Reading Guidance and Motivation—Young Adult Literature.

Monson, Dianne L., ed. *Adventuring with Books: A Booklist for Pre-K–Grade 6, New Edition.* **NCTE, 1985. 395 pp. ISBN 0-8141-0076-7 (pap.).**

PURPOSE

This selective list was prepared as a guide for teachers and parents. School librarians will also find it helpful.

CONTENTS

Some 1,700 books were selected from about 7,000 published from 1981 to 1984, and submitted by their publishers to the Committee on the Elementary School Booklist of NCTE. Criteria were literary merit and artistic quality as determined by the committee and their potential for use in the classroom and at home.

Organized by genre, the entries provide critical annotations of about 50 words, identification of awards, information about illustrations, and suggested age level. A separate list for young children includes wordless books, ABC books, concept books, and some additional titles. The main list is divided into broad categories further divided into subheadings. These include traditional folklore, contemporary fantasy, historical fiction (subdivided by time period and place), modern realistic fiction, language books, and social studies, which includes careers, cultures, government, handicapped, social issues, and the like. Also included are biographies (subdivided by vocation), books about the sciences (space, animals, computers, prehistoric life, and others), fine arts, crafts and hobbies, sports and games, and holidays.

A list of professional books is also provided; author and title indexes complete the book.

COMMENT

This is a continuing series; an earlier edition was published in 1981, with selections being made by an ongoing committee. While the books have been carefully selected and thoughtfully annotated, and their subject arrangement makes for ease of use, this guide must be supplemented by more recent professional journal selections.

Paulin, Mary Ann, and Susan Berlin, comps. *Outstanding Books for the College Bound.* SEE Chapter 11, Reading Guidance and Motivation—Young Adult Literature.

Pilla, Marianne Laino. *Resources for Middle-Grade Reluctant Readers: A Guide for Librarians.* SEE Chapter 11, Reading Guidance and Motivation—General Works.

Richardson, Selma K. *Magazines for Young Adults: Selections for School and Public Libraries.* **ALA, 1984. 329 pp. ISBN 0-8389-0407-6 (pap.).**

PURPOSE

This annotated list of popular and curriculum-related magazines was prepared to aid librarians serving young adults in school and public libraries in the selection and acquisition of magazines for students' leisure reading and research.

CONTENTS

An introduction describes the purpose and use of the publications in both school and public libraries. Criteria for inclusion are explained and the categories of excluded magazines are also provided. Among the criteria are conformance with the purpose stated by the publisher, content that reflects the concerns and capacities of young people, clarity, organization, and intelligibility of treatment, and quality of illustrations and format. All titles annotated in the author's *Periodicals for School Media Programs* (ALA, 1978) that are still being published are included, as well as all those indexed in *Readers' Guide to Periodicals*. The author also comments on the annotations, accuracy of publication information, and grade levels.

A chapter on the role of periodicals in school library media programs describes the many uses of magazines in support of the curriculum and for recreational reading. Comments on selecting, acquiring, storing, and displaying periodicals are provided, and ease of location is stressed. Promotional strategies for fostering magazine use are also discussed.

The magazine titles are presented in a single alphabet. A subject index using 60 fairly broad subject headings that reflect the curriculum and recreational interests of students enables the user to locate magazines according to their primary subject emphasis. Subjects range from "Aeronautics and Astronautics" to "World Affairs" and also cover automobiles, journalism, dance, earth science, nature study, economics, sports, and technology, to name a few.

Entries include title, publisher, editorial and subscription address, frequency of publication, and subscription price for libraries. A sprightly annotation ranging from about 150 to 250 words follows and gives a description of the target readership, scope, subject, and/or special emphasis. Comments on design and format are included and an evaluation indicates the magazine's suitability and appeal for young adults, the nature of the authorship of articles, quality of articles and illustration, and other information of pertinence. Publications in which the magazine is indexed are also identified.

AUTHORITY

The author is an associate professor in the Graduate School of Library and Information Science at the University of Illinois and author of *Periodicals for School Media Programs* (ALA, 1978) and *Magazines for Children* (ALA, 1983).

COMMENT

Lively and informative annotations and comprehensive coverage representing a wide range of student interest contribute to the effectiveness and convenience of this selection guide. Its publication date, however, precludes the reflection of changes in magazine publishing that have occurred since 1983.

Roman, Susan. *Sequences: An Annotated Guide to Children's Fiction in Series.* SEE Chapter 11, Reading Guidance and Motivation—General Works.

Rudman, Masha Kabakow. *Children's Literature: An Issues Approach,* **2nd ed.** SEE Chapter 11, Reading Guidance and Motivation—General Works.

Sader, Marion, ed. *Reference Books for Young Readers: Authoritative Evaluations of Encyclopedias, Atlases, and Dictionaries.* **Bowker, 1988. 615 pp. ISBN 0-8352-2366-3.**

PURPOSE

Designed to serve both librarians and the general public, as well as mature students, this guide to general reference sources can be used as both a reference and a selection tool. It will enable the user to find the works best suited to a particular need and to compare reference sources with those of similar purpose and format.

CONTENTS

What would a reference book be without a history of its subject? True to form, *Reference Books for Young Readers* begins with a history of encyclopedias, starting with the first writing systems and continuing into the present day. Similar treatment is accorded atlases, dictionaries, thesauruses, and other wordbooks. Other introductory chapters discuss salient points about choosing reference books, and report on a survey of 250 public, elementary, middle school, and high school libraries, which drew 69 responses, with the resultant data tabulated. In addition, comparative charts are presented that provide statistical and other brief descriptive data about the reference books evaluated.

An introductory chapter to the encyclopedia section describes how the encyclopedias were evaluated and defines and explains the importance of the concepts used: scope, authority, currency, accuracy, clarity, objectivity, accessibility, special features, and format. Reviewers checked preselected entries for currency, and subject experts compared coverage of selected topics for accuracy. Excerpts from published reviews are also included in each evaluation. Fifteen multivolume, three on-line, and four small-volume encyclopedias are evaluated with care, precision, and objectivity. A somewhat reduced sample page is reproduced in most evaluations, and various features are highlighted and captioned.

Following a chapter on what to look for in atlases, which also includes a glossary of primarily cartography terms, are evaluations of 42 atlases. These include an introduction, and discussions of format, special features, geographic balance, scale and projections, accuracy, currency, legibility, and accessibility. The evaluations are descriptive and concise, and comparisons are made between atlases for particular users, suggesting why one might be a better choice than another for a given group.

Dictionaries and other wordbooks receive the greatest coverage, because there are so many of them. The comparative chart, arranged by grade level, can be used as an index to the alphabetical evaluation section. The introductory "What to Look for in Dictionaries and in Word Books" provides a superb minicourse in dictionary evaluation, analyzing and comparing entries, pronunciation systems and symbols, and commenting on graphics and format, among other important aspects of the subject. A glossary of lexicography terms is also provided.

One hundred and two dictionaries, both paperback and hardbound, and 27 wordbooks have been evaluated according to authority, comprehensiveness, quality and currency of entries, syllabication and pronunciation, special features, accessibility, and graphics and format. Captioned facsimiles of entries are used to illustrate reviewers' comments. The evaluations are thorough and informative. A final chapter evaluates large-print reference books—14 dictionaries, 2 thesauruses, and an atlas—with the same care and criteria used in evaluations of the other categories and with special concern for the visually impaired and learning disabled user.

Appended are a bibliography and a list of reference book publishers. An index completes the work.

AUTHORITY

Marion Sader, currently publisher of Professional and Reference Books at R. R. Bowker Company, and also a librarian and author of other reference works for the library markets, together with some 32 reviewers, contributors, and consultants combined their expertise to produce this authoritative guide. The reviews were prepared by librarians and subject matter specialists, and three librarian-consultants determined the criteria and examined the reviews.

COMMENT

The results of the contributors' labors are not only definitive evaluations but a clearer understanding of the many aspects of reference works that must be considered in the selection process. Expertise oozes out of every sentence, and the clarity of the writing is exceptional. Even the makeup of the book has been carefully conceived, including the provision of a highlighted "Facts at a Glance" section that precedes each review. It is a valuable tool not only in school and public libraries but also in graduate library school courses in reference work and book selection. *Best Encyclopedias* by Kenneth Kister (reviewed in this chapter) covers the same general ground, but also provides evaluations of specialized encyclopedias, an area not covered here. Also available from Bowker is *General Reference Books for Adults*.

Schon, Isabel. *Basic Collection of Children's Books in Spanish.* **Scarecrow, 1986. 230 pp. ISBN 0-8108-1904-X.**

PURPOSE

This core collection of reference and trade books in Spanish for preschool through sixth grade children was assembled for the use of librarians in schools and public libraries that serve Spanish-speaking or bilingual children.

CONTENTS

The books that make up this collection were selected primarily from the output of publishers in Spain, Mexico, Argentina, and the United States. Other Spanish-speaking countries, the author states, are for the most part either too poor or too inclined to moralize in their children's books to have produced more than a few that were worthy of inclusion. A directory of dealers in books in Spanish is provided in an appendix.

Each entry includes a descriptive annotation in English, an English translation of the title, complete bibliographic information, including ISBN, where available, price (as of 1986), and grade level. The entries are arranged in Dewey order, beginning with reference books, and concluding with separate lists of Publishers' Series, Fiction, Easy, and Professional books. Author, title, and subject indexes are also provided.

Many of the books are Spanish translations of works that originated in other languages, including such popular English-language books as Judy Blume's *Blubber,* Beverly Cleary's *Ramona the Pest,* and H. A. Rey's *Curious George,* and some not-so-well-known stories by Hemingway, *The Good Lion* and *The Faithful Bull.*

AUTHORITY

Schon is professor of library science at Arizona State University, Tempe, and several other of her guides to children's books in Spanish have been published by Scarecrow Press. Two of the latest of these are described next.

COMMENT

Librarians who do not know Spanish and are in need of a recommended list of books for their Spanish-speaking clientele will find this a comprehensive guide. The author attributes some gaps in subject coverage to the unavailability of suitable material at the time of the book's publication.

Schon, Isabel. *Books in Spanish for Children and Young Adults, Series III; Books in Spanish for Children and Young Adults, Series IV.* **Scarecrow, 1985, 1987. 208 pp., 301 pp. ISBN 0-8108-1807-8, ISBN 0-8108-2004-8.**

PURPOSE

These are the most recent in a series of guides for adults—teachers, librarians, counselors, parents, and others—to literature in Spanish for young people that has been published since 1987.

CONTENTS

The books listed and annotated in these collections include those that "highlight the lifestyle, folklore, heroes, history, fiction, poetry, theatre, and classical literature of Hispanic cultures as expressed by Hispanic authors" (Preface, p. v.). Also included are bilingual books and translations into Spanish of popular books originating in other languages.

Each entry is marked with a symbol in the margin that indicates the author's judgment of its quality, and this is further elaborated in the annotation. Also added to the bibliographic information are ISBN and tentative grade level. The countries whose publications receive the greatest representation are Spain, Argentina, and Mexico, but also included are books from Bolivia, Chile, Colombia, Costa Rica, Cuba, Equador, Peru, Puerto Rico, the United States, and Venezuela.

The arrangement is first by country, then by type of book (fiction, folklore, health, historical fiction, history, poetry, religion, science and technology, sports, and theater make up most of the subjects included) within each of the countries represented. Author and title indexes are provided, along with lists of book dealers in Spanish-speaking countries as well as in the United States.

Annotations range from 50 to 100 words, and are both descriptive and evaluative. The author has no hesitation in skewering those books that fall short of her standards. Although the criteria that Schon used are not stated, it is clear that moralizing, cuteness, didacticism, and pedantry draw withering scorn when they appear. And who would argue with that? While some of her criticisms are understated, others are extremely forthright.

In Series IV, a book of songs draws the comment, "Songs like these are certain to take the joy out of singing," and a story collection is characterized thus, "Collection of seven disgustingly melodramatic stories about an old cart, silent birds, heartless people and

other such topics that have nothing to offer readers of any age."
Obviously there is no equivocating here.

Recommended books are received with equally notable directness, and there are many of them.

AUTHORITY

Schon is professor of library science at Arizona State University,
Tempe, and several other of her guides to children's books in Spanish have been published by Scarecrow Press.

COMMENT

Schon's impatience with the meretricious is quite clear. She has succeeded in conveying her admiration of Hispanic customs and culture, and her appreciation of the Spanish language. These books
are a trustworthy guide to all of these as addressed in young people's books. The negative annotations are unfailingly mordant, direct, and fun to read.

Shapiro, Lillian L., ed. *Fiction for Youth: A Guide to Recommended Books*, **2nd ed. Neal-Schuman, 1986. 264 pp. ISBN 0-
918212-94-4.**

PURPOSE

An annotated, alphabetical listing of fiction for adolescents, this
book is a selection guide for librarians, teachers, and parents to use
in providing fiction for the capable and, most likely, college-bound
reader.

CONTENTS

The thought that many of the books in this discerning collection will
never be read by the capable young people for whom they have
been written is a disquieting one. Yet, as Shapiro notes, the decline
in reading of fiction not only among high schoolers but also among
adults is an unhappy reality. In her introduction, she suggests ways
of reviving the fiction reading habit and urges that school librarians
return to the booktalk, revive book clubs, and provide the kinds of
special programs (dramatic productions, readings, guest authors)
that will encourage reading. Scheduled free reading time is a further suggestion.

Also in the introduction she describes the reader for whom the
list is intended, and sets forth the criteria used in selecting the 619
titles: only twentieth-century fiction is included; the books must
deal with adolescent interests; most titles should be books for adults;
juvenile books are to be of lasting quality; titles must have literary

value; and "sexual explicitness or obscene language were considered within the overall impact of the book and were not reasons for eliminating a title" (p. xviii), but their presence is indicated in the annotations.

The bibliography was prepared under Shapiro's editorship by a committee representing regions across the country who examined various selection tools as the list was prepared. Selected out-of-print titles are included in a separate section, and title and subject indexes are provided. Subjects range from abortion to farm life, immigrants, love stories, satire, trials, and World Wars I and II. Most annotations are about 80 to 100 words long.

AUTHORITY

Lillian Shapiro is a consultant and reviewer. She has been director of media services at the United Nations School in New York City, an assistant professor in the St. John's University School of Library Service, and assistant director of the Bureau of School Libraries at the New York City Board of Education.

COMMENT

Fine critical judgment has been exercised in the excellent selection of titles. The annotations are clear and succinct, and consist primarily of plot descriptions rather than literary analysis.

Shawn, Karen. *The End of Innocence: Anne Frank and the Holocaust.* SEE Chapter 13, The Library Media Center and the Curriculum.

Sheehy, Eugene P., ed. *Guide to Reference Books,* **10th ed.** SEE Chapter 10, Reference Services.

Smith, Robert M., and Phyllis M. Cunningham. *The Independent Learners' Sourcebook: Resources and Materials for Selected Topics.* **ALA, 1987. 306 pp. ISBN 0-8389-0459-9.**

PURPOSE

Written for librarians, teachers, and other professionals concerned with assisting independent adult learners, this guide to learning resources also provides assistance for the learners themselves. Advanced and gifted high school students will find it a helpful resource for independent study.

CONTENTS

Many of the 34 subjects selected for coverage have a contemporary ring, responding to current curiosity about such areas of inquiry as futurism, ecology/environment, computers and robotics, parapsychology, peace/arms reduction, and self-awareness. Others are more traditional: art appreciation, automobiles, bird-watching, history, law, and photography. Almost all topics covered lend themselves to independent study projects by high school juniors and seniors. Of particular interest to those who are approaching graduation and adulthood are work/careers/jobs, postsecondary education programs, and parenting.

For each subject the authors provide an introduction to the topic, references and introductory materials, other useful books, government documents, magazines and journals, on-line data bases, and agencies and organizations. Brief annotations describe the kind of coverage provided by each source. An author-title index and an index to agencies and organizations conclude the book.

AUTHORITY

The authors are professors of adult continuing education at Northern Illinois University, DeKalb. Both have written on topics in adult education.

COMMENT

This sourcebook will help high school librarians assist students in their search for information sources on subjects of personal as well as educational interest, and provides them with an approach to the types of resources that may be used in investigating a topic.

Software for Schools 1987–88: A Comprehensive Directory of Educational Software, Grades Pre-K through 12. Bowker, 1987. 1,085 pp. ISBN 0-8352-2369-8.

PURPOSE

A comprehensive list of instructional and professional software, with sources, this book was prepared for the use of building and district personnel involved in the purchase of computer software.

CONTENTS

Several indexes provide access to software and related information:

software for classroom use: by computer type/subject/grade level
software for professional use: by computer type/subject
software by title: alphabetically arranged and with extended entries

publishers index: arranged alphabetically, provides addresses and
phone numbers of 900 software publishers

computer periodicals directory: arranged alphabetically, provides address, phone numbers, brief description of contents, frequency of
publication, editor, subscription price

Main entries are found in the alphabetical title index. They provide the following information: grade level, release date, compatible
hardware, memory and other requirements, programming lan-
guage(s), price, number of disks, availability of manual and war-
ranty, order number and producer, and a description of contents. A
total of 8,800 currently available software packages are included. A
"How to Use This Book" section explains the book's organization
and displays each type of entry, identifying each element. Additional aids are the subject headings list, checklists for hardware and
software, and a glossary.

Introductory articles deal with the selection and evaluation of software; classroom use of computers, past and future; management
concerns in the use of computers in schools; and networking in
schools, definitions, benefits, and how-to's. Written by experts in
their respective fields, these articles are both practical and farsighted.

AUTHORITY

Prepared by R. R. Bowker Company's Database Publishing Group
in collaboration with the Systems Development Department, the
book includes not only software from their existing data base but
additional products that emerged from a search of catalogs, magazines, and press releases, as well as contact with producers.

COMMENTS

This book is clearly the result of careful planning and much forethought. The entries, while nonevaluative, provide thorough descriptions, and the indexes provide ready access by several useful
means. One possible flaw, however, is the lack of indication whether
the software requires color or monochrome monitors and adapters,
information that might affect purchasing decisions. *Software for
Schools* promises to be the standard work in its field.

Stanford, Barbara Dodds, and Karima Amin. *Black Literature for
High School Students.* SEE Chapter 11, Reading Guidance and
Motivation—Young Adult Literature.

Sutherland, Zena, ed. *The Best in Children's Books: The University of Chicago Guide to Children's Literature, 1979–1984.* Univ. of Chicago Press, 1986. 511 pp. ISBN 0-226-78060-0.

PURPOSE
School media specialists and public library children's and young adult specialists will find a rich source of children's and young adult literature of all kinds in this book.

CONTENTS
The 1,400 recommended children's and young adult books in this compilation were selected by the editor from reviews that appeared in the *Bulletin of the Center for Children's Books* (University of Chicago Press). The list includes books from the United Kingdom as well as the United States. An advisory committee of teachers and librarians in public and private schools and libraries met regularly with the editor to discuss the reviews, and recommended evaluation by an expert when the subject required it. Literary quality was the primary determinant of selection, rather than a search for balance either among age groups, subjects, or genre.

In the introduction, Sutherland stresses the importance of offering children a discriminating choice of books because of the other activities and interests that compete for their attention. With so little time left for reading and so many series books, mass market books, and comics to distract them from quality materials, a caring adult can make a difference by encouraging the reading and discussion of good books.

Criteria used for selecting the books are consistent with those applied to adult books, and are not unfamiliar to librarians and teachers. Adults are cautioned, however, against letting their own biases get in the way of objective judgment. An important precept in the evaluation of books chosen for the *Bulletin* is that they be judged on their own merits, and not be eliminated for some weaknesses if they have important strengths.

The entries are arranged alphabetically by author, are numbered consecutively, and include an age range, LC card number, ISBN, and price (which is no longer particularly relevant). Annotations are about 150 words long, comment on theme and plot, and manage to convey a sense of the author's style. There are indexes for title, developmental values, curricular use, reading level, title, and author. The subject index includes both fiction and nonfiction titles.

AUTHORITY
Sutherland is professor emeritus, Graduate Library School at the University of Chicago, and former editor of the *Bulletin of the Center for Children's Books.*

COMMENT

While not a core collection, this guide will lead to books for a particular subject area or age level or books related to such themes as family relations, intercultural understanding, self-appraisal, cooperation, and courage, to name a very few of those included in the developmental values index. It is an authoritative and effective selection tool for those searching for a retrospective guide to recent best books for young people.

That All May Read: Library Service for Blind and Physically Handicapped People. SEE Chapter 12, Serving Special Learners.

Tway, Eileen, ed. *Reading Ladders for Human Relations,* **6th ed. NCTE, 1981. 398 pp. ISBN 0-02-933040-8 (pap.).**

PURPOSE

Since its inception as a pamphlet in 1947, *Reading Ladders* has been guiding educators and parents in selecting books to foster improved human relations and, as a prerequisite to that, self-understanding.

CONTENTS

More than 1,600 titles are annotated and grouped into five major categories, or "ladders": Growing into Self, Relating to Wide Individual Differences, Interacting in Groups, Appreciating Different Cultures, and Coping in a Changing World. Each of these ladders is further subdivided. The first deals with understanding and valuing the self: self-image, maturity, cultural heritage, and values. The second is concerned with diversity: the aging, the handicapped, the gifted, male and female, and differences in economic circumstances. The third ladder presents books about different kinds of relationships: families, friends, peers, and other social groups. The fourth steps into cultural diversity: ethnic, religious, regional, and world cultures. The last completes the cycle with books that help young people deal with change: birth, growth, nurturing, and death; understanding the past; and dealing with crises, political realities, technology, and a challenging future world.

Books in each chapter are divided into age groups, which range from early childhood to mature adolescence. Both fiction and non-fiction titles are included. Introductory texts offer generalizations about the contents of *Reading Ladders* as a whole and of each of its sections. A list of professional references concludes each section, and a directory of publishers and title and author indexes round out the book.

AUTHORITY

The editor is chair of the Department of Teacher Education at Miami University of Ohio. The team members responsible for book selection and annotations represent different geographic areas, age specialization, and literary interests.

COMMENT

If continuity of publication is any indication of value, *Reading Ladders'* continuous existence for almost 40 years is emphatic testimony. Its thematic approach, combined with the advancement to greater maturity as readers work their way up the ladders' steps, provides a unique way of teaching about literature while nurturing humane values. The 1981 publication date is, of course, a drawback, although many of the recommended books are still in print. If the publication cycle (every nine years) is maintained, a new revision is just around the corner.

Walker, Elinor. *Book Bait: Detailed Notes on Adult Books Popular with Young People*, 4th ed. ALA, 1988. 166 pp. ISBN 0-8389-0491-2.

PURPOSE

A guide to selection and a booktalk resource for librarians working with seventh to ninth grade students, this book provides detailed information on quality adult books recommended by young people.

CONTENTS

The fourth edition of a work initiated by Walker in 1957, this book continues to include books recommended by young adult librarians throughout the United States. Approximately one third of the titles have appeared in previous editions.

Books were selected that would help young readers to understand and learn about the problems that they were facing. It was thought that by reading of love and courage and brotherhood the readers would be better able to find acceptable resolutions for their own problems. In keeping with the spirit of this selection process, selectors were particularly judicious in avoiding books with questionable language or scenes that might be objectionable. The titles that were finally included here can be used to motivate young teens to continue to read. They are not only of good quality but capable of opening new vistas for their readers and enhancing their pleasure in reading. The group of young teenage readers who recommended the almost 400 titles did so enthusiastically.

Each main entry consists of a detailed plot summary and includes background information about the author, the story, or some other information that will help librarians introduce the book. Hints for booktalking and specific pages that lend themselves to inclusion in booktalks are also provided, as are titles and information about related books.

A subject index to the main entries ranges from adventure to World War II, and includes such topics as danger, death and disaster, humor, handicapped, love stories and marriage, various genres such as fantasy and humor, social issues, and a variety of subjects that engage the interest of teenagers. A title index is also provided.

AUTHORITY

The author has been working with young people for over 50 years, as a teacher, a young adult librarian, and coordinator of young adult services at Carnegie Library, Pittsburgh. She also authored *Doors to More Mature Reading* (ALA, 1981).

COMMENT

A useful selection tool, this book will also help find that "other book just like this one," and has added use for planning booktalks.

Walton, Robert A., and Nancy Taylor. *Directory of Microcomputer Software for Libraries.* SEE Chapter 16, Technology and Automation.

Wilson, George, and Joyce Moss. *Books for Children to Read Alone: A Guide for Parents and Librarians.* **Bowker, 1988. 184 pp. ISBN 0-8352-2346-9.**

PURPOSE

While Wilson and Moss have found books that direct adults to good books for reading to children, there has been nothing available to help them identify good books that young children can read themselves. To fill this gap, they have prepared this annotated list.

CONTENTS

The books presented in this bibliography were chosen on the recommendations of young readers and a children's librarian, then examined by the authors. Using readability scales, and their own understanding that children's interests and these scales do not necessarily coincide, the authors organized the books by grade level and concept level.

After the first chapter, which presents wordless or nearly wordless books, the succeeding six chapters present books for each half-grade, from first to third. Separate lists of easy, average, and challenging books for that half-grade reading level precede more detailed entries, which include bibliographic information and an annotation of about 100 words, and a designation of genre and subject.

An appendix lists books in series: Madeline, Petunia, Amelia Bedelia, and so on. Indexes provided are by subject, readability, author, and title.

AUTHORITY

George Wilson is a former high school teacher who also recruited and trained science teachers for the Los Angeles City schools. Joyce Moss is a writer and editor in educational publishing.

COMMENT

This unpretentious guide makes no claims to presenting literary criticism of books for young readers or of definitiveness. What it does offer is a well-organized descriptive list of time-tested, popular and appealing books for the early grades, useful both to parents and librarians as a selection guide.

Wise, Bernice Kemler. *Teaching Materials for the Learning Disabled: A Selected List for Grades 6–12*. ALA, 1980. 64 pp. ISBN 0-8389-0311-8.

PURPOSE

Despite the flurry of publishing activity that followed passage of the Education for All Handicapped Children Act of 1975, there still exists a lack of material of practical value in selecting current books for learning disabled young people. This 1980 compilation was prepared to help teachers and librarians locate both professional materials for themselves and learning materials for their sixth to twelfth grade students, and many of the materials may still be available.

The introduction presents an accurate description of learning disabled youngsters and enumerates the criteria used in selecting materials for them. A separate section on reading programs lists a variety of kits, texts, and workbooks designed to motivate reading with high interest, low reading level materials.

The major portion of the booklet lists books, magazines, and nonprint media in various subject areas that will help meet the educational needs of learning disabled students. Among the topics are health and sex education, industrial arts and home economics, handwriting (particularly needed by many in this group), math and science, social sciences, sports, survival, and vocational guidance. Materials not necessarily related to the curriculum, such as fiction, biography, cars, and racing, are also included. Entries are descriptively annotated.

A brief bibliography, a directory of publishers, and an author-title index, complete the publication.

COMMENT

This guide would have been recommended unreservedly if this were 1981 or 1982. In 1989, it is useful for some recommendations in those areas that don't require currency, and because it will lead the user to publishers that specialize in materials for the learning disabled.

Winkel, Lois, ed. *The Elementary School Library Collection: A Guide to Books and Other Media, Phases 1-2-3*, **16th ed. Brodart, 1988. 1,048 pp. ISBN 0-87272-091-8.**

PURPOSE

Essential for creating a new media center collection, this resource will also serve librarians as they continue to develop and maintain presently existing collections. It covers materials suitable for pre-kindergarten to sixth grade children. A professional collection section lists materials on aspects of child development and curriculum planning for elementary schools.

CONTENTS

A total of 10,847 titles for children are included in the collection, consisting of 8,374 books, 123 periodicals, 120 computer software, and 2,147 audiovisual materials. The classified arrangement combined with indexes permits quick access, and the entries are cataloged fully, allowing for their use as a cataloging source. Foreign-language materials are included also, and users are advised to use the subject index for access.

Criteria for selection are listed in the opening pages, which also include descriptions of trends in elementary education. Among the criteria are accuracy and appeal of individual titles, a comparison with others on the same subject, and a determination of need for the title in the collection. Books in series, for example, the "Great Brain" books, are listed together in "omnibus" entries, and abridgments and simplified versions of books have been omitted from the collection. Policies are also described for special collection areas and specific formats.

The book is divided into three sections. The first is the classified catalog, in which audiovisual materials (videocassettes, computer software, filmstrips, kits, recordings, art and study prints) are integrated with the print materials (reference and trade books and periodicals). Omitted from the collection are 16mm films, packaged learning programs, textbooks, and workbooks. The collection includes older titles judged still to be useful, either newly added or continued from the previous edition, and selected new titles published between April 1985 and April 1987. In all, 2,625 titles have been added. Brief annotations are provided along with subject headings and readability and interest level codes.

Section 2 consists of separate author, title, and subject indexes, and Section 3 is the appendix, which includes materials for preschool children and books recommended for independent reading. Materials are identified for purchase for building collections in accordance with three phases: Phase 1 is recommended for all media centers, phase 2 for continuing development, and phase 3 materials are usually less important for the collection but still recommendable.

AUTHORITY

Winkel, a former New York City elementary school librarian, is currently affiliated with the graduate library school at the University of North Carolina at Greensboro.

COMMENT

Its continuance through 16 editions testifies to the value of this publication, which is put together by a committee of consultants. It continues to be a prime selection source for upgrading and maintaining elementary school library media collections, and is particularly valuable for its integration of nonprint media as well as cataloging information.

Wynar, Bohdan S., ed. *Recommended Reference Books for Small and Medium-Sized Libraries and Media Centers, 1988.* **Libraries Unlimited, 1988. 261 pp. ISBN 0-87287-682-9.**

PURPOSE

Small public and college libraries and school resource centers are the target institutions for this review source, which covers recommended reference books published in 1987.

CONTENTS

The 517 reviews presented in this eighth volume of an annual series were selected from 1,809 titles reviewed in *American Reference Books Annual (ARBA)*, which covers Canadian as well as American publications. General reference sources such as encyclopedias and dictionaries, geographic references, indexes, directories, bibliographies, guides, selected indexing and abstracting services, and selected government publications are among the types of works included. Code letters indicate whether a source is recommended for small college libraries (C), public libraries (P), or school library media centers (S), and all titles included in this publication are recommended, although some reservations may have been expressed in the reviews.

Four major sections are divided into 36 subsections, and each of these is further subdivided either by type of reference work or by subject. The general organization within the book, and within chapters, moves from the general to the specific. Part I provides reviews of general reference works, and the chapters included are arranged alphabetically by chapter title, from acronyms to quotation books. The second section includes reference works in the social sciences, the third section reviews publications in the humanities, and the fourth covers science and technology. "Subdivisions are based on the amount of material available on a given topic and will vary from year to year" (Introduction, p. xii).

The entries are numbered, simplifying access from the author/title index, and include ordering as well as bibliographic information. Reviews range in length from approximately 150 to 500 words, with an occasional longer one appearing for a lengthy or encyclopedic work, and are both descriptive and evaluative. Each review is signed, and concludes with a citation of other reviews that appeared in one of the ten professional journals used as additional reviewing sources.

In addition to the author/title index, a subject index is provided, which includes helpful see and see also references.

Wynar is editor of *American Reference Books Annual,* and received ALA's Isadore Gilbert Mudge Citation for his contributions to reference librarianship and publishing. The respected *American Reference Books Annual* is the source for the reviews selected for inclusion in this publication. Contributors include over 200 subject specialists in American libraries and universities.

An excellent selection tool for small libraries, this publication can be used to update Christine Gehrt Wynar's *Guide to Reference Books for School Media Centers* (also reviewed in this chapter). A minor flaw here is the use of letter codes to highlight recommendations for particular types of libraries. Users may overlook reviews of suitable publications if they are not coded for their type of library. Two of several such cases are *Lives of the Great Twentieth Century Artists,* which is recommended for college and public libraries but seems suitable also for high school library media centers, and the *Biological and Agricultural Index,* which is recommended for high school use but lacks the letter code for school libraries. These minor flaws aside, this is a highly recommended source.

Wynar, Christine Gehrt. *Guide to Reference Books for School Media Centers*, 3rd ed. Libraries Unlimited, 1986. 407 pp. ISBN 0-87287-545-8.

This guide to selection of recommended current reference books for school libraries encompasses several user groups: students in elementary, junior, and senior high schools; school library media specialists and teachers in those schools; and postsecondary school teachers of preservice and in-service education and library/information science courses.

Among the 2,011 entries are reference books for students in all grades, selection guides and information sources in a variety of formats for school library media specialists, and reference materials for teachers in general, special, and bilingual education. Selection was dependent on whether the publication is appropriate to the K–12 curriculum; reflects the current interests of potential users; and is appropriate to strategies of instruction, reading and interest level, the treatment and accuracy of information presented, the format and ease of locating information, and comparisons with other available works that treat the same topic.

Consecutively numbered entries provide full bibliographic and ordering information and a descriptive and analytical annotation. Citations of reviews in one or more of six publications listed in the front of the book are enclosed in brackets and appear at the end of the annotation. Codes indicate books for early and upper elementary grades only; books for middle and high schools are uncoded.

The first chapter presents general sources of print and nonprint media and software (review journals, catalogs, selection guides and indexes), and the second covers general reference materials, including data base services. The major part of the book provides coverage of 54 subjects, divided into chapters that are arranged alphabetically. Within each chapter, entries are organized first by type of reference work (bibliographies, directories, handbooks), then alphabetically by author or title. The subjects that are included are primarily curriculum-related (chemistry, earth sciences, social studies, careers, health and family), and topics of general interest (hobbies and games, occult, pets) are covered as well.

Materials of professional interest and use are listed in subject chapters, as well as in the opening chapters, and those entitled "Children's Literature," "Education," and Library Science."

A system of cross-references leads the user to related subjects or subsections. Where works may be searched for in more than one subject listing, a title is given in one and a see reference leads to the annotated main entry. An extensive introduction describes the scope and purpose of the book and explains how to use it. The index combines authors, titles, and subjects in a single alphabet, which simplifies searching.

AUTHORITY

The author has been district librarian for the Alamitos School District in California and a contributing editor for *School Library Media Quarterly*.

COMMENT

This comprehensive guide is an invaluable aid to the selection of reference materials for school libraries. It goes beyond the bounds suggested by its title by providing materials for school professionals as well as students, and that is all to the good. While its format can be somewhat confounding, help is provided by the cross-referencing system, the combined author, title, and subject index, and the introductory use instructions.

ADDITIONAL READINGS

Austin, Mary C., and Esther Jenkins. *Promoting World Understanding through Literature, K–8.* Libraries Unlimited, 1983. 266 pp. ISBN 0-87287-615-2. Annotated entries on children's literature about blacks, native Americans, Hispanics, and other American ethnic groups are supplemented by listings of historical events important for each group.

The Best Science Books and Films for Children. Susan M. O'Connell and Valeria J. Montenegro, eds. American Association for the Advancement of Science, 1987. ISBN 0-87168-316-4. Books, films, filmstrips, and videocassettes recommended for children from kindergarten to junior high school reviewed in selections that first appeared in *Science Books and Films,* the AAAS quarterly publication, between 1982 and 1987.

Books for the Teen-Age. NYPL, Committee on Books for Young Adults, annual. This is an excellent collection of about 1,250 titles chosen for their appeal to teenagers.

Bookwaves: A Compilation of Reviews of Books for Teenagers. San Francisco: Bay Area Young Adult Librarians, biennial. These brief critical and descriptive reviews of books of interest to a young adult audience are subdivided into subject categories for both fiction and nonfiction books.

Breen, Karen, ed. *Index to Collective Biographies for Young Readers,* 4th ed. Bowker, 1988. ISBN 0-8352-2348-5. Over 1,000 collective biographies have been indexed by occupation, title, and name of biographee to enable users to locate briefer than book-length biographies about contemporary and historical notables.

Gillespie, John T. *Publishers and Distributors of Paperback Books for Young People,* 3rd ed. ALA, 1987. 190 pp. ISBN 0-8389-0471-8; *Elementary School Paperback Collection.* ALA, 1985. 256 pp. ISBN 0-8389-0419-X; *Junior High School Paperback Collection.* ALA, 1985. 256 pp. ISBN 0-8389-0470-3; *Senior High School Paperback Collection.* ALA, 1986. 544 pp. ISBN 0-8389-0454-8. These four paperback volumes combine to make definitive acquisitions and selection tools for retrospective purchasing of paperback books, until updated versions are published.

Horner, Catherine Townsend. *The Single-Parent Family in Children's Books: An Annotated Bibliography,* 2nd ed. Scarecrow, 1988. 339 pp. ISBN 0-8108-2065-X. This annotated bibliography of 600 titles covers fiction, primarily, with some nonfiction, and is subdivided into such categories as divorce, desertion, separation, and the like.

Howard, Elizabeth F. *America as Story: Historical Fiction for Secondary Schools.* ALA, 1988. 156 pp. ISBN 0-8389-0492-0. Novels as they reflect American history are listed in this annotated bibliography that also includes student report ideas and follow-up activities.

Kennedy, DayAnn, Stella Spangler, and Mary Ann Vanderwerf. *Science & Technology in Fact and Fiction: A Guide to Children's Books*. Bowker, 1990. ISBN 0-8352-2708-1. Entries on fiction, nonfiction, and picture books provide summaries and evaluations, reading levels, and ISBN or out-of-print status. Indexes by author, title, subject, illustrator, and readability (using the Fry formula) provide access to the recommended books.

Kies, Cosette. *Supernatural Fiction for Teens: 500 Good Paperbacks to Read for Wonderment, Fear and Fun*. Libraries Unlimited, 1987. 127 pp. ISBN 0-87287-602-0. The popularity of this genre among young readers makes this a particularly appropriate selection tool for secondary schools. Included are 500 briefly annotated tales of magic, horror, the occult, psychic phenomena, and similar subjects.

Lima, Carolyn W., and John A. Lima. *A to Zoo: Subject Access to Children's Picture Books*, 3rd ed. New York: Bowker, 1989. 940 pp. ISBN 0-8352-2599-2. Nearly 12,000 fiction and nonfiction titles cataloged under 700 subjects. Includes subject headings, subject guide, bibliographic guide, title index, and illustrator index.

The following three classified core lists of books for school libraries provide unparalleled subject access and cataloging information. New editions are published every five years and yearly supplements are provided.

Children's Catalog, 15th ed. Richard H. Isaacson, and others, eds. Wilson, 1986.

Junior High School Catalog, 5th ed. Richard H. Isaacson, ed. Wilson, 1985.

Senior High School Catalog, 13th ed. Ferne E. Hillegas and Juliette Yaakov, eds. Wilson, 1987.

Serving Student Needs

9
The School Library Media Program

"School library media program" is difficult to define because its meaning has gone slack. For some, it describes everything that goes on in a school library media center. For others, it signifies what is left after the basic management functions are factored out. And still others take it to refer to just those special activities that are planned to create and maintain public awareness of the media center and otherwise enliven and lighten the library landscape. This chapter includes some books that touch on each of these definitions.

Exemplary programs are discussed in the government publication *Check This Out*, Margaret McDonald's *Towards Excellence,* and Lillian Shapiro's *Serving Youth.* Jane Smith discusses a middle school's curriculum support program in *Library Media Center Programs for Middle Schools,* and Patricia Wilson and Ann Kimzey offer some programming suggestions in *Happenings*. Additional books about special library programs can be found in Chapter 4, "Publicity and Public Relations."

Baker, D. Philip, and David R. Bender. *Library Media Programs and the Special Learner.* SEE Chapter 12, Serving Special Learners.

Check This Out: Library Program Models. **U.S. Department of Education, 1987. 319 pp. ISBN 0-318-23543-9 (pap.).**

PURPOSE

The National Diffusion Network, a program within the U.S. Department of Education, sought to identify exemplary programs within libraries and media centers that could be adapted or replicated elsewhere. Among the goals of this effort were to encourage self-evaluation, to collect and disseminate information about the selected programs, and to assist those who wish to replicate the programs.

CONTENTS

Effective school librarians are always searching for new ways to meet the needs of special populations within their schools and to enhance their services to all users. Professional journals provide some answers, and this book proffers additional ideas.

Descriptions of 62 programs are presented in *Check This Out,* most of them in elementary and secondary school library media centers, but also including programs in public and academic libraries. Particular aspects of a library program have been selected for dissemination rather than an entire library program itself.

The examples included here were selected from the results of a nationwide search, and represent such program areas as services to populations without or with inadequate library media centers, community information and referral services, services to the disadvantaged and handicapped, effective uses of technology to expand services, programs that teach library media skills, and models for teacher-librarian cooperation in planning for and implementing student learning.

The checklist used in evaluating the programs is reproduced in the book to encourage and help librarians in reviewing their own programs to assess their strengths and weaknesses. Those programs that exemplify the criteria in the checklist are listed under each criterion. Among the programs that are included are offering special tutoring for migrant students; using stations for learning library skills; using an open media center as the focal point for individually prescribed instruction; using media for learning and communication; rewarding students who read at home; enriching a school with Great Books, philosophy, art museums, and more; introducing parents to the books their teenage children are reading; having students meet authors in the school library; integrating information skills into the high school curriculum; instituting a public relations program to create awareness of media center services; videotaping through microscopes; and using microcomputers, electronic bulletin boards, electronic research tools, and so on.

Each listing describes the needs assessment, goals and objectives, implementation, staff required and costs, evaluation results, dissemination services, and funding sources for the program. The name, address, and telephone number of a contact person are also provided.

AUTHORITY

All programs were reviewed by a team of prominent librarians, library administrators, library educators, and U.S. Department of Education officers.

COMMENT

Reading the model program descriptions is a first step in implementing innovative programs. Readers of this source should call or write to the contact people of programs in which they are interested for more information.

Liebold, Louise Condak. *Fireworks, Brass Bands, and Elephants: Promotional Events with Flair for Libraries and Other Nonprofit Organizations.* SEE Chapter 4, Publicity and Public Relations.

McDonald, Margaret Marshall. *Towards Excellence: Case Studies of Good School Libraries.* **British Library Association, 1985; dist. by ALA. 92 pp. ISBN 0-85365-856-0.**

PURPOSE

Exemplary school libraries in British schools have been described in order to demonstrate the advantages to students and staff that are offered by effective school library programs.

CONTENTS

Ten school library programs of varied geographic distribution and school level were chosen for these case studies because they represent the best in school library service in the United Kingdom. Each study describes the policy, finances, staffing, use, organization, and other relevant features of the library under discussion; photographs, floor plans, and other visual material supplement the written word.

There appear to be no national boundaries, neither to excellence in service nor to the problems that hinder it, at least between Britain and the United States. The school libraries that are effective there, as here, are those with knowledgeable and enthusiastic librarians or teacher-librarians who reach out constantly to the entire school community, and with head teachers, or principals, who support the program unreservedly. Teachers, students, and parents are all involved in one way or another in each of these school library's activities and recognize its importance in the life of the school. However, nationwide, "Desperation is voiced by librarians and teachers about the shortage of books, staff, time, space and assistance" (Introduction, p. vii).

In addition to commitment, other qualities common to these high-functioning library programs include clerical and technical support; efficient use of space; coordination of library resources with curriculum; adequacy of the collection to meet school as well as individual students' needs; presence of a "local education authority adviser," that is, district coordinator or supervisor; instructional program in library user skills; positive relationship and liaison between school and public library; local mandates requiring a school librarian; and a school bookshop to encourage the reading habit.

In the secondary schools, the librarian is accorded status equivalent to that of subject department head, attending staff meetings and relating to faculty at a departmental level. Nevertheless, clerical tasks are often given over to student or parent volunteers, on the ground that they provide pupils with good experience. Interestingly, such experience is not offered in the school kitchen or by the school secretary, nor are teachers expected to depend on student assistants, a point well taken by the author.

AUTHORITY
The author has served as school and academic librarian, and lecturer in librarianship. She has authored many books and articles.

COMMENT
Although there are differences in terminology to stumble over, it is enlightening to read about and note the striking similarities between British and American model school libraries. But one cannot help wondering what there is in both national characters that denies adequate funding for school libraries in spite of their demonstrably positive effect on so many of the children in their schools.

Shapiro, Lillian L. *Serving Youth: Communication and Commitment in the High School Library*. Bowker, 1975. 268 pp. ISBN 0-8352-0763-3.

PURPOSE
Although it was published 15 years ago, *Serving Youth* is remarkably reflective of the current scene in school library media programs. While some of its references to then current issues are somewhat

162

outdated, it still offers a lively perspective of the school library's role and a critical view of what might be done to enhance it.

CONTENTS

Shapiro begins with a look at the societal forces that affect the attitudes and activities of young people. What were trends in the 1970s have become unpleasant reality today as urban areas, particularly, are beset with all the ailments that the misuse of drugs and alcohol and the loosening of public morality and family structure can bring. The obvious next question is what influence can schools, and more particularly, school librarians exert to help bring about change? That this question still remains unanswered must give pause to all proponents of school reform in the 1980s and 1990s.

Shapiro proceeds to examine the secondary school library and the librarian's role in the school. Her lists of teachers' and librarians' respective views of each others' job duties and performances will strike a spark of recognition in most readers. In spite of task analyses, studies, and job classifications, many of which were conducted shortly before her book was published, Shapiro still notes a lack of definition of the school librarian's role, except to observe that it is a hybrid one. School librarians are neither fully teachers, although they work in schools, nor librarians, although they manage libraries, and this dichotomy has been a costly one in terms of achieving an identity.

That the role can be a creative and decisive one, however, is demonstrated by the exemplary programs discussed in the book, where several are described in considerable detail. Some of the factors common to these programs are listed and include the principal's positive attitude, the flexibility of teachers, adequacy of budget, student involvement in determination of policies, minimal regulations about student access, mutual understanding of faculty and media staff roles, stress on continuing education of school staff members, emphasis on student-produced materials in varied formats, prompt information service and use of interlibrary loan, and regular evaluation combined with continuing adaptation. Support by the community might have been included, although it is not mentioned here. Suggestions for focusing on the community in order to gain its support are, however, discussed in a later chapter.

In all of this Shapiro sees a need for school librarians to shift from a reactive attitude to a proactive one and to become more visible, more responsive, and more service-oriented.

AUTHORITY

Shapiro has served as director of media services in the United Nations International School, as a supervisor of high school libraries in

163

the New York City school system, and on the faculty of the St. John's University Department of Library and Information Science, Queens, New York.

COMMENT

The paucity of books dealing with the underlying reality of being a school librarian in a high school provoked Lillian Shapiro to write *Serving Youth*. Her observations, while somewhat outdated in some respects, will evoke some nods of recognition from most school library media specialists, and her views on the school librarians' role are astute. Perhaps the role of curriculum consultant that some current observers of the scene are trying to shape will be the most comfortable one, in the long run, but it looks like librarians will have to act the role before they are named to fill it.

Smith, Jane Bandy. *Library Media Center Programs for Middle Schools: A Curriculum-Based Approach.* **ALA, 1989. 150 pp. ISBN 0-8389-0500-5 (pap.).**

PURPOSE

The role of the school library media center in middle schools is explored here for school library media specialists and library school students.

CONTENTS

As middle schools and school library media programs have evolved from junior high schools and school libraries, their parallel development has been an interactive one, and the media program is, or should be, an integral part of middle school education. Smith develops this theme as she works through the four component parts of her book: offering a model for planning, correlating library media services and skill development, demonstrating the library media role in human development, and suggesting a model for evaluating the support of school goals provided by the media program.

Middle schools, no longer emulating high schools, which center on the group, set their focus on meeting individual needs. Because of its unique ability to respond to individual learning styles, the media center can support the delivery of personalized instruction. Because of the rapid growth and change of students of middle school age, their developmental diversity requires a wide range of learning materials, also supplied by the school library media center. With a function so clearly established, it remains only for the school library media specialist to begin planning the support program that has been outlined.

The library media specialist's role is defined in a threefold pattern, as administrator of the facility and collection, as instructor in media skills and literature, and as consultant in information retrieval and supporter of instruction. Planning the library media program is a first step in filling this role. Planning, in this author's view, involves three steps, defining, developing, and evaluating. In the first phase, information is gathered, the school program is analyzed, and program priorities are established. After activities are planned and coordinated with class schedules, implementation of activities can begin. The evaluation phase applies to activities and services, then the total program and finally dissemination of the results of the program.

Going beyond a theoretical approach, the author offers sound, practical advice, suggesting ways of involving teachers in the selection process, reminding school library media specialists of the importance of relevant and up-to-date materials, and describing the need to convince faculty members of the librarian's ability to serve as an instructional resource person, partner in guidance, and effective teacher of library and information skills. Smith presents a sequence of media skills in six areas to be covered in grades 5 through 8 and shows how to correlate and integrate the skills with coursework in English, social studies, science, and math. She discusses the relationship between the guidance program and books and media. Finally, she presents methods and sources of information about evaluation and provides several forms for conducting the evaluation.

Appendixes list regional accrediting agencies and provide a bibliography of materials for bibliotherapy. An index concludes the book.

AUTHORITY
Smith is an education specialist in the State Department of Education, Montgomery, Alabama, and managing editor of *School Library Media Annual, 1988* (Libraries Unlimited).

COMMENT
While this book is uniquely applicable to middle school media centers, it also offers planning, implementation, and evaluation tools that are adaptable for any school setting. Its clarity, succinctness, and practicality recommend it to all school library media specialists, and especially those in middle schools.

Tuggle, Ann Montgomery, and Dawn Hansen Heller. *Grand Schemes and Nitty-Gritty Details: Library PR That Works.* SEE Chapter 4, Publicity and Public Relations.

Velleman, Ruth A. *Serving Physically Disabled People: An Information Handbook for All Libraries.* SEE Chapter 12, Serving Special Learners.

Wilson, Patricia, and Ann C. Kimzey. *Happenings: Developing Successful Programs for School Libraries.* **Libraries Unlimited, 1987. 124 pp. ISBN 0-87287-522-9.**

PURPOSE

Ideas, programs, and directions for establishing the school media center as a lively and creative center of activity are provided for the inspiration of school library media specialists.

CONTENTS

Successful programs designed to provide curriculum enrichment, promote awareness of the school library media center, and foster good school-community public relations are the substance of this book. The opening section presents a rationale for program development and describes the types of programs and their goals. They include programs for specific target groups, programs that develop specific themes, meet curricular needs, enhance school community relations, and promote involvement of students and staff in library activities.

Some opening advice suggests that planners avoid publicizing private businesses and controversial topics (unless materials are used that express every point of view), and include preparations for security, among other things. Themes can be based on student interests, the school curriculum, special events in the community and common situations, besides the usual holiday and anniversary celebrations. A variety of formats and idea sources are suggested as well.

Considerations in planning are identified, and resources are described. Maintaining a community resource file simplifies the process, and other sources of help and ideas are included. Some of them are questionnaires, the media, public libraries and other institutions, organizations and clubs, and special events.

Three sample programs are offered for each of the three school levels and include crafts and storytelling for elementary schools, programs with an international flavor and introducing sports stars for middle school, and paperback swapping, teleconferencing, and space explorations for high schools. Each program description includes objectives, materials, and procedures; an appendix supplements this with an entire program plan, including these three elements and adding follow-up activities and correlation and evaluation procedures.

The niceties of postprogram activities are mentioned, such as thank-yous, adding to the resource file, and securing evaluations from staff and students. The overall effects of the program can be examined as well, from circulation and use statistics and analysis of other data. Keeping records and including program descriptions in reports are also advised.

A second appendix presents a bibliography. An index concludes the book.

AUTHORITY
Patricia Wilson is a lecturer on curriculum and instruction at the University of Houston and Ann Kimzey is a lecturer on children's literature at the University of Houston, Texas.

COMMENT
All aspects of program planning are included in this handbook, and some ideas for effective programs are offered as well.

10

Reference Services

While one of the goals of school library media programs is to teach young people to find information for themselves, occasions always arise where the school librarian's own reference skills are brought into play. For inexperienced library media specialists or students of library service, some groundwork in reference techniques must be laid. Assembled here are some books that will help develop reference skills and help select books for the reference section. There is even a book on reference interviewing to polish the technique of learning what the questioner really wants, an important necessity in all school libraries, and another designed for teachers and administrators searching for that perfect quotation.

A basic introduction is offered in the two-volume *Introduction to Reference Work* by William Katz. In the second volume, *Reference Services and Reference Processes,* he discusses a subject that will engage the interest of the more experienced school library media specialist, on-line searching. When the librarian does it, it is a reference service; when students do it, it is called end-user searching. Whoever does on-line searching, using automated data bases as information sources or bibliographic tools is an important new addition to the searcher's repertory of skills. The use of on-line data bases, however, also raises a number of issues, creates management problems, and requires the infusion of additional budgetary resources. Two of the books included here offer discussion and elucidation of these issues, management problems, and budget, and provide information on developing trends as well: Fred Batt's *Online Searching for End Users* and Martin Kesselman and Sarah Watstein's *End-User Searching.*

ALA, Reference Books Bulletin Editorial Board. *Purchasing an Encyclopedia: 12 Points to Consider,* **2nd ed. ALA, 1988. 40 pp. ISBN 0-8389-3351-3.**

PURPOSE

Encyclopedia reviews assist the busy librarian or parent seeking purchasing advice, with criteria and content analysis.

CONTENTS

This pamphlet not only presents evaluative criteria for determining quality of encyclopedias but also provides brief reviews of ten of the most commonly used adult and children's encyclopedias. Each review is modeled after the criteria that have been established and indicates where a more detailed analysis may be found. Despite its small size, this publication packs a wealth of descriptive and evaluative information into the reviews, and a comparison chart adds to its utility.

Purchasing an Encyclopedia is a particularly useful source for busy school librarians, for parents seeking a recommendation of what to buy for home use, and for students who are learning how to evaluate information sources. ALA is planning a biennial update.

AUTHORITY

Reviews were written by the expert members of the Reference Books Bulletin Editorial Board of ALA.

COMMENT

This quick reference source will help older students and parents understand the niceties of encyclopedia evaluation, and provide school media specialists with current reviews.

Robert M. Pierson, *Desk Dictionaries: A Consumer's Guide,* also published by ALA (1986), provides, in the same size package, a similar evaluation of seven highly rated desk dictionaries along with a section on reference aids dealing with new words and familiar words whose uses have recently changed.

Aversa, Elizabeth S., and Jacqueline C. Mancall. *Management of Online Search Services in Schools.* SEE Chapter 16, Technology and Automation.

Batt, Fred. *Online Searching for End Users: An Information Sourcebook.* **Oryx, 1988. 116 pp. ISBN 0-89774-394-6.**

PURPOSE

Information, sources, and bibliographies are provided in this sourcebook for librarians who use or teach the concepts and techniques of on-line searching, as well as students in library and information science courses.

CONTENTS

The books and articles on major trends and concepts of on-line searching are analyzed and annotated in this guide to the literature, which also presents introductory overviews of each subject considered. Also included are selected lists of on-line data base vendors, software and user interface systems, periodicals on data base searching, and advantages and disadvantages of on-line searching. A total of 510 entries are included, numbered consecutively for ease of location. An introduction describes the content of the book and defines the terminology.

After school library media specialists, particularly in high schools, developed skill in on-line searching, they began to discover the value of teaching the skills to student searchers, thus changing their focus on on-line data bases from serving as intermediary to training end users. These two aspects of on-line searching are considered in the first two chapters, the first offering a historical overview of librarian (intermediary) searching, a list of commonly used data bases, some general sources of information on the state of the art, and annotations of 41 books and journal articles. Chapter 2 provides articles and books about teaching end users and other aspects of end-user searching.

Searching strategies and styles are the subject of Chapter 3, which also provides sources on downloading, cost-effectiveness, and various search techniques. Data bases and vendors are described, equipment considerations discussed, and future trends and prospects considered, notably the growing utilization of CD-ROM. The final chapter, Chapter 4, offers a core library collection, including bibliographies on on-line searching, directories, and selected books. Author, title, and subject indexes complete the book.

AUTHORITY

The author is head of the reference department and associate professor at the University of Oklahoma at Norman.

COMMENT
While an introductory course or seminar can get librarians started with on-line searching, issues and problems that are involved may need further examination. The succinct chapter overviews in this guide offer perspective on many of these, and the selections that have been annotated present further avenues of exploration.

Epler, Doris M. *Online Searching Goes to School.* SEE Chapter 14, Teaching Library and Information Skills.

Farber, Bernard E., comp. *A Teacher's Treasury of Quotations.* **McFarland, 1985. 370 pp. ISBN 0-89950-150-8.**

PURPOSE
This collection simplifies finding appropriate quotations on education and related subjects.

CONTENTS
Over 4,600 quotations about education, its providers, its objects, its subjects and aims, and analogous topics are arranged alphabetically by subject, with author and subject indexes provided for help in locating the apt bon mot. From the earliest recorded thinkers (Confucius, Aristotle) to more recent notables (George Santayana, Harry Golden, John Dewey), the quotations are often striking in their truth or irritating to those who disagree. Remarkably contemporary is this thought, quoted from the Talmud, and written before A.D. 400: "If you see cities uprooted, know that it came about because they did not maintain teachers' salaries."

Books, learning, censorship, pornography, perfection, and paperwork are only some of the subjects of quotations that will be of particular interest to school library media specialists. Teachers and administrators will find a wealth of relevant quotes to amuse, inspire, and spark a discussion.

AUTHORITY
Farber is a former teacher and school administrator.

COMMENT
Keep a copy of this book on the professional shelf for yourself, teachers, and administrators to browse through and use.

Hede, Agnes Ann. *Reference Readiness: A Manual for Librarians and Students,* **3rd ed., rev. and updated. Library Professional, 1984. 187 pp. ISBN 0-208-02001-2.**

PURPOSE

Designed for library science students, practicing librarians, and researchers, this book introduces a variety of selected reference sources, enabling the user to select the most appropriate source for a particular information need.

CONTENTS

Hede has selected approximately 145 standard reference sources, both general and special, and provided summaries of their contents and arrangement, advice about how they may be used, and their Library of Congress classification. Each section also provides additional citations of related works. Entries are arranged in chapters according to the type of source: dictionaries; encyclopedias; yearbooks, annuals, and almanacs; handbooks and manuals; indexes, serials, and directories; bibliographies; biographical sources; atlases, gazetteers, and guidebooks; and computer sources and services. Entries are alphabetically arranged, for the most part, the exception being those that are in a series or in an interrelated sequence.

Some major sources suitable for use with children are included where appropriate, and identified as "Children's Sources," but Hede rightly notes that "these constitute only an introduction to the basic titles that are available" (Introduction, p. xiv). Youngsters in secondary schools are considered close enough to adulthood to be served by the adult sources.

The final chapter provides search questions for each type of reference source, allowing for practice, first in determining which source(s) to use and then in using whatever has been selected. A single index combines author, editor, and title entries.

AUTHORITY

Hede is an adult reference service librarian with the Los Angeles Public Library.

COMMENT

Less forbidding than the more comprehensive guides to reference sources, this manual will serve student and beginning librarians, as well as beginning researchers, as a gentle introduction to reference materials of various kinds. It describes accurately what reference books contain, how they are arranged, and how and when to use them and then encourages the user to examine the source while

172

reading about it. This is a painless initiation for the inexperienced and a useful review for those who need that.

Hillard, James M. *Where to Find What: A Handbook to Reference Service,* rev. and updated. Scarecrow, 1984. 357 pp. ISBN 0-8108-1645-8.

PURPOSE

"A ready-reference source for the harried librarian" (p. v.) and for the librarian inexperienced in reference service, this book will also help the library user to find the answer to reference questions when the "Harried One" is not immediately available.

CONTENTS

This revision of an earlier work provides an alphabetical listing of subjects likely to have prompted reference questions and then provides recommended sources of information about them. Citations include trade as well as reference books. Topics range from Abbreviations and Acronyms to Zoos and include such esoterica as Brands on Cattle, Carving of Meats, Demons, and Solitaire, as well as the mostly commonplace, for example, Cats, Calendars, and Caves. In all, 595 subject headings are included. Recommended titles are well annotated, and the user is rarely burdened with more than a half dozen sources. See and see also references facilitate finding the correct subject heading for locating the appropriate reference sources.

While Hillard lays no claim to offering a buying guide, he has provided the bibliographic information needed for purchases. An exhaustive bibliography of the subjects covered was not his purpose either, as the brevity of the list under each subject heading will attest.

AUTHORITY

The author is director of the Daniel Library at the Citadel in South Carolina. He acknowledges his use of the suggestions of reference librarians and critics of his earlier version of this book.

COMMENT

This unpretentious book is a handy guide to the resources that might help to answer a tough reference question, particularly for the novice. It is, however, far from comprehensive. On the other hand, one might well wonder what, short of a complete library subject catalog, would be comprehensive enough. Nevertheless, there are some annoying flaws. Under religion, for example, only

Christianity and Islam are listed, but there are separate entries for Mennonites and Buddhism. Where are Judaism and Hinduism, among others? The subject Music and Musicians provides see also references to several related topics, but not to Jazz, which is a separate entry. A look into Audiovisual Materials will lead to four cited books, none with a publication date more recent than 1975. Perfection, alas, has still eluded James Hillard. Nevertheless he has carried a promising idea to a somewhat useful conclusion.

Hunter, Beverly, and Erica K. Lodish. *Online Searching in the Curriculum: A Teaching Guide for Library/Media Specialists and Teachers.* SEE Chapter 14, Teaching Library and Information Skills.

Jennerich, Elaine Zaremba, and Edward J. Jennerich. *The Reference Interview as a Creative Art.* **Libraries Unlimited, 1987. 107 pp. ISBN 0-87287-445-1.**

PURPOSE

It is a rare patron indeed who knows how to state reference needs clearly, without help, and this is particularly true in school libraries. This book describes the basics in reference interviewing for all librarians as well as students in library science courses.

CONTENTS

Interviewing patrons to determine their needs is an essential step in providing effective library service. The Jennerichs present the appropriate techniques in a minidrama format, replete with theatrical terms as chapter headings. They begin with "Setting the Stage," in which a historical and philosophical context is provided, and continue with "The Actor's Tools," a discussion of the skills involved in conducting the interview. These include listening attentively, asking open questions, restating the response, and using encouragement for further explanation. Nonverbal skills involving eye contact, tone of voice, and facial expression are discussed as well. An interviewing test and checklist are provided.

A discussion of reference librarian characteristics sets the stage for an analysis of various types of interviews, such as teaching, directional, information, circulation, and others. Interviewing for on-line search requirements is a separate skill, and a set of prescribed questions is often used to facilitate formulation of a search strategy.

The physical setting influences the interview's outcome either by creating barriers or providing visibility, and the importance of proximity to entering patrons and ease of identification of the reference librarian is stressed. The roles and responsibilities of student assistants and paraprofessionals are described, and the wisdom of providing training suggested.

Additional chapters discuss librarians working alone, dealing with handicapped and non-English-speaking patrons, and suggestions for follow-up and handling complaints. A final chapter sums it up with a list of skills and a reprise of the earlier action, suggesting evaluation techniques and noting characteristics of successful interviewers, among other points. A bibliography and an index conclude the book.

AUTHORITY

Elaine Zaremba Jennerich is library director at Emory and Henry College, Emory, Virginia. Edward J. Jennerich is vice president for academic affairs, Virginia Intermont College, Bristol, Virginia.

COMMENT

For those librarians who experience difficulty or frustration when trying to determine just what it is a patron wants, this book offers a good deal of practical advice. Another helpful source is William Katz's *Introduction to Reference Work, Vol. 2* (reviewed in this chapter).

Katz, William A. *Introduction to Reference Work, Vol. 1: Basic Information Sources*, 5th ed. McGraw-Hill, 1987. 397 pp. ISBN 0-07-033537-0.

PURPOSE

Written for librarians, students, and general users, this text was designed to familiarize them with those sources of information that will help in making effective use of library resources.

CONTENTS

This updated and revised version of earlier guides to reference materials by Katz presents sources of information on a wide range of topics. Chapters are arranged according to the type of material being discussed rather than by subject, enabling the author to provide explanations of how to use that form of reference source and to compare sources of that type.

The book consists of three parts, the first of which introduces, in its first chapter, general information about reference services, its role in the library, the role of the reference librarian, and general comments on information sources. Chapter 2 acquaints the reader with on-line reference services, explaining terminology and discussing advantages of on-line searching.

Part 2 describes the basic forms of works that provide initial access to information. Chapter 3 introduces the subject with discussions of evaluation guidelines for bibliographies, selection aids, indexes to reviews, and guides to reference books. Among the forms discussed in the following chapters are union catalogs, retrospective bibliography, and bibliographies of periodicals and newspapers, microforms, nonprint materials, and bibliography of bibliographies. Indexing and abstracting services and their forms are discussed in Chapters 4 and 5.

Part 3 presents analyses of information sources. General information sources are considered in Chapters 7 and 8, and evaluation criteria are discussed. Included are general and subject encyclopedias for adults and children, ready reference sources such as almanacs and yearbooks, handbooks and directories, and so forth. The remaining chapters, 9 through 12, are more subject-specific, and include biographical sources, universal and current, dictionaries of various kinds, geographic sources, and government documents.

All chapters begin with an introduction, most discuss evaluation of the particular form being considered and include comparisons of sources, and all conclude with a list of suggested reading. A comprehensive index ends the work.

AUTHORITY

Bill Katz is a professor at the School of Library and Information Science, State University of New York at Albany, editor of *The Reference Librarian,* and a columnist for *Library Journal.* He has authored a number of books for the use of librarians, primarily about magazines and reference service.

COMMENT

This basic text, now considered a standard for general reference work, is thorough and comprehensive enough for most school librarians' needs. Particularly helpful are the introductions to each section, in which the author demonstrates how particular reference sources are used for answering questions and reference problem solving. More expansive coverage of reference materials is provided by Eugene Sheehy's *Guide to Reference Books,* also reviewed in this chapter.

Katz, William A. *Introduction to Reference Work, Vol. 2: Reference Services and Reference Processes,* **5th ed. McGraw-Hill, 1987. 397 pp. ISBN 0-07-033538-9.**

PURPOSE

Addressed to librarians as well as students of library service, this second volume of *Introduction to Reference Work* provides an overview of the changes in reference services that have been wrought by the computer, as well as assisting in the upgrading of skills required for reference work.

CONTENTS

As with Volume 1, Katz has added significantly to the contents of earlier versions, not only in the areas of on-line searching and the overall impact of microcomputers, but also in networking, library instruction, and the evaluation of reference services. References, footnotes, and suggested materials for further reading have also been updated.

The role of libraries as information centers for the communities they serve is the subject of Part 1, whose two chapters describe information and referral services and services to adults and students, as well as changes in patterns of communication and the information industry, packaging of information, and changes that have occurred in the positions of reference professionals.

Part 2 is concerned with working with patrons on reference or research problems. In Chapter 3, techniques of conducting reference interviews are discussed. An example of an actual interview is presented, and the dialogue demonstrates how a skilled reference librarian can ascertain a patron's precise need and fill it. Also discussed are the levels of reference service that a library might choose to offer. Developing a search strategy and manual searching techniques are the subjects of the fourth chapter.

On-line reference services are described in Part 3, which, in Chapters 5 and 6, explains the elements of on-line searching, provides extensive information about data bases and their evaluation and use, and includes a guide to vendors. Some of the major changes that have occurred in this area are discussed and trends are analyzed. Chapter 7 is devoted to microcomputers, and includes information on CD-ROM, software, and important sources of information about them. In Chapter 8, bibliographic networks, the bibliographic utilities currently in use and their reference possibilities, and their applications in interlibrary loan are discussed.

The concluding section focuses on bibliographic instruction and program evaluation, with recommendations for planning and carrying out both kinds of programs. Separate portions of Chapter 9 deal with instruction for the on-line searcher, and aids to searching are provided. Evaluation of the reference program is the subject of the final chapter. Guidelines for service, defining goals and objectives, and evaluation techniques are discussed, as well as evaluation of librarians who perform reference services.

AUTHORITY

Bill Katz is a professor at the School of Library and Information Science, State University of New York at Albany, editor of *The Reference Librarian*, and a columnist in *Library Journal*. He has authored a number of books for the use of librarians, primarily about magazines and reference service.

COMMENT

Beyond its obvious usefulness in introducing students to reference services, this book will refresh practitioners on the fundamentals of reference services and trends that are overtaking traditional methods of providing service. The questions that are raised and the discussions of various issues are provocative and informative. Librarians in secondary schools, particularly, will find it a helpful source.

Kesselman, Martin, and Sarah B. Watstein, eds. *End-User Searching: Services and Providers.* **ALA, 1988. 230 pp. ISBN 0-8389-0488-2 (pap.).**

PURPOSE

With the proliferation of microcomputers in homes and businesses, an increasing amount of data base searching is being done by people without librarianship training. This book considers some issues raised by this shift, and was written to help librarians find the best means of defining and helping to serve the needs arising from this change.

CONTENTS

School library media specialists, particularly in secondary schools, have witnessed, and perhaps have encouraged, the expanding population of data base end users by teaching search techniques to their students. Data base vendors have increasingly aimed at this growing market by simplifying search procedures, providing menu-driven user interfaces, and offering other services to improve accessibility. While this book is aimed at all librarians, its specific application to secondary school library media specialists is clear as it defines the need to plan and develop end-user services.

The opening chapter describes the increasing demand and the issues that arise in developing an end-user program. Chapter 2 considers the factors involved in implementing such a program, including determining which services to subscribe to, deciding on policies and procedures, selecting hardware and software, promoting the program, and developing support systems (documentation, instructions for use, schedules, forms). Chapter 3 is concerned with the training and instruction of users and provides some hints, advice, and an outline of objectives.

Chapters 4, 5, and 6 describe the services that are available to end users from BRS, Dialog, H. W. Wilson, and Information Access Company (IAC). Each chapter includes an introductory section, descriptions of the data bases covered by the service, its access and availability, and evaluation of the documentation and support provided for users. An overview of search features and commands indicates the ease with which searches may be accomplished and reactions of searchers to the service. Information on pricing and other services offered by the vendor is also provided.

Services for business, law, and human resources are described in Chapter 7, among them Dow Jones, Lexis, and Newsnet. Chapter 8 is concerned with services in science, technology, and health, such as Chemical Abstract Service (CAS Online), Biosis, and Medline, and the software interface provided with them. Consumer services include Compuserve, Delphi, The Source, and Bulletin Board Services (BBS) and are described in Chapter 9.

A number of software products have been developed to simplify searching and to provide simultaneous access to several data base services. These "front-end" and "gateway" products are described in Chapter 10. The laser disk, an increasingly important alternative to on-line data bases, is discussed. Included in Chapter 11 are descriptions of compact disk read-only memory (CD-ROM), compact disk-interactive (CD-I), optical read-only memory (OROM), write-once read-many (WORM), and laser cards, and the services and data bases based on these technologies.

Each chapter has footnotes and bibliography. An annotated bibliography, a list of books and journals for end users, a directory of on-line products and services, and an index conclude the book.

AUTHORITY

Martin Kesselman is coordinator of on-line and instructional services at the Library of Science and Medicine at Rutgers University and author of a monthly column on on-line searching for *Wilson*

Library Bulletin. Sarah B. Watstein is head of reference services at Hunter College Library, author of many articles on reference services and artificial intelligence, and an active ALA member.

COMMENT

Secondary school library media specialists who are teaching their students how to perform on-line searching and providing them with access to data bases appropriate to their needs are already leading the way in creating end-user programs and services. Those who are moving in that direction will find invaluable assistance and guidance in this book.

Kister, Kenneth F. *Best Encyclopedias: A Guide to General and Specialized Encyclopedias.* SEE Chapter 8, Selection Guides and Resources.

Parisi, Lynn S., and Virginia L. Jones. *Directory of Online Databases and CD-ROM Resources for High Schools.* SEE Chapter 13, The Library Media Center and the Curriculum.

Sader, Marion, ed. *Reference Books for Young Readers: Authoritative Evaluations of Encyclopedias, Atlases, and Dictionaries.* SEE Chapter 8, Selection Guides and Resources.

Sheehy, Eugene P., ed. *Guide to Reference Books,* **10th ed. ALA, 1986. 1,560 pp. ISBN 0-8389-0390-8.**

PURPOSE

Targeted primarily for the academic and research librarian, this comprehensive guide also is of interest to school librarians and the general reader.

CONTENTS

Divided into five major sections with subdivisions and subsections of each, this work offers brief descriptive annotations of reference works covering the widest conceivable range of subjects. In the preface Sheehy offers a brief history of the publication and explanatory notes concerning the descriptive and subject cataloging employed, as well as other information pertinent to the use of the publication.

The first section, "General Reference Works," includes general and special bibliographies, encyclopedias, dictionaries, genealogy, and sources for librarians in all categories. The second section presents reference materials on the humanities, including such subjects as linguistics and languages, philosophy and religion, literature, fine and applied arts, and sports, recreation, and travel.

Sources included in the third section are in the social sciences, and representative topics include education, anthropology, mythology and folklore, statistics, economics, law, political science, and geography. General works on history, archaeology and ancient history, and a range of reference materials and studies of American and world history as well as area studies make up the fourth section. The final section comprises science and technology, on such topics as medical and health sciences, engineering, mathematics, and the several pure sciences, each further subdivided.

Each entry includes a bibliographic description of the work, an annotation that describes the contents, and other forms in which the work may be available (for example, *World Book Encyclopedia* is available on cassette tapes for visually impaired users). In addition, review sources and comments are cited where appropriate, and evaluative comments are also provided by the annotator in many cases. A Library of Congress classification number and identification number for locating the annotation are given. Introductions to many subsections describe the general content and comment on some of the titles and their reference uses. The cutoff date for inclusion of books in this guide was 1984, but the editor and his associates also made room for some 1985 publications. While no statement of the total number of entries is provided, a very rough estimate would suggest that approximately 13,000 entries are included. Authors, titles, and subjects are indexed in a single alphabetical list.

AUTHORITY
The author is head of the Reference Department of the Columbia University Libraries and editor of the ninth edition of the *Guide to Reference Books*. He has been editor of the "Selected Reference Books" column in *College & Research Libraries* for a number of years.

COMMENT
This indispensable reference book selection tool may be more inclusive than school library media specialists need for elementary and middle schools. Those in secondary schools will want a copy for the reference desk.

Wolf, Carolyn, and Richard Wolf. *Basic Library Skills*, 2nd ed. McFarland, 1986. 141 pp. ISBN 0-89950-228-8.

PURPOSE
Prepared for advanced high school and beginning college students, this guide to finding and using library research tools will serve also as an orientation for teachers without library experience who have

been assigned to a school library and for substitute teachers filling in for an absent school librarian.

CONTENTS

A brief history of libraries prepares the user for the first step in an orientation, an investigative tour of the library, to locate its resources and facilities, and to determine its policies, hours of service, and other regulations. A series of lessons then follows, which begins by introducing the reader to the card catalog, bibliographic tools, classification systems, subject headings, and filing rules. The basic reference sources are then introduced, followed by information about using indexes and abstracts of periodicals and newspapers.

Among the more specific research tools covered are those for literature and criticism, government manuals and documents, biographical references, business and consumer references, and microforms. Computers and their use in libraries are touched on briefly, just enough to provide an overview and to provide some familiarity with terms.

Each of the chapters provides learning objectives, practice exercises, a list of important terms, and lists of related, additional resources. The final chapter deals with writing the paper, emphasizing the importance of primary sources, describing how to take notes and add footnotes, and adding a cautionary note about plagiarism and copyright. The authors have estimated that students can work their way through the guide in 15 to 20 hours. The book concludes with answers to the exercises and an index.

AUTHORITY

Carolyn Wolf and Richard Wolf are head of public services at a college library and an associate professor of educational psychology, respectively.

COMMENT

Clear and inclusive descriptions of library tools combined with thoughtfully planned practice in using them make this a useful guide for the untutored.

Wynar, Bohdan S., ed. *Recommended Reference Books for Small and Medium-Sized Libraries and Media Centers, 1988.* SEE Chapter 8, Selection Guides and Resources.

Wynar, Christine Gehrt. *Guide to Reference Books for School Media Centers,* **3rd ed.** SEE Chapter 8, Selection Guides and Resources.

11
Reading Guidance and Motivation

The literature on this subject offers an abundance of materials, many of them worthy of attention. While an attempt was made to concentrate on recent publications, there are some books of enduring worth that could not be omitted. A supplementary list of briefly annotated sources appears at the end of this chapter. Librarians may want to keep on hand some books that were written primarily for parents and teachers to ensure that inspiration and guidance in reading are offered outside the library as well as within it.

The section on children's literature includes some standard works of literary criticism and the texts that have introduced library science students to the subject over the years. For further study of the subject, see Rita Kohn's annotated resource guide, *Once Upon . . . a Time for Young People and Their Books*.

Young adult literature has not received as much critical attention as children's literature. Two notable sources are *Reaching Adolescents* by Arthea Reed and *Literature for Today's Young Adults* by Alleen Nilsen and Kenneth Donelson, both reviewed in the section on young adult literature. Northrop Frye's *The Educated Imagination* is a discerning introduction to literary criticism with applications to young adult literature. Some of the latest selection guides for young adult reading are also included here, and others may be found in Chapter 8, "Selection Guides and Resources."

Storytelling and booktalking, being separate and distinct arts, are treated in separate sections in this chapter, and the most noteworthy books on these subjects are included.

GENERAL WORKS

Bauer, Caroline Feller. *Celebrations: Read-Aloud Holiday and Theme Book Programs.* **Wilson, 1985. 301 pp. ISBN 0-8242-0708-4.**

PURPOSE

This sourcebook for programs in public libraries and school library media centers suggests some delightful ways of bringing children and good literature together.

CONTENTS

As Bauer notes in her preface, the 16 programs are "pre-packaged and ready to go." What is more they offer inspiration enough to start librarians off on new events of their own devising. Included are programs to celebrate holidays and nonholidays, and such activities and obsessions as fishing, baseball, and "pigmania." Among other comments in the preface, Bauer notes that many of the "celebrations" can be moved around the calendar—for example, the one on baseball can help celebrate opening day or World Series time and the first program, "The Art of Art," can be presented at any time. In addition, she advises the user to concentrate on the reading, then follow with the activities, which are just an adjunct to the literary experience, and to provide enough time for browsing.

Each program begins with some comments, which include advice on how to begin, discussion of what is in the selections, and illustrations in the margin that can be photocopied and distributed as bookmarks. All the chapters follow the same general order: a story or two, some poems, treats and activities, and a reading list. The programs are generally suited to fourth through seventh grade, but can be stretched in either direction, depending on the audience being served. Suggestions for bulletin boards and food treats are also included in many of the programs. Where creative writing activities are suggested, they are for the purpose of encouraging children to write, not for grades but for sharing their thoughts voluntarily.

Typical of the programs is the one on art, which provides two stories, five poems, souvenirs, treats, a bulletin board idea, a list of book illustrators and their birthdays, suggested field trips, and a reading list of about 90 books. This reviewer was particularly taken with the Halloween celebration, on a theme of monsters, which presented an excerpt from Robert Nye's retelling of Beowulf. A particularly delightful illustration of a monster shyly grinning and holding his tail stands in the margin, waiting to become a bookmark. Three poems follow, and among the activities is face painting; some jokes and a funny monster story are also included.

AUTHORITY

Bauer has written from a rich background that includes working with children in school and public libraries, teaching library students in the graduate program at the University of Oregon, and appearing on radio and television on her own weekly storytelling program. She has written several books about literature programs for children.

COMMENT

These excellent read-aloud programs are ready-made for busy school librarians, and will provide their audiences with quantities of literary enrichment, joy, and motivation to read.

Benedict, Emma Lou, and Darla Shaw. *The Reading Consultant/ Library Media Specialist Team: Building the Reading Habit.* **Library Professional, 1987. 200 pp. ISBN 0-208-02102-7.**

PURPOSE

The book describes an interdisciplinary program that deals with skills in reading, gathering information, and writing. Teachers, librarians, and school administrators will find descriptions that encourage the development of a motivation to read and the acquirement of lifelong habits of effective library use.

CONTENTS

This school library media specialist and reading consultant partnership, often joined by classroom teachers, provides a program of reading, library, English, and social studies experiences. Part I describes how each team member provides motivation and instruction in his or her own special area of expertise. Reference and research skills are geared to goals and objectives established by state, district, and school. Exercises are presented for such skills as scanning and skimming, using indexes and reference books, finding the main idea, and outlining. The comprehension skills are taught by the reading consultant. After these isolated skills have been taught, the classroom teacher provides the assignment that will call the skills into use.

Part II discusses the reading program and the interconnection of books that have been selected by theme or setting. The respective roles of each team member are described. Advice for conducting book discussion programs is provided, and book report formats and questionnaires are included. An appendix lists study guides, supplemental materials, and books about reading and literature.

Motivational activities are the subject of Part III. These include booktalks, sustained silent reading, book fairs, computers, and audiovisual production. Parents are involved in the program as well. Activities to involve the community are presented in Part IV, and methods of organizing and planning, as well as program ideas and guidelines, are provided. Also included are storytelling and family folklore, and a conference day for student authors and readers. After-hours programs provide opportunities to the community for increasing reading rates, test preparation, storytelling, and learning about search techniques for using on-line data bases. An index concludes the book.

AUTHORITY
Emma Lou Benedict is a school library media specialist and Darla Shaw is a reading consultant in the Ridgefield, Connecticut, schools.

COMMENT
There is no denying the worth of a team approach to supporting a school's reading program and involving subject teachers and parents in a unified effort to promote reading and the learning of library skills. As described in this book, however, the skills are taught in an isolated fashion rather than in the context of the curriculum, a practice that many school library media specialists have discarded because of its ineffectiveness. This approach has marred an otherwise useful description of an effective partnership effort that reaches beyond the school population and into the community.

Bernstein, Joanne E., and Masha Kabakow Rudman. *Books to Help Children Cope with Separation and Loss: An Annotated Bibliography,* **Vol. 3.** SEE Chapter 8, Selection Guides and Resources.

Bettelheim, Bruno, and Karen Zelan. *On Learning to Read: The Child's Fascination with Meaning.* **Knopf, 1982. 306 pp. ISBN 0-394-51592-7.**

PURPOSE
The authors examine the origins of reading blocks among children with severe reading disabilities and place a good deal of the blame

on primers and other textbooks used to teach children how to read. The intended audience is the general reader, and school library media specialists will find much corroboration of their own inclinations to replace basal readers with children's literature.

CONTENTS

In looking for the causes of children's reluctance to read and the presence of actual reading disabilities, Bettelheim and Zelan have examined the preprimers and primers with which children are introduced to the joys of reading, and found them sadly lacking. Even the most reputable among them, the Bank Street Readers, have serious shortcomings, and most reading textbooks provide a number of different ways to ensure failure: boring text, senseless repetition, attractive illustrations that distract the child from the mindless stories, and frequent allusion to the fact that it would be better to be playing outdoors than enduring the vapid material they are required to attend to. By way of contrast, the authors examine the emotional and intellectual appeal of children's literature, and describe some positive examples of children's responses to books.

The authors and six co-workers observed some 300 children in eight schools over a period of four years. Viewing children's misreading of words from a psychoanalytic perspective, Bettelheim theorizes that the errors originate in a deeper understanding of the material than had been supposed, which was sometimes combined with emotional connotations that were unknown or not understood by the reading teacher. Unconscious needs or anxieties often surfaced in this way, although it was not the authors' purpose to become involved in analyzing them. In many cases children revealed their unconscious rebellion against the material by misreading some of it, thus showing their resentment at being required to read dull, meaningless pseudostories that insult their intelligence. Among other conclusions was the conviction that literacy could be promoted by teachers who refrain from correcting errors, but simply talk reassuringly with the child.

That children need to find meaning in the stories they read is obvious. That a lack of meaning in their reading material will actually hinder their ability to become readers is one of the important points that Bettelheim makes. He spends the last chapter describing at length some primers and preprimers used in Austrian, Swiss, and French schools and showing their superiority to the American variety in a number of respects. While still somewhat removed from literary excellence, their appeal is clearly in accordance with Bettelheim's precepts. Perhaps American textbook publishers will take note.

Bettelheim is a world-renowned psychologist and distinguished professor emeritus at the University of Chicago. Another of his books, *The Uses of Enchantment,* is reviewed in this chapter under "Children's Literature." Karen Zelan is a child, adolescent, and adult psychologist who trained with Bettelheim at the Orthogenic School of the University of Chicago and was senior staff psychologist at Children's Hospital at the Boston Medical Center.

The authors have succeeded in getting to the heart of what is wrong with how American schools teach reading. Fortunately, children are still enchanted with the magic of words, and can find meaning and joy in books that stir their emotions and excite their imaginations. School librarians can take pleasure in continuing to provide them with such literature.

Carroll, Frances Laverne, and Mary Meacham, eds. *Exciting, Funny, Scary, Short, Different and Sad Books That Kids Like about Animals, Science, Sports, Families, Songs, and Other Things.* **ALA, 1984. 192 pp. ISBN 0-8389-0423-8 (pap.).**

The annotated lists in this book are for children's librarians' and elementary school library media specialists' use with children who "want another book just like . . ." or ask for books about topics that especially interest them.

Currently recommended books that can be offered to children in response to their not-too-well-defined requests about something special are arranged in lists that will help librarians respond to their needs. While this book is not a buying guide, most of the titles will be found in *Children's Books in Print* (Bowker). No age or reading level is given, but the emphasis is on books for children in grades 2 through 5.

In the preface, the editors carefully explain how the lists and books were assembled and why they were arranged as they appear. In response to a request to a large number of children's librarians, many of them suggested topics, and working with the approximately 100 subjects that were finally selected, several submitted lists of briefly annotated books. Contributors were asked to list both fiction and nonfiction titles. Among those included some were out of print, and the editors retained those that children still love to read.

The list of topics and annotated books leads off with islands, mummies, and snakes as the first three chapters, and included among the others are family stories, monsters, pets, cars, holidays, how-to books, mysteries and animals, and books in series. Annotations rarely exceed four lines, and the lists usually have five to fifteen titles, with few picture books included. Many of the topics use the questions children ask when making their requests, resulting in chapters ingenuously headed "I like to read about families" or "Where can I find out how to do things?"

AUTHORITY

Carroll is professor of library science at the University of Oklahoma, where she teaches courses on children's literature and international librarianship. Meacham is a free-lance writer and editor and a doctoral candidate at Texas Woman's University. She has previously worked as a children's and young adult librarian.

COMMENT

This gem of a book will serve parents, teachers, and children, who can use it as a guide for their own personal reading, as well as librarians in public library children's rooms and elementary school library media specialists.

Dreyer, Sharon Spredemann, ed. *The Bookfinder, Vol. 2: A Guide to Children's Literature about the Needs and Problems of Youth Aged 2–15.* **American Guidance Service, 1981. Unp. ISBN 0-913476-3.**

PURPOSE

Written for parents, teachers, librarians, and guidance and therapy professionals, this guide helps to locate books that may aid children as they cope with the problems and challenges in their lives.

CONTENTS

Printed and bound in a split-page format, this book annotates 723 children's books in its lower half; the extensive indexing in the upper half makes the annotations readily accessible and permits simultaneous skimming of indexes and annotations. An annotation of about 300 to 400 words provides a synopsis of the book and commentary on its strengths and limitations, its potential use, literary merit, and points of special concern. In addition, the general reading level is indicated and other forms in which the book is available are indicated (film, tape, formats for blind and other physically disabled users).

Bibliographies and reviewing sources for children's books were used in the selection process; the 723 books that were finally selected were gleaned from 2,500 that were reviewed, making for a highly selective process. Criteria for selection are described in the introduction. Fiction books represent 90 percent of the total and biographies the other 10 percent, with a few factual books also included.

Dreyer recommends that teachers and/or school library media specialists read aloud from selected books and conduct small group reading and discussion activities to help children understand disabilities, sibling and other family problems, aging, fear, prejudice, and other concerns and values.

Dreyer comments on bibliotherapy as a way of using literature to help solve problems and develop the ability to cope with those that cannot be solved. Selecting the right book to recommend to a child can help provide comfort after the loss of a loved one, adjustment to a new school situation or neighborhood, traveling, growing up, illness, prejudice, and many other of the trials that beset children and arouse their fears and anxieties. Through identification, catharsis, and insight, children fill their needs for self-concept, gain relief from conflicts, clarify their values, and improve their understanding of other people.

Lists are provided for further professional reading and for aid in book selection. A directory of publishers and producers is also included.

There are three volumes in this series. The first, published in 1977, includes then-current books; the second is the one reviewed here; and the third, covering books published from 1979 to 1982, appeared in 1985.

AUTHORITY
Among those contributing to the book and evaluating the selections were librarians, editors, book reviewers, and school library media specialists.

COMMENT
Dreyer recommends placing a copy of this guide on or near the card catalog or in another accessible place for children to examine by themselves. This concern for children's needs and feelings permeates the book, the selections, and the author's opening comments.

She has created a publication that should be available in all school libraries.

Eble, Mary M., and Jeanne Renton. *New Dimensions in School Library Media Service.* SEE Chapter 13, The Library Media Center and the Curriculum.

Freeman, Judy. *Books Kids Will Sit Still For: A Guide to Using Children's Literature for Librarians, Teachers, and Parents.* **Freline, 1984. 210 pp. ISBN 0-913853-02-X (pap.).**

PURPOSE
Recommended books for reading aloud and suggestions for other book-related activities are featured in this idea book for beginning elementary school library media specialists, teachers, and parents.

CONTENTS
Anyone needing a rationale for reading books aloud to children will find it in the introduction, which also promises ideas for enlivening children's education by using books in curriculum-related ways. Freeman also notes the value of storytelling, booktalking, creative dramatics, and other activities based on children's literature that will motivate reading, help teach writing, advance reading comprehension, and foster children's creativity.

Some practical tips on reading aloud are included, such as keeping the group small enough and close enough so that children are able to see the pictures, holding the book in the right position so that eye contact can be maintained, using good vocal expression and pitch, and making sure you like the book by reading it carefully before reading to children. Her advice to change the author's language if one finds it inappropriate is also found in other books about reading aloud. However, several other writers feel that readers to children who are uncomfortable with any part of a book should either not be reading it to them or should conquer their squeamishness.

A chapter on booktalking announces that anyone can do it, and proceeds to demonstrate how, aptly comparing a booktalk with film coming attractions trailers. Her advice to practice the talk before delivering it, to keep records of talks that are given, and to teach the techniques to children is well taken. Freeman's useful tips on creative dramatics include the use of a tape recorder for preparing sound effects, encouraging children to pantomime, and providing opportunities for children to conduct interviews of others in the role of story characters.

The lists of books for reading aloud provide brief annotations and a suggested grade level, and include fiction, folk and fairy tales, myths, legends, and poetry among the thousand titles. The book concludes with a list of 50 ways to celebrate books, among them discussing, visualizing, writing about them, dramatizing and selling them, and creating a variety of other projects. Author, title, and subject indexes complete the book.

AUTHORITY

The author has served as librarian for ten years at the Van Holten school in Bridgewater, New Jersey, and is an adjunct staff member at Rutgers University's School of Communication, Information and Library Studies.

COMMENT

Library school students, newly appointed librarians, and those more experienced who want to renew their skills will find some new ideas here for bringing children and books together. For more detailed coverage of booktalking alone, see *Booktalk!2* by Joni Bodart in this chapter under "Booktalking."

Frye, Northrop. *The Educated Imagination.* SEE this chapter under Young Adult Literature.

Graves, Ruth, ed. *The RIF Guide to Encouraging Young Readers.* **Doubleday, 1987. 324 pp. ISBN 0-385-23632-8 (pap.).**

PURPOSE

This book is a parents' guide to encouraging children to read. Many of the activities can be adapted for use in classrooms and school libraries.

CONTENTS

Reading Is Fundamental (RIF) is a nonprofit organization that has brought many millions of books into homes across the country, and claims to be the "largest reading motivation program in the United States" (back cover). This guide will continue these motivational activities in print form. The suggested activities and book annotations represent the collective work of scores of volunteers who support RIF.

Graves leads off with some advice on how to use the guide and gives tips for encouraging children to read. Among the suggested activities are reading aloud, including reading on family trips; using the newspaper as a source for reading games; combining reading with crafts; using television and movies to inspire reading; using museum, zoo, library, and other visits to spark reading; and creating reading activities for family and peer groups.

A chapter on writing activities suggests a variety of things to do, such as encouraging young children to dictate stories, which are then typed and gathered together in a book; keeping a family journal; writing games that invite children to add, in turn, a paragraph or sentence to a starter paragraph, the whole to be read aloud after all have had a turn; writing sequels to favorite books; and so on. Many of these have been used in schools but some have an innovative twist.

An annotated suggested reading list of about 200 books ranges in age coverage from infancy to 11, and the annotations are imaginative springboards to reading. Lists of added resources include books and periodicals for parents, book lists, magazines for children, and children's book clubs and other organizations.

AUTHORITY
Ruth Graves is president of Reading Is Fundamental.

COMMENT
While many of the activities will be familiar to teachers and librarians, there is enough novelty here to inspire creative adaptations. Parents who ask, "How can I get my child to read?" can be answered with some of the suggestions in this book. And the baby-sitters' shelf in high school libraries will be enriched by this addition.

Laughlin, Mildred Knight, and Letty S. Watt. *Developing Learning Skills through Children's Literature: An Idea Book for K–5 Classrooms and Libraries.* **Oryx, 1986. 270 pp. ISBN 0-89774-258-3 (pap.).**

PURPOSE
Believing that learning about literature should begin in kindergarten and progress through the elementary grades, with classroom teachers and librarians acting as partners in its presentation, Laughlin and Watt have put together a guide for such a program.

CONTENTS
Following an introduction that explores the need for a structured program in literature at the earliest school level, the authors give

their ideas for what activities might be included. For the youngest children, they believe, the best approach is to group together several books by a particular author. To acquaint children with each of the authors, some biographical material is introduced. Among the authors so treated are Tana Hoban, Mother Goose, Pat Hutchins, Marie Hall Ets, John Burningham, and Rosemary Wells. For each of these units the book offers student objectives, biographical sources, a group introductory activity, and follow-up activities.

As the children advance in maturity, some units are grouped around a theme or genre, and activities become more numerous and more advanced. Such author-artists as Robert McCloskey and Ezra Jack Keats can now be introduced, as well as Maurice Sendak and Roger Duvoisin. By grades 3 and 4 the children are acquainted with Caldecott Medal winners, and the folktales retold and illustrated by Marcia Brown. Poetry is introduced, with the verses of Karla Kuskin, Myra Cohn Livingston, Jack Prelutsky, and Aileen Fisher. By fourth and fifth grades the children encounter the old standards: works of Laura Ingalls Wilder, Scott O'Dell, Elizabeth Speare, William Steig, and Betsy Byars, American folklore as found in the works of Richard Chase, Steven Kellogg, and Adrienne Stoutenberg, and hobbies. Where audiovisual materials are available and appropriate, their use is suggested.

AUTHORITY

Laughlin is a professor in the School of Library and Information Studies at the University of Oklahoma, Norman, and has published several books and articles about children's literature. Watt is an elementary library media specialist at Jefferson Elementary School, Norman, Oklahoma.

COMMENT

The detailed descriptions of activities provide ready-made lesson plans for those inexperienced in teaching literature to children; the experienced librarian, though, in search of innovation or inspiration is unlikely to find them here. Materials on a given theme or author are brought together, a systematic approach that will save much time for the user of this book. While some of the books suggested seem inappropriately below the grade levels for which they are suggested, the learning experiences are suited to the suggested grade levels and offer variety and insight. Altogether the authors have provided a useful handbook for introducing children's literature to their classes, and the idea of delving into books by way of a thorough investigation of one author at a time offers some novelty. Some adults did it in college literature courses. Why not start in kindergarten?

Leonard, Phyllis B. *Choose, Use, Enjoy, Share: Library Media Skills for the Gifted Child.* SEE Chapter 12, Serving Special Learners.

LiBretto, Ellen V. *High/Low Handbook: Books, Materials, and Services for the Problem Reader,* **2nd ed.** SEE Chapter 12, Serving Special Learners.

MacDonald, Margaret Read. *Booksharing: 101 Programs to Use with Preschoolers.* **Library Professional, 1988. 251 pp. ISBN 0-208-02159-0.**

PURPOSE

To bring joy into story time, MacDonald has added a wealth of music, poetry, art, creative dramatics, puppetry, exploration, and other activities to help children's librarians, teachers, and parents enrich the story-sharing experiences of young children.

CONTENTS

True to the title, 101 programs are provided that will energize the story hour and enhance children's enjoyment of books. Although some of the programs are for the youngest of the preschool set, most are suitable or adaptable for kindergartners and first graders. As a matter of fact, none of the programs is labeled as to age.

The program descriptions are arranged in eight sections, each of which is devoted to a particular focus and most of which are further subdivided. The focal points are science, the seasons, holiday celebrations, self-understanding, and imaginative adventures, which make up most of the programs; these are followed by a handful of programs on foreign countries, simple art ideas, and music.

Each session begins with some songs and continues with the reading of two or three books. This is followed by some lively activities and some songs to close with. For the program leader there are a brief list of related books, suggested reading to provide background information, and follow-up activities for home or school.

MacDonald describes how she has used the programs in a brief introduction, and provides some good advice about conducting them, such as to build a program on the books themselves, not with a theme; to use recordings and films where it is appropriate to do so, rather than as a substitute for books or your own involvement; and not to mistake the production of "crafties and freebies" for the real outcome, "the small bit of joy you left inside each child" (p. 12).

The author has offered these programs in her capacity as children's librarian at Bothell Public Library in the Seattle, Washington, area.

COMMENT
Elementary school library media specialists are bound to enjoy presenting these programs for the enrichment of their early childhood classes. In high schools, classes in family living and students who baby-sit will find a gold mine of ideas.

Mahoney, Ellen, and Leah Wilcox. *Ready, Set, Read: Best Books to Prepare Preschoolers.* SEE Chapter 8, Selection Guides and Resources.

Matthews, Dorothy, ed. *High Interest-Easy Reading for Junior and Senior High School Students,* **5th ed.** SEE this chapter under Young Adult Literature.

Paulin, Mary Ann. *Creative Uses of Children's Literature.* **Library Professional, 1986. 730 pp. ISBN 0-208-01861-1.**

PURPOSE
This encyclopedic book of ideas sprang from a conference workshop for school library media specialists, designed to demonstrate how literature and nonprint media can be combined with the performing and visual arts, music, and poetry to stimulate and guide children's reading.

CONTENTS
Each of the six chapters is packed with ideas and resources for sparking children's enthusiasm for books. Chapter 1 presents ways of introducing books—and booktalks and storytelling are only two of many—including book discussion panels, reading aloud, relating books to television programs, introducing holiday and birthday programs, using various media and even basal readers, to name a few. The chapter begins with a list of 36 objectives, and then presents the steps for developing and delivering a booktalk, along with suggested subjects and themes, and the books that may be used to explore them. Other methods of introducing books are also described. A section on storytelling provides methods, objectives, some programs, and numbered references to the bibliography at the back of the book.

Objectives and techniques start off Chapter 2, "Experiencing Art through Picture Books," and the author introduces the various art techniques in book illustrations. Art projects are described and various groupings by subject inspire many of them, including piñatas and kites, art media, color and line, collage, alphabet books, wordless books, individual illustrators and their styles, and many more.

Combining music with books is the subject of Chapter 3, which also suggests ways of coordinating filmstrips, records, and other nonprint media with stories and verse. Objectives, techniques, and an introduction again lead off the chapter, and the uses of song are explored. Folk songs, nursery rhymes, ballads, lullabies, and holiday songs are the sources of many activities described here. Such books as *Mary Poppins, The Wizard of Oz,* and *Chitty Chitty Bang Bang* are forever bound with the musical versions they inspired, but many other books are also associated with songs, and the author establishes the links.

Poetry and verse in picture books, on recordings, and in anthologies inspire a number of creative ideas in Chapter 4, among which are illustrating poems, writing them, and exploring some on particular topics (dogs and cats, food, holidays). Choral reading and writing haiku are included here as well.

Finger plays, flannel boards, pantomime, and puppets are among the mainstays of dramatizing stories included in Chapter 5. The different kinds of puppets, how to make them, and how to use them are discussed. Integrating puppetry in its various forms with play development and craft activities provides many outlets for creative self-expression, and the author offers many suggestions in this area and provides some math and science tie-ins as well.

Chapter 6 brings an abundance of humor into play, providing activities based on folk themes and comparing various versions of riddles, jokes, and noodlehead stories. Codes, pig Latin, rebuses, hieroglyphics, pictograms, and other kinds of language symbols are also explored. Magic and magic numbers in folk literature form the base of numerous other activities.

Bibliographies list 4,045 books and 785 nonprint media, and title and subject indexes lead to information in the text and bibliographies.

AUTHORITY

The author is a media specialist in the Negaunee, Michigan, public schools. She has been active in professional associations and has given conferences and workshops throughout the country.

COMMENT

An enormous amount of creativity and forethought has gone into the preparation of this book, which was created for all those who work with young children. With some changes in the titles used, readers will find applications for older children as well. Librarians looking for a single source on a number of approaches to exploring literature with children will be more than satisfied. Those seeking greater depth will want also to examine sources on individual topics, such as storytelling, music, art, folklore, and puppetry.

Paulin, Mary Ann, and Susan Berlin, comps. *Outstanding Books for the College Bound.* SEE this chapter under Young Adult Literature.

Pilgrim, Geneva Hanna, and Mariana K. McAllister. *Books, Young People, and Reading Guidance*, 2nd ed. Harper & Row, 1968, o.p. 241 pp.

PURPOSE
Written for those who are concerned with guiding the reading of junior and senior high school students, this book has organized information about the development of young people, their interests, problems, and aspirations and the contributions that books can make as they reach toward maturity.

CONTENTS
The reading experience and its influence on intellectual and emotional growth is the subject of the introductory chapter. The need for leading young people, even those who are academically successful, to the delights of literature offers challenges to the adult guide. Reasons why people choose to read or not to read are described, and characteristics of the mature reader are examined. A brief history and description of books for young adults follow, and some genres are introduced in the following chapter.

Cultural and physical factors in the growth of young people are described, and their reading interests explored, in the next two chapters. Chapter 5 discusses books in relation to young people's needs and lists some of these needs. Included are the need for reassurance about their normality and the drive to become independent of adults, to establish satisfactory relationships with their peers, to experience success, and others. Examples of books that help meet these needs are provided; while some are no longer read very much, others are still popular among teens.

The elements of book selection are considered in Chapter 6, which includes discussion of novels, poetry, plays, essays, and some nonfiction. Censorship and aids to book selection are also commented upon. "Escape" reading can have constructive effects—

increased ability to face problems, development of sound values—as well as negative ones—escaping from oneself, a taste for the sensational and cheap, superficial emotionalism. These are further elaborated in Chapter 7.

Chapter 8 stresses the importance of knowing students as individuals and of becoming familiar with their potential reading interests through the use of interest inventories, personal discussion, and teacher-librarian conferences. Knowing the books is, of course, another essential. The challenge of reading guidance and some methods of doing it are discussed in the final chapter, which also touches on instruction in the library and the importance of cooperation between teacher and librarian. Booktalks and displays are two methods for sharing books that are described in this chapter.

Classified reading lists and selection and evaluation aids are provided, but while some are available now in later editions, others are obsolete. Of the books referred to in the text and listed at the end of the book, many have been succeeded by more current titles; a few, though, are still of interest to teens. An index concludes the book.

AUTHORITY

Pilgrim was an associate professor in the College of Education of the University of Texas, Austin. McAllister was a visiting lecturer in the University of Texas Graduate School of Library Science, Austin.

COMMENT

It is always a pleasure to go back to an older book (out of print, but still available in libraries) and find that it is still relevant to its purpose. Written with sensitivity and understanding of the adolescents who are its subject, this book still provides guidance for the adults who would help lead them to maturity.

Pilla, Marianne Laino. *Resources for Middle-Grade Reluctant Readers: A Guide for Librarians.* **Libraries Unlimited, 1987. 122 pp. ISBN 0-87287-547-4.**

PURPOSE

The professional groups addressed here are elementary school teachers of reluctant and/or disabled readers in grades 4 through 6 and elementary school library media specialists.

CONTENTS

On the theory that children who choose not to read or whose reading disabilities prevent them from reading books at their chronological age level, Pilla has assembled a bibliography of books that are easy and fun or exciting to read. The bibliography is preceded by textual material that examines some aspects of learning disabilities and reluctant readers and suggests possible interventions by librarians that may help to motivate reading.

The first chapter considers the nature of learning disabilities and the characteristics of reluctant readers, examining the role of librarians and areas of professional cooperation. Chapter 2 emphasizes the importance of recreational reading and discusses characteristics of books suitable for reluctant or disabled readers. The influence of libraries and librarians on motivating reading, and ways of determining individuals' reading interests, are also included in this chapter. In Chapter 3 reading formulas and the advantages and disadvantages of their use are examined, along with book selection criteria and processing considerations. Successful programs used by teachers and librarians to motivate reading are the subject of Chapter 4; among them are booktalks, storytelling, book discussion groups, creative book reporting, and read-aloud programs. Ways in which schools and public libraries can cooperate in meeting the needs of these children are also discussed.

Chapter 5 explores the use of computers with reluctant readers, describing how to evaluate and build collections of software, listing selection tools and reviewing sources, and noting some future uses. An annotated bibliography of about 120 books is presented in Chapter 6, which also includes magazines, read-alongs, series books, and recommended software.

AUTHORITY

Pilla is a children's librarian at Long Beach Public Library, New York.

COMMENT

The introductory material is helpful for the most part, but lacks clarity in discussing the relative roles of school and public librarians. Of particular value are the suggestions for computer utilization and the accompanying lists of selection aids and review sources. The bibliographic entries provide ordering information and interest and reading levels, and the annotations are readable and clear; however, the number of books included is disappointingly small. For another point of view about meeting the needs of reluctant and disabled readers, see Bruno Bettelheim and Karen Zelan, *On Learning to Read: The Child's Fascination with Meaning,* reviewed in this section.

Polette, Nancy. *Books and Real Life: A Guide for Gifted Students and Teachers*. McFarland, 1984. 117 pp. ISBN 0-89950-119-2 (pap.).

PURPOSE

Books that reflect the losses, problems, and uncertainties of life have been selected for use with gifted children by parents, teachers, and school library media specialists.

CONTENTS

Children derive meaning from fiction when they can identify with the characters in books. Leading gifted children through discussions of the lifelike situations they encounter in the literature they read helps them form values and make decisions that are applicable to their own lives. This is the premise on which Polette builds a series of questions for discussion and other activities, based on the themes of books that are listed and annotated here.

In a brief introduction Polette discusses these assumptions about the uses of literature, and assures the reader that bibliotherapy is not her purpose. This is followed by the book annotations and guides to discussion. The section for the preschool and primary grades includes 83 such discussions; for upper elementary grades 47 books are presented. Among the topics discussed are death, family life, friendship, rejection, divorce, handicaps, and aging. Discussion questions often encourage children to identify with the characters. For example, What do you think it feels like to be. . .? is a question that is repeated frequently. The questions are thought-provoking and probing and help children better understand not only the books but themselves and others as well.

The discussions center on values and ideas rather than literary analysis of plot, character, and setting. Also stereotyping is not only avoided but dealt with in a way that will have positive effects on children's understanding and, it may be hoped, their behavior as well. Many of the questions introduce problem-solving situations, a good approach to use with gifted children. The introductory plot summaries can be used for booktalks, leaving discussion of the books for later—after the children have read them or heard them read aloud.

AUTHORITY

Polette is professor of education and director of the campus laboratory school at the Lindenwood Colleges, Missouri. She has authored many books and other publications.

COMMENT

Using books as a springboard for exploring values and practicing decision making stimulates imagination, empathy, and thought. Many librarians and teachers already use this technique in book discussions. This book offers ready-made material for initiating and broadening a series of probing discussions that are bound to enhance the values of children from grades 1 through 9.

Polkingharn, Anne T., and Catherine Toohey. *More Creative Encounters: Activities to Expand Children's Responses to Literature.* **Libraries Unlimited, 1988. 116 pp. ISBN 0-87287-663-2.**

PURPOSE

The authors have provided ideas for extending children's responses to books for the use of elementary school teachers and library media specialists.

CONTENTS

Library media specialists and teachers who are at a loss for follow-up activities after sharing books with a class may find useful suggestions here, written for use with children in grades K through 4. This collection provides activities that are based on the content of 50 books, most of which are available in school libraries. Each entry provides a brief book summary and describes the purpose of the activity, materials to use, and instructions for presenting the activity. Notes list other books by that author and other books related to the theme or subject.

Activities involve drawing, cutting, pasting, sewing, and the like, and most are suitable primarily for the early childhood grades. Children also make books and quilts, explore maps, dramatize stories, and respond in other ways to the books that have been read. These enjoyable activities, the authors feel, make reading a more pleasurable experience than drill or practice would.

A bibliography of the books discussed and an index conclude the book.

Creative Encounters (Libraries Unlimited, 1983), by the same authors presents activities for grades K through 6.

AUTHORITY

Anne Polkingharn is a librarian and Catherine Toohey is the reading product manager for Scribner Educational Publishers in New York City.

COMMENT

These activities will get new teachers and librarians started toward encouraging children's responses to the books they read. Neither the books chosen nor the activities that extend them are particularly remarkable, however.

Roman, Susan. *Sequences: An Annotated Guide to Children's Fiction in Series.* **ALA, 1985. 134 pp. ISBN 0-8389-0428-9.**

PURPOSE

This selected list of the best fiction in series and sequences written for children and young adults was designed to help librarians in guiding children's reading and as a selection aid.

CONTENTS

Roman defines sequences as books in which plot elements and character develop and change from one book to the next; sequels are those series that have the same characters as earlier books, but no observable relationship to each other except for the identity of the characters. The books here vary in genre, but picture books and easy-to-read books have been omitted.

Both sequences and sequels are included in this listing, which reflects Roman's careful choice of stories in which the growth and development of characters have been achieved. That children favor these books and enjoy following favorite characters through adventures and crises is evident; and the care with which the author has selected the best of these is evident as well.

The selections are arranged alphabetically by author, and the books are numbered to show the order in which they should be read. Each series is introduced with the author's comments on the quality of writing and reasons for selection, and a grade recommendation is a general guide to age suitability. An annotation is supplied for each book, and books related to the series but not a part of it are described in a note. Indexes include one for book titles, one for series titles, and one for main characters. Approximately 80 series and 500 titles are included.

AUTHORITY

Susan Roman is head of youth services at Northbrook Illinois Public Library, has taught courses on children's literature, and has spoken on standards for children's services.

COMMENT

A good many of these series will be familiar to most school library media specialists. The advantage of using this book is the ease with which recommended reading order can be found and the help it provides in locating those books in a series that are needed to complete a group. Thus it is an aid to acquisition and in reading guidance for children and young adult readers as well.

Rudman, Masha Kabakow. *Children's Literature: An Issues Approach,* **2nd ed. Longman, 1984. 476 pp. ISBN 0-582-28398-1.**

PURPOSE

Both a reference and a selection guide, this is an aid for teachers and other caring adults in understanding and selecting books for certain problem areas in children's lives and in society in general.

CONTENTS

Advocating an issues rather than a genre approach to the study and teaching of children's literature, Rudman presents important issues in the lives of children and in society in general. Moving from the personal (the family) to the global (death and war), Rudman explores the issues in terms of children's emotional and intellectual development and then provides lists of books that explore each issue. The issues include family: siblings, divorce, foster care, and adoption; sex; gender roles; cultural heritage: Native American, African-American, Hispanic, Asian, Jewish, and other Americans; special needs: learning and physical disabilities, and special categories (child abuse, substance abuse, appearance and giftedness); old age; death; and war.

Each of these issue sections includes selection criteria, discussions of the topic and related books, suggested activities, adult reference materials and sources, and the annotated bibliographies of recommended books for children and young adults. A final chapter discusses methodology, describing the principles of the reading program, grouping, scheduling, record keeping, and activities. Appendixes include a directory of publishers, a selected list of children's book awards and their winners, and a bibliography of references on children's literature. Author-illustrator, title, and subject indexes complete the book.

AUTHORITY

Rudman teaches children's literature at the University of Massachusetts at Amherst, and has written other books on children's literature.

"Bibliotherapy" is a word much used in this book, a questionable approach according to some authorities. On the whole, however, the suggestions for encouraging reading and teaching comprehension, critical reading, and thinking skills have much to recommend them. Although many of the suggested activities will be familiar to many school librarians, most of the discussion questions are provocative and will produce enlightenment for teachers as well as students. The bibliographies provide excellent resources for collection development as well as for further professional reading.

Stanford, Barbara Dodds, and Karima Amin. *Black Literature for High School Students.* SEE this chapter under Young Adult Literature.

Trelease, Jim. *The Read-Aloud Handbook.* **Penguin, 1985. 243 pp. ISBN 0-14-046727-0 (pap.).**

PURPOSE

The power of stories, read aloud by a caring parent or teacher, to inspire in children a love of books and reading is captured in this book. While written for parents and teachers primarily, it serves to remind librarians as well of the pleasures of sharing books in this way.

CONTENTS

Regaling the reader with apt quotations about stories and books and anecdotes that describe the positive effects of reading books aloud, Trelease makes an enthusiastic and persuasive case. He points to research studies that demonstrate higher reading scores among children who were read to as compared with a control group with no reading aloud. Not only will children be motivated to learn to read and then continue reading, their language skills will advance, their imaginations stimulated, and their emotions released. These are only some of the reasons advanced for reading aloud in the first chapter.

The next chapters consider when to begin reading aloud and discuss the stages of offering books; declaring that it is never too early, Trelease offers six months as a suitable time to start. As for teachers, they are advised to begin on the first day of school.

Dos and don'ts of reading aloud are listed in Chapter 4, and the next two deal with home and school interaction and the home/library connection. Trelease cites the example of a school in Massachusetts where parents are encouraged to celebrate a child's birthday by donating a book to the school library to commemorate the event instead of keeping the child home on that day. He even urges pediatricians to replace the dog-eared and worn children's magazines in their waiting rooms with some new books, and suggests placing advertisements for libraries on cereal boxes.

Television viewing is to be discouraged, in favor of reading aloud, and house rules, firmly enforced, are advised. Other comments on television are to be found in Chapter 7. Sustained silent reading is discussed in the next chapter, and the practice is advocated in home and school.

The rest of the book consists of a "Treasury of Read-Alouds" with instructions for its use. The annotated list consists of anthologies, poetry, novels, and wordless and picture books and is arranged alphabetically by title. Age levels are suggested, and other books by the author of the cited book are listed as well. Footnotes, a bibliography, and an author-illustrator index complete the book.

AUTHORITY

The author, an avowed reader-aloud, started as a journalist for the *Springfield* (Massachusetts) *Daily News*. The first edition of this book, published in 1982, became a best-seller. Trelease lectures frequently to parents and professional audiences. (His lectures are available on film and audiocassette.)

COMMENT

What with computers and curriculum support and other distractions, it is easy to neglect the reading guidance function that school libraries also have. Trelease provides an eloquent reminder. And school library media specialists who don't need reminding might keep a copy or two available for the teachers and parents for whom the book was written.

Tway, Eileen, ed. *Reading Ladders for Human Relations*, 6th ed. SEE Chapter 8, Selection Guides and Resources.

CHILDREN'S LITERATURE

Bettelheim, Bruno. *The Uses of Enchantment: The Meaning and Importance of Fairy Tales.* **Knopf, 1976; pap. Vintage, 1977. 328 pp. ISBN 0-394-49771-6.**

PURPOSE

Bettelheim explores the place of fantasy, as it exists in folktales, in a child's world. His book aims to demonstrate the developmental role of folktales in children's lives by showing how they first attract children by their art and then lead them to inner growth by their imaginative appeal. Because their imaginations are engaged, children can experience vicariously the growth processes that the characters and events in these stories symbolize. In this way, fairy tales make "great and positive psychological contributions to the child's inner growth" (Introduction, p. 12).

CONTENTS

What explains the enormous appeal to children of the folk/fairy tales that are our cultural heritage? What inner needs do they satisfy? What is their value in the difficult process of maturation? Bringing his background in psychoanalysis and Freudian theory to an examination of that supreme art form, the fairy tale, Bettelheim seeks answers to these questions.

Describing children's emotional needs, their fears, and conflicts, he demonstrates how children use fairy tales to conquer their anxieties and resolve the internal conflicts that beset them. Because of the psychological truth of these stories, children can respond to them at many levels of their development, taking from them the consolation that they may need. How this is so is analyzed by Bettelheim, using some of the best known tales of folk literature, each taken up in turn and subjected to a scrutiny that is dominated by Freudian interpretation. The result is a reaffirmation of the power of these tales and a deeper understanding of their fascination.

Bettelheim insists that only the folk/fairy tale has this ability to heal, perhaps because he lacks familiarity with some of the other great literature for children. In asserting that authored stories may delight and entertain children but will not help to release them from conflict and anxiety as fairy tales do, he may be overlooking the fact that the fairy tale's power derives from the ability of all great imaginative literature to transform human experience and reach into the soul of the reader. But this objection should not diminish Bettelheim's accomplishment in raising the fairy tale to the level at which it belongs as a vital expression of human imagination and psychological truth, not to be denied children as they set out to accomplish the developmental tasks that life has set for them.

AUTHORITY

A world-renowned child psychologist, known particularly for his work with autistic children and for his writings, Bettelheim is distinguished professor of education and professor of psychology and psychiatry at the University of Chicago.

COMMENT

This landmark book helped stem the opposition to encouraging children to read fairy tales because of the violence that some of them portray. While some may quarrel with the author's reliance on Freudian theory, he argues convincingly for the importance of the folk/fairy tale in the imaginative lives of children and in the cultural heritage of all people.

Carpenter, Humphrey, and Mari Pritchard. *The Oxford Companion to Children's Literature.* **Oxford Univ. Press, 1984. 587 pp. ISBN 0-19-211582-0.**

PURPOSE

This encyclopedialike compendium of information about children's literature was prepared for students of the subject.

CONTENTS

Fairly brief articles cover a variety of subjects pertaining to children's books in English. Authors, titles, characters, folklore, childhood lore, and related information are the topics covered in the articles. A gracefully written introduction explains how the book came to be written, and a generally lively style characterizes the writing as a whole.

Such article headings as cowboys, cotton-tail, Wyatt Earp, games-rhymes, and Homeric legends indicate the range of subject matter. Many articles deal with authors and illustrators and some of the aspects of book production, while others are headed by book titles. Book characters, cartoons, magazines, and comics are other types of subject matter.

Although American literature is far from neglected, there is a strong emphasis on things British, a bias that is clearly indicated by the relative length of the articles on King Arthur (three and one-half pages) and the Homeric legends (about 100 words). Selected book illustrations accompany some articles, along with an occasional relevant photograph. A generous array of cross-references aids the reader in locating information.

AUTHORITY

The articles were written by the collaborators and were checked by "advisers."

COMMENT

This reference work supplies some pleasant browsing along with authoritative information on many aspects of children's literature.

Chambers, Dewey W. *Children's Literature in the Curriculum.* SEE Chapter 13, The Library Media Center and the Curriculum.

Cullinan, Bernice E., et al. *Literature and the Child.* Harcourt Brace Jovanovich, 1981. 594 pp. ISBN 0-15-551110-6.

PURPOSE

The approach used by the authors is based on the principles of child development proposed by Jean Piaget, as well as other research on language learning and reader response theory. Written for teachers, librarians, and parents, this work discusses outstanding books for children and suggests ways of introducing them and eliciting creative response.

CONTENTS

The book is divided into three main sections. The first dwells on the child, who is viewed as a being that gains knowledge as an outcome of interaction with his or her environment. Children's literature participates in the influence of the environment when it is included in it, affecting the development of language and socialization as well as of cognition. Using examples from children's literature, Cullinan and co-authors Mary Karrer and Arlene Pillar demonstrate how a sense of story develops from simple repetition of events to the ability to identify and discuss themes. Encouraging a variety of responses to literature, what the authors call "creative interaction" (p. 21), allows time for reflection and includes activities related to the book, which may include art, drama, and discussion, oral or written.

The many dimensions of literary exploration are described, and include concept development, relating books to children's lives, investigating themes, and considering books as reflectors of life. The various types of children's literature are listed here, and in Section 2 each becomes the subject of a separate chapter. The second chapter in Section 1 presents a comprehensive historical view of children's books. The third describes the authors' concept of how literature expands children's language and presents criteria for selecting books that extend language development.

In Section 2 the focus is the books, and they are discussed by type. In their discussion of picture books, the authors consider picture book art, and how these books reflect on and touch the child's inner world and self-concept, the social world of family and friends, the natural world that surrounds the child, and the aesthetic world. Criteria for selection are presented here and in each of the following chapters.

The next few chapters offer discussions of the various genres of children's literature, always relating them to the lives, minds, and emotions of the readers. They include folklore, fantasy and science fiction, poetry and verse, contemporary realism, historical fiction, and biography. Informational books are discussed in terms of how they can be integrated in the curriculum, and units are presented as examples: My Body and How It Works, for primary grades, Using the World's Resources in a More Resourceful Way, for middle grades, and Endangered Species, for advanced grades. Many books are cited within the chapters, and notes and a professional reference list are also provided.

The four chapters in the third section deal with the children and the books in combination. Their subjects are literature and children with special needs, ways of presenting books in the classroom, such as reading aloud, storytelling, booktalks, and audiovisual materials, and activities such as drama and art. A literature curriculum providing aesthetic experiences, exploration of book structure, language expansion, and values that demonstrates an integrated approach is proposed, and basic books for a literature program are listed. The final chapter deals with issues in the world of books, such as racism, sexism, censorship, abridgments, and the influence of television.

Appendixes list book awards, selection aids, books about authors and illustrators, publishers, holiday books, birthdays of authors and illustrators, and National Children's Book Week. Subject and author/title indexes complete the work.

AUTHORITY
Bernice E. Cullinan is a professor of children's literature at New York University; Mary K. Karrer and Arlene M. Pillar are associated with the Worthington, Ohio, public schools and the C. W. Post Center of Long Island University, respectively.

With this book, Cullinan and her collaborators helped to lay the groundwork for the whole language approach to teaching reading and communication arts. It was written for classroom teachers rather than school library media specialists, and the consequent emphasis is on using books in the curriculum rather than presenting them to children simply as objects of enjoyment. Having made this distinction, I am not sure how much it matters. If it encourages teachers to turn away from basal readers, skills workbooks, and limited vocabulary versions of classics and toward books that will have meaning in children's lives, it will have accomplished an important purpose. It certainly will help teachers, and librarians as well, make that vital connection between literature and children.

Egoff, Sheila, ed. *Only Connect: Readings on Children's Literature*, 2nd ed. Oxford Univ. Press, 1980. 457 pp. ISBN 0-19-540309-6 (pap.).

This diverse collection of the thoughts of leading American and British writers and critics of children's literature is intended for use by librarians, parents, teachers, students, and others with an interest in the subject.

The book is organized around five themes, Books and Children; Fairy Tales, Fantasy, Animals; Some Writers and Their Books; Illustration; and The Modern Scene. Among the distinguished authors and illustrators are Roger Lancelyn Green, John Rowe Townsend, Jason Epstein, J. R. R. Tolkien, Donnarae Mac Cann, Lillian H. Smith, P. L. Travers, C. S. Lewis, Elizabeth Janeway, Graham Green, T. S. Eliot, Clifton Fadiman, Edward Ardizzone, and Sylvia Engdahl. Others with less readily recognized names are represented as well.

One may expect a high level of thought and discussion from these writers, and the expectation is not disappointed. In his thoughtful essay, John Rowe Townsend questions those who find racism and sexism in some children's books, who suggest that *Cinderella* ought to be rewritten to eliminate its sexist attitudes, that Pippi Longstocking is not a girl at all but really a boy in disguise, and that *Sounder* is racist because it depicts a black family as submissive, at a time when such behavior was necessary for survival. He notes that authors and publishers have an obligation to maintain their artistic

211

freedom in the face of ill-conceived efforts to curb their freedom of expression.

In "Good Bunnies Always Obey" Jason Epstein observes how children's literary choices often reflect their desire to escape organized society. Their preference for books like *Gulliver's Travels, Robinson Crusoe, Alice in Wonderland, Huckleberry Finn,* and *Catcher in the Rye* is an indication of this propensity and represents a further refusal to buy the world that parents and teachers and other experts are trying to sell them. In "Only Connect," the title of P. L. Travers's essay, presented at a colloquium sponsored by the Library of Congress, Travers describes the connecting links that led to the creation of Mary Poppins. T. S. Eliot presents an absorbing critical study of Huckleberry Finn.

Other topics discussed include the children's book trade, the pleasure and problems of children's book illustration, problem novels, young people in the space age, fables and fancy, Babar and Narnia, historical novels, didacticism, juvenile series books, and others.

AUTHORITY

Sheila Egoff is a professor in the School of Librarianship at the University of British Columbia. She coordinated the First Pacific Rim Conference on Children's Literature in Vancouver in 1976, and edited its papers, entitled *One Ocean Touching.*

COMMENT

The pleasure of spending some time in the company of such authors, illustrators, and critics is well worth the price of admission. Their ideas are stimulating, and will offer fresh insights into the ever-fascinating study of children's literature.

England, Claire, and Adele M. Fasick. *Child View: Evaluating and Reviewing Materials for Children.* **Libraries Unlimited, 1987. 207 pp. ISBN 0-87287-519-9.**

PURPOSE

For reviewers of children's books, whether for preparatory or in-service courses or on the job, there are many aspects and issues to consider that are inherent in the task. This book presents general principles and the authors' views on these matters to help sharpen librarians' and teachers' evaluation skills. It also discusses the writing of reviews.

The art of evaluation and reviewing encompasses a number of issues and abilities, and these are discussed in the first section. First among these is the capacity to perceive a book not only from an adult point of view, but from the child's as well, understanding what the child's eyes see, what the child's mind and imagination will absorb, and what response a book may evoke.

Second, the reviewer must consider what role in children's lives is played by print and nonprint materials. What an adult may expect of materials for children, to what extent adult standards and tastes should be imposed on children, and how adult values and concerns often conflict with the child's actual perspective are also important considerations. Do children really exhibit behaviors they read about? Certainly reading encourages reflection through vicarious participation in events and the sharing of characters' thoughts and emotions. Will children exercise judgment or blindly imitate what book or media characters do? These and related questions concerning children's freedom to read, as well as the issue of popularity versus merit, are also considered.

Third, the reviewer requires an understanding of children's development from a theoretical point of view. The authors discuss Piaget's theories of cognitive development, and also consider language development and growth in values and discrimination. Finally, reviewers need to be aware of the importance of reviewing and evaluating in collection development and be familiar with the major reviewing journals. These are also considered in the book, along with aspects of the reviewer's craft.

The second section considers the books and nonprint media themselves, in all their variety. Special characteristics of different types and formats are discussed in separate chapters. These include early childhood materials, traditional materials (folklore and fairy tales), fiction, poetry, biography, information materials, dictionaries and encyclopedias, and nonprint materials. Appended information on finding reviews includes bibliographies and indexes to reviews and reviewing journals. An index completes the book.

England and Fasick are on the Faculty of Library and Information Science, University of Toronto.

Competent evaluation of books and other communications media is an essential ingredient in the training and performance of school library media specialists. The ability to write reviews is another step on the road to professional fulfillment. *Child View* is a fine traveling companion with much to say about some essentials of collection development as well.

Field, Carolyn W., and Jacqueline Shachter Weiss. *Values in Selected Children's Books of Fiction and Fantasy.* **Library Professional, 1987. 298 pp. ISBN 0-208-02100-0.**

PURPOSE

That the books they read can play an important role in helping children develop positive values is the underlying premise of this guide to the literature for librarians, teachers, and parents.

CONTENTS

Books for early (grades pre-K to 2), middle (grades 3 and 4), and later (grades 5 to 8) years are commented on in ten chapters, each devoted to a single value. The values (and chapter titles) are co-operation, courage, friendship and love of animals, friendship and love of people, humaneness, ingenuity, loyalty, maturing, responsibility, and self-respect. While recent titles have been emphasized in the selection, the books included were published between 1930 and 1984. Over 700 annotations are provided.

Each chapter begins with a brief introduction, and annotations are written discursively rather than separately for each book, and often include brief quotations from the book that is being discussed. Bibliographic information is provided in the alphabetical listing at the end of the chapter in which the book is discussed, and other values that play a part in the book's theme are also mentioned, where appropriate. Title and author indexes are provided.

AUTHORITY

Carolyn W. Field, retired from her position as director of Work with Children at the Free Library of Philadelphia, is president of the United States Board on Books for Young People. Jacqueline Shachter Weiss is a senior associate professor at Temple University, and has written other materials about children's books.

COMMENT

Although selection criteria are not specified in this collection, the books that have been included do have literary merit and are not merely didactic. While bibliotherapy is one of the suggested uses of the books annotated in this guide, there are other purposes that they will serve as well. The grouping of the recommended books simplifies selection by thematic material, so that suitable subjects for booktalks and discussions may be readily identified. The variety of cultural, national, and ethnic backgrounds represented in the selections ensures appeal on another level.

Hazard, Paul. *Books, Children and Men*. Trans. by Marguerite Mitchell. Horn Book, 1972. 176 pp. ISBN 0-87675-059-5 (pap.).

PURPOSE

An eminent literary scholar, Hazard wrote this loving survey of literature for children. It was translated and published as a memorial to him after his death during World War II and it remains a beacon to those who work with children and their books.

CONTENTS

With admiration and affection, Hazard is introduced to his readers by his publisher, his translator, and his former colleague. A man of spirit and principle, Hazard left the safety of New England during World War II to return to his work as professor at the College de France in Paris. The translation of his work into English marks a critical path to understanding what makes for the best in children's books.

Hazard takes his readers with him as he travels from country to country in Europe, capturing its essence and describing what in its literature has captivated the young. In the Latin countries, he notes, children are considered "future men," but in the Nordic lands a "truer truth" is understood, that adults are but children who have grown up (p. 110). The French fondness for observing the proprieties is illustrated by Cinderella's godmother, whose ideas follow a correct sequence, thus pleasing that nation whose people "are less fond of being dazzled than of seeing clearly" (p. 123). About Pinocchio, he comments that doing what is forbidden has a greater attraction than doing what he is bidden to do. As a result, "repentance follows close on sinning, but sinning follows close on repentance" (p. 112).

Hazard has more to offer, however, than grace of expression, and that is a critical depth that seeks out and exposes the meretricious as it discerns and salutes the meritorious. From Perrault to Barrie to Perseus, Hazard describes those touchstones of literature that children have made their own and the nature of their appeal, and relegates to the rubbish heap the didactic products of lesser imaginations.

AUTHORITY

Literary scholar, member of the French Academy, faculty member of the Sorbonne, possessor of two American doctorates (Harvard and Columbia universities), Paul Hazard shared with children a love of inner truth and a delight in the magic of language and the "dignity of play."

One may understand the joys of children's literature without having read this book. One can develop criteria for selecting the best without having read this book. But those who do not read it will have missed the grace and intellect of this man who not only loved literature but also the people who produced it and the children who continue to enjoy it.

Kohn, Rita. *Once Upon . . . a Time for Young People and Their Books: An Annotated Resource Guide.* **Scarecrow, 1986. 211 pp. ISBN 0-8108-1922-8.**

PURPOSE

This listing of available resources for the study or selection of children's literature provides access to books and journal articles about that topic.

CONTENTS

Well over 800 entries covering a variety of subjects in the field of children's literature are presented alphabetically by author or title main entry where there is no author. The entries are numbered to facilitate their location by way of the title or subject index.

In her preface Kohn states that the list is neither comprehensive nor critical, being simply a guide to what is available if still in print or can be found in a library if out of print. Subjects range from academic library, basic collection to young adult literature, and book types include selection guides, textbooks, and critical works. Nonprint resources are included also, according to the author, but are not accorded a separate entry in the subject list, making it difficult to locate any by that approach. A search did turn up an audiocassette by Morton Schindel, *Voices from the Wilderness: The Art of Recording Children's Stories* (Weston Woods, 1979).

Entries include a brief annotation and provide ISBNs as well as the usual bibliographic information. Appendix A offers a supplementary list of such resources as agencies and organizations that provide lists, reviews, and other publications on literature for young people. Appendix B is a list of review sources, and Appendix C provides names and addresses of publishers.

The author has been an instructor in children's literature at Illinois State University and Butler University, Indiana.

Students in graduate courses on children's literature or librarians seeking further expertise or selection tools will find this book a helpful, though far from exhaustive, guide.

Leonard, Phyllis B. *Choose, Use, Enjoy, Share: Library Media Skills for the Gifted Child.* SEE Chapter 12, Serving Special Learners.

Meigs, Cornelia, ed. *A Critical History of Children's Literature,* **rev. ed. Macmillan, 1969, o.p. 700 pp.**

This critical survey of English and American literature for children is a reference work for librarians, teachers, and parents, providing an overview of the rich body of works written expressly for children and those for adults that children have appropriated for themselves.

Beginning with the ancient world and the folk origins of stories, this book's four authors carry the reader to the mid-1960s. Part One, written by Cornelia Meigs, describes the earliest folklore, and the beginning of drama in the mystery and morality plays of the Middle Ages, as well as the tales of that era. A new age was ushered in by the printing press, and the influence of Caxton and the books he printed, among them *Aesop's Fables* and Malory's *Morte D'Arthur,* are described. Meigs carries the reader through the eighteenth century in England and into the beginnings of children's literature in America, stopping at the early nineteenth century.

The next 50 years saw the first flowerings of a body of work written especially for children (Part Two), and includes the revitalization of folktales by Jacob and Wilhelm Grimm, Hans Christian Andersen, and others and the beginnings of adventure and realistic fiction. Illustrators now appeared who combined visual images with words, for example, Walter Crane, Randolph Caldecott, and Kate Greenaway. Anne Thaxter Eaton, who wrote this section, also covers children's magazines and poetry for children.

A new era for children's literature (Part Three), from 1890 to

1920, was ushered in by the author/illustrator Howard Pyle and continued to bring forth new riches for the young with the works of Robert Louis Stevenson, Rudyard Kipling, Beatrix Potter, and Kenneth Grahame.

Under the authorship of Elizabeth Nesbitt, this portion of the book brings the reader to the early historians and biographers for children, the poets who wrote of childhood, the early picture books, the blossoming of public library children's rooms and their influence, and the recognition that children's literature was important enough to merit serious literary criticism. On that subject Nesbitt writes eloquently, seeking a return to the fundamentals of literary criticism that recognize that literature of a distinctive type should be treated according to its own content and style, that didactic books rarely persuade the heart and reach the emotions, that literature respects reality and interprets human life, and that children who seek to escape from problems through literature are pursuing "the rightful heritage of children" (p. 308).

Part Four, written by Ruth Hill Viguers, brings us into the fruitful years, when the production of children's books became a lucrative industry, spurred on by the governmental largess provided by the National Defense Education Act (NDEA) and the Elementary and Secondary Education Act (ESEA), which poured millions of dollars into newly recognized school libraries. The proliferation of new books for children allows Viguers only to skip from one highlight to another in her introductory survey. In subsequent chapters of this section she discusses fiction belonging to various genres and outstanding nonfiction in science, history, biography, and poetry.

As family-owned publishing companies were swallowed up by megacorporations, the concern for profits began to overtake the search for quality, a trend that has continued into the present. The hope is that from this outpouring of books, some of quality will prove as durable as have those of the more distant past.

Bibliographies are included at the end of each chapter, and an index is provided.

AUTHORITY

The authors, under the overall editorship of Meigs, have had distinguished careers, variously as writers of and about children's books, children's librarians in school and public libraries, and teachers of children's literature in graduate library schools.

COMMENT

This critical literary history has put the venerable lineage of children's literature, culminating in the current superabundance, into some perspective. The selection process becomes all the more important as librarians face the mountains of books that issue forth each year. Knowing what children have taken for themselves in the past, and why, will help in guiding them by the choices made in the present. A book of this scope is bound to displease in some small way. Perhaps a future edition will recognize that boys are not the only people who love the likes of *Treasure Island, Kidnapped,* and *Robinson Crusoe.*

Rudman, Masha Kabakow. *Children's Literature: An Issues Approach,* **2nd ed.** SEE this chapter under General Works.

Sayers, Frances Clarke. *Summoned by Books: Essays and Speeches.* **Comp. by Marjeanne Jensen Blinn. Viking, 1965, o.p. 173 pp.**

PURPOSE
Compiled by Marjeanne Jensen Blinn, this collection of essays and speeches provides the opportunity for future readers to meet Sayers by reading her thoughts as expressed in the pages of this book. It is an encounter to be treasured by all who share her passion for books and her understanding and love of children.

CONTENTS
Selections include Sayers's thoughts on being a librarian, on such notables of the profession as Anne Eaton and Anne Carroll Moore, on storytelling, and the art of writing for children. Among the writers for children she discusses are Eleanor Estes, Eleanor Farjeon, and Ella Young. The book concludes with essays that describe the appeal to children of those books that have endured.

Because a soupçon of Sayers is more eloquent than any summary of her thoughts can be, this review of that excellent children's librarian and storyteller will leave the pleasures of encountering her to the reader and simply summarize a bit.

In a speech entitled "The Belligerent Profession," Sayers admonishes librarians to avoid the predisposition of those sociologists and psychologists who would examine literature from their social science perspective and to embrace it with their sensibilities and intuition. She reminds them of the worth of their profession, which is to know books and to remind readers of their enduring value. In "Writing for Children: A Responsibility and an Art," Sayers urges writers of children's books to ignore the scientific studies of children's and adolescents' reading interests and to write from their inner experiences of childhood. Forget the taboos, don't write to order, but remember that children live by what you feed them, and they should have the best you can offer. "Feel as deeply as you can," she says, "and then try to convey that feeling to your reader" (p. 114).

In another selection, about children's literary classics, she describes a child's delight in some of the books she has read as she shares her enthusiasm for them with another child, unconscious that she has been praising some "classics." Sayers reminds her readers what classics are, and why children delight in reading them.

AUTHORITY

Frances Clarke Sayers has been a children's librarian and member of the faculty of the School of Library Services, University of California, Los Angeles. Her professional writings have appeared in many professional journals, notably *Horn Book.*

COMMENT

In this time of information output and input, as the school library moves from media center to information center, and librarians concentrate on such esoterica as teaching about search strategies and on-line data bases, it is easy to forget what brought so many to school librarianship in the first place: the love of books and the desire to share them with children. Sayers reminds all librarians of this and refreshes one's sense of the value of this endeavor.

Smith, Lillian H. *The Unreluctant Years: A Critical Approach to Children's Literature.* **ALA, 1953, o.p. 193 pp.**

PURPOSE

Forgoing the lists of recommended books that provide the substance of many critical studies of children's literature, Smith has limited herself to a precious few. She uses these to distill those qualities that distinguish children's literature from ordinary writing for children, so that they may be used wisely in book selection.

CONTENTS

Literary critics have endeavored, since Plato's time, to determine what constitutes literary merit. The literary criticism of children's books, however, is a more recent phenomenon. Asserting that children's books and stories have a literary importance of their own that sets them in the firmament of universal literature, Smith proceeds to explore those books that exemplify the beauty and truth that move children by their power.

A brief historical chapter precedes the exploration of what principles may be established to explain the universal appeal of those masterpieces of children's literature that have endured. These principles are applied in succeeding chapters to fairy tales, Greek and Norse mythology, and the epics, sagas, and hero stories of the Mediterranean and Germanic peoples. The author compares different versions of these tales, demonstrating why one is superior to another.

Poetry, picture books, stories, fantasy, and historical fiction are analyzed for those creative qualities, inner truthfulness and beauty and universality of theme and expression, that establish their claims to immortality. Quotations, summaries, and explication provide those touchstones by which other writings may be judged. A final chapter on "books of knowledge" concludes this critical journey through children's literature.

The author deals briefly with the importance of selecting only the best, and urges those who choose the books always to ask themselves whether a book is truly good enough for children. When children are moved to laugh or cry by a book, they demonstrate a response far deeper than one that can be prompted by the formula stories that some allow to pass for literature. Children respond to what is "fundamentally true and good" with honest emotion, and librarians should be guided in their selections by this principle. Book selection and use should be based on a sound literary philosophy founded on carefully nurtured values, standards, and perceptions. A library with such a collection "sustains and fosters the spirit of literature" (p. 190).

AUTHORITY

Smith was head of the Boys and Girls Division of the Toronto Public Library. She is a recipient of the Clarence Day Award for outstanding work in encouraging a love for and reading of books.

COMMENT

Slim in size but large in persuasiveness, this book is an invaluable reminder of the need to exercise critical integrity in selecting books for children. The means for doing so having been placed in librarians' hands by this gifted critic, there is no excuse for failing to use it.

Sutherland, Zena, and May Hill Arbuthnot. *Children and Books*, 7th ed. Scott, Foresman, 1986. 751 pp. ISBN 0-673-18069-7.

PURPOSE

Covering the developmental stages and reading interests of children from the early years to beginning adolescence, *Children and Books* was written to serve as a textbook in the preservice training of teachers, librarians, and others whose lives and work touch children.

CONTENTS

There are not many school library media specialists who have not encountered and been guided and enriched by some earlier version of *Children and Books,* and no bibliography of this kind can fail to include it. In the 1957 revised edition, Arbuthnot admonished librarians to "know your child and know his books, because for every child there is the right book at the right time." Building on that time-honored concept, this latest edition provides summaries of leading child development theories in the context of the best in children's literature and what it has to offer to the growing child.

Included in the text are an overview of children's literature, a history and chart of milestones in its development, an exploration of various types of literature, and discussions of criteria for evaluating both the written word and illustrations. This is followed by discussions of techniques and methods of bringing children and books together and fostering children's response to and understanding of what they read. Some of the issues that have emerged in relation to children's literature today are explored.

An additional feature is "Viewpoints," relevant comments by other authorities that reflect on the chapters' contents. Extensive bibliographies of "Adult References and Book Selection Aids" are appended to each chapter, and listed, with annotations and full bibliographic information, in appendixes at the end of the book.

AUTHORITY

Zena Sutherland is a well-known expert in children's literature. She has used her own background and knowledge and that of authorities in the areas covered by the book to build on the strong foundation laid by the late May Hill Arbuthnot, who was a renowned critic and writer on children's literature.

COMMENT

Children and Books provides an overview of the vast field of children's literature and an ordering of its many parts and fosters an understanding of how children's developmental needs can be met by the best of the books for children that have been published. The well-informed chattiness of earlier editions, under Arbuthnot's authorship, have given way to the more objective and intellectual approach of Sutherland, and many of the selections that Arbuthnot used to illustrate her comments are gone. In their place are more extensive bibliographies and discussions of more recently published books and their authors. This is still the best way to get to know the basics of children's literature.

Townsend, John Rowe. *Written for Children: An Outline of English-Language Children's Literature.* **Lippincott, 1975. 368 pp. ISBN 0-397-32298-4.**

PURPOSE

Covering roughly the same territory as Cornelia Meigs's *A Critical History of Children's Literature* (reviewed in this section), this book describes the history, variety, and uses of children's literature through the ages.

CONTENTS

A quick summary of the early history of children's literature brings the reader into the nineteenth century. The meat of the book is its coverage of the last two centuries, which has been divided into manageable chunks: 1840–1915, 1915–1945, and 1945 to the early 1970s. Unconcerned with the vast store of folk and fairy tales, Townsend writes about the genres peculiar to the times and places in which they appeared, from adventure to didactic books, fantasy, realism, picture books, and verse.

Townsend approaches children's literature with a personal view and a sharp and discriminating critical eye. While books are grouped into types for convenience, he disdains classification by genre and avoids the use of age labels. Also avoided are those books that are merely popular but also unimportant and have fallen short of literary significance.

Not surprisingly for an English critic, Townsend devotes considerable attention to modern English and Australian books not too familiar to American readers, although few American writers of quality are overlooked. And in a brief quarrel with Meigs he scorns the revered Howard Pyle and commends instead the oft-neglected and frequently rejected Frank Baum and his Oz books.

In a brief afterword, Townsend considers the future of children's books, noting the intrusion of the audiovisual world, the spread of paperback publishing, and the internationalization of children's literature, particularly the picture book. He concludes with the optimistic picture of a child "lying on the hearthrug or whatever may by then have replaced the hearthrug, light years away from his surroundings, lost in the pages of a book" (p. 334). May his optimism be fulfilled.

Notes, an index, and a comprehensive bibliography with a decidedly British cast conclude the book.

AUTHORITY
Townsend is an acclaimed writer for young people.

COMMENT
Like his American counterparts, Townsend bestows credibility and importance on children's literature by treating it with the same seriousness of purpose devoted to adult literature. He expresses his views with vigor and clarity of style. Less comprehensive than the Meigs work, lacking as it does any treatment of folk literature and nonfiction, *Written for Children* nevertheless provides an important critical view of imaginative writing for children.

Trelease, Jim. *The Read-Aloud Handbook.* SEE this chapter under General Works.

YOUNG ADULT LITERATURE

Abrahamson, Richard F., and Betty Carter, eds. *Books for You: A Booklist for Senior High Students*, 10th ed. NCTE, 1988. 507 pp. ISBN 0-8141-0364-2 (pap.).

PURPOSE
This reading list for teens was compiled from the contributions of members of the Committee on the Senior High School Booklist of NCTE for the use of senior high school students. It can be used by high school librarians as a tool for both reading guidance and selection.

CONTENTS
The committee members examined 4,000 books of varied subject matter and genre over a three-year period and selected approximately 1,200 for listing in this book. In the introduction, addressed to the student, the editors explain how to use the indexes to find books by a favorite author or a title that a friend may have mentioned. They also explain the arrangement, which is in sections that

represent young people's reading interests, and suggest how to locate material of interest by moving from one section to related ones.

The books are arranged alphabetically by author, and the entries indicate if the book is illustrated, along with original publication date and book type (fiction, biography, and so on). The annotations, averaging about 100 words, are descriptive teasers that pique the readers' curiosity; they can also serve librarians and teachers as booktalk material.

Books for You has 47 chapters, alphabetically arranged, and each headed by a subject interest of teenagers, among them "Dating and Sexual Awareness," "Airplanes and Automobiles," "Computer Technology," "Drugs and Alcohol," "Personal Grooming and Self-Improvement," "War," "Your Health and Your Body," and the like. A directory of publishers and separate author and title indexes complete the book.

AUTHORITY

Abrahamson and Carter are co-chairs of the Committee on the Senior High School Booklist of NCTE. The reviewing committee is composed of dedicated and accomplished teachers, librarians, administrators, and university professors.

COMMENT

The list is inclusive and up to date, consisting of books published between 1985 and 1987, and some new editions of earlier works are also included. The subject matter is wide ranging, and the annotations are excellent sales pitches. Its continuing popularity indicates the book's appeal to teenagers and its usefulness to high school library media specialists.

Campbell, Joseph, with Bill Moyers. *The Power of Myth.* **Doubleday, 1988. 231 pp. ISBN 0-385-24773-7.**

PURPOSE

This synthesis of several televised conversations between Joseph Campbell and Bill Moyers presents Campbell's views on the significance of myth. In these pages Campbell explores the commonality of certain themes in all mythologies, and his interpretations should be of interest to all readers.

CONTENTS

This book is offered as an antidote to those librarians, teachers, and others who persist in explaining to young people that myths are merely the prescientific attempts of early peoples to explain natural phenomena. In it Campbell responds to Moyers' probing comments and questions with his interpretations of the myths and rituals that have guided the lives, social systems, and religions of humankind.

In the first chapter, Campbell considers the collapse of meaning, in a mythical sense, in contemporary life. He discusses the emptiness of those rituals that still persist, and the absence of real heroes such as those celebrated in myths. The sense of wonderment at the mystery of human existence, and of the universe, the setting in place of a social order, and the ethical dimension of human reason have all been lost, and the consequences of this loss are examined by both Campbell and Moyers.

The origin and functions of myth are considered in Chapter 2, along with the symbols and archetypes that are used metaphorically to symbolize the mysteries of creation and of life and death. "The First Storytellers," Chapter 3, continues the exploration of myth, discussing the mythic significance of the early cave paintings, comparing them with medieval cathedrals as symbols of man's reverence for the transcendent, and recounting myths and describing the rituals that are defined as an enactment of the myths.

The inner meanings of "Sacrifice and Bliss," Chapter 4, and of the hero and his adventures and death, of the "Goddess" as the epitome of women's life-giving and nurturing power, and of love and marriage continue the exploration of myth. Finally, in the last chapter, Campbell discusses religions and their mysteries and their power to reflect the "spiritual potentialities" (p. 207) of humankind.

AUTHORITY

Joseph Campbell, who died in 1987, was a teacher at Sarah Lawrence College, Bronxville, New York, and a scholar and author of several classic books about mythology. He was also a skilled storyteller. Bill Moyers is a well-known television journalist for CBS News and PBS (Public Broadcasting System).

COMMENT

It is impossible to distill Campbell's thought, and these incisive and often profound conversations, into a few brief paragraphs. Before embarking with students on an investigation of mythology, however, the reader is urged to read this book, and may wish to follow the experience with a study of Campbell's *The Hero with a Thousand Faces* (Princeton Univ. Press, 1968) and *The Masks of God: Creative Mythology* (Viking, 1972).

Carlsen, G. Robert. *Books and the Teenage Reader: A Guide for Teachers, Librarians and Parents*, 2nd rev. ed. Harper & Row, 1980. 290 pp. ISBN 0-06-010626-3.

PURPOSE

This commentary on young people and the books they choose to read also provides extensive lists of recommended books as an aid in selection by parents, teachers, and librarians.

CONTENTS

The opening chapter describes the reading experience of adolescents, which includes the books written for teens as well as the adult books that they have adopted, and the kind of environment and reading materials that help to support and foster the development of the reading habit. The developmental tasks that teenagers must accomplish as they reach toward maturity—growth in human relations, understanding their sexuality, developing self-esteem and a sense of values, and making vocational choices—are described in the second chapter. Books that help in this maturation process are listed in this section.

The stages of adolescent growth and the kinds of books that appeal during these stages are described in the third chapter. Series books (Nancy Drew, The Hardy Boys, et al.), adult romance and adventure novels, film and television tie-ins, and the nature and appeal of this "subliterature" are discussed in Chapter 4. While the author notes the disadvantages of young people's getting stuck in this stage of reading development, he also finds some positive results of the inevitable appeal of these books, and recommends the use of literary ladders to move readers toward more mature taste.

The adolescent novel and its various genres are the subject of Chapter 5, and these are the books that are found on junior and senior high school library shelves. A substantial list of these concludes the chapter, and while the list will need updating, many of the titles remain remarkably durable.

As adolescents continue to mature they begin to turn toward the popular adult novels, pausing along the way for such almost-adult books as *A Separate Peace* and *Mr. and Mrs. Bo Jo Jones*, now fading from popularity. Carlsen discusses the various genres and distinguishes the popular adult novel (*Gone with the Wind, Rebecca, Mutiny on the Bounty, Shane*) from the more significant modern literature (*Catcher in the Rye, Member of the Wedding, Lord of the Flies, Catch-22*).

The chapters that discuss these books are separated by another that deals with students' right to read and attempts to abridge that right. Carlsen discusses language and sex in this regard, and also the leanings toward censorship of feminist and gay groups and religious and political censorship attempts. The place of the classics, some significant biographies, nonfiction books, poetry and drama, literature about women, and science fiction and fantasy are briefly touched on in the concluding chapters. Reommended books in these areas are listed in generous supply.

Briefly annotated entries complete each chapter; an appendix lists bibliographic tools and review sources, and an index concludes the book.

AUTHORITY

Carlsen is professor and head of high school English at the University of Iowa. A past president of the National Council of Teachers of English, he has written several books and articles.

COMMENT

Discussion of literature and teenage reading from an English teacher's perspective, practical guidance, useful summaries, and sensible advice add up to a good book for parents and a helpful one for teachers and librarians.

Frye, Northrop. *The Educated Imagination.* **Indiana Univ. Press, 1964. 156 pp.**

PURPOSE

Addressed to teachers of literature and the general reader, this book seeks to define the uses and value of literature so that young people may be led to value it as well.

CONTENTS

Northrop Frye, a literary critic and scholar, is also a writer with a rare ability to couch profundity in simple phrases. Here he examines the uses of literature, explaining in metaphorical terms what it is and why the experience of it is necessary. The book consists of six talks, each dealing with aspects of literature, language, and the imagination. He separates the use of language into three levels, the first of which is the language of awareness, a language that names things and defines them. The second level is language of practicality, which describes actions and movement. It is the language of science and the practical arts. On the third level is that language used to project a vision of reality, a model of the interpretation of experience, an imaginative construct. This is the language of literature, which speaks in metaphor and, reflecting the literary artist's imagination, appeals to the imagination of the reader.

All of literature, Frye says, emerges from the same impulse, and while *Huckleberry Finn* may appear to be very different from *The Odyssey,* it follows the same patterns of disguises and adventures, of strangeness and familiarity, and of the strength of human comradeship that surmounts disaster. He examines poetry and drama as expressions of the imagination within accepted conventions. Literary writing is not intended to impart information, and has nothing to do with teaching morality or explaining reality. Literature allows one to stand apart from what it depicts while at the same time being absorbed by it.

One of Frye's talks is concerned with myth, which he defines as a "simple and primitive effort of the imagination to identify the human with the nonhuman world" (p. 110). In teaching about literature, he notes, one should begin with myths, starting with the biblical ones, and continue with classical mythology, to build a foundation for the literature that follows.

Literature, as all art, is man's way of searching for, and finding, his place in his environment. Literature is the means Frye prescribes for allowing man to cope better with the problems of the world by educating his imagination.

AUTHORITY

Frye is professor of English and principal of Victoria College at the University of Toronto. He has taught at many American universities, including Harvard, Columbia, Princeton, Indiana, and Washington.

COMMENT

Frye's deceptively simple prose hides the perceptive mind of a literary critic, and is inordinately difficult to summarize. It is, however, worth more than one careful reading for those who want to understand better the power of literature.

Matthews, Dorothy, ed. *High Interest-Easy Reading for Junior and Senior High School Students*, 5th ed. NCTE, 1988. 115 pp. ISBN 0-8141-2096-2 (pap.).

PURPOSE

Written by members of the NCTE Committee to Revise *High Interest-Easy Reading*, this 1988 edition offers some 400 books for the entertainment and information of reluctant teenage readers. Among the 23 subjects treated are adventure, careers, fantasy and science fiction, ghosts and the supernatural, love and friendship, problems, self-improvement, and wheels and wings.

An introduction addressed to the young people for whom the book was compiled describes how to use it, suggesting the use of the cross-references that have been provided and inviting the readers to explore several sections before deciding on a choice. Users are also advised that books have not been labeled for junior or senior high school readers, since all are easy to read, and that it is all right to discard a book that they dislike.

Most of the entries are books published between 1984 and 1986, and "juvenile books have not been listed" (p. viii). Some older worthwhile titles are also included. Annotations are about 80 to 100 words long and offer enough description to capture the interest of the potential readers. They can be used by librarians to introduce the books in talks to groups or individuals. The carefully selected titles constitute a "hi-lo" guide for purchasing, and ISBNs are supplied for ordering convenience.

AUTHORITY

Matthews is chair, Committee to Revise *High Interest-Easy Reading* of NCTE. Committee members who contributed reviews were not identified, but one may assume that they include school librarians and English teachers.

COMMENT

The low-key introduction assures the reader that "there's something here for you," and that appears to be the case. The selections reflect the diverse reading interests of this age group, and yet the level of difficulty will not be too great for those seeking an easy read.

Nilsen, Alleen Pace, and Kenneth L. Donelson. *Literature for Today's Young Adults,* **2nd ed. Scott, Foresman, 1985. 661 pp. ISBN 0-673-15033-7.**

PURPOSE

This book updates the authors' first edition, published in 1980 in response to the need expressed by many teachers and librarians for a book that would take a scholarly approach to providing a readable background source on literature for young adults.

CONTENTS

Literature for young adults has occupied a gray area between the acknowledged artistry of children's literature and that of literature for adults. Only fairly recently have books written specifically for young adults emerged as a literature worthy of serious consideration. Nilsen and Donelson have organized their study around four major focal points: understanding young adults and books, what young adults are reading now, adults and the literature of young adults, and a history of what young adults have read in the past.

Young adult literature includes those books that young people have freely chosen to read, whether books written specifically for them or adult books that they have made their own. The first chapter further defines this literature and discusses prevalent myths, such as that young adult literature is antiadult, that the books avoid taboo topics, and that they are all the same. Chapter 2 discusses such literary aspects as plot, theme, mood, character, point of view, and style, establishing some common ground for further discussion. It also presents a theory of reading development from early childhood to adulthood.

Part 2, Chapters 3 through 9, discusses the books that young adults are reading now. These include realistic stories about parent/ child relationships, friendships, societal problems, explorations of sex roles, and self-identity; adventurous romances and love stories; action novels; the supernatural; and historical fiction. Also considered are science fiction, fantasy and utopias, and "life models," which include stories of heroes in sports, death, war, and the Holocaust. These are primarily autobiographical and biographical works. Among the other nonfiction books are those that treat health, sex, and drugs; careers and vocations; and how-to books. A new chapter is devoted to poetry, drama, and humor, and also comments on video games and music video, as well as films.

Part 3 describes how adults can influence young adults' reading with booktalks and other programs that motivate and guide reading, and how books can be promoted in reading, social studies, and English classes. The literature's contribution to clarification of values and enhancing understanding of others and the self is also discussed.

An important issue for adults to consider is finding a basis for evaluating young adult literature, and the authors provide some criteria for evaluating nonfiction books in the earlier chapter on that category (Chapter 8). How the literature deals with questions about ethnicity—whether differences or commonality should be stressed— is also considered. A section on religious themes in young adult books is included, along with a discussion of new trends in publishing that affect the young adult market.

Censorship issues are dealt with in Chapter 12, new to this edition, which includes a brief history of censorship, a list of recent court decisions, and a briefing on the state of censorship in classrooms and libraries today. The authors also touch on censorship within schools themselves, by teachers, administrators, and librarians.

Chapters 13, 14, and 15 offer a historical overview, condensing a considerable amount of material into its 60-odd pages. The periods covered are the nineteenth century, 1900 to 1940, and 1940 to 1966. The last of these chapters covers such topics as bibliotherapy, the paperback tide, nine outstanding writers for young adults, and the rise of criticism of young adult literature.

Interspersed throughout the pages are comments about the future of YA literature, written by authors, editors, teachers, critics, and librarians. Each chapter uses books appropriate to the topic to illustrate the comments and presents a bibliography of the books discussed.

Appendixes include "Honor Sampling," a list of books published from 1967 to 1983 that were highly recommended by several major reviewing sources; a list of selection guides; and a bibliography of books and articles about young adult literature. Acknowledgments, author, title, and subject indexes, and an index of critics and commentators conclude the book.

AUTHORITY
The authors are faculty members of Arizona State University at Tempe.

COMMENT
This thorough and well-organized text has raised the level of discussion of young adult literature to a high plane, bringing scholarship and clear thinking to an important subject. It is recommended reading for all secondary school library media specialists, and offers an excellent introduction to the subject for library school students.

Paulin, Mary Ann, and Susan Berlin, comps. *Outstanding Books for the College Bound*. ALA, Young Adult Services Division, 1984. 92 pp. ISBN 0-8389-3302-5 (pap.).

PURPOSE
Bringing together a number of previously published lists compiled by the Young Adult Services Division committee members, the compilers of this book have responded to the need for combining them in a single book. It is a selection and reading guidance tool for librarians, and will be used by teenagers as well.

CONTENTS

The annotated lists are presented in five sectons: fiction, nonfiction, biography, theater, and other performing arts. Each section has an alphabetical arrangement by title, except that the individual biographies are arranged alphabetically by the biographee, and the plays are arranged chronologically, by publication date. An index of authors and titles is provided for ease in searching.

The annotations are brief but descriptive, and the bibliographic information is current as of the 1983–1984 edition of *Books in Print*. Out-of-print status is indicated where appropriate, and the number of times a book has been included on previous lists is indicated parenthetically. The year of the book's original publication is indicated at the end of the annotation, and the year of the most recent edition appears in the imprint.

A brief comment introduces each section, and the approximately 600 selections are primarily classics, covering a broad range of interests.

AUTHORITY

Mary Ann Paulin is a media specialist with the Negaunee, Michigan, public schools, and the many contributors to the individual lists are experienced professionals.

COMMENT

By its nature, this selection guide does not require currency, since the titles need to reflect choices that have stood the test of time. Thus the five-year-old publication date is of no consequence, nor is the age of the lists on which the book is based. This compilation will serve well the purposes for which it was prepared.

Reed, Arthea J. S. *Reaching Adolescents: The Young Adult Book and the School*. Holt, 1985. 487 pp. ISBN 0-03-069342-X.

PURPOSE

This book was designed to provide secondary school library media specialists and teachers and students in education and library science courses with practical assistance in making young adult literature a part of the instructional program in a variety of subject areas.

CONTENTS

In her preface Reed describes her first ineffectual attempts to get her teaching career off to a satisfying start and her quick discovery that listening to her students and using the books they were reading might be her catalyst for effective teaching. They were, and this book summarizes what she has learned, not only from her own experiences but also from those of other outstanding teachers who have shared their own perceptions with her.

The book comprises four parts. In the first part, Chapter 1 provides a rationale for integrating young adult books with classroom instruction and also includes discussions of the stages of reading development, adolescent needs and interests, and the teacher's role in using books to bridge them. Motivation of reading and learning and the interrelationship among reading activity, motivation, and achievement are discussed in Chapter 2.

Young adult literature is the topic of Part 2, in which various genres are discussed in Chapter 3, and themes in young adult literature in the next two chapters. Developmental and emotional needs of young readers and their responsiveness to various kinds of novels are among the topics explored. This part concludes with an examination of biographies and other nonfiction, poetry, and short stories. Comments are descriptive rather than critical and offer a reference point for teacher planning.

Part 3 focuses on methods of combining young adult literature with studies in various subject areas. It is introduced with a discussion of "thematic teaching" and offers techniques for integrating young adult books with subject matter. A suggested framework is offered in Chapter 7 that also differentiates single discipline from interdisciplinary thematic units and presents a model thematic unit. Additional chapters discuss specific subject areas such as English, social studies, reading, science, mathematics, music, and art. Unit plans are featured throughout these chapters, and Chapter 11 considers ways of experiencing and sharing books with young adults.

Part 4 presents selection sources for young adult books, including best books and awards lists, reviewing sources, and bibliographies. The final chapter discusses censorship, some differing views about it and methods of dealing with it.

Each chapter has a bibliography of the titles discussed in it, many of them organized by theme or genre. Also included are suggested sources for further study, as well as audiovisual materials to augment the reading materials.

AUTHORITY

Reed is an associate professor of education at the University of North Carolina at Asheville and is editor of *The ALAN Review,* an international journal for the study and review of young adult literature and related media, published by the National Council of Teachers of English.

COMMENT

This book's approach to young adult literature is less comprehensive than the Nilsen-Donelson text (see this section) and lacks the critical and scholarly edge of that book. However, it provides some very practical guidelines and actual units of study that incorporate the books read by adolescents with the actual subject matter taught in secondary schools. Librarians have two excellent sources to choose from, and can best be guided by their own needs.

Stanford, Barbara Dodds, and Karima Amin. *Black Literature for High School Students.* **NCTE, 1978. 273 pp. ISBN 0-8141-0330-8 (pap.).**

PURPOSE

This book was written to guide English teachers in the presentation of black literature, and the bibliographies it includes will guide school librarians in selection of books to implement such courses and generally to expand existing collections.

CONTENTS

Black literature, like all literature, has an influence on the development of values and social attitudes. The sharing of human experiences, in thought and emotion, develops awareness of human similarities as well as ethnic differences in how these experiences might be perceived. Within this conceptual framework, the authors present a survey of black American literature in the first section of the book and some literature units for classroom use in the second.

The first section begins with a discussion of aspects of teaching black literature in high schools today (in 1978, when the book was published). Chapter 1 discusses this literature as a separate tradition and considers its affective aspects, then outlines the goals and objectives for courses in the subject. The second chapter presents an overview of black American writers from pre-Civil War to the present. Chapter 3 considers fiction by black authors and the black experience as filtered through the perceptions of white writers; and Chapter 4 deals with biographies and autobiographies of historical and modern figures. Chapter 5 offers bibliographies of African literature, novels and plays by blacks, and annotated bibliographies of sports literature and recordings of black American literature.

Section 2 presents several literature units, each of which concludes with a bibliography. Subjects included are the journey from Africa to America, slavery in narrative and autobiography, black

235

poetry and short stories, black literature and human relations, the world of the imagination, myths and legends, prose nonfiction, and a senior elective course. The final chapter offers motivators for writing and discussion, ideas for role playing, and other supplementary activities.

A directory of publishers and author and title indexes complete the book.

Barbara Dodds Stanford is an associate professor in the teacher education program at Utica College of Syracuse University, New York, and has written and edited books about literature, black literature, and related subjects. Karima Amin is a language arts teacher in the Academy for the Visual and Performing Arts, a magnet school in Buffalo, New York.

Stanford and Amin differ not only in their ethnic backgrounds but also in their responses to the black experience and its literary manifestations. Each preserves her viewpoint and both present a sensitive rendering of their subject. The bibliographies offer selection guidance and the curriculum units provide a source for replication or adaptation.

STORYTELLING

Baker, Augusta, and Ellin Greene. *Storytelling: Art and Technique,* **2nd ed. Bowker, 1987. 182 pp. ISBN 0-8352-2336-1.**

This manual highlights the importance and value of storytelling and provides all the information needed for the successful practice of the art in a variety of settings and with a wide range of audiences. The authors' goal is to provide teachers and librarians with the confidence they need as storytellers to be able to share stories regularly with children.

A brief background sketches the beginnings of storytelling and describes its introduction into libraries by the great storytellers who originated and continued library story hours: Marie Shedlock,

Anna Cogswell Tyler, Mary Gould Davis, Ruth Sawyer, and Gudrun Thorne-Thomsen.

The uses of storytelling and story selection are the subjects of Chapters 2 and 3. How to learn stories and then present them, styles of storytelling, and approaches recommended for use in special settings and for children with special needs continue the presentation. Additional chapters are devoted to the planning and conducting of storytelling programs, including storytelling by children and teens, and in-service education in storytelling for librarians, teachers, and other potential storytellers.

Each chapter concludes with a bibliography. An appendix provides an extensive list of story sources, recommended stories for different age groups, reference sources on the art of storytelling, and a list of storytelling recordings.

AUTHORITY

The authors are recognized storytellers in the library tradition, with much successful experience in practicing their art as well as teaching it.

COMMENT

Baker and Greene offer guidance to the beginner in the practical aspects of getting started, reassurance to those who might stumble, and inspiration for those who might doubt the importance of the endeavor. The coverage is wide ranging, with excellent advice and good anticipation of problems. All in all this is a succinct and useful guide.

The opening chapter, while generous with the history of modern library storytelling, is quite sketchy in dealing with early history. That may be enough in a handbook of this practical nature, but some will seek more detail on this subject. More thorough and colorful coverage is found in Ruth Sawyer's *The Way of the Storyteller* (see this section), in her chapter entitled "Patterns of the Past."

Bauer, Caroline Feller. *Handbook for Storytellers*. ALA, 1977. 381 pp. ISBN 0-8389-0293-6 (pap.).

PURPOSE

Bauer explores the various facets of planning and presenting storytelling programs, using storytelling as a means of presenting literature to children and adults.

CONTENTS

The goals presented here are somewhat different from those of traditional storytellers, who are constrained to keep alive and transmit an oral tradition of great antiquity, and who are gifted with the special talent and compulsion that enables them to do it successfully. Bauer uses storytelling as entertainment with a purpose: that of inspiring a love of literature. And who can fault that?

Her book ranges ebulliently from finding a place, planning a program, and promoting it to learning a story and reading aloud, and presents a wealth of source material to choose from, including such nonnarrative sources as poetry, riddles, rhymes, and tongue twisters. She adds media to the mix, and describes how to use puppets, films, magic tricks, overhead projectors, felt and chalkboards and other kinds of boards, slides, and other communications tools.

All aspects of program planning are explored and for all age groups, from preschool to adult. Activities described include not only storytelling but also booktalks, book parties, creative dramatics, and book exhibits, even field trips to be followed up with a related story hour. In short, Bauer has produced, not a storytelling handbook but a library programming guide in which storytelling plays a major role. Perhaps a more inclusive title would have helped to set things straight.

AUTHORITY

Bauer has written from a rich background that includes working with children in school and public libraries, teaching library students in the graduate program at the University of Oregon, and appearing on radio and television on her own weekly storytelling program.

COMMENT

Written with zest and a you-can-do-it emphasis, the book provides myriad ideas for library programs and activities. It will be an inspiring addition to the professional library. However, use Augusta Baker and Ellin Greene's *Storytelling: Art and Technique* (see this section) for guidance in storytelling techniques.

De Wit, Dorothy. *Children's Faces Looking Up*. ALA, 1979. 156 pp. ISBN 0-8389-0272-3.

PURPOSE

Creating vital storytelling programs is the basic subject of this book, written principally for the novice storyteller, whether in a school or public library.

238

CONTENTS

Although the pages of this book are relatively few, the format is large, permitting the author to explore a variety of tangential subjects. Before discussing program building, De Wit explores the origins of storytelling, presents pointers and sources for selection, discusses and demonstrates how stories may be modified, and explains methods of learning stories.

Deciding on a theme for a series of programs is only the first step. One then has to find the stories that fit the theme, and De Wit suggests a variety of techniques, ranging from internal brainstorming to research involving a variety of library tools. Not available when she wrote this book was Margaret MacDonald's *The Storyteller's Sourcebook* (reviewed in this section), which would make the job much easier. De Wit analyzes and reviews some important principles to consider in creating programs, some of which are balance, variety, and mood. Her real gift to the reader, however, is the six story programs she presents, complete with tales, sources, and annotations, and followed by suggestions for further enrichment.

A summary completes the text, which is followed by bibliographies of sources cited in the text, anthologies and other story sources, and professional reading and guides. A brief index is also provided.

AUTHORITY

De Wit, head of children's services in a regional library, is a book reviewer for professional publications. She is the author of the children's book *The Talking Stone* (Greenwillow, 1968).

COMMENT

School librarians with the time and the inclination to offer series of storytelling programs rather than occasional individual stories will find a wealth of information and guidance here. In schools where children participate in storytelling programs, they can be taught some of the techniques for finding stories appropriate to a selected theme so that they can build programs by themselves individually or in a group.

Livo, Norma J., and Sandra A. Rietz. *Storytelling: Process and Practice*. Libraries Unlimited, 1986. 462 pp. ISBN 0-87287-443-5.

PURPOSE

Livo and Rietz have captured the art of storytelling and pass it on to those who would continue or at least understand the oral transmission of cultural traditions and the stories and folkways that inform it. Their purpose in storytelling is to save the stories by telling them to others: "We give away what was given to us. We can keep it only by handing it on" (p. xvi).

CONTENTS

Magic, enchantment, fairy gold—these words have all been used to describe the fairy tale and the art by which it and other folktales are transmitted orally. How this art can be nurtured, possessed, and practiced is described in this book.

What it means to be a storyteller, the function of story, and the art of storytelling are discussed in the opening pages of the book. In subsequent sections the authors develop their analysis of the process of becoming a storyteller, taking up the procedure by which stories are learned and analyzing story structure and describing how stories may be prepared, developed, and delivered to an audience. Included here are such techniques as creating a map of the structure and extending and expanding stories. Such nonlanguage aspects of storytelling as movement, eye contact, mood, rate of telling, breathing, and props are also considered.

Because the audience is an essential part of the storytelling process, Livo and Rietz discuss techniques of working with an audience and the ritual aspects of storytelling. The game elements of storytelling are defined, and the nature of the audience treated. This section concludes with a discussion of educating the audience: developing its competence in oral literacy, providing ritual, and building story readiness.

Next considered are the resources a storyteller may use as the basis for a storytelling program: variants of stories, types of stories, local folklore, personal experiences, and family stories. Other folklore forms such as games, ballads, swapping songs, and even dances are described and examples provided. Of special interest to school librarians are the next chapters: "Storytelling at Home and School" and "Planning and Arranging Storytelling Events." Here the authors present an article describing how a father concocted stories for his children, providing opportunities for their participation in developing the stories.

The values of conducting storytelling programs in the school include an appreciation of stories as literature and an enhancement of speaking, listening, reading, and writing abilities. Related activities in language arts, social studies, science, and math are suggested, but with the sound advice that storytelling has its own reason for being, and is not to be considered as a means to achieving curriculum goals.

There are some good suggestions here, except the one that recommends that children "investigate myths as the encyclopedia of scientific information of preliterate societies." Students of mythology have other interpretations of myth than that particular oversimplification. Among the best of these interpreters are Robert Graves and Joseph Campbell.

Appendixes provide amplification of material in the text: from units of instruction to conference programs and course syllabi (seven appendixes in all). There are reference and resource lists with each chapter, and a detailed index.

AUTHORITY

Livo and Rietz have had lifelong experience as storytellers.

COMMENT

Accomplished storytellers, like musicians and painters, are the recipients of a special gift. Those who nurture the gift, and practice it, bring great pleasure to their audiences. Those who try to impart the substance of their art by writing about it bestow a further gift. Reading this book and practicing its suggestions will not only make for better storytelling in school libraries but will add immeasurably to understanding what storytelling is all about. Storytellers might be considered living libraries of folklore, which they constantly expand as they take versions from printed sources and translate them into oral language. The authors suggest adding a storyteller to the library collection, which is not a bad idea at all.

MacDonald, Margaret Read. *The Storyteller's Sourcebook: A Subject, Title and Motif Index to Folklore Collections for Children.* **Neal-Schuman/Gale, 1982. 818 pp. ISBN 0-8103-0471-6.**

PURPOSE

An index to folktales in children's collections, this reference work is the first to provide brief descriptions and ready access by subject, collection, geographic area, ethnic origin, and variants. It was "designed for quick and easy access by teacher or librarian."

CONTENTS

The preface indicates that 556 folktale collections and 389 picture books have been indexed, and the book includes all the folktale titles that appeared in *Children's Catalog* from 1960 through 1980. Omitted are epic, romance, and tall-tale hero tales, as well as modern fairy tales by such authors as Eleanor Farjeon, Rudyard Kipling, and Hans Christian Andersen, except for *The Princess and the Pea.*

There is no textual material, except a brief guide to how the sourcebook may be used; the rest is all index. The first, and longest, of these is a motif index, which is preceded by an outline of the motif groups. This index provides synopses of each story cited and refers the user to the tale title, author, and ethnic or geographic index listing. A subject index leads to the motif listing. The several indexes allow the user to locate stories through a variety of means: by motif, ethnic origin, country, title, subject, and variants. A bibliography of the collections and single titles that have been indexed is also provided.

AUTHORITY

MacDonald refers to the ten years that went into the book's preparation, and credits the assistance of the Folklore Institute and the Graduate Library School at Indiana University. She has written extensively about storytelling.

COMMENT

Librarians with a serious interest in storytelling will find this book invaluable for locating stories by subject or motif and then the collections in which they may be found. It is also useful in verifying the folk origin of a particular tale. Whether it should be included in the professional collection of a school library will depend on budgetary and other considerations. It is certainly a tool of great value to school librarians, and one to become familiar with, especially where folk literature and storytelling are of high priority.

MacDonald, Margaret Read, ed. *Twenty Tellable Tales: Audience Participation for the Beginning Storyteller.* **Wilson, 1986. 220 pp. ISBN 0-8242-0719-X.**

PURPOSE

This how-to book for beginning storytellers was written also for those school library media specialists who want to tell stories but lack the time to learn them.

CONTENTS

It was inevitable that as folklore scholars committed folktales, which belonged to an oral tradition, to writing, their basic simplicity would be altered by the complexities of the written word. With this as justification for returning to the unembellished directness of the oral tradition, MacDonald suggests that a first step in learning stories for oral telling is to simplify them. Besides, she comments, there are as many variants of each tale as there are tellers.

As examples of the outcome of this process, she presents 20 stories of homely virtue, easy to learn and tell, and enjoyable for all. These versions capture the cadence and brevity that speak directly to young children, and encourage their participation in the telling as well. Among the stories are "A Whale of a Tale," "Little Crab and His Magic Eyes," "Old One Eye," and "Sody Sallyrytus." Some of the tales that are included are American variants of European tales, and others are Native American tales. All have simple refrains that children will be anxious to repeat, enabling them to participate actively in the storytelling event.

Supplementing the stories themselves are the author's recommendations for learning these stories and telling them. She notes the importance of maintaining eye contact with the audience, speaking to each child individually, of using body language to demonstrate one's own enjoyment of the story, and of pacing the telling with care. Of greatest importance is to retell them as often as possible.

In her comments on creating a written version of an oral tale, MacDonald urges the writer to reflect the storytelling occasion itself, including audience reactions, and the songs and chants that would accompany an actual event, and singles out Diane Wolkstein's *The Magic Orange Tree* (Random House, 1978) as an example of this.

In the final chapter MacDonald explains how to research variants of tales and lists type and motif indexes that can be used in the search. She also lists story collections with texts that are close to their oral origins, picture books that are good story sources, and stories that have been told on recordings, films, and videotapes.

The book concludes with recommended books for beginning storytellers and a bibliography of the works consulted.

AUTHORITY

MacDonald is an acknowledged authority on folklore. She is the author of *The Storyteller's Sourcebook* (reviewed in this section), and has written extensively about storytelling.

COMMENT

It really does seem possible to learn the stories in this book in little more than an hour, and they will delight both storyteller and audience. Moreover, children can learn to tell them too.

Painter, William M. *Musical Story Hours: Using Music with Storytelling and Puppetry.* **Library Professional, 1989. 158 pp. ISBN 0-208-02205-8.**

Using (mostly) classical music to provide a background for story-telling and adding puppets to the mix are the innovative contributions of Painter to storytelling programs, particularly recommended in elementary school libraries and early childhood programs.

Music has been accompanying storytelling since Orpheus first fingered his lute, but Painter has a different twist. In his foreword, Spencer Shaw, renowned storyteller and professor emeritus of the University of Seattle's Graduate Library School, discusses some aspects of combining music with storytelling and offers a few provisos about such programming. Painter's introduction provides his rationale for using music, noting how effective an appropriate musical background can be in setting the mood and enriching a story. The use of puppets adds another fillip to the story hour.

Painter's method is to pluck a story out of the air or off the shelf, build a program with stories having a similar theme or subject, then find some suitable music. This enables him to spend many happy hours listening to records, and he always seems to come up with just the right piece of music. Along the way to his description of the complete program he manages to relate the story and some of the others that will be included. The whole thing is done in a charmingly casual way, and programs are introduced with an appropriate song or verse, which children may sing or recite along with the storyteller. Most of the songs are variations of "Ten Little Indians," altered to match the story characters. Games and other activities are also suggested, and suitable audiovisual materials are often introduced.

Some of the pairings of story and music are more than obvious: *Swimmy* (Random House, 1973) and "The Blue Danube Waltz," for example. Others are more subtle: *Crictor* (Harper & Row, 1958) and Mozart's Clarinet Concerto, for another. All told, there are 21 programs in the book, and a quick reference section at the end lists the story and music pairings. In the concluding chapter, Painter cites a research study that indicated the effectiveness of storytelling in encouraging reading and preparing children to learn how to read. He is convinced that providing musical accompaniment simply adds to the enjoyment of the story hour.

William Painter is youth services librarian and assistant director of the North Miami Public Library.

Painter makes a persuasive case for dressing up the storytelling program with music, puppets, flannel boards, and anything else that might enrich the hour. Judging from the reactions he describes, they have been successful additions that the reader is encouraged to try. Elementary school librarians seeking to embellish the story hour with an innovative twist, and other adventurous souls, will find inspiration here.

Pellowski, Anne. *The World of Storytelling.* Bowker, 1977, o.p. 296 pp.

PURPOSE
Written for all who are interested in storytelling and its history and traditions throughout the world, this book takes the reader through many cultures and into many settings where the oral tradition continues to thrive.

CONTENTS
Whether storytelling is truly as old as man's ability to speak will no doubt always remain a supposition. That evidence for its practice exists in early historical records is shown in quotations from early Egyptian papyri from around 1600 B.C. Quoted writings of the ancient Greeks and Romans, a bit more recent, also refer to storytelling.

Starting with these early beginnings in the historical record, Pellowski takes the reader into the Middle Ages, when bards, scops, and minstrels continued the oral traditions. They are identified and described, not only as written records have shown them to have existed in the Western European countries but also in other areas of the world, such as Eastern Europe, India, the Orient, Africa, and the Middle East.

Continuing with folk storytelling, in the home and at work, at the market and in the streets, Pellowski takes the reader to the settings where they occur, introducing the Indian *kathakas,* the *kamishibai* of Japan, and other itinerant storytellers. Religious, theatrical, and institutional (in libraries, primarily) storytelling complete her description of purposes and types.

It is not surprising to learn that the rituals of storytelling vary from culture to culture. What these rituals are—opening and ending the session, the style and gestures used, changes of voice, and audience participation—are also portrayed. In some cultures music, objects, and pictures are used, and these are presented also.

Final chapters include a history of methods used in the training of storytellers and suggestions for bringing greater authenticity into storytelling programs and published folktales. A multilingual dictionary of storytelling terms, notes, a bibliography, and an index complete the book.

AUTHORITY

Pellowski has written extensively about storytelling and children's literature. She has held positions at several major libraries and universities, including director-librarian at the Information Center on Children's Cultures, U.S. Committee for UNICEF, and is herself a storyteller.

COMMENT

The house of storytelling has many rooms. There is one for how to do it, another for what it is like to devote one's life to the storytelling art, a third for the ethnological study of it, a fourth for its effectiveness in teaching children about their cultural heritage, and so on. This book belongs in the living room, where all the world's peoples and their experiences with storytelling are gathered, and the phenomena of their oral traditions may be explored. While it includes no folktales, it does provide the background for understanding how the tales have been transmitted from times long past, each in the context of its own culture. This is knowledge well worth having and easy to acquire from this well-written account.

Sawyer, Ruth. *The Way of the Storyteller*. Viking, 1966. 356 pp. ISBN 0-14-004436-1 (pap.).

PURPOSE

Sawyer has written this book in order to share the spiritual experience of being a storyteller. Along the way there is talk about the hows and whys of storytelling, but this is incidental to the passing along of "fairy gold," for an explanation of which the book must be read.

CONTENTS

Beginning with the folk origins and antiquity of storytelling, the book encompasses all that underlies the storyteller's art, sweeping the reader into the experience with the force of the author's convictions but gentled with a helping of wit. Sawyer describes her delight in the sharing of stories, both as a listener, when she was a child, and as a beginning storyteller and later as an accomplished artist.

She shares with the reader not only the joy and satisfactions of her art but also the wide range of knowledge and hard work that go into its development, likening the preparation and discipline of the storyteller with that of a musician. She describes how the "power of creative imagination" may be developed, and how the speaking voice, the storyteller's instrument, can be improved. Commenting on the art of story selection, Sawyer emphasizes that it depends not only on powers of discrimination but also on a large and diverse acquaintanceship with stories.

The use of storytelling to acquaint children with a variety of books and a consideration of poetry during the story hour are the final concerns of the book. It concludes with a delightful selection of stories and an informative list for further reading.

AUTHORITY

Recognized as a master of the art of storytelling, Ruth Sawyer has also written books for children.

COMMENT

Sawyer sets a high standard for storytellers, but at the same time gives good reason for doing so. This is not a book to read for a step-by-step approach to learning how to tell stories. But for a deeper understanding of a living art, for inspiration to attempt to practice that art, and for sheer joy in the exercise of that art it is unequaled.

Shedlock, Marie L. *The Art of the Storyteller*. Dover, 1951. 290 pp. ISBN 0-486-20636-1.

PURPOSE

Written for the potential storytellers among those who work with children, this book emphasizes the value of storytelling as an art form and provides advice on practicing that art.

CONTENTS

Shedlock, a master storyteller, came to the United States in 1900, after ten years spent as a storyteller in England and France. She toured the country with her stories and lectured and trained storytellers, inspiring those who heard her, teachers and librarians, to continue the oral tradition. This book is a collection of her lectures to teachers.

She begins with some of the difficulties that storytellers encounter in perfecting their art, among them getting involved in issues not relevant to the story, using unfamiliar words, altering the story, and obscuring the point of the story with details, and discusses ways of overcoming them. Shedlock continues with a reminder of the importance of submerging oneself in the story, and provides some practical advice on telling stories to individuals and groups, sharing such techniques as pacing and pausing for emphasis.

Selecting stories is the subject of another lecture, and she advises her audience against choosing overly analytical stories, and those that use sarcasm, or display an excess of sentimentality. Start with the child's world, she suggests, and avoid stories that are outside their interests and experience.

In sharing her enthusiasm for the art of storytelling, she insists that stories be allowed to stand on their own for children to experience rather than be used as the basis for any kind of assignments. Let the words tell the story, and avoid the use of pictures or any explanation beyond the narrative, and avoid asking questions about the story.

The lectures are followed by written versions of 18 classic stories that the author recommends for telling. Among them are "The Stone Cutter," "The Water Nixie," "The Blue Rose," "The Proud Cock," and some tales of Hans Christian Andersen. An additional feature of the book is an annotated list of stories, including myths and legends, fanciful stories, folktales, poetry and nonsense, and more.

AUTHORITY

Shedlock is one of those artists whose name is forever linked with the storytelling art. She inspired the development of storytelling in the children's rooms of libraries across the nation, and especially in the New York Public Library, where storytelling is a tradition that still retains its vitality.

COMMENT

This book of lectures is Shedlock's written legacy to teachers and librarians, one that stands beside the more ephemeral artistry with which she continued and transmitted the oral storytelling tradition. That facet of her art is lost to those who will never have the opportunity to hear her, but this book remains and it is considered a classic by storytelling artists.

BOOKTALKING

Bodart, Joni. *Booktalk!2: Booktalking for All Ages and Audiences,* **2nd ed. Wilson, 1985. 388 pp. ISBN 0-8242-0716-5 (pap.).**

Written primarily for public librarians but with much relevance for school library media specialists, this book describes how to give a booktalk, and provides the substance of many in the talks written by librarians across the country.

CONTENTS
Although the booktalk has been traditionally the province of young adult public librarians, giving booktalks is certainly within the capabilities of school library media specialists. Larry Rakow, a school librarian in Shaker Heights High School in Ohio, has been doing it successfully ever since he gave a talk at an in-service meeting of the English department in his school, and teachers began asking him to do the same for their classes. His article about how he finds time to prepare, and occasions to deliver, booktalks in his school library is one of the selections in this book, and a persuasive one, at that. Other chapters discuss why to do it: Basically because it is such an effective way of getting young people to read books; second, according to Rakow, because it helps keep the library at the front and center of people's minds.

How to do it follows the opening chapter's rationale. It begins with writing the talk, with two unbreakable rules established at the outset: Do not give away the ending and always read the book before attempting to talk about it. The rest of the advice is presented in detail in the second chapter. The next two chapters discuss planning the booktalk, which includes setting the books aside and making sure that no one removes them, and may include the use of slides and music, and surely includes making all the scheduling and other arrangements and giving the presentation. Presenting the talk involves learning how to control interaction with the audience, controlling stage fright, and handling other details that can interfere with your presentation.

Giving booktalks in schools (addressed to booktalkers who are not teachers or school librarians) and booktalking for children are the subjects of the next two chapters. Rakow's article and another about evaluating one's effectiveness are followed by a third that offers suggestions for giving workshops and other methods for teaching booktalking. A final chapter describes how other librarians, both school and public, prepare, present, and share booktalks, and how the popularity of this form of sharing books can spread to community groups and special settings, such as schools for the deaf and the blind and juvenile detention centers.

The rest of the book consists of over 200 pages of booktalks, collected from some 80 librarians around the United States. The talks are arranged alphabetically by title, and bibliographies in the appendix help the reader locate books by age level and by theme and genre. Also included in the appendix are lists of publishers and short films, and various handouts and forms that booktalkers may find useful.

AUTHORITY

Bodart is assistant professor at the School of Library and Information Management at Emporia State University in Kansas, and is editor of *Top of the News* and a columnist for *Voice of Youth Advocates*. She has lectured and led workshops on booktalking and young adult literature.

COMMENT

Bodart's writing style is breezy and engaging, and the advice and booktalking suggestions she offers are unexceptionable, detailed, and practical. The booktalks themselves are briefer than those offered in R. R. Bowker's booktalking series, but many more of them are offered in a single book. Librarians who need help in getting started will find it in *Booktalk!2*.

Bodart-Talbot, Joni, ed. *Booktalk!3: More Booktalks for All Ages and Audiences*. Wilson, 1988. 371 pp. ISBN 0-8242-0764-5 (pap.).

PURPOSE

Building on the success of her two earlier booktalk guides, plus some booktalks that wouldn't fit into *Booktalk!2* and the new ones that kept coming in, Bodart-Talbot has compiled a new set of booktalks for the use of elementary and secondary school librarians.

CONTENTS

Close to 300 booktalks make up this new volume, among them several "flashtalks," which are brief teasers that can be interspersed among those of greater length, or used to start off a booktalk program. Gone are the booktalk pep talks and the how-to advice for giving booktalks that appeared in *Booktalk!2*. This publication starts with the booktalks themselves right after the list of contributors and a two-page introduction.

The talks are well-written summaries of book plots that succeed in giving their flavor and creating enough suspense to make listeners want to read the book. Several were written by Bodart-Talbot, while the rest represent contributions of her Emporia State University colleagues and a nationwide scattering of librarians. Most of the books described are 1980s publications, but a few are old standbys from the 1970s and 1960s. Books fall into such varied categories as aging, eating disorders, biography, humor, minorities, romance, and working, to mention a few.

Following the talks are the bibliography of all the books included, alphabetically arranged by author with grade level; a title list arranged by age level; a "selective bibliography by theme and genre"; a list of publishers, with addresses; and an index to both this book and *Booktalk!2.*

AUTHORITY

Bodart-Talbot is assistant professor at the School of Library and Information Management at Emporia State University in Kansas. She is nationally known among librarians for her workshops and lectures on young adult literature and booktalking, and has served ALA's Young Adult Services Division as head of the Best Books for Young Adults Committee.

COMMENT

The booktalks are time-savers for those librarians who prefer not to write their own, but as Bodart-Talbot noted in her earlier compilation, it is vital to read the books before giving a talk about them. These talks lack the features in R. R. Bowker's booktalking series, but there are many more of them in a single book. (See the books in this section by Gillespie and Lembo, *Introducing Books* and *Juniorplots;* Gillespie and Naden, *Juniorplots 3* and *Seniorplots;* Spirt, *Introducing Bookplots 3;* and Thomas, *Primaryplots.*)

Gillespie, John T., and Diana L. Lembo. *Introducing Books: A Guide for the Middle Grades.* **Bowker, 1970. 318 pp. ISBN 0-8352-0215-1.**

PURPOSE

This booktalk guide has been prepared for elementary school library media specialists and teachers of upper elementary grades.

CONTENTS

Following the same general organization as the *Juniorplots* titles (reviewed in this section), this book's content is based on the developmental goals and interests of a 9- to 12-year-old readership. Themes include making friends, developing values, learning to think abstractly, reading for fun, and similar concerns of this age group. The plots and supplementary information about 88 well-chosen books are included, along with author, title, and subject indexes.

AUTHORITY

John Gillespie and Diana Lembo were both professors of library science in the Palmer School of Library and Information Science, C. W. Post Campus of Long Island University. Each has written numerous books, many of them selection guides and booktalk manuals.

COMMENT

The books selected are still being read by their young audience, making this handbook current. If only one of the bookplot series is to be bought, however, the most recent one, *Introducing Bookplots 3*, by Diana Spirt, should be the first choice (see review in this section).

Introducing More Books: A Guide for the Middle Grades (Bowker, 1978, 240 pp.) by Diana L. Spirt (formerly Lembo) continues in the same vein. This book summarizes 72 titles; themes include getting along in the family, formulating a worldview, and understanding social problems.

Gillespie, John T., and Diana L. Lembo. *Juniorplots: A Book Talk Manual for Teachers and Librarians*. Bowker, 1967. 222 pp. ISBN 0-8352-0063-9.

PURPOSE

An aid for preparing booktalks, *Juniorplots* has been designed to help teachers and librarians guide students' reading by introducing readable and relevant books.

CONTENTS

Focusing on eight basic developmental goals for adolescents, this book is organized around the following themes/chapters: Building a World View, Overcoming Emotional Growing Pains, Earning a Living, Understanding Physical Problems, Making Friends, Developing Self-Reliance, Evaluating Life, and Appreciating Books. Each chapter presents plot summaries of ten books that carry out its theme. After the plot summary are a brief explanation of the thematic material, suggestions for pages to read aloud as part of the booktalk, and suggestions for related books that can be included in the booktalk or for further reading. The authors indicate the age group for which the titles are appropriate.

Neither a critical work nor a best-books list, *Juniorplots* suggests books that are useful for booktalking around the themes selected. It also includes an author/title index and a subject index. An introductory chapter written by Doris M. Cole describes the purposes, planning, and delivery of booktalks. The authors caution the user against substituting the booktalk material for a careful reading of the books.

More Juniorplots (Bowker, 1977, 253 pp.), written by John T. Gillespie alone, provides summaries of 72 additional books for young adolescents, using, again, a thematic approach.

AUTHORITY

John Gillespie and Diana Lembo were both professors of library science in the Palmer School of Library and Information Science, C. W. Post Campus of Long Island University. Each has written numerous books, many of them selection guides and booktalk manuals.

COMMENT

The titles selected for this book have remained popular with young readers and are still to be found on library shelves. *Juniorplots* is still being offered by its publisher and, budget permitting, it is a worthwhile purchase. For those librarians who can only afford one, the more recent *Juniorplots 3*, by Gillespie and Naden, is recommended (reviewed in this section).

Gillespie, John T., and Corinne J. Naden. *Juniorplots 3: A Book Talk Guide for Use with Readers Ages 12–16.* **Bowker, 1987. 352 pp. ISBN 0-8352-2367-1.**

PURPOSE

Twenty years after its initial appearance, a new *Juniorplots* made its appearance with a new title, new appearance, and, of course, new book summaries. The basic purpose remains the same, but there are changes in content and amplitude of the entries.

CONTENTS

The introductory chapter on the art of booktalking has been omitted here. A new layout makes for a more attractive book. The entries have been expanded to include an introduction of the book and its author's output, a longer plot summary, more about the theme and more passages recommended for reading aloud, and reference sources for biographical material about the author. The number of books presented, however, is still 80, and the authors still stress the importance of reading the book before introducing it in a booktalk.

The books are now arranged by subject and genre, and the new chapters include Teenage Life and Concerns, Adventure and Mystery Stories, Science Fiction and Fantasy, Historical Fiction, Sports Fiction, Biography and True Adventure, Guidance and Health, and

The World Around Us. Author, title, and subject indexes complete the book.

AUTHORITY

John Gillespie was a professor of library science in the Palmer School of Library and Information Science, C. W. Post Campus of Long Island University, and has written numerous books, many of them selection guides and booktalk manuals. Corinne Naden is a free-lance editor and children's book author.

COMMENT

Once again, this is an excellent selection of new titles for introduction to potential readers. Other variations for different age levels are described elsewhere in this chapter. All are recommended.

Gillespie, John T., and Corinne J. Naden. *Seniorplots: A Book Talk Guide for Use with Readers Ages 15–18.* **Bowker, 1989. 386 pp. ISBN 0-8352-2513-5.**

PURPOSE

A source of story summaries and other aids for booktalks for 15- to 18-year-olds, this book was written to assist senior high school librarians in introducing some outstanding contemporary books and a few classics to their students.

CONTENTS

Summaries of 80 books, divided into 12 subject areas or genres, constitute the substance of this book. In his introduction Gillespie presents a guide to giving booktalks and describes the primary and some secondary purposes of booktalking. He discusses how to prepare for a booktalk, what to include, and how to deliver it, and suggests some sources for further investigation.

The entries themselves include a summary of the plot (usually about two pages long, depending on the complexity of the plot), comments on the theme, recommendations for portions of the book that might be read aloud as part of the talk, related books with brief annotations, sources of reviews of the book, and information about the author. While some of the books require a considerable degree of maturity (Alice Walker's *The Color Purple*, Charles Dickens's *Hard Times*), most are less demanding. The nonfiction titles include a few biographies, autobiographies, and some health and guidance titles.

The books are divided into 12 chapters that reflect the concerns of older adolescents: Growing Up, Interpersonal Relations, Challenging Adult Novels, Stories of Other Lands and Times, Possible

Worlds, Fantasy, Adventure Stories, Suspense and Mystery, Sports in Fact and Fiction, Interesting Lives and True Adventure, The World Around Us, and Guidance and Health.

Separate author, title, and subject indexes are provided.

AUTHORITY

John Gillespie has been a professor of Library Science in the School of Library and Information Science, C. W. Post Campus of Long Island University, and has written 17 books, many of them selection guides and booktalk manuals. Corinne Naden is a free-lance editor and a children's book author.

COMMENT

Recent movements toward embracing computer technology and emphasizing library management concerns and the school library media center's curriculum support role suggest that reading guidance may be losing ground as an important function in school libraries. It may be hoped that *Seniorplots* will come to the rescue before booktalking becomes a lost art in high school library media centers. It is distinguished by complete, concise, accurate, and sensitively written plot summaries. It is highly recommended.

Kimmel, Margaret Mary, and Elizabeth Segel. *For Reading Out Loud! A Guide to Sharing Books with Children*, rev. and expanded ed. Delacorte, 1988. 266 pp. ISBN 0-385-29660-6.

PURPOSE

Written for parents and teachers primarily, this book can be helpful to school librarians as well.

CONTENTS

Several chapters introduce this collection of stories for reading aloud. Each focuses on a different aspect of the subject. Chapter 1 provides a rationale, with many authoritative and persuasive quotations that encourage reading aloud in school and at home. It is followed by a discussion of when, in an infant's life, reading aloud can begin, and offers reasons for starting at an early age. Why continue reading to children when they can read themselves is answered in Chapter 3, which offers a host of reasons. Chapter 4 suggests ways of finding time in the midst of busy lives at school and at home for reading aloud, and suggests limiting television viewing as one of them. Chapter 6 describes how to read aloud and offers practical suggestions for the classroom setting. Anticipated questions are answered in the next chapter, and Chapter 8 provides a general discussion of what to read as an introduction to the recommended books. In a conversational way the authors present an admirable view of selection criteria.

Some 300 books are presented for reading to children from preschool to eighth grade. Each book entry includes bibliographic information, a descriptive and evaluative annotation, and a suggested listening level, using age ranges for preschoolers, grade level for older children. The entries are arranged alphabetically by title. Indexes list books for school-age children by subject, length, type, and setting. A brief appended list of poetry, with equally brief annotations, completes the offerings. A combined author, title, subject index ends the book.

AUTHORITY

Margaret Mary Kimmel is a professor in the School of Library and Information Science at the University of Pittsburgh and coordinates the Children's Literature Certificate Program, University of Pittsburgh. Elizabeth Segel is co-director of Beginning with Books, an outreach program connected with Pittsburgh's Carnegie Library, and is a review editor of *Children's Literature in Education.*

COMMENT

Many books that are fine silent reading companions are not necessarily successful read-alouds, as librarians are often chagrined to discover after they have started to read one aloud. That is not the case with the books included in this guide, which makes it an excellent selection tool for read-alouds. The annotations will also lend themselves to use in booktalks. The opening chapters will convince parents and teachers, as well as school administrators who need convincing, that read-aloud time in classrooms is well spent. It belongs with the professional collection, alongside Jim Trelease's *The Read-Aloud Handbook* (reviewed in this chapter under General Works). There is very little overlapping of titles in the two books, but the textual matter covers pretty much the same ground.

Rochman, Hazel. *Tales of Love and Terror: Booktalking the Classics, Old and New.* **ALA, 1987. 120 pp. ISBN 0-8389-0463-7.**

PURPOSE

The booktalking techniques and sample booktalks presented here are designed to introduce the art of booktalking and to inspire school library media specialists and library school students to practice it.

CONTENTS

Sharing with others one's pleasure or excitement over a book is at the heart of giving a booktalk. Because the substance of literature is the human condition, books should be offered, not as good medicine, but as good partners in exploring oneself. Therefore, books that raise questions, that bring discomfort, that move deeply while they absorb the reader are the ones worth talking about.

A first step in building one's confidence before giving a booktalk is to share parts of books by reading aloud. Select a scene to read that has dramatic action, a quarrel, a suspenseful or mysterious incident, or a comic situation. Booktalks can be given in a classroom as well as the library. Rochman recommends bringing along a cart full of books and letting the class examine and borrow the books afterward.

A variety of styles are used by booktalkers, and Rochman discusses some, along with different ways of preparing for the talk. She offers some recommendations that are worth heeding, such as to avoid overselling, to build the talk around the basic situation rather than reveal the entire plot, and not to avoid material in a book that might shock or arouse controversy.

Specific books are used as examples throughout this introductory section. The author explores the many possibilities offered by *Wuthering Heights* for thematic approaches, such as love, rage, family conflict, survival, and others, and notes the variety of themes suggested by other titles as well. She demonstrates how to connect several books about a single theme, using war as an example, and shows how poetry can help make graceful transitions from one book to the next.

The second part of the book offers a variety of booktalks built around such themes as animals, survival, love, and terror, among others.

An appendix lists titles by theme and genre. A selected bibliography and an index complete the book.

AUTHORITY

Rochman is assistant editor of the "Books for Young Adults" section of *Booklist*. She has taught English and served as young adult librarian at the University of Chicago laboratory schools.

COMMENT

An enthusiastic and sensitive tour through the booktalking art, this book offers many effective booktalks that hold a promise of bestirring young adults to read.

Spirt, Diana L. *Introducing Bookplots 3: A Book Talk Guide for Use with Readers Ages 8–12.* **Bowker, 1988. 352 pp. ISBN 0-8352-2345-0.**

PURPOSE

Prepared for school and public librarians who work with children in elementary, middle, and junior high schools, this book provides summaries and related material for guiding the reading of some of the best books for this age group.

CONTENTS

This new and expanded version of *Introducing Books* and *Introducing More Books* (both Bowker, 1970; 1978) discusses books published between 1979 and 1986. Focusing on the developmental goals and concerns of children in the middle years between early childhood and adolescence, this booktalking guide features 81 plot summaries and related information, plus a total of 1,225 recommended fiction and nonfiction titles, as well as audiovisual materials, organized in nine chapters: Getting Along in the Family, Making Friends, Developing Values, Understanding Physical and Emotional Problems, Forming a View of the World, Respecting Living Creatures, Understanding Social Problems, Identifying Adult Roles, and Appreciating Books.

In her foreword, Marilyn Berg Iarusso, New York Public Library's assistant coordinator of children's services, emphasizes the importance of guiding children in the middle years to good books. Noting that this is the age when the love of books, so carefully nurtured during early childhood, is easily lost to more convenient pastimes, she urges librarians to continue to offer appropriate books to these children.

Following the preface, a Reading Ladder has been added, which lists titles in each chapter by degree of difficulty. A brief introduction to each chapter comments on the developmental task on which it is focused. A detailed summary, analysis of theme, suggested passages for reading, and related materials are presented for each book.

There is a Directory of Audiovisual Publishers and Distributors, a Biographical Index, a Title-Author-Illustrator Index, and a Subject Index.

AUTHORITY

Spirt was professor of children's books and materials, Palmer School of Library and Information Science, C. W. Post Campus of Long Island University.

COMMENT
This series continues to promote good reading for children by providing assistance to the professionals who guide them. The titles are well selected, and the summaries and related materials are accurate and well chosen.

Thomas, Rebecca L. *Primaryplots: A Book Talk Guide for Use with Readers Ages 4–8*. **Bowker, 1989. 392 pp. ISBN 0-8352-2514-3.**

PURPOSE
Recommended books are described for elementary school librarians and teachers in presenting booktalks for the 4- to 8-year-old age group. Because many of the titles are recent, this guide also helps to familiarize oneself with new early childhood books and their non-print adaptations.

CONTENTS
The 150 highlighted titles were selected from books published between 1983 and 1987 after an examination of several selection tools and recommended lists. The book summaries are organized into eight chapters, each focusing on a theme or subject appropriate to the reading interests of this age group: friends and family, personal identity, common experiences, picture book humor, the past, the world, understanding the illustrator's art, and folk literature.

Each entry includes the level for suggested use as well as reading level, in addition to the bibliographic information. Plot summaries average about 100 to 150 words, followed by a brief exploration of the theme. Suggestions for introducing the book, activities, and discussion ideas follow, and audiovisual materials based on the book are also included. Related titles are annotated briefly, and sources of biographical information about the author and illustrator are an added feature.

The suggested activities emphasize the development of such critical thinking skills as comparing, analyzing, and ordering. Often they lead to further exploration of the library's resources. The discussions of illustrators' contributions to picture books are particularly good, helping children analyze the use of color, art and photography techniques, and other aspects of the art. Mapping, videotaping, writing, drawing, making charts, and exploring the natural environment are among the recommended activities. Correlations with curriculum in science, social studies, art, and language arts are also suggested.

AUTHORITY
Rebecca Thomas is an elementary school librarian at the Boulevard
Elementary School in the Shaker Heights (Ohio) schools.

COMMENT
One might well wonder what could be the point of offering plot
summaries of picture books, which, after all, require very little reading time of librarians. An examination of this guide, however, dis-
pels all doubts of its usefulness. For one thing, it is a timesaver.
Combining a featured book with the recommended related titles
equals a full, ready-made booktalk program. Using the recommended audiovisual version at another time offers program variety.
The activities are thoughtfully developed and will elicit discussion
and thought and promote insight. The analyses of the illustrations
will uncover details often overlooked in a cursory inspection. Most
important, it will help bring the joy of reading and talking about
good books to your school library and classrooms.

Walker, Elinor. *Book Bait: Detailed Notes on Adult Books Popular with
Young People,* **4th ed.** SEE Chapter 8, Selection Guides and Resources.

ADDITIONAL READINGS

American Storytelling Series. Wilson, 1986. 8 videocassettes, color/VHS/Hi-Fi,
with viewer's guides, approx. 30 min. each. Included in the set are stories
adapted from classic literature, Native American myths, and folktales
from other lands. Each volume includes two or three storytellers using
varying styles and some musical accompaniment. Some of the tellings
seem overly dramatic, perhaps the effect of the television medium.

Bader, Barbara. *American Picturebooks: From Noah's Ark to the Beast Within.*
New York: Macmillan, 1976. 615 pp. ISBN 0-02-708080-3. Covering
books produced from the early twentieth century up to the late 1960s,
Barbara Bader provides historical perspective and discusses individual
artists, social change, publishers, and various types of styles and techniques in this well-illustrated critical study.

Butler, Francelia, and Richard Rotert, eds. *Triumphs of the Spirit in Children's
Literature.* Library Professional, 1986. 26 pp. ISBN 0-208-02111-6. Essays on such authors as Hans Christian Andersen, Robert Cormier, Judy
Blume, Madeleine L'Engle, and Maurice Sendak illustrate the spiritual
effects of their work and demonstrate the influence of literature on the
emotional lives of readers.

Egoff, Sheila. *Thursday's Child: Trends and Patterns in Contemporary Children's Literature.* ALA, 1981. 340 pp. ISBN 0-8389-0327-4. A survey of the development of children's literature from the "golden age" until today. *Thursday's Child* examines such contemporary genres as realistic fiction, fantasy, science fiction, and historical fiction. Poetry, picture books, and English translations of European books are also discussed.

Greene, Ellin, and George Shannon. *Storytelling: A Selected Annotated Bibliography.* Garland, 1986. 125 pp. An overview of storytelling in American libraries introduces the annotated entries, which cover history, selection aids, and storytelling techniques. Entries number 250 and cover 1890 to the present.

Huck, Charlotte S. *Children's Literature in the Elementary School.* 3rd rev. ed. Holt, Rinehart & Winston, 1979. 785 pp. ISBN 0-03-046086-7. While in some need of updating, this standard text considers the uses of children's literature in the classroom within a framework of child development and educational research.

Lukens, Rebecca J. *A Critical Handbook of Children's Literature.* 2nd ed. Scott, Foresman, 1982. 264 pp. ISBN 0-673-15504-1. This textbook for students of children's literature focuses on critical methods and standards, examining such elements as theme, setting, plot, and character. Standards for evaluating poetry and nonfiction are also discussed, and samples from the literature illustrate the author's observations.

Rosenberg, Betty. *Genreflecting: A Guide to Reading Interests in Genre Fiction.* 2nd ed. Libraries Unlimited, 1986. 298 pp. ISBN 0-87287-530-X. Defining the genres and identifying their characteristics, *Genreflecting* also discusses authors. Grouped by type and subject, the genres include westerns, thrillers, romance, and horror fiction.

Wilson's instruction and demonstration videos of storytelling by Caroline Feller Bauer and booktalking by Joni Bodart are considerably more successful than Wilson's *American Storytelling Series* (see p. 260).

Booktalking with Joni Bodart. Wilson, 1986. videocassette, color/VHS/HiFi, with viewer's guide, 28 min. ISBN 0-8242-0740-8. How to create and present booktalks are demonstrated by Bodart and colleagues Larry Rakow and Jacqueline Brown Woody. The talks are lively and well received, and offer a variety of styles, books, and approaches.

Storytelling with Caroline Feller Bauer. Wilson, 1986. videocassette, color/VHS/HiFi, with viewer's guide, 28 min. ISBN 0-8242-0740-8. Combining voice-over instruction with storytelling before a live audience, Bauer demonstrates how captivating storytelling can be. She discusses how to find and learn stories, how to involve the audience and use props, and how to find a style and use voice and gesture effectively.

12
Serving Special Learners

While library services to the blind were begun just before the turn of the century, people with other disabilities had to wait much longer for libraries to respond to their special needs. In recent years schools have been prompted to address the needs of disabled children by the passage of the Education for All Handicapped Children Act (P.L. 94-142) in 1975, and supplemented by the Education Amendments of 1978. While many severely disabled children remained in self-contained classrooms, others with milder disabilities were now placed in mainstream classes. Whatever their placement, children with physical, emotional, and learning disabilities are an acknowledged responsibility of school library media programs.

This chapter is designed to help school library media specialists meet their own information needs so that they might better serve the needs of the disabled population in their schools. Included here are some background readings on many types of disabilities and their effects on learning. Particular attention is given to children with learning disabilities because they make up such a large part of the disabled population. Gifted children have special educational needs as well, and they are discussed in the two books by Corinne Clendening and Ruth Ann Davies. Clearly, books about people with disabilities should be provided in the school library collection for the information and personal needs of disabled children in the school. But it is equally important to provide them for nondisabled children, to assist them in the formation of wholesome values and positive attitudes about the disabled. The selection guides reviewed here will help library professionals to achieve these goals.

Baker, D. Philip, and David R. Bender. *Library Media Programs and the Special Learner.* **Library Professional, 1981. 384 pp. ISBN 0-208-01846-8 (pap.).**

PURPOSE

The conviction that the mandates to schools given by P.L. 94-142 offer opportunities to school library media programs to reach beyond their traditional instructional purposes and extend services to disabled learners has prompted Baker and Bender's exploration of how school library media specialists may address this challenge. They have identified exemplary special programs and analyzed some of the factors in their positive impact.

CONTENTS

The significance for school library media specialists of the Education for All Handicapped Children Act of 1975 (P.L. 94-142) is the object of attentive and extensive scrutiny here. Special learners, who had heretofore been taught in groups separate from their non-disabled peers, were now to be placed into the least restrictive environment in which they might function successfully. As a result, many now are in the educational mainstream. Individualized educational plans designed to provide learning opportunities tailored to their needs are being used to help them overcome obstacles to learning imposed by their disabilities.

The possible responses to the new demands placed on the school library media program can range from indifference to alarm to enthusiasm. That the authors advocate what is the only desirable one, a caring commitment to meeting the learning needs of these special young people, should go without saying. They have, in fact supplied a host of telling arguments for that response, first in a lengthy introduction and then in their discussions about the legal and historical precedents for P.L. 94-142 and on teaching the special learner.

The major part of the book consists of descriptions of exemplary programs of various kinds. In the first of these sections, the authors describe 14 state, regional, and district programs and networks designed to assist teachers and learners by providing materials and/or staff development programs. Included in these descriptions are the various centers' goals and objectives and those qualities that conferred exemplary status.

A chapter headed "The Learning Disabled and Mentally Retarded" is actually broader in scope than the title would imply, as it discusses physically disabled and emotionally disturbed populations as well. A public library program is included among the eight described in this section. "Learning disabled" is a term with very specific applications, and in actuality, none of the programs described in this section is specifically geared to provide services for this group.

The following chapter describes five programs for gifted and talented students, one of them being the Lewis Research Center, operated by NASA, in Cleveland, Ohio. It offers resources, public awareness programs, and access to gifted and talented learners, as well as their teachers and, in fact, the general public. With 10,000 visitors a month, this program is not exactly typical of a library media program for gifted youngsters in a school setting. Of the others, two reflect school system approaches to educational services to this group, and only two actually describe real in-school programs, one in an elementary school and the other in grades 9 and 10.

Appendixes supplement the book's contents as follows: Appendix I is a listing of associations and organizations that provide services and information related to special learners; Appendix II lists 20 "Selected Special Education/Learning Disabilities Programs," each of which identifies the target population and contact person, and describes the project, not necessarily related to school library media programs; Appendix III defines and clarifies P.L. 94-142; and Appendix IV gives the site observers and sites and outlines the criteria that were used for evaluation. An index completes the book.

AUTHORITY

D. Philip Baker is coordinator of instructional media programs for the Stamford, Connecticut, schools, a past president of the American Association of School Librarians (AASL), and author of *School and Public Library Media Programs for Children and Young Adults* (1977). David R. Bender has been executive director of the Special Libraries Association and is the author of *Learning Resources and the Instructional Program in Community Colleges* (1980).

COMMENT

Baker and Bender combine exuberance and sensitivity in their discursive treatment of the subject. To do the right thing can be more difficult than to know what is the right thing to do, as they point out. School librarians who want to know what are the right things to do need an authoritative and practical guide to school media services for youngsters with learning disabilities. Clear, precise, and concise descriptions of the various types of handicapping conditions are required; suggestions for appropriate media center services need to be outlined; Individualized Education Programs (IEPs) must be defined and examples presented; specific learning needs must be identified; and applicable hardware and software listed or at least described. This book may change attitudes toward helping disabled young people, but it does not provide the intellectual tools required to assist these children in the school library media center.

Baskin, Barbara H., and Karen H. Harris. *More Notes from a Different Drummer: A Guide to Juvenile Fiction Portraying the Disabled.* SEE Chapter 8, Selection Guides and Resources.

Clendening, Corinne P., and Ruth Ann Davies. *Challenging the Gifted: Curriculum Enrichment and Acceleration Models.* **Bowker, 1983. 482 pp. ISBN 0-8352-1682-9.**

PURPOSE

This follow-up to the authors' *Creating Programs for the Gifted* (reviewed in this chapter) offers librarians and teachers a combination of the basic steps of designing and carrying out instructional programs for the gifted and model programs of varying length and subject matter.

CONTENTS

Part I includes the basics of program design and implementation. Included in its two chapters are guidelines for program goals, curriculum planning and strategies, accompanied by checklists and guidelines.

Part II is the major section of the book and presents the model programs, for grades K–12, which are of unusual breadth and depth. This extensive scope provides opportunities for choice: The teacher may select portions, adapt for grade level or the amount of time available, and students may choose options for independent study. The models provide goals and objectives, checklists, instructional strategies, handouts, and a multiplicity of resources, both print and nonprint. Several of these courses of study are based on textbooks, parts of which are reproduced. Others use guides or manuals. Model 7, for example, reproduces an article from *The World Book Encyclopedia,* "How to Do Research" (Vol. 22, 1982 ed.), and uses it as a learning resource for students studying that unit, *Independent Study.*

Occasionally, worthwhile strategies are overlooked, and some questionable ones included. Model 4, *Exploring the United States,* for example, includes a unit on the westward movement, but there is little on the rich folklore of these times and events, such as cowboy ballads and tall tales. Authors like Scott O'Dell and Jack London and their works are introduced via filmstrips. Why not have gifted children read *Island of the Blue Dolphins* or *The Call of the Wild* instead of viewing abridgments of them? And surely, gifted learners can be asked to explore the reasons why people were uprooting themselves and moving their families and possessions to an unknown wilderness, and to note the courage that it took.

Such criticisms, aside, however, this book brings together a variety of approaches to teaching gifted children ranging in grade levels from kindergarten to twelfth grade and adds a wealth of resources and teaching tools. Added to the text are a directory of producers, publishers and distributors and an index. The table of contents directs the user to locations of various checklists, examples, handouts, and bibliographies.

AUTHORITY

Clendening and Davies have experienced many years of teaching and preparing curriculum for gifted children of all ages. They have conducted workshops and served as consultants in the United States and Canada and both are writers in the field of education.

COMMENT

The models are useful starting points for developing programs of instruction for gifted children. Viewing these models with a critical eye, the experienced librarian will know where to add or substitute. Less experienced librarians will find in them ready-made practical approaches to providing challenges and resources for the gifted learners in their schools.

Clendening, Corinne P., and Ruth Ann Davies. *Creating Programs for the Gifted: A Guide for Teachers, Librarians, and Students*. Bowker, 1980. 574 pp. ISBN 0-8352-1265-3.

PURPOSE

That gifted and talented children are as much in need of specially designed educational programs as are children with physical, emotional, or other learning handicaps is the basic premise of this book. A guide for all who are concerned about and involved in the education of gifted children—teachers, librarians, school administrators and board members, and parents—it is designed to help in initiating new programs or improving existing ones.

CONTENTS

Education programs for gifted and talented children received a boost in 1975 with the passage of P.L. 94-142, the Education for All Handicapped Children Act, which guarantees a free and *appropriate* public education to all exceptional children. This was followed by P.L. 95-561, Education Amendments of 1978, which provides state and local educational agencies with financial assistance for the development and implementation of programs to meet the special educational needs of gifted children.

How can these special children be identified? What are their needs, generally and individually? How can their special abilities and talents be encouraged and nurtured? These questions are explored in the opening chapters of the book, which also describes strategies for program design and various types of programs for the gifted that may be developed. The book then presents model state guidelines (Pennsylvania) and a model district program (North Hills School District) whose curriculum goals and strategies focus on critical thinking skills, independent learning, and the development of communication skills.

The role of the school library in the acquisition of these skills and in the emphasis on individualization of instruction is clearly delineated. The model programs on every grade level reflect the importance of school library involvement in every aspect of teaching these children. These models are adaptable, with objectives and strategies of widespread applicability.

Throughout are references to the seminal works in educational theory and particularly in the education of gifted and talented children. A bibliography of these is provided. Of equal value are the appendixes, which include the text of the Marland report, *Education of the Gifted and Talented,* fact sheets, testing instruments, information resources, and directories. Figures, tables, checklists, and examples are listed in the table of contents. An index is provided.

AUTHORITY

Clendening and Davies have experienced many years of teaching and preparing curriculum for gifted children of all ages. They have conducted workshops and served as consultants in the United States and Canada and both are writers in the field of education.

COMMENT

The imperative to educate gifted children in accordance with their special needs and traits is clearly set forth here, and the role of the school library media center in supporting this enterprise is a vital one. The program models that are presented are exemplary, and their having been field-tested adds to their credibility. With its

267

wealth of information, resources, and practical guidance, this book remains a valuable resource in the education of the gifted.

Cruickshank, William M., et al. *Learning Disabilities: The Struggle from Adolescence toward Adulthood.* **Syracuse Univ. Press, 1980. 285 pp. ISBN 0-8156-2221-X.**

PURPOSE

Written for teachers and parents of learning disabled youngsters, this book sets out to develop understanding and recognition of learning disabilities so that they can detect behavioral clues and identify environmental and organic causes. It presents recommendations for school programs that will meet the cognitive and affective needs of these special adolescents.

CONTENTS

Using the case histories of five young men, Cruickshank and his co-authors, William Morse and Jeannie Johns, trace the observation and diagnosis of their learning and behavioral problems and follow up the results of a clinical teaching program with interviews conducted many years later. The interviews are preceded by a section called "Adolescence as a Time of Life," a brief but discerning look at adolescence and the particular difficulties faced by learning disabled young people. The interviews themselves offer insight into the lives and thoughts of these young people, and the influence of the clinical teaching program on their development and ability to cope.

The final section puts learning disabilities into a school context. What does it feel like for a learning disabled youngster to encounter life in a high school? What does he look like to others? How can the school meet his needs? Can education meet the challenge? The authors provide some perceptive and humane answers.

AUTHORITY

Cruickshank is a prominent psychologist whose work in special education is well known to educators.

COMMENT

This treatment of learning disabilities in adolescence is a sympathetic introduction to the subject, and offers practical recommendations that junior and senior high schools may implement. It combines a humane concern and empathy for troubled adolescents with the results of years of research and often effective treatment. While there are no specific tie-ins to school library media programs, librarians who read the book may infer for themselves ways in which they may fulfill a role in the provision of sound educational assistance for these youngsters, particularly those with reading disabilities.

Friedberg, Joan Brest, et al. *Accept Me as I Am: Best Books of Juvenile Nonfiction on Impairments and Disabilities.* **Bowker, 1985. 363 pp. ISBN 0-8352-1974-7.**

PURPOSE

For use by parents, teachers, counselors, and young people, this annotated bibliography seeks to provide sources of accurate information and understanding about physical, emotional, and mental disabilities and the stories of real people who have been affected by them.

CONTENTS

In preparing this selective guide, Friedberg and co-authors June B. Mullins and Adelaide Weir Sukiennik sought out nonfiction books that foster positive attitudes of openness and tolerance toward the disabled and that demonstrate to nondisabled and disabled people alike that people can lead constructive lives in spite of their disabilities. Some 300 titles have been subdivided according to type of disability and, within each type, are arranged alphabetically by author. The books cited are biographies and autobiographies and factual explanations of particular disabilities. Those that were chosen avoid the use of stereotypes in language, attitude, or representation. Citations include reading level and disability, followed by a summary of the book's contents and a critical analysis.

Introductory chapters set the tone of the selections. Chapter 1 explains why the authors limited their selections to nonfiction: "[It] has the power to say to its audience: 'This is what really *is* out there' " (p. 1). Chapter 2 describes changes in attitudes toward disabilities, along with the language that describes them. Chapter 3 discusses how printed sources view disabilities, and includes descriptions of stereotypes and guidelines for evaluating the language used and the attitudes expressed. The final introductory chapter, Chapter 4, discusses current trends and patterns in books of this type: in the subject matter, types, and themes, and who writes and reads them. The book is rounded out with a Professional Bibliography, Author Index, Title Index, and Subject Index.

AUTHORITY

Friedberg is co-director of Beginning with Books, a family literacy program, in Pittsburgh.

The authors' attitudes toward disabilities are perhaps best expressed in the title they have chosen for their book. Their no-nonsense approach, devoid of sentimentality and critical of excess, both of scorn and of pity, is what their subject merits. Their selection of books reflects their attitudes well. The summaries and analyses of the books are clear, forceful, and thorough, ranging in length from a short paragraph to a page or more. Location of books by type (biography, explanation, memoir) would have been simplified by further subdivision.

Leonard, Phyllis B. *Choose, Use, Enjoy, Share: Library Media Skills for the Gifted Child.* **Libraries Unlimited, 1985. 153 pp. ISBN 0-87287-417-6.**

The school library media center should be playing a central role in educating gifted and talented children. This book was designed to demonstrate the media center's potential importance by describing the program implemented in the author's school.

Emphasis on skills and technology in school library media centers, combined with cutbacks in funding, have tended to deemphasize a focus on books and reading. The school library media center is often overlooked by teachers of gifted children, even as they seek for them the exposure to the best in human thought, imagination, and intellect that is provided by great books. With these facts in mind, Leonard has selected books and activities that will bring these youngsters into the library: to Choose materials, Use them proficiently, Enjoy doing it, and Share the results with others—the process exemplified by C.U.E.S.

Associating the hierarchy of library skills with the important teaching strategies models that have emerged in the past decade, Leonard urges library media specialists to get involved in teaching the higher order skills as part of the media center's instructional program. An ensuing chapter dwells on grouping and setting rules for the group. It is followed by suggestions for exploring language and literature via the media center's resources.

Ventures into language begin with an exploration of its sources and structure and include various kinds of wordplay and storytelling. Books that will aid in this effort are discussed and listed, including easy books for the youngest. A voyage through classification and learning about scientists is precipitated by a discussion of *Harriet the Spy* (Harper & Row, 1964). Suggestions for nurturing curiosity follow, along with a list of reference materials, ranging from *The Concise Columbia Encyclopedia* (Columbia Univ. Press, 1983) to *You Can't Eat Peanuts in Church and Other Little Known Laws* (Doubleday, 1975). "Literary Capers" is a chapter that suggests connections between disparate books, topics, people, and places and advocates a kind of literary hopscotch for linking previously unconnected ideas and facts. A final chapter introduces the computer as an adjunct in the library media center's effort to release the creativity and refine the thought processes of gifted and talented children.

AUTHORITY

Leonard, a library media specialist in a Maryland elementary school, has taught gifted and talented children and has written curriculum materials for them.

COMMENT

Neither guidebook nor manual, this collection of ideas and recommended books for introducing literature and language to gifted and talented children brings a playful spirit to the enterprise and combines it with creativity and joy in the endeavor.

Lerner, Janet. *Learning Disabilities: Theories, Diagnosis, and Teaching Strategies,* 4th ed. Houghton Mifflin, 1985. 581 pp. ISBN 0-395-35775-6.

PURPOSE

The complex subject of learning disabilities is introduced in this basic textbook. It was written to provide a background in the subject for teachers, educational administrators, language pathologists, school psychologists, and other professionals who work with learning disabled youngsters and for those who are preparing for careers in those and related fields.

CONTENTS

The book is composed of four parts, each dealing with a major aspect of learning disabilities. It opens with an overview of the subject, a summary of the growing awareness, concern, and study that contributed to its increasing importance, and the culmination of national concern: P.L. 94-142, the Education for All Handicapped Children Act.

The second part is concerned with procedures used to assess problem learners, the influence of P.L. 94-142 on this process, and the clinical teaching methods used to meet the needs of learning disabled children. Part 3 expands the theoretical framework, dealing with the psychological and medical aspects of learning disabilities and widening the age range with discussion of at-risk preschoolers and adolescents with learning disabilities. The last part surveys specific areas of learning disabilities: motor and perceptual problems; oral, writing, and reading disabilities; disabilities in mathematics; and the social and emotional malaise that often accompanies learning disabilities.

A brief look at promising new developments is followed by several appendixes: a case study, an introduction to the concepts and vocabulary of phonics, a list of tests, a directory of publishers of tests and other materials, and a glossary. The bibliography, while inclusive, is without subdivisions, making it difficult to locate appropriate sources for a particular subtopic.

AUTHORITY

Lerner has been a teacher of reading and learning disabled children and has taught college and university courses on learning disabilities. The advice and comments of both colleagues and students have been incorporated into this outcome of her work.

COMMENT

"Learning disabled" is a label that has been applied to close to 2 million children in the United States, almost 5 percent of the school population in 1984, and these figures continue to rise. School library media centers, dedicated as they are to serving the needs of all the children in their schools, have a role to play in helping to meet these children's needs. The clarity and objectivity that Lerner has brought to her writing on this subject will update the knowledge required by all school librarians and especially those who work with learning disabled children. *Learning Disabilities* is an effective introduction to the subject.

LiBretto, Ellen V. *High/Low Handbook: Books, Materials, and Services for the Problem Reader,* **2nd ed. Bowker, 1985. 264 pp. ISBN 0-8352-2133-4.**

PURPOSE

Written for those who work with reluctant and/or disabled readers, this handbook not only provides an annotated list of appropriate titles but also describes ways of meeting the needs of these young people and lists resources for locating materials and services.

CONTENTS

Part I presents, from varying perspectives, the problems of getting readable books into the hands of adolescents with reading difficulties. How does a publisher go about developing a series of high/low books? How does a writer use special interests to create readable books for youngsters with reading problems? How does a librarian develop a collection for a special user group in a unique school/jail setting? Who are these disabled adolescent readers, and can they be reached? How effective are sustained silent reading programs in countering disabilities and reluctance to read? Ann Durell, publisher at Dutton; Daniel Cohen, popular writer about the occult; Stephan Likosky, librarian at Spofford, a correctional institution for adolescents, Bronx, New York; Jean Rossman, a reading consultant; and Steven G. Levine, a special education teacher, provide some answers.

Part II of the book deals with selection and evaluation. Julie M. T. Chan describes the use of computers for this population, enumerates selection criteria, recommends a core collection of computer programs, lists sources of reviews, and provides a directory of producers. Judith Goldberger provides a reviewer's perspective on book evaluation, and Patsy Perritt describes how readability formulas are used to determine reading grade levels. LiBretto concludes this section with a description of staff training in selection and evaluation.

In Part III, "The Core Collection," a list of 286 high/low books with descriptive and evaluative annotations is presented, followed by a periodicals list. In a supplementary chapter Leslie Charles, a public librarian who works with youngsters in New York City's vocational schools, describes booktalking, shares her experiences, and offers a supplementary list of titles.

Title and subject indexes conclude the book.

AUTHORITY

Ellen V. LiBretto is young adult consultant at Queens Borough Public Library.

COMMENT

Junior and senior high school librarians will find in this book a variety of useful titles for disabled and reluctant readers. Equally important is the inspiration provided by the dedicated contributors who have found ways in their various professions to combat the growing tide of teenagers' indifference to books and inability to read them.

273

Needham, William L., and Gerald Jahoda. *Improving Library Service to Physically Disabled Persons.* **Libraries Unlimited, 1983. 135 pp. ISBN 0-87287-348-X.**

PURPOSE

Based on research, studies in the field, and personal experience, this book was designed to help librarians in all types of libraries in their efforts to improve services to physically disabled people.

CONTENTS

Library services to people with physical disabilities, those who are blind or visually impaired, deaf or hearing impaired, and those who lack physical mobility, require planning and evaluation. Their informational needs for school, work, and recreation are the same as those of the general population, but they have additional informational needs as well. Information and related books about their disabilities, legal information about governmental responsibilities and their rights, travel information, and information about assisting devices constitute the special information needs of this population.

The means for accessing the available information will, of course, depend on the disability, and architectural, physical, and other barriers may impede access as well. In their introduction Needham and Jahoda describe potential barriers to service and outline and discuss the elements of library service that should be evaluated: awareness and identification of the users, arrangement of facilities, provision of services, nature of resources, presence and attitudes of staff, adequacy of funding, and relations with external resources such as special collections, referral centers, networks, and the like. Checklists are provided to help libraries identify the quality of their response to each of these management aspects and requirements. Each item is based on the elements described above, and is presented as a question, with a response that states the applicable standards and offers additional comments. An initial checklist presents general standards, and separate checklists, including one for school library media centers, supplement it.

A chapter on resources lists and describes organizations, sources for materials, aids, and devices, bibliographic sources, periodicals, and a professional bibliography for further reference. A number of appendixes provide additional assistance, including a sample policy on library services for the physically disabled, a job description for librarians who serve the physically disabled, methods and reference sources on obtaining funding for special projects, information on conducting surveys, standards and legislation, goals for service, and a directory of special libraries for the blind and physically handicapped arranged by state.

AUTHORITY

The authors are faculty members at Florida State University, Tallahassee. They conducted a survey entitled *The Current State of Public Library Service to Physically Handicapped Persons,* a U.S. Office of Education Final Report.

COMMENT

Concise and practical, this book provides the reader with knowledge of evaluation standards to assist in improving library services of all types.

Petrie, Joyce. *Mainstreaming in the Media Center.* Oryx, 1982. 219 pp. ISBN 0-912700-73-4 (pap.).

PURPOSE

One important effect of the Education for All Handicapped Children Act was to increase the number of disabled children who were to be educated in the mainstream. Some modifications of media center programs and environments needed to be made as a result, and this book was written to provide some guidelines for media personnel and the staffs they work with so that they might better meet the needs of mainstreamed children with disabilities.

CONTENTS

School library media centers have a vital role in the education of disabled children not only because they are the information center of the school, but also because they provide so many different forms of communications media. To assist school library media specialists in fulfilling this role, *Mainstreaming in the Media Center* discusses P.L. 94-142 (Education for All Handicapped Children Act), the value of mainstreaming and its implications for the school media center, the purpose and philosophy of the school media center in general education, and characteristics of students with particular disabilities.

The book presents a media center program model, argues for a commitment to mainstreaming, describes the nature of various kinds of disabilities and the special needs resulting from them, and shows how adaptations of specific programs and services and modifications of the physical environment can meet these needs. It offers specific guidelines for staff roles and attitudes, and suggestions for planning library instruction, processing and use of library materials, programming activities, and purchasing of specialized equipment and facilities.

In the form of goal statements, guides are presented to assess the media center program, staff attitudes, the instructional program and its role in enhancing the school's educational program, the collection, and the media center's overall responsiveness to special needs. This is followed by a planning guide for developing newly formulated goals and objectives.

Appropriate resources accompany the various chapters, and a bibliography, a list of organizations, and an index are appended.

COMMENTS

Mainstreaming in the Media Center is a well-organized overview of the responsibilities of the school library media center in educating mainstreamed children who are disabled. Petrie offers solidity and strength in her view of the school library media center's role in the school as a whole and mainstreaming in particular. She demonstrates a keen understanding both of the needs of children who are disabled and of the changes in the media center environment that are necessary to foster their growth and learning.

Polette, Nancy. *The Research Book for Gifted Programs K–8*. SEE Chapter 14, Teaching Library and Information Skills.

That All May Read: Library Service for Blind and Physically Handicapped People. **Library of Congress, 1983. 518 pp.**

PURPOSE

Prepared under the editorship of Frank Kurt Cylke, director of the National Library Service for the Blind and Physically Handicapped (NLS), this book describes the needs of people who are unable to use print materials and tells how those needs are being met currently and have been met in the past.

CONTENTS

In 1897 the Library of Congress opened a reading room for blind people in the local area, which provided some 40 titles, typewriters, writing slates, and other devices. From this small beginning developed a collection of embossed books that circulated nationally and the talking book project that in the 1930s began to provide for national distribution of recorded books and the devices for playing them, without cost to the user. It was not until 1953, however, that children's books became available in braille and recorded form. Soon after, a regional network for library service to the blind emerged, and in 1966, physically handicapped people were included in the service. By 1980, there were 160 participating libraries, and close to 800,000 people had borrowed nearly 17 million items. Among those eligible to use NLS services are the learning disabled, who may apply for the use of talking books.

Part One describes the history of library services for the blind and physically handicapped, the national legislation that made possible the expansion and improvement of these and other services, and the pioneer work of the Library of Congress.

Part Two describes the clientele and the materials they use and identifies the publishers of braille, large type, and recorded books. It also describes the services provided by NLS, beginning with outreach and extending to reference work and the Reader-Transcriber Registry, which matches blind readers with volunteers who are willing to transcribe for them. Music services are also offered, which provide braille and large print scores, books, and magazines about music. Various types of informational recordings about music are also available, as is reference service. This part continues with a discussion of reading aids and devices, state services, and the NLS network.

Part Three describes services to the blind and physically handicapped in school media centers and public and academic libraries. The chapter on school media centers discusses barriers to service, both attitudinal and physical, and describes the nature of the population as well as reading interests, sources of materials, and programs. A chapter deals with training and research toward improving library services for the handicapped and urges further effort in this direction.

The book concludes with chapters that discuss services in other countries and the status of international cooperative efforts in the field. A lengthy and comprehensive bibliography is provided, and an index concludes the book.

AUTHORITY

The book was prepared by NLS staff, and consultants and librarians who work with vision impaired and physically disabled people.

COMMENT

This comprehensive work is an important addition to the literature on library services for the handicapped. It provides an overview of past and present accomplishments, describes materials and devices available for the use of the blind and physically handicapped, and points the way to future achievements in understanding and meeting the needs of this special group of library users.

Thomas, Carol H., and James L. Thomas, eds. *Meeting the Needs of the Handicapped: A Resource for Teachers and Librarians.* **Oryx, 1980. 479 pp. ISBN 0-912700-54-8.**

PURPOSE

Articles with ideas, techniques, and programs for developing the potential of children with various disabilities are collected here for the use of school administrators, teachers, and library media specialists.

CONTENTS

Children of all ages, and with many kinds of disabilities, are the subject of this resource for school professionals. The book is organized into seven parts, each dealing with a specific type of disability, except for the first and last. Each section includes introductory comments and several articles on various aspects of its subject.

Part 1 offers an article about the Education for All Handicapped Children Act (P.L. 94-142) and Section 504 of the Vocational Rehabilitation Act Amendments of 1973. In question and answer format the authors discuss the provisions of this legislation and their implications for educational services, civil rights of the handicapped, and other issues. A second article discusses provisions of additional legislation for opportunities for vocational training for young people with disabilities. The potential for library service to special children is the subject of a third article, which insists on their right to be served as part of the school population, and describes the difference in these children's lives that the library media center program has made.

Three of the articles in Part 2, devoted to mentally retarded children, are about library services to this group, one in which listening skills are taught through storytelling and reading aloud, a second discussing cooperative planning between librarian and teachers of mentally retarded junior high school students, and a third describing a toy library designed for the developmentally disabled. Children's learning disabilities are the subject of Part 3, which includes articles about the use of talking books for teaching children how to read, the use of bibliotherapy with learning disabled adolescents, and the use of films for meeting the affective needs of learning disabled children. Annotated lists of films are included.

Part 4 provides articles about emotionally disturbed children and adolescents, and includes a description of a school designed to promote self-esteem, another on autistic children, and three of special interest to school library media specialists: on creative dramatics, poetry therapy, and filmmaking. Children with hearing impairments are the subject of Part 5, which offers articles about public library story hours for the deaf, the use of photography to develop communication skills, and the use of recent silent films to educate hearing impaired children about personal health, love, ecology, and other subjects.

Students with visual disabilities and orthopedic impairments are discussed in Part 6, which includes articles about programs in art and music, language arts and math for the visually handicapped, and juvenile fiction about the orthopedically disabled. Part 7 offers articles about prevocational and vocational programs for young people with disabilities.

A bibliography for further professional reading also includes audiovisual materials for use with children with various disabilities. The appendixes include information on materials selection, with a separate list of criteria; a directory of producers of materials for special children; and organizations and publications about the handicapped.

AUTHORITY

Carol Thomas and James Thomas have edited several books published by Oryx, among them *Academic Library Facilities and Services for the Handicapped* (1981), *Bilingual Special Education Resource Guide* (1982), and *Directory of College Facilities and Services for the Disabled,* 2nd ed. (1986). The articles are written by teachers, librarians, consultants, administrators, and college faculty members with expertise in the various areas of special education programs.

COMMENT

An anthology of this kind always leaves some blank spots where one would have liked to find information and a sequence of thought. The editors, however, have done a fine job of fitting the pieces together, and the ideas and programs described in the articles are readily adaptable to individual situations.

Velleman, Ruth A. *Serving Physically Disabled People: An Information Handbook for All Libraries.* **Bowker, 1979. 392 pp. ISBN 0-8352-1167-3.**

PURPOSE

Librarians who work with physically disabled people, students preparing to work as librarians and/or teachers, and students of rehabilitation counseling will find in this book guidance toward an understanding of the information needs of this group and the professional's role in meeting them, as well as familiarity with available resources, both human and informational.

CONTENTS

In 1979, when this book was written, some 8 million children and 30 million adults were counted among the disabled. In its first part, Velleman provides the background information that is needed for an understanding of societal attitudes toward the disabled, their attitudes about themselves and others, and the physical and attitudinal barriers that separate the disabled from access to opportunities that the nondisabled take for granted.

Physically disabled people include the deaf, blind, and those with loss of various physical functions due to disease or accident. These include people with missing limbs, arthritis, congenitally curved joints, cerebral palsy, cystic fibrosis, hemophilia, multiple sclerosis, muscular dystrophy, paraplegia and quadriplegia, and spina bifida, among others. The disabilities are enumerated and described, with information provided about their nature and effects.

Library services are described in separate sections, each of which discusses the different types of libraries and the kinds of services they can provide. In Part II, six chapters discuss public libraries and such matters as legal benefits and civil rights of the disabled, the informational context of meeting their needs, and the design requirements for removal of physical barriers to the use of library facilities. The special needs of, and services available to, blind and deaf patrons are described. Special equipment and their sources and a core collection of reference materials, periodicals, and directories complete the part.

Three chapters in Part III are devoted to the special rehabilitation library. Librarians have been recently added to the team whose goal is to help the disabled person achieve maximum self-sufficiency. Librarians in this role provide information sources to patrons and the professionals who work with them. The history, philosophy, and current scene in rehabilitation facilities are presented here and a model rehabilitation library is described.

School and university libraries are treated in Part IV, which begins with a history of special education, including information about teacher preparation, legislation affecting the disabled, the role and services of library programs for disabled children in the mainstream and in special programs, research programs, and advocacy and information organizations, such as the Council for Exceptional Children. A core reference collection for special education provides professional resources for teachers and others who work with these children, and includes directories, catalogs, and bibliographies, medical and psychological sources, and materials for parents, among other resources.

Appendixes include professional and volunteer agencies, government offices and agencies, rehabilitation and independent living centers, special education resource centers, and sources for aids and equipment. A detailed index concludes the book.

AUTHORITY
Velleman's many years of service as library media center director in a school and rehabilitation center for physically disabled young people and adults provided the experiential background for this book.

COMMENT
Well-organized, informative, and thoroughly professional best describe this book. While special education programs may have changed some in the ten years since its publication, the comprehensive coverage it provides of a long neglected area of library service continues to be valuable. The core collections will, however, need updating.

Wise, Bernice Kemler. *Teaching Materials for the Learning Disabled: A Selected List for Grades 6–12*. SEE Chapter 8, Selection Guides and Resources.

Educating the Library User

13
The Library Media Center and the Curriculum

Beyond the need to plan a viable library and information skills curriculum for educating young people, an additional responsibility has evolved for school library media specialists. Implicit in the concept of resource-based teaching that David Loertscher has introduced in his "Taxonomy" is the involvement of the school library media specialist in curriculum planning for many subjects taught in the school. Going beyond textbooks and workbooks, this involvement brings into the curriculum the resources of the library and makes them a part of the learning process. The search for information is not only the basis of learning library and information skills; it is also part of learning subject matter and provides additional opportunity for learning and practicing critical reading and thinking skills.

A number of publications in this chapter are based on this premise or refer to it. As far back as 1971, Dewey Chambers recognized this, and his *Children's Literature in the Curriculum* is included here as a reference point. Also published that year, *Teaching and Media* by Vernon Gerlach and Donald Ely deals with media as an essential resource in a systems approach to teaching. The advent of on-line searching and other computer capabilities has further extended these concepts, as discussed in other books reviewed in this chapter.

Books about other curriculum imperatives that are not necessarily related to these concepts are also cited here. Among the areas they deal with are bilingual and multiethnic studies, and the Holocaust. Other issues that might bear curriculum consideration are included in Chapter 17, "Issues in School Library Media Services,"

including AIDS and child abuse. Additional sources, briefly annotated, will be found at the end of this chapter.

Allen, Adela Artola, ed. *Library Services for Hispanic Children: A Guide for Public and School Librarians.* **Oryx, 1987.
201 pp. ISBN 0-89774-371-7 (pap.).**

PURPOSE

As librarians and teachers respond to the increasing demand for
library services and books for Hispanic children that reflect their
cultural heritage, the need for evaluation and selection aids has
become evident. This book offers the tools to help librarians provide long overdue library services and materials to this growing
population.

CONTENTS

Part I begins with an overview of library services to Hispanics from
a historical perspective, one that has been considerably hindered by
a lack of documentation before 1970. In that year a three-day workshop brought together some 70 public and school librarians in the
Southwest to consider ways of bringing to Hispanic children library
services that would incorporate Hispanic values and a bilingual approach. Bilingual legislation and affirmative action policies have
added to the impetus, and encouraged the entry and promotion of
Hispanic librarians into middle management positions. Cataloging,
subject access, and selection criteria are among the areas that have
needed special attention. Despite the demonstrated need, a decline
in concern and funding has endangered the continuing provision of
quality library services to this population.

Another article deals with issues of learning style and bilingual-
ism within the context of social and cultural orientation. Preconcep-
tions and stereotypes notwithstanding, an approach to understanding individual children and their lives demonstrates that many
factors influence Hispanic children's intellectual development, that
their language and culture do not impede academic success, and
that it is in the classroom that success is determined.

Part II presents some of the issues involved in providing library
services to this group. For librarians to function successfully in a
bilingual setting, it is vital to be aware of the degrees of the mixture of
Spanish and English in the children's language abilities and how
proficient they are in either or both languages. Such factors as vocabulary, syntax, listening skill, oral language proficiency, and when and
in what language reading was introduced will influence success and

determine the kinds of materials that will best meet needs. The most important attitudinal qualities needed by professionals are commitment, agreement on goals and objectives, and adequate resources. Intellectual requirements are an understanding of Hispanic culture, familiarity with materials sources, an acquaintanceship with the literature, and the vagaries of publishing practices in Hispanic countries. Note, for example, that children will better understand the Castilian Spanish used in books published in Spain than the Spanish of a Latin American country different from their own country of origin. An appendix lists and annotates general sources of information on Spanish-language books for children.

Strategies for getting children involved in reading literature and a resource list are provided. Also presented are Spanish equivalents of library terms and procedures, and vocabulary for encouraging cooperation and responsibility, for motivating students, and for developing library skills. A summary of Dewey classes is also given in Spanish.

Part III presents several annotated lists, including recommended English-language books about Hispanics for children, recommended recent children's books in Spanish, bilingual nonprint materials, selected software for Spanish-speaking children, information sources for librarians on library services for Hispanics, sources for reviews and for information about specific Hispanic countries, and a directory of publishers and distributors of Spanish-language materials. An index completes the book.

AUTHORITY

Allen is head of the Language, Reading, and Culture Division of the College of Education, University of Arizona, Tucson. Contributors include librarians, administrators, and faculty members of universities and other institutions that serve and are otherwise involved with Hispanic youth, literature, language, and culture.

COMMENT

This guide brings a rich mix of knowledge, understanding, and access to resources that will help librarians and teachers in their quest to enrich and educate Spanish-speaking children using their own language and literature, and English-speaking children as well, in the cultural heritage of their friends and neighbors who speak Spanish.

Ambert, Alba N., and Sarah E. Melendez. *Bilingual Education: A Sourcebook*. Garland, 1985. 340 pp. ISBN 0-8240-9055-1.

PURPOSE

Primarily a bibliographic guide to the professional literature, this book also provides information about some of the major issues in bilingual education, with a strongly stated bias in its favor.

CONTENTS

The book is divided into 11 chapters, each of which includes an introduction to the subject followed by a list of references and an annotated bibliography. Topics covered include model programs in bilingual education, legal issues and legislation, English as a second language (ESL), assessment, reading, bilingual special and vocational education, program evaluation, parental involvement, teachers and teacher training, and antibilingualism.

The introduction notes that 23 million residents in the United States speak a language other than English at home, of whom 11.1 million are Spanish speaking. The authors argue that many bilingual programs existed throughout U.S. history until World War I, when the spirit of nationalism and isolationism determined that English was to be the dominant language of instruction and assimilation a major goal in American education. The 1970s and 1980s saw the litigation and legislation that brought bilingual and ESL instruction into the nation's classrooms, but not without opposition.

COMMENT

The literature in favor of bilingual education is presented in a well-organized fashion, and the introductory comments are cogently argued. The reader, however, will not receive an evenhanded view of this still controversial subject.

American Foundation for AIDS Research (AmFAR). *Learning AIDS: An Information Resource Directory,* **2nd ed.** SEE Chapter 8, Selection Guides and Resources.

Banks, James A. *Teaching Strategies for Ethnic Studies,* **4th ed. Allyn & Bacon, 1987. 555 pp. ISBN 0-205-10344-8 (pap.).**

PURPOSE

Written for teachers and education students, this book also provides background for school librarians on a curriculum in ethnic studies. In an America that has become increasingly aware of the diversity of its people, this content can be integrated into the curriculum of the school.

CONTENTS

The idea of America as a melting pot, where ethnic groups and immigrants give up their cultural identity and merge with the mainstream, is no longer valid, in the author's view. Ethnicity persists, he states, because of prejudice and discrimination, because of the continuing stream of new immigrants, and because continuing ties to a cultural heritage fulfill human needs.

To help young people understand the cultural diversity that exists in American society today, "[t]he total school curriculum should be transformed" (p. 11). The ethnic studies curriculum has been developed to promote understanding and respect for the many cultural groups that have contributed to national growth, and to provide for improved educational opportunities and self-awareness of all cultural groups. This curriculum is interdisciplinary, centered on higher-level concepts, and is values-oriented. It utilizes children's books to an important degree, and provides excellent bibliographies for each of the ethnic groups covered, both for teachers and for students.

Study units have been written for the largest groups, Native Americans and Afro-Americans, European Americans, Hispanic Americans, and Asian Americans, and their major subgroups receive separate treatment. Each unit includes the concepts to be emphasized, recommended strategies, and materials. A time chart and historical summary of each group's experience in America are presented along with other important factual information.

A final chapter explains how to combine key concepts with their related disciplines, how to prepare objectives, and how to evaluate results. Appendixes include a chronology of key events of ethnic groups in American history, a list of nonprint materials, 20 classic books in ethnic literature, the Carter G. Woodson Award books, and an evaluation checklist. A detailed index completes the work.

AUTHORITY

James Banks, of the University of Washington, has written extensively about multicultural education, and his colleague, Spencer Shaw, who prepared the bibliographies, is known to many school librarians as a master storyteller and children's services specialist.

COMMENT

Although written for classroom teachers, this book is commended to school librarians for several reasons: it provides guidelines and a framework for implementing a multiethnic curriculum; its annotated bibliographies present excellent sources for collection development; its overviews of ethnic groups' histories in America present the facts in concise and convenient form; and many of the suggested activities lend themselves to book discussions, research, and other library adaptations. Proactive librarians may wish to try leading the way toward providing ethnic studies in their schools.

Bradley, Leo H. *Curriculum Leadership and Development Handbook*. Prentice Hall, 1985. 158 pp. ISBN 0-13-196056-3.

PURPOSE

Written primarily for curriculum leaders, that is, directors of curriculum and instruction, principals, and district level curriculum coordinators, this book offers guidelines and practical assistance also to teachers, media specialists, and others who participate in curriculum planning.

CONTENTS

The school curriculum has two major functions: It is the backbone of instruction, providing direction for teachers and supervisors, and it facilitates change in instruction, when goals and objectives are modified and other strategies introduced. Planning curriculum, as described here, is a group decision-making process, initiated and led by the curriculum administrator.

The book begins with a discussion of the importance of curriculum, the curriculum leader's role in its planning and implementation, and the requirements for effective performance in that role. The curriculum leader is a generalist and is not required to have expertise in content; rather, his or her expertise lies in the process of planning, developing, implementing, and evaluating. Where teachers participate in curriculum planning, it is their subject expertise that is called on for providing content.

The process involves deciding on a philosophy, determining goals and objectives for the content area, preparing a scope and sequence, deciding on resources and strategies, and determining methods of evaluating progress. Bradley explains the steps in completing these tasks, establishes guidelines, and provides sample forms and statements that readers may adapt.

Subsequent chapters are devoted to defining the tasks of the curriculum leader, clarifying the various elements in making decisions about the curriculum, and describing styles of leadership and the human needs that a leader must be aware of and plan to fulfill. These needs are arranged in a hierarchical pattern, and their importance in facilitating the planning process is discussed. Each of these needs is defined and their implications for curriculum leadership discussed. Concluding chapters talk about the premises that under-lie curriculum change and the major aspects of planning for change, and the indicators of successful leadership in curriculum development.

A number of sample forms, charts, and worksheets are scattered throughout the chapters where they are relevant, and footnotes accompany most of the chapters. An index concludes the book.

AUTHORITY
Bradley is the assistant superintendent for curriculum and instruction at the Clermont County Board of Education in Batavia, Ohio, and adjunct professor of educational administration at the University of Cincinnati. He has had many years of experience as a teacher and administrator.

COMMENT
The importance of library media specialists' participation in curriculum planning and development has been emphasized in countless books about their role in the school and in implementing its curriculum. Those who agree with that assessment will become participants in the curriculum development process. This book will help them play a leading role as goals and objectives are defined and strategies for their accomplishment are worked out. Those who are effective leaders will assure a central place for the school library media program in implementing the curriculum of every subject in whose planning they are involved.

Chambers, Dewey W. *Children's Literature in the Curriculum.* Rand McNally, 1971, o.p. 227 pp.

PURPOSE
Writing for elementary school teachers and consultants and students of elementary education, the author was an early advocate of the integration of children's literature with every subject in the school curriculum.

CONTENTS
Chambers derides the tradition of allowing children to read books at their desks after they have completed their workbooks and other class assignments on the grounds that this practice diminishes the importance of reading and of children's literature. In the first section, Chambers discusses the role of literature in the elementary school curriculum, comparing reading programs using basal read-

ers and those providing for individualized reading. He suggests that features of both be combined, leaving to teachers the development of an actual curriculum.

In the several sections Chambers explores ways of incorporating children's literature in all aspects of the curriculum, demonstrating how social studies learning can be enhanced by the use of factual books, biographies, and fiction. In the elementary science program books are used to encourage research and experimentation, for checking facts, and for pursuing science hobbies. He suggests ways of utilizing books to foster appreciation of the arts, to help in the formation of good taste in literature as well, and to develop oral and writing skills. Illustrations in picture books help develop an under-standing of what makes for good art; poetry collections, stories that inspire creative drama, and folk literature all provide the substance for encouraging skill in reading critically.

Many values and positive qualities are nurtured by good chil-dren's literature, as school librarians are certainly aware. Children gain from their literature a greater depth of understanding about their fellow human beings, be they peers, parents, siblings, or oth-ers. Books help expand cultural horizons, promote a sense of re-sponsibility, and instill a respect for other cultures, genders, and ethnic groups. They stimulate the imagination and help nurture creative talent. The author demonstrates enthusiastically how this can be accomplished.

In a final chapter on special issues, Chambers discusses the impor-tance of selection, and reminds his readers that books that have won awards, or that have shiny covers and special gimmicks, are not necessarily those that will be best for young readers. He heartily disdains abridged or rewritten versions of classics, and is not too fond of the traditional book report either.

Suggested readings follow many chapters, and a bibliography and an index conclude the book.

AUTHORITY

Chambers has been an elementary school teacher for ten years and a supervisor of teacher interns after that.

COMMENT

Chambers has provided an enthusiastic rationale for integrating children's literature with many curricular areas, and has shown a fine understanding of the uses of good books for children. His work was a precursor of the view that permeates Bernice Cullinan and her co-authors' much more extensive and expanded treatment of the same theme in *Literature and the Child,* which appeared ten years later (for a review, see Chapter 11, "Reading Guidance and Motivation" under Children's Literature).

Clendening, Corinne P., and Ruth Ann Davies. *Challenging the Gifted: Curriculum Enrichment and Acceleration Models.* SEE Chapter 12, Serving Special Learners.

Clendening, Corinne P., and Ruth Ann Davies. *Creating Programs for the Gifted: A Guide for Teachers, Librarians, and Students.* SEE Chapter 12, Serving Special Learners.

Davies, Ruth Ann. *The School Library Media Program: Instructional Force for Excellence,* **3rd ed. Bowker, 1979. 580 pp. ISBN 0-8352-1244-0.**

PURPOSE

To set the school library in its proper context as a powerful force for excellence in education, Davies has drawn on a multiplicity of sources. She fleshes out this philosophical framework with practical illustrations of the librarian-teacher partnership in action, which cannot fail to enlarge the understanding of all educators.

CONTENTS

Writing at a time when the nation's educational system was at a low point in public approval, Davies begins with a discussion of the nation's disenchantment with its schools, then places public education in perspective, describing present goals and principles and premises for the future. Focusing on the school library as an innovative force in promoting excellence in education, she asserts that the school library media specialist is responsible for creating a humane environment, satisfying a multiplicity of student needs, and providing a variety of learning experiences. The rest of the book is an elaboration of this theme.

The weakness of a textbook-centered curriculum was described in the Harvard Report (*General Education in a Free Society,* 1945) and quoted by Davies. It states that the weakness of textbooks as learning instruments is that they present a summary of what is to be learned rather than the experience of learning itself. Students mistake this summation for the substance, perhaps memorize it, but never really go through the learning steps that will bring them knowledge that a genuine learning experience will offer.

The school library media center, however, can engage students by providing them with the substance of learning. This alternative to teaching by textbook was recognized as early as 1578, when an ordinance was passed in England that schools should include "a library and gallerie . . . furnished with all manner of books, mappes, spheres, instruments of astronomye and all other things apperteyninge to learning." The author details the progress from that point to the joint American Association of School Librarians (AASL)/Association for Educational Communications and Technology (AECT) standards, published in 1975, and presents some illustrative case studies.

The next chapter asserts the necessity for schools to individualize, humanize, and personalize instruction and nurture creativity and, by implication, underscores the role of the school library in fostering this approach. It is not the strength of the media collection that will turn the trick, however, but rather the ability of the school library media specialist to infuse energy and leadership into the educational program, working with teachers and students to facilitate and enhance learning opportunities.

How library media specialists function in their various roles, as teachers, as instructional technologists, and as managers of curriculum support, is detailed in the next chapters. Here, the author provides a generous supply of checklists, examples, and goals, along with descriptions of a typical day in an elementary and secondary school library in exhausting detail.

Specific details are also provided in succeeding chapters, which portray the library's supportive relationship in the teaching of English, social studies, science and math, the humanities, and developmental skills. These are followed by a chapter on evaluating the school library media program, which supplies the tools for evaluation: checklists on the media program, its staff, resources, organization, and utilization. Included also is a checklist of criteria for excellence. *Illinois Standards for School Media Programs* (1972) is also included, providing a benchmark for evaluation.

In the final chapters the competencies and functions of the district supervisor of school media programs are delineated, with emphasis on the twin roles of leadership and change agent. An epilogue looks to the future. The final third of the book consists of appendixes, definitions of terminology, a comprehensive bibliography, and an index. Included in the appendixes are some basic background readings, sample teaching units, and various guides, guidelines, and statements that supplement the text.

Davies has been influential in her various roles as librarian, library administrator, and educator of librarians, and has written widely about school libraries and school librarianship.

COMMENT
Davies has given voice to the aspirations toward excellence and toward a major role in the education of children that have been experienced by so many school librarians. She has offered a mirror in which practitioners can see themselves in relation to an ideal of performance of their educational role. She has set the school library media center in a position of prominence on the educational scene that can neither be denied nor overlooked. It remains for librarians, teachers, and administrators, experienced, beginning, or preparing for careers, to put the principles into practice.

Eble, Mary M., and Jeanne Renton. *New Dimensions in School Library Media Service.* **Scarecrow, 1988. 468 pp. ISBN 0-8108-2115-X.**

PURPOSE
A presentation of literature study units for grades 7 through 12, this book provides school library media specialists with a recipe for effective librarian-teacher partnerships in offering students a wealth of learning experiences and the motivation to pursue them.

CONTENTS
An entire school, encompassing grades 7 through 12, participates in the Books Unlimited Reading Program at Fairview, Ohio, Junior/Senior High School. A district grant (amount undisclosed) made possible the purchase of multiple copies of books for student use in this successful effort to produce literate graduates with a permanent love of reading. The program, described in careful detail in this book, includes several units of study, and everything that is needed to replicate them is provided. Although the reading and small group discussion of books begin in third grade, the program's implementation in elementary school is not included in order to provide ample description of the secondary school program.

Younger students learn to prepare review cards for each book they read, citing book title, author, type, subject, reference aids for the reader, and an evaluation. In the secondary grades, students concentrate on setting, point of view, and theme. In all grades, informal discussion of the book focuses on the literary elements: plot, character, setting, and theme, the author's style and knowledge of the subject, and the appeal of the book. Students are provided with a discussion outline and annotated bibliographies geared to their developmental level.

Various special projects branch·off from this basic approach to literature. For a photo essay project, used in grades 11 and 12, students select a topic, write an essay developing a theme or thesis, illustrate it with slides or photographs, create or select a musical accompaniment, and coordinate these elements in a multimedia product. A list of provocative topics is provided; a few examples are values in a technological age, the adolescent's search for identity, creation vs. evolution, and peace in our time. An individualized program is offered by Reading Ladders, which provides increasingly sophisticated books about a particular theme, based on the interests and needs of each student. Among the subjects are alienation, death, friendship, love, fantasy, and unforgettable women. Books are recommended by librarian and/or teacher after individual conferences with each student.

A unit on Comparative Literature provides the students with groups of titles with related themes that they will read and compare as to purpose, theme, characterization, and overall literary quality. The classroom teacher provides the grounding in literary criticism, and the librarian provides supplementary guidance, along with the book. Other literature units included are Censorship, The Magic of Film, World Biography, and Two Books and a Theme, in which students select a book and identify its theme and the librarian suggests a companion book. A volunteer Pre-College Reading Program is offered during study hall, when students discuss the selections they have read. The Enchanting World of Children's Literature, The Classic and the Contemporary Novel, Utopian Thought (for gifted students), Book Evaluation by Seniors, and Contemporary Thought (developed in relation to a social studies course on current issues) are also presented.

Perhaps the most satisfying experience, both for students and librarians, is an independent study project offered to eighth grade gifted students. Students who are mature enough to engage in self-directed research plan their own projects, gather and take notes on their materials, prepare an outline, and present their results in a self-determined form. A few of these projects are summarized by the authors, and a list of topics is also presented.

The book concludes with Library Media Information and Research Skills, a section that includes goals and objectives, copies of student handouts, and a scope and sequence for grades K through 12. An index is also provided.

The authors have drawn on many years of experience in the service of literature, learning, students, and teachers, at the Fairview Park Junior/Senior High School, Ohio.

COMMENT
An enormous amount of thought, planning, and preparation has obviously been expended on the programs that the authors have described. Materials handed out to students, bibliographies, goals and objectives, procedures, and questions for discussion are all shared with the reader of this book. The units are adaptable for different grade levels, with some changes in the bibliographies and procedures. If the execution is as good as the preparation was pains-taking and thorough, these courses of study cannot fail to produce literate and thoughtful people.

Eisenberg, Michael B., and Robert E. Berkowitz. *Curriculum Initiative: An Agenda and Strategy for Library Media Programs.* **Ablex, 1988. 180 pp. ISBN 0-89391-486-X.**

PURPOSE
Written for practicing school library media professionals and li-brary school students, this book offers both the concepts that un-derlie the school library's curriculum support role and their practi-cal applications.

CONTENTS
Curriculum and the library have a twofold interrelationship: First, the library offers materials and other resources for implementing curriculum in the subjects taught in the school; second, the library provides an instructional program of its own, teaching students how to use the resources that the library provides. Neither of these func-tions is independent of the other, since the teaching of library and information skills is based on curriculum needs, and in order to use the resources provided for mastery of the various subjects, students must be skilled in search techniques and other library and informa-tion skills.

Eisenberg and Berkowitz focus on the various elements involved in providing a library instructional program within its curriculum support framework. In the first section of the book they discuss their concept of the school library media specialist's changing roles, and describe some of the management aspects of this shift in role. The second section offers a "Six-Stage Strategy" for the implementation of the library's curriculum support role, which is a systematically organized management process. The stages include a review of what currently exists, the definition of goals and objectives, the provision of "support systems," an analysis of available resources and time, the planning phase, and plans and procedures for evaluating progress and accomplishments.

The third section is concerned with information about the curriculum in the school, as well as the curriculum for teaching library and information skills. "Curriculum mapping" is the authors' term for the process of collecting and organizing information about the curriculum, a process that requires the use of a computer with a data base management program. The authors provide a worksheet for preliminary preparation, data base definitions, and some sample curriculum maps. They describe the library's role in providing curriculum support and the curriculum in library and information skills and provide a scope and sequence for teaching these skills. Suggestions are offered for developing unit and lesson plans, and a look to the future is given.

AUTHORITY

Eisenberg is an assistant professor at the School of Information Studies at Syracuse University. He is a frequent speaker at conferences and a trainer and workshop leader. Berkowitz, currently a library media specialist at Wayne Central School District, New York, has worked in both rural and urban schools, and is a co-founder of SCAN, School Library Career Awareness Network, in New York State.

COMMENT

This well-organized presentation of the authors' ideas about curriculum and its many aspects in school library media programs offers a carefully arranged sequence and practical guidance. Their concept of curriculum mapping, however, is another matter. The mere question of available time for school librarians to do the mapping raises doubts about its practicality, to say nothing of its necessity. Nevertheless, this book has some important points to make about the library media center's proper involvement in curriculum, and merits school library media specialists' careful attention.

Eisenberg, Michael B., and Robert E. Berkowitz. *Resource Companion for Curriculum Initiative: An Agenda and Strategy for Library Media Programs.* **Ablex, 1988. 161 pp. ISBN 0-89391-486-X (pap.).**

PURPOSE

This book was intended for use with Eisenberg and Berkowitz's *Curriculum Initiative* (see above) and for the same audience.

CONTENTS

Librarians who are ready for the plunge into curriculum measurement and the other tasks assigned them in *Curriculum Initiative* will find the tools for doing it in this book. Included here are worksheets and masters to assist in the implementation of the strategies conceived by the authors. They are designed to help in gathering information, analyze situations, plan for change, set a course, and evaluate the process and what has been achieved. While the tools the authors provide are linked to the text, they do not follow the text chapter by chapter, but the authors do explain the context in which the tools are to be used. They encourage users to make use of the computer technology that is now available in the innovative ways they suggest.

Their premises are that the school library media center is no longer a passive collection of materials waiting to be used, but an active support service that must reach out to teachers and administrators with programs that serve curriculum goals. To do this, librarians must analyze the curriculum that is taught and meet those needs of teachers and students that their analysis enables them to perceive. The integration of the library media program with the school curriculum will be the inevitable and desired result.

AUTHORITY

Eisenberg is an assistant professor at the School of Information Studies at Syracuse University. He is a frequent speaker at conferences and a trainer and workshop leader. Berkowitz, currently a library media specialist at Wayne Central School District, New York, has worked in both rural and urban schools, and is a co-founder of SCAN, School Library Career Awareness Network, in New York State.

COMMENT

Some useful tools are provided here for information gathering and other tasks required by the authors' agenda. While they require a good deal of time for analysis of the results, they offer a good beginning for the integration the authors rightly urge.

Felsted, Carla Martindell, ed. *Youth and Alcohol Abuse: Readings and Resources.* **Oryx, 1986. 219 pp. ISBN 0-89774-251-6 (pap.).**

This compilation of articles provides information and resources for education professionals, counselors, community leaders, and parents on various aspects of alcohol abuse among young people, using an approach that is somewhere between a popular and a scientific one.

Facts and statistics are provided as background for a comprehensive discussion of the issues that surround teenage drinking. An introductory chapter presents statistical and demographic information and identifies the gradations of drinking behavior. The next chapter poses and answers questions about patterns of teenage drinking.

Section I explores the influences that contribute to teenage drinking and the varying schools of thought about the seriousness of alcohol use, separating occasional consumption of alcoholic beverages from drunken behavior, problem drinking, and alcoholism. Family and social influences are also considered. Identifying, remedying, and preventing alcohol abuse are the subjects of Section II, which provides guidelines on detecting the signals and helping actual or potential abusers. Teaching how to handle alcohol responsibly is the subject of one of the articles in this section, and several statewide efforts are identified and described in another.

Section III considers such special issues as family patterns of alcoholism and the effects of alcohol abuse by parents on their children. The serious problem of drunk driving, especially among teenagers, is addressed in three articles. The first article presents the facts in its opening statement that drunk driving is the single greatest cause of death among 15- to 24-year-olds, and the rate of 45 deaths per 100,000 the highest among all age groups. Additional data are provided in a follow-up article, and the third describes the crusade against drunk driving and its effects. A final article presents resources for promoting sober driving habits.

Section IV provides annotated lists of resources for adults who work with teenagers, for children, and for young adults. Audiovisual and other educational materials are also listed. A directory of agencies and publishers is included, and appendixes offer recommendations on how to refuse a drink, a self-test about alcohol, and excerpts from a 1982 survey of drug abuse. An index concludes the collection.

Felsted is a staff member of the Texas Institute on Alcohol Studies, Austin. Contributors include leading authorities from university faculties and the fields of psychology and social work.

COMMENT

There is a wide range of opinions about teenage alcohol use, from those who accept it as a phenomenon of youth that will be outgrown to others who see it as a fundamental national problem that must be addressed. While the issues are debated, thousands of young people will die in drunk driving accidents, or become problem drinkers or alcoholics. This book offers informed guidance and insight into the issues, and presents information sources that belong in school libraries.

Gerlach, Vernon S., and Donald P. Ely. *Teaching and Media: A Systematic Approach.* Prentice-Hall, 1971. 395 pp. ISBN 0-13-891358-7.

PURPOSE

The elements of teaching are presented in a systematic way, and the use of media is treated as a basic element in the design of instruction. Written for classroom teachers, the book has important applications for library media specialists both in their roles as teachers and as leaders in the use of instructional resources.

CONTENTS

Gerlach and Ely assume that the best teaching is that which is done in a systematic way, beginning with carefully described objectives and ending with evaluation and feedback. Using the book itself as a model of an instructional system, they present objectives for each chapter that the reader may expect to achieve after reading that portion and participating in the exercises that are part of it. A graphic model of a teaching system is presented, and each of its elements is explained and justified.

Since behavioral objectives are considered the most essential element in the design of instruction (all the other elements of the system proceed from the objectives), their preparation receives the most attention. Objectives are defined, analyzed, and classified, and the reader is encouraged to participate in writing and improving them. After proceeding through nine chapters on objectives, the reader is ready to consider the other elements of the system: instructional strategies, organizing groups, allocation of time, allocation of space, selection and use of instructional resources, and evaluation. Particular attention is given to audiovisual media categories, selection, and use. The basic rule for its use is emphasized, that "a medium of instruction must be selected on the basis of its potential for implementing a stated objective."

Diagrams and photographs generously illustrate and explain the various concepts treated in the book, and the practice exercises are effective. Bibliographies and sources for media are also included.

AUTHORITY

The authors are recognized authorities in the design of instructional systems and the use of audiovisual media.

COMMENT

While much of the material may be old hat to practicing library media specialists, this book provides a rational basis for using media in classroom and library. Mastering and applying the elements of instructional design provide a framework for utilizing library resources and a structure for instruction in library and information skills. This effective textbook not only presents a usable system for instruction, it uses it to instruct. Although bibliographies and sources are somewhat outdated, the basic content is still valid, if somewhat lacking in recognition of the book as a prime instructional resource.

Gilbert, Martin. *The Holocaust: A History of the Jews of Europe During the Second World War.* SEE Chapter 17, Issues in School Library Media Services.

Gong, Victor, and Norman Rudnick, eds. *AIDS: Facts and Issues,* **rev. and updated ed.** SEE Chapter 17, Issues in School Library Media Services.

Havlice, Patricia Pate. *Oral History: A Reference Guide and Annotated Bibliography.* SEE Chapter 8, Selection Guides and Resources.

Hirsch, E. D., Jr. *Cultural Literacy: What Every American Needs to Know.* **Houghton Mifflin, 1987. 251 pp. ISBN 0-394-75843-9.**

PURPOSE

Advocating nothing less than a reformulation of the content of American education, Hirsch examines the nature of cultural literacy and demonstrates its importance in laying the foundation on which is built the ability to read and communicate.

CONTENTS

At last! A definitive explanation of why illiteracy in America is continuing to rise, and a sensible theory about what can be done about it. The controversy aroused by this book may have abated, but its challenge to reexamine the causes of illiteracy remains.

According to Hirsch, the possession of a network of information, cultural literacy, is the missing prerequisite to the attainment of literacy. Without the common knowledge that is basic to our culture, children are demonstrably unable to proceed from decoding words to reading with comprehension. Effective communication depends on the assumption that speaker and listener, or writer and reader, possess the common information that provides meaning to their message.

The author's arguments are built on a convincing framework of linguistic studies and experiments, which he cites and explains with clarity and power. If reading skills and critical thinking skills are inoperable without the shared background of a common cultural heritage, it follows that fact, content, information ought to be returned to the curriculum. Once agreement is reached on what this content should be, it remains only for educators to devise the appropriate curriculum changes.

Hirsch proposes a "national vocabulary" list, compiled with his colleagues Joseph Kett and James Trefil, around which a revised curriculum can be built. He states that "[m]ore than one hundred consultants reported agreement on over 90 percent of the items listed," but invites further comments and suggestions. The list includes items of popular culture and folklore as well as literary, historical, and scientific names and terms.

AUTHORITY

Hirsch is William R. Kenan Professor of English at the University of Virginia. Kett and Trefil are professors of history and science, respectively, at the University of Virginia.

COMMENT

While it is hard to imagine a national consensus forming on the contents of Hirsch's list, it is easy to be persuaded of the soundness of his argument. In any case, this book merits the serious attention of all educators, especially those concerned with libraries, which are, after all, the repositories of cultural literacy.

Langhorne, Mary Jo, et al. *Teaching with Computers: A New Menu for the '90s.* Oryx, 1989. 213 pp. ISBN 0-89774-481-0 (pap.).

PURPOSE

Appropriate uses of computers for instruction and management applications for administrators and teachers are the principal concerns discussed here for all school professionals.

CONTENTS

The first phase of computer use in schools occurred as a response to parent demand and a sudden outpouring of newly available funds. The typical reaction to these powerful forces was a rush by school administrators, check in hand, to the nearest computer vendors, and the (usually) subsequent development of courses in computer programming and/or literacy. This initial burst of enthusiasm has resulted in the presence of 2 million computers in the nation's schools, an average of one for each 38 students, according to statistics quoted by the authors, who now suggest some rational planning for proper instructional use of these tools for learning.

The book is organized in three logical sections, the first of which discusses planning and organization for use beginning at the district level. Rather than attempt to devise a computer curriculum, Langhorne, together with co-authors Jean Donham, June Gross, and Denise Rehmke, urges school and district decision makers to plan for computer use as another of the learning tools, albeit a particularly powerful one, available for implementing curriculum design and for administrative purposes. Computer literacy then becomes an intended outgrowth of integration with the curriculum in several subject areas. Software can be selected with these curriculum support purposes in mind and teacher in-service programs will focus on using computers as integral parts of the curriculum. District decision makers can now base hardware and software acquisitions decisions on identified curriculum requirements. Software should be acquired after suitable evaluation, and managed by the school professional whose training and functions are most appropriate to that task, the school library media specialist.

The second section discusses the integration of computers in the curriculum, with chapters on introducing computers in elementary schools, teaching keyboarding and word processing, and introducing data bases in junior high schools. A number of suggestions and observations for teaching these skills are offered; computer hardware needs are outlined and several lesson plans are provided. The teaching of information skills involving computer use, primarily data base searching and including CD-ROM use, are treated, followed by descriptions of computer use in teaching thinking skills and software that is useful for problem-solving practice. Additional discussions examine the integration of computers with curriculum in mathematics, social studies, science, and elective subjects.

The third section discusses administrative uses of computers and trends and issues in instructional computing. Appendixes list relevant periodicals, conferences on new developments, and a small number of consultants in instructional computing. A list of software producers whose products are cited in the book is also provided. An index concludes the book.

AUTHORITY
Mary Jo Langhorne and Denise Rehmke are library media specialists, and Jean Donham is district library media coordinator, all in Iowa City schools; June Gross is library media specialist, St. Louis Park Junior High School, St. Louis, Minnesota.

COMMENT
A sensible approach to the proper utilization of computer technology in schools has been a long time coming, and this reasonable and readable book offers a persuasive and timely perspective on the subject. This excellent plea for sanity in using computers, making them an integral part of curriculum design, should be read by all school library media specialists and then rushed to the principal's office.

Leonard, Phyllis B. *Choose, Use, Enjoy, Share: Library Media Skills for the Gifted Child.* SEE Chapter 12, Serving Special Learners.

Lerner, Janet. *Learning Disabilities: Theories, Diagnosis, and Teaching Strategies,* **4th ed.** SEE Chapter 12, Serving Special Learners.

Levine, Michael P. *How Schools Can Help Combat Student Eating Disorders: Anorexia Nervosa and Bulimia.* **NEA, 1987. 280 pp. ISBN 0-8106-3290-X.**

PURPOSE
The rising incidence of eating disorders among adolescents, particularly girls, suggests a need for those who work with this population not only to learn about it but also find ways of helping to prevent it. While this book is directed primarily at teachers and school mental health professionals, school library media specialists are also a part of this effort.

CONTENTS

Because of the difficulties of curing eating disorders, the attention of mental health professionals is turning to ways of preventing them. Both anorexia nervosa and bulimia are disturbances with cyclical patterns—recurrent episodes of dieting, binging, and purging—and with anorexics, particularly, the cycle is difficult to interrupt.

Many factors contribute to the development of eating disorders. Sociocultural factors contribute to an intense desire to be thin, and the stigma against obesity and the equating of femininity with a thin appearance further create an urge to diet. Among the familial factors are conflict, stress, emotional isolation, history of affective disorders within the family, and a tendency to magnify cultural trends. Among the predisposing factors of individuals themselves are problems with identity, mood variation, depression and impulsiveness, low self-esteem, weight problems, and inflexibility. These and other factors are discussed in the book, which also presents interviews with victims of eating disorders and their parents.

The role of school personnel in preventing the onset or continuance of eating disorders and identifying those in need of further professional help is discussed. Teachers are urged not to involve themselves in attempts at counseling and to examine their own motives and attitudes toward eating disorders before embarking on a teaching program. Signs of anorexia nervosa and bulimia are listed and general principles for teaching and referral are offered. School library media specialists are urged to provide materials for students as well as school professionals, with the warning that materials for students must be examined carefully and borrowers' privacy protected.

Appendixes provide a list of national and regional organizations and clinics and a list of films, books, and pamphlets.

AUTHORITY

Levine is associate professor of psychology at Kenyon College and author of *The Psychology of Eating Disorders: A Lesson Plan for Grades 7–12* (National Anorexic Aid Society, 1983). Consultants in the preparation of this work included leaders in eating disorder organizations, teachers, and psychologists; an advisory panel consisted of teachers, school counselors, and school library media specialists.

COMMENT

The first step in preventing anorexia and bulimia or identifying their victims is to understand these eating disorders. Teachers, counselors, and school library media specialists can begin to help by reading this book.

Loertscher, David V., ed. *Measures of Excellence for School Library Media Centers.* SEE Chapter 5, Evaluating the School Library Media Program.

Loertscher, David V. *Taxonomies of the School Library Media Program.* **Libraries Unlimited, 1988. 336 pp. ISBN 0-87287-662-4.**

PURPOSE

Loertscher has constructed a model and a set of taxonomies of "resource-based teaching" for viewing the curriculum-support role of library media programs in schools. Although this book is primarily for school library media specialists, teachers and school administrators will also find it an instructive experience.

CONTENTS

A taxonomy is a classification scheme; as used here, a model is the graphic representation of a theory and its parts in a unified scheme. Loertscher's taxonomy orders school library media programs in accordance with their involvement in "resource-based teaching." Programs in which there is no involvement in curriculum are at the bottom; the pinnacle is reserved for programs in which the school library media specialist contributes actively to the planning and development of curriculum in school and district.

The model is pictured as a building. At its foundation are three functions: "solid warehousing support," "direct services to teachers and students," and "resource-based teaching." The pillars that support it are the various activities conducted in the center: "reading motivation," "research skills," "information analysis," "technology skills," "cultural literacy," "targeted student groups," and/or other features that make up individual programs. The structure's capstone is the program itself.

The taxonomies relate program and services to the different roles that exist in the school community, and there is one each for the school library media specialist, the teacher, the student, and the principal. A self-evaluation checklist enables individuals to examine their role in relation to the media program. The foundations of the model are considered in succeeding chapters. "Resource-based teaching" derives from a planning partnership of media specialist and teacher, and requires a collection of sufficient depth to support instruction and the achievement of objectives. The planning steps are outlined, and charts, checklists, evaluation methods, and a case study are provided.

Services provided by the library media center are another basic supportive element. They are outlined and described, and methods for evaluating their quality are suggested. "The warehouse" is the third element that supports the edifice, and encompasses the collection, staff, facilities, and technology and the operations needed for their development and maintenance. The warehouse function should not be mistaken for the program, however, as it has been in the past, although it is vital to the successful functioning of the school library media program. Some arcane statistical methods are used to determine the collection's adequacy for meeting curriculum needs, its prime purpose; other elements belonging in this category are analyzed as well.

In the following chapter concepts and examples are presented for fostering various skills, providing reading motivation, working with targeted groups, imparting cultural literacy, and offering other features of a media program. Evaluation methods are suggested. The book's final two chapters present a discussion of other models of school media programs and evaluation methods and instruments that are recommended for use in determining the success of the school media program. Appendixes A and B provide sample state and school district evaluation instruments and self-evaluation systems for appraising services, functions, and collection. Appendix C offers a comprehensive list of additional readings. An index completes the work.

AUTHORITY

Loertscher is senior acquisitions editor for Libraries Unlimited, and is a former professor at the University of Oklahoma Graduate School of Library and Information Studies, Norman, as well as at the University of Arkansas, Fayetteville, and Purdue University, West Lafayette, Indiana.

COMMENT

Loertscher premises his model on the conviction that the school library media program's principal role resides in curriculum support with a librarian-teacher partnership planning instruction together. This new and greater prominence for curriculum planning carries the library program one step farther into the mainstream of instruction, giving it a central place in the school. While there are some flaws that have to be worked out, it is a construct that school library media specialists should study carefully.

Loertscher, David V., and May Lein Ho. *Computerized Collection Development for School Library Media Centers.* **Hi Willow Research, 1986. 180 pp. ISBN 0-931510-19-8.**

PURPOSE

This system for providing ongoing evaluation and development of library media collections using AppleWorks and accompanying template disks is presented as a step-by-step guide for school librarians, and also can be used as a handbook by workshop leaders who are introducing the system.

CONTENTS

The premise that the school library media collection exists for the sole purpose of supporting the school curriculum provides the underlying philosophical framework of the collection development system described in the six chapters of this book. The materials that support recreational reading and related activities are considered part of the reading program in this schema, and everything purchased for the library should have a positive relationship with the curriculum.

It follows, then, that the existing collection should be evaluated for its ability to serve curricular needs, and policies, budgeting, and strategies for improvement should be defined in terms of this purpose. Evaluation of the collection is facilitated by an automated system that employs collection mapping to determine how well each segment of the collection supports curricular needs, and every aspect of collection building becomes part of the total system.

Standards based on the foregoing premise for evaluating collections, budget practices, and acquisition procedures are outlined in the first chapter. Methods of documentation are introduced, and the evidence needed for the evaluation is developed through the use of the computerized system. Chapter 2 presents an overview of computerized collection development. The implementation of the system is phased in over a two-year period, and the components are collection mapping, mapping the collection in depth, the computerized acquisition system, and collection evaluation. These terms are examined in detail and the process for accomplishing each phase is spelled out, with examples provided at each step. The use of the template disks along with AppleWorks to map the collection is introduced, and procedures for evaluating the collection are outlined.

Collection mapping is examined in further detail in Chapter 3, which provides questionnaires for developing data, instructions for creating the map, and ways of using it. Chapter 4 emphasizes the importance of familiarity with the curriculum as the first step in analyzing the collection in curricular terms, and describes how to achieve it. Curriculum and collection are matched as the in-depth mapping proceeds, and acquisitions policies and budget will be determined by the outcome of this process.

Chapter 5 describes the computerized acquisitions system, and demonstrates its use in creating consideration files, preparing purchase orders, and maintaining received files. Chapter 6 is concerned with evaluating the collection, and explores other methods of evaluation than the usual practice of comparing it with national and/or state standards.

This innovative approach suggests that evaluation be based on an examination of the collection's adequacy in meeting the curricular needs of the school, and collection mapping is an important tool for doing this. It turns the focus of evaluation away from comparing the school collection with an outside standard to the actual library's potential for support for the school's curriculum. Collection mapping provides for the presentation of evidence that the collection is either able to meet the school's needs, or requires some fine tuning, or is in need of an infusion of additional funding if learning is to proceed with proper media center support.

The six appendixes provide transparency masters, forms, and other materials that extend the usefulness of each chapter, and each is numbered to correspond with the chapter to which it is tied.

AUTHORITY

Loertscher is senior acquisitions editor for Libraries Unlimited, and is a former professor at the University of Oklahoma Graduate School of Library and Information Studies, Norman, as well as at the University of Arkansas, Fayetteville, and Purdue University, West Lafayette, Indiana. Ho is author of *AppleWorks for School Librarians* (see the review in Chapter 1).

COMMENT

The system described in this book is the culmination of years of collaboration and testing in the 80 school library media centers in which it has been piloted. Its applicability in other schools will be determined by the amount of time available to school library media specialists for its implementation and the willingness of the teaching staff to devote the time required in filling out the questionnaires and otherwise contributing to its execution. Its concepts and innovative perspective, however, cannot be ignored, and all school library media specialists should become familiar with them.

Malinowsky, H. Robert, and Gerald J. Perry, eds. *AIDS Information Sourcebook*, **2nd ed.** SEE Chapter 8, Selection Guides and Resources.

Miller, Inabeth. *Microcomputers in School Library Media Centers.* SEE Chapter 16, Technology and Automation.

Parisi, Lynn S., and Virginia L. Jones. *Directory of Online Databases and CD-ROM Resources for High Schools.* ABC-Clio, 1988. 136 pp. ISBN 0-87436-515-5.

PURPOSE

An introduction to the use of commercial data bases for high school library media specialists, teachers, and students, this book describes the data bases that can be used for research in the subjects of science, social studies, English, and more general topics.

CONTENTS

An introductory chapter explains data bases and their place in high school education, identifies equipment necessary for accessing data bases, discusses telecommunications networks, describes and compares data base vendors and CD-ROM, and explains how to use the book and the criteria used for selecting the data bases.

Each of the major subjects and the recommended data bases that relate to them are taken up in the next three chapters. A table is provided for each subject, which indicates the data base format and the information it supplies (bibliographic only, bibliographic plus abstract, full text, directories, or statistics) and which curriculum area it is most suitable for.

Social studies data bases are U.S. government, world geography and culture, economics, law, and similar subjects; 25 related data bases are listed in all. The text that follows provides a general description of each data base and indicates the scope, the user for whom it is intended, its suitability as a research tool in high school, frequency of updating, and vendor(s) that provide access. Seventeen data bases are provided for the sciences, which include health, general science, earth science, biology, and so forth. Descriptions offer the same kinds of information as in social studies data bases. For the curricula in English: American, English, and world literature, composition, speech, journalism, and the like, there are ten data bases. For general subject areas there are general data bases, such as Academic American Encyclopedia, available on CD-ROM as well as through several vendors, Magazine Index, and similarly general sources, as well as Who's Who and National College Databank. A glossary, data base index, and subject index complete the book.

Parisi is a staff associate and project director of the Social Science Education Consortium in Boulder, Colorado, and the compiler of *Creative Role-Playing Exercises in Science and Technology* (1986). Jones is social studies specialist with the Colorado Department of Education.

High school library media specialists who have been searching data bases with and/or for their students will probably be familiar with these data bases. For those librarians who are new to data base searching and for students who are getting started, this book provides an informative introduction.

Pennsylvania State Library. *Integrating Information-Management Skills: A Process for Incorporating Library Media Skills into Content Areas.* **Pennsylvania Department of Education, 1988. 66 pp.**

This manual for integrating the teaching of "information-management" skills with the school curriculum provides instruction and direction for school library media specialists.

The imperative for transforming the teaching of library media skills from isolated lessons in using library tools to integrated units that enhance subject teaching and learning is stated in the opening page of this curriculum guide. The challenge presented to library media specialists is to plan for all teaching of skills in a curriculum context rather than waiting for opportunities to arise. School media specialists and teachers, working in concert with the blessing and support of the school administrator, are charged with designing such integrated instruction.

"Information-management skills" is the term used in this guide to describe what traditionally has been called library or library media skills. Among the nine objectives of attaining these skills are understanding the library environment and its behavior requirements, locating materials efficiently, using critical thinking and problem-solving skills, knowing and using the steps involved in doing research, and so on. The critical thinking skills that are enhanced in the process are listed here as well.

A rationale and planning methods are presented, and results of research are outlined to provide the theoretical basis. The necessity for administrator and teacher involvement is discussed and their roles described. Librarians begin by developing an "information-management" scope and sequence list, which includes goal statements and the skills that will be taught. Having identified the skills, librarians can now plan for their incorporation in the various subjects taught in the schools.

The guide continues by supplying step-by-step applications of the principles of curriculum writing: determining the format, deciding on content, defining the process of instruction, selecting resources, determining evaluation methods, and providing for staff development. The resultant curriculum, reflecting the collaborative efforts of teachers and library media specialists, will enhance the school library media center's curriculum support role and provide for instructional improvement.

AUTHORITY

This guide was prepared by a committee of school library media specialists and supervisors under the direction of the Pennsylvania Department of Education, Doris M. Epler, director of school library media services.

COMMENT

The process for planning for the integration of library skills with subject content areas has been analyzed and presented in a logical and detailed sequence, with a carefully considered and persuasive rationale. School library media specialists are urged to follow these steps so that they can better contribute to effective teaching and learning, and demonstrate the essential role of the school library media center in the instructional program of their schools.

Reed, Arthea J. S. *Reaching Adolescents: The Young Adult Book and the School.* SEE Chapter 11, Reading Guidance and Motivation— Young Adult Literature.

Shawn, Karen. *The End of Innocence: Anne Frank and the Holocaust.* **International Center for Holocaust Studies, Anti-Defamation League of B'nai B'rith, 1989. 102 pp.**

PURPOSE

An increasing number of schools are including units on the Holocaust in English, social studies, or world history classes. *The End of Innocence* was designed to serve as a curriculum for the study of the Holocaust in junior and senior high schools.

CONTENTS

Although it is called a curriculum, this book is actually more of a sourcebook, providing excerpts from Anne Frank's diary and from the memoirs of survivors and witnesses of the war against the Jews conducted by the Nazis before and during World War II. It presents a narrative of events that led up to the Holocaust and continues with eyewitness accounts and dramatizations of actual events that punctuate the descriptive material.

Five lessons are included, and marginal notes in the text refer to appended readings. Italicized words, names, and events are explained in notes at the bottom of the page. Questions at the end of each lesson will prompt discussion and suggest further areas for study and research. There are 23 additional readings in the appendix, including poems, dramatic readings, a short story, charts and a map, and excerpts from the personal narratives and accounts of survivors and witnesses. Photographs accompany the text.

The first lesson is a brief summary of events beginning in 1918 and continuing until 1933. Lesson 2 covers the period from 1933 to 1940, describing the Nuremberg laws and the events of *Kristallnacht,* the "night of broken glass" which announced Nazi intentions to an unheeding world. Lesson 3 uses Anne Frank's words as a point of departure for considering some of the events between 1940 and 1943, and raises some questions about the diary excerpts and the outside world. The year of 1944 is the subject of lesson 4, which focuses on events in Holland; 1944 to the present are explored in the final lesson. The fate of Anne and her family are revealed, and the lasting effects of the Holocaust on humankind's view of itself are examined.

Among other matters touched on in this account are Jewish resistance to the Nazis, the heroism of many non-Jews who risked their own lives to try to save them, and the all-consuming question of the human capacity for evil.

A chronology of key events, a glossary, and a briefly annotated list of books, films, and videos complete the book.

AUTHORITY

Karen Shawn is an English teacher at Lawrence Middle School, New York. She completed a summer study course on the Holocaust at

Yad Vashem in Israel. Currently, she is developing a Holocaust curriculum for her doctoral dissertation at New York University.

COMMENT

With all the books, documentaries, dramas, and studies of the Holocaust that have been produced, it is still an event that eludes comprehension. There are no answers supplied in this book, but a good many questions that need to be raised and discussed. Focusing on Anne Frank and a limited number of passages from other accounts allows young readers to perceive the human dimensions of this tragedy that statistics tend to obscure. The selections were chosen with sensitivity to young readers' reactions, and do not exceed their ability to handle them.

Two other sources available from the International Center for Holocaust Studies are *The Holocaust: Catalog of Publications and Audio-Visual Materials, 1988–1990,* biennial. This annotated bibliography, with age level designations, includes books and materials from several publishers and producers that are available from the Center. The other source is Judith Herschlag Muffs, ed., *The Holocaust in Books and Films: A Selected Annotated List,* 3rd ed., 1986.

Smith, Jane Bandy. *Library Media Center Programs for Middle Schools: A Curriculum-Based Approach.* SEE Chapter 9, The School Library Media Program.

Smith, Jane Bandy, ed. *School Library Media Annual,* **Vol. 6.** SEE Chapter 17, Issues in School Library Media Services.

Stanford, Barbara Dodds, and Karima Amin. *Black Literature for High School Students.* SEE Chapter 11, Reading Guidance and Motivation—Young Adult Literature.

Van Vliet, Lucille W. *Media Skills for Middle Schools: Strategies for Library Media Specialists and Teachers.* SEE Chapter 14, Teaching Library and Information Skills.

ADDITIONAL READINGS

Clay, Katherine, ed. *The School Administrator's Resource Guide.* Oryx, 1988. 104 pp. ISBN 0-89774-446-2. This annotated list of books, articles, and reports, drawn mostly from ERIC, covers publications about such subjects as staff development, supervision, and evaluation and management practices.

Goodman, Kenneth. *What's Whole in Whole Language?* Heinemann Educational Books, 1986. 80 pp. ISBN 0-435-08254-X (pap.). The basis, features, and future of the whole language movement are discussed, with examples of whole language programs that are already at work and suggestions for building new programs.

Jweid, Rosann, and Margaret Rizzo. *The Library-Classroom Partnership: Teaching Library Media Skills in Middle and Junior High Schools.* Scarecrow, 1988. 246 pp. ISBN 0-8108-2191-5. To assist the school library media specialist-teacher instructional team, this book offers lessons in coordinating library and information skills with classroom learning in 11 disciplines, providing objectives, strategies, lists of materials and activities, as well as tests and bibliographies.

Newman, Judith M., ed. *Whole Language: Theory in Use.* Heinemann Educational Books, 1985. 204 pp. ISBN 0-435-08244-2 (pap.). Putting into practice the whole language theory is demonstrated through teachers' own experiences.

Troutner, Joanne. *The Media Specialist, the Microcomputer and the Curriculum,* 2nd ed. Libraries Unlimited, 1988. ca.175 pp. ISBN 0-87287-610-1. Keeping up with the expansion of microcomputer use in schools, this edition promises information on the integration of computer use with the curriculum, and discusses CD-ROM, telecommunications, and interactive video. Discussions of computer literacy and ethics are also included, as are a glossary, bibliographies, and funding sources.

Turner, Philip M., ed. *A Casebook for Helping Teachers Teach.* Libraries Unlimited, 1988. 150 pp. ISBN 0-87287-615-2. Designed to accompany Turner's earlier *Helping Teachers Teach* (see below), this collection of case studies illustrates the school library media specialist's involvement in assisting teachers.

Turner, Philip M. *Helping Teachers Teach: A School Library Media Specialist's Role.* Libraries Unlimited, 1985. 259 pp. ISBN 0-87287-456-7. The school library media specialist's support role for instruction is carried beyond supplying media for teachers to providing them with help in planning instruction. This book offers practical suggestions for media specialists involved in the design of instruction.

14
Teaching Library and Information Skills

The futility of trying to teach library media and information skills in isolation from the real world of curricular, social, and personal needs has been demonstrated in classrooms and libraries across the nation for many years. Unless children have a need for using library tools, they will not learn how to use them. The school curriculum provides the natural context for teaching and learning the location, use, and selection of library materials appropriate to a particular purpose.

From building reference skills in upper elementary grades to developing search strategies and using on-line data bases in secondary schools, the emphasis of information skills instruction is placed squarely on a curriculum framework. This is the frame of reference, to varying degrees, of the books included in this chapter. While all grades are covered, the greatest number of books deal with the middle years, followed closely by books about high school learners. Lillian Wehmeyer's *The School Librarian as Educator* is the most comprehensive, depicting the school library media specialist as a teacher, not only of young people but of teachers as well. Teaching the research process is adeptly presented by Carol Kuhlthau, who is as much concerned with students' affective responses to preparing a research paper as the cognitive outcomes. On-line searching is the subject of no less than three books reviewed here.

Breivik, Patricia Senn. *Planning the Library Instruction Program.* ALA, 1982. 146 pp. ISBN 0-8389-0358-4 (pap.).

Although academic librarians are the principal audience for this book, it will provide guidance for high school librarians as well, in planning and conducting instruction in library skills, not on a one-to-one basis but in a group (class) setting.

CONTENTS

Library instruction is a key activity in school library media centers, and an increasingly important one in academic libraries. Equipping young people with the ability to learn independently in libraries, and working with the school faculty to provide opportunities for library instruction within the framework of the curriculum, will secure for the library a heightened prominence as a vital contributor to the educational enterprise. Following this rationale, Breivik describes the nature of effective instruction: It is reality-based, provides for active involvement, allows for individual differences and learning styles, recognizes the importance of process as well as content, and is conducted in a nonthreatening environment.

The political elements of planning for a library instructional program involve securing a positive attitude on the part of the library staff, administrators, faculty, and students. How this may be accomplished is discussed in Chapter 2. In describing the elements of the planning process, in the next chapters, Breivik takes a more leisurely route than one might think possible, let alone desirable, providing a planning schedule that will consume several months. The important points are that goals and objectives and target groups are to be identified and matched with each other, priorities established, and then program objectives may be set in order.

Good library instruction is based on responding to students' perceived needs, rather than consisting of explanations of library tools. It is focused on the students, their learning style and speed, and it recognizes the potential need for a variety of learning experiences. It provides activities for students to do, rather than lectures for them to listen to. It is flexible, and it provides for evaluation.

Preparing instructional objectives determines what is to be learned and under what conditions, and out of them grow methods of instruction, the content, and the means for evaluating whether and how effectively the skills have been learned. The author explains objectives, describes various methodologies, discusses content and timing, and explores evaluation in terms of, first, what must be evaluated— what the learner has achieved, effectiveness of the learning experiences, the quality of instruction, affective outcomes, and the program as a whole—and, second, what evaluation methods may be used.

Afforded the luxury of a sizable staff, an academic library may designate a head of library instruction and a standing committee on instruction. All of these roles will most likely be shared among the staff of most school library media centers. The joint responsibilities include planning, developing positive relationships within and outside the library media center, implementing evaluation procedures, and keeping records of instructional activities. Chapters on the library's public relations program and its instructional mission conclude the book. Accomplishing that mission requires "conviction, commitment, and cooperation" (p. 132), qualities that define the effective practitioner whatever the mission might be.

An appendix provides guidelines for bibliographic instruction. Footnotes and an index complete the book.

AUTHORITY
Breivik is director of the Auraria Library at the University of Colorado, Denver. She has served as dean of library services at Sangamon State University, Springfield, Illinois.

COMMENT
Although it is geared toward college librarians, this book has enough meat to satisfy the teaching appetites of high school library media specialists as well. The author's theory that involving students and staff in a productive instructional program will ensure that they will be transformed into advocates of the library and allies in the struggle to keep it viable may be encouraging, but that is not where the decision-making power resides, outside of academe. While it is always helpful to have allies, school library media specialists should not make the mistake of believing that that is all they need. They must still aim their persuasive efforts directly at school and district administrators and school boards, all of whom make the real decisions and control the budget.

Epler, Doris M. *Online Searching Goes to School.* **Oryx, 1989. 149 pp. ISBN 0-89774-546-9 (pap.).**

PURPOSE
According to research quoted by the author, although schools nationwide own an average of two to three computers, the average expenditure for on-line searching per school is only $17. This tends to indicate that many schools have not yet joined the on-line searching revolution in school library services. A strong advocate of its use in schools, Epler presents approaches to the integration of on-line

searching into the curriculum and the programs of school library media centers.

CONTENTS

Although on-line and CD-ROM data bases have not replaced traditional printed sources of information, and will not in the foreseeable future, their value as an adjunct to the print collection is clear. To the end user, they offer speed of access to a multiplicity of information resources that supplement books and periodicals. For the school library media specialist who uses them to provide expanded information services, they offer a new image of the professional who is comfortable with new technology and who has thrown off the burdensome characterization as the stamper and warehouser of books. Of greatest importance, however, is the need to give students the ability to function proficiently as adult users of on-line information sources. Thus the school librarian must know not only how to search on-line but also how to teach youngsters to do it. *Online Searching Goes to School* introduces school librarians to the concepts, information, sources, and guidelines for introducing on-line searching in their schools. Advantages and disadvantages are discussed, budget and management considerations are presented, and some of the major on-line data bases are described.

The author discusses how to fit on-line searching into the school library media center and its program, and how to involve both the media center staff and the teaching staff in its use. The planning and implementation of an on-line curriculum, the role of networking, and other means for obtaining documents are also explored, and methods of evaluating the on-line search program are described as well. A brief final chapter looks into the future and sees new developments in data storage and retrieval, the need for more in-service training opportunities in this skill for librarians, and an increase in network services and sharing of resources.

An appendix lists products and services and their sources. A bibliography and an index complete the book.

AUTHORITY

Epler is the director of Pennsylvania's Division of School Library Media Services, Department of Education. Under her direction, Pennsylvania's on-line searching network has reached well over 200 members, and a union catalog of the collections of 375 schools is available on compact disk.

COMMENT

The power and the promise of automation technology is to bring information of great variety and abundance into the grasp of students. Although it doesn't teach the skill of on-line searching, this book does suggest ways of taking the first steps toward the use of information technology in school libraries. The value of using this technology exists on several levels: First, it will improve service to library patrons; second, it provides opportunities for increased interaction and collaboration with teaching colleagues; third, it provides an avenue for leadership in a new venture; and finally, it furnishes the chance to establish the library's function as the information center of the school. To miss these opportunities is to risk creating a vacuum that others will rush in to fill.

Hunter, Beverly, and Erica K. Lodish. *Online Searching in the Curriculum: A Teaching Guide for Library/Media Specialists and Teachers.* **ABC-Clio, 1989. 219 pp. ISBN 0-87436-516-3 (pap.).**

PURPOSE

On-line searching as part of the research process that students should be learning in secondary schools is a technique whose time has come. This book was written to help library media specialists and teachers enable students to conduct their own searches of on-line data bases.

CONTENTS

Learning to locate information by searching on-line data bases is only part of the process taught by the examples in this book. Its real import is in their design, which fosters the cooperation of student teams as they work on each project, requires them to analyze, to think critically and creatively, and to organize their information to accomplish a purposeful goal.

Four projects have been carefully worked out: "Interpreting Students' Rights" is a project in government and law. Students are given a case description that they must investigate as if they were lawyers developing a legal brief, searching out precedents in previously adjudicated court cases, finding relevant constitutional provisions, and identifying the conflicting issues in the case. "Creating Historical Exhibits" is a history project, in which students plan a museum exhibit that illustrates a historical "puzzle." In the example used, the subject is Edison's invention of the incandescent light bulb, and the problem is to determine whether he deserved sole credit for its invention. "Designing an Outer Space Habitat" is a science project that encompasses earth science and astronomy. Students must design a life support system for a mission to a planet or satellite in the solar system. Working in teams, they develop an artificial habitat that will protect human life in the environment they have chosen to investigate. "Pollution Task Force" is an environmental studies project with a knowledge of chemistry and biology as its base. Working in teams, students must decide what to do about a steel drum found in a lake near a city, which is filled with an unknown chemical compound. They must identify the compound from the formula printed on its label, examine the policy issues regarding it, prepare a set of recommendations, and develop a presentation for explaining them to the city council.

Each project is worked out in careful detail. Included in the project descriptions are learning objectives and tasks the students will perform, materials required, instructional activities, handouts, forms for analyzing the problem and working out search strategies, lists of data bases suggested for searching, printouts of actual searches, checklists for evaluating search results, worksheets, plans for helping students evaluate, analyze, and synthesize the information they have found, and descriptions of team members' responsibilities.

The final chapter suggests additional projects in science, social studies, and other subjects. Each of these projects includes a brief description and a list of suggested data bases; some also have transparency masters of sample searches. An index concludes the book.

AUTHORITY

Beverly Hunter has been involved with computer literacy and education for over 20 years, and has written over 100 books, articles, and technical reports. Erica Lodish is an educational media generalist at Montgomery Blair High School, Maryland, and has had articles published in computer and education journals.

COMMENT

This masterful presentation for school library media specialists in secondary schools offers some superb examples of how to integrate on-line searching with curriculum in social studies and science and provide for the exercise of a variety of critical thinking skills. All the planning and development and forms and outlines that went into the preparation of these projects have been gathered together in this one source. Even the spiral binding of the book is helpful, permitting easy photocopying of forms and transparency masters. Teachers, computer coordinators, and school administrators will find in this treasury of ideas and applications for on-line searching a revelation of teaching and learning possibilities.

Jay, Hilda L. *Stimulating Student Search: Library Media/ Classroom Teacher Techniques.* **Library Professional, 1983. 176 pp. ISBN 0-208-01936-7.**

PURPOSE

A handbook for school library media specialists and teachers engaged in teaching the search process to secondary school students, this book points the way to improved instruction in how to find, use, organize, and present information.

CONTENTS

Amid the growing recognition that a cooperative planning partnership between subject teachers and the school library media specialist is an essential factor in student achievement not only of skill in using library resources but also of mastering subject material itself, Jay has prescribed some ways of leading students to precisely those accomplishments. Most library media specialists understand that learning search skills occurs when opportunities are provided for practice that stems from curriculum-based needs for information. An important leadership function for them is to influence teacher attitudes toward that understanding and to foster the development of a team approach.

Jay has provided some stimulating ideas for motivating search practice, and they involve the major subject areas. Before getting into these, however, she offers some workable solutions to problems that have plagued many library media specialists, particularly those with limited budgets and consequently limited collections. Details of her collection-stretching ideas can be found in Chapter 2. They involve creative scheduling, changing search project requirements and design, and intradepartmental planning. One of the factors that contribute to teacher resistance to the assignment of research papers is the extra time and work they entail, and Jay has some answers to that problem as well.

The greatest obstacle that students encounter in getting started is often that of choosing a topic, and then facing that great unknown, "Now, where do I begin?" The answer, of course, is in the careful preparation of students for the tasks ahead, and Chapters 3 through 6 detail the helping steps to follow, from selecting and narrowing a topic to understanding various types of filing rules and alphabetizing methods, organizing the project, taking notes, outlining, and diagnostic testing of students' search skills, which are themselves mini search projects.

The suggested search projects are centered primarily on English and American literature and other language arts topics, with a few provided also in social studies, science, and mathematics; a list of search projects in art is also included. Projects involve students in using primary sources, specialized encyclopedias and dictionaries, handbooks, yearbooks, indexes, and other reference sources. The assignments employ some ingenious devices, requiring students to imagine themselves in contemporary situations but planted in earlier historical contexts—for example, you are food editor of a popular women's magazine. Write an article on Queen Elizabeth's state dinner for Sir Francis Drake to celebrate the destruction of the Spanish Armada. Such devices can be adapted to a number of subject contexts, and most of the projects are equally adaptable.

AUTHORITY
Hilda Jay is former director of the library media program at Ridgefield High School, Connecticut.

COMMENT
Jay's long experience with this kind of instruction has provided her with a keen insight into the problems inherent in using this approach for teaching search skills. She provides some sound advice that will help library media specialists, teachers, and students cope successfully with the difficulties peculiar to their roles. While this book was a forerunner to the concept of total integration of the school library media center program with the curriculum, it does not quite go that far. It does, however, bridge the gap between the passe practice of teaching library skills in isolation from any curriculum context and using curricular and classroom needs as the basis for the learning of search skills.

Jay, M. Ellen. *Motivation and the School Library Media Teacher.* **Library Professional, 1988. 201 pp. ISBN 0-208-02171-X.**

PURPOSE
Jay offers to school library media specialists a variety of practical ideas and projects for motivating learners in the acquisition and practice of library and thinking skills.

CONTENTS
There comes a time in every elementary school library media specialist's life when creative ideas for motivating children to learn runs dry. The author has come to the rescue with a wealth of activities that will spark enthusiasm and create learning opportunities that go beyond the usual location skills and into the realm of reasoning.

Many of the activities are outgrowths of problem situations that arise from unreasonable teacher assignments, unreasonable because they don't take certain limitations into account. Examples are the teacher who assigns to an entire class a book report requiring the reading of fiction published during the 1940s; another who wants a class to read biographies of at least 250 pages about business tycoons of the industrial revolution. Jay has worked out some ingenious solutions that will work, with consultation and compromise. See her chapter on book reports.

Beyond this, however, she has described bulletin boards that not only involve children in acquiring facts but also motivate them to think critically, to work independently, and to develop search skills. She has created activities for schoolwide contests and celebrations of special events. "Thinking Skills of the Month" provides motivation and practice for understanding analogies, grouping, classifying, and other thinking processes. "Writing Spinoffs" suggests some writing and media projects that are built on children's reading, slides, and other experiences. Computer activities include the use of word processing and newsletter production programs, and several thinking skills programs are included, along with descriptions and a bibliography. Puzzles and games round out the offerings.

A final chapter presents several mini-units, based on themes that are expanded in a multidisciplinary way. They can be based on objects, people, and places, they give rise to varied activities, and they provide opportunities for learning both in the media center and in the classroom.

AUTHORITY

M. Ellen Jay is a school library media teacher in the Montgomery County, Maryland, schools. She has written several practical guides for school library media specialists, some with Hilda L. Jay as co-author (see, for example, the next entry).

COMMENT

The activities suggested in this book are not only creative but practical as well. Children love puzzles, games, and contests, and many are provided. The inescapable book reports are made palatable and workable by spreading out the demand for resources over lengthy periods of time. Materials, procedures, and specific examples are provided for all activities. The ideas that are suggested are adaptable and will spark the reader's imagination and creativity to further inventiveness.

Jay, M. Ellen, and Hilda L. Jay. *Building Reference Skills in the Elementary School.* **Library Professional, 1986. 187 pp. ISBN 0-208-02098-5.**

PURPOSE

In order to function successfully in this era of rapid change, students must be equipped to find information for themselves, to analyze and evaluate what they find, and to use it in a thoughtful way. These and other thinking skills are successfully taught when library and information skills are integrated with the curriculum in various subject areas. This book suggests ways of accomplishing this goal in elementary school libraries.

CONTENTS

The opening chapters argue for starting in the early grades to provide students with tools for coping with change, for using library skills instruction to teach thinking and intellectual skills, and to integrate this instruction with subject matter. Activities for teaching the use of various reference sources follow, although many of these depend on children's interests rather than school subjects for teaching search skills. Subject reference works (science encyclopedias, art and music dictionaries, atlases and almanacs) are used in an integrated way, however, and all suggested activities may be adapted easily for use with particular subjects.

Learning how to take notes and then what to do with them is a most difficult task for young researchers. There are excellent suggestions here for teaching these skills, as well as how to recognize relevant facts, how to organize notes, and how to write and revise the final paper. The value of peer conferencing is discussed and its successful use described. A project writing checklist accompanies these chapters, along with suggestions for its use to encourage students to take a step-by-step approach to their research. The checklist can be used as is or adapted to teacher/student requirements, but it is a helpful ingredient.

A bibliography of suggested resources to present to children is inclusive and can also be used as a buying list.

AUTHORITY

Both authors have written books for practical use by school library media specialists. M. Ellen Jay is a school library media teacher in the Montgomery County, Maryland, schools. Hilda Jay is former director of the library media program at Ridgefield High School, Connecticut.

After presenting convincing arguments for integrating instruction in library skills with classroom instruction, the authors proceed to negate their argument by presenting isolated skills in a somewhat improved package. In spite of this flaw, however, the book excels in its treatment of note-taking skills and organization of information and in its advocacy of integrated instruction and teaching of thinking skills in elementary schools. By adapting suggested activities to what is actually being taught in their schools, librarians can put this book to good use.

Kuhlthau, Carol Collier. *School Librarian's Grade-by-Grade Activities Program: A Complete Sequential Skills Plan for Grades K–8.* **Center for Applied Research in Education, 1981. 204 pp. ISBN 0-87628-744-5.**

PURPOSE

Kuhlthau has presented a curriculum for grades K through 8 to "strengthen and revitalize library skills instruction" (p. viii). The book provides a sequence of activities and guidelines for each grade designed to be adaptable to curriculum content.

CONTENTS

A brief introduction provides a rationale and overview of the book's content and organization. This is followed by eight chapters, one for each grade from kindergarten through the sixth and one that combines the seventh and eighth grades. Each includes a description of children's needs and developmental abilities at that grade level, a checklist of skills to be developed, and activities for carrying out the teaching program. Each chapter begins with a brief description of what the children are like at that age, physically, emotionally, and intellectually. This is followed by a few paragraphs of advice on coordinating the library media program with classroom instruction, and then some sections on what skills are covered in the next pages.

The activities are described in detail: the amount of time needed and number of sessions, what materials and preparation are required, and how to proceed with the activity. Where relevant, appropriate titles are suggested. The activities are geared to the development stage of the children for whom they are proposed, and are keyed also to the checklist of library and information skills for that grade. Ideas for follow-up are also presented.

The checklist for each grade includes location and interpretation skills, and each skill is stated in behavioral terms. They are presented in outline form, which simplifies locating particular skills in the list. Like the activities, the skills have been carefully chosen to match the developmental stage of the grade for which they are suggested. They vary in number from 2 location skills in kindergarten to 46 in sixth grade, and each level builds on the previous year's work.

The book is not limited to research skills, but includes activities that will deepen children's understanding of literature and enhance their enjoyment of books. Abilities to evaluate and select suitable materials, to use and produce audiovisual materials, and to analyze and synthesize information are among those that are fostered here.

AUTHORITY

Kuhlthau is currently on the faculty of the School of Communication, Information and Library Studies, Rutgers University. She was also a school library media specialist in elementary and secondary schools.

COMMENT

Library media specialists will appreciate the care with which this book has been made, from the thoughtful organization of its content to the readability of its print and suitability of its format. The content is of equal quality: All the ingredients needed for the development of a superior instructional program in library and information skills have been brought together and blended with skill and intelligence. It is well organized and comprehensive, and demonstrates how skills can be integrated with subject area assignments.

Kuhlthau, Carol Collier. *Teaching the Library Research Process: A Step-by-Step Program for Secondary School Students.* **Center for Applied Research in Education, 1985. 190 pp. ISBN 0-87628-804-2.**

PURPOSE

Writing a research paper is a complex task for students. Teaching them how to do it and helping them through the process can be an intricate task even for the most experienced of secondary school library media specialists. This book was written to guide the perplexed through the complexities of research, from start to finish.

CONTENT

Kuhlthau has divided the research assignment into seven stages, and each of these is explored in a separate section of the book. Her underlying thesis is that working with students through the process itself, and monitoring their reactions and problems at various phases, are as important as preparing students for the cognitive tasks they will perform. Providing guidance during each step of the process is vital if they are to succeed. Putting this premise to work, Kuhlthau has studied what high school students thought and felt as they moved from one phase to the next, and advocates requiring that researchers keep a journal in which they note what they are thinking and feeling as they work, and a timeline for keeping track of their progress.

Each section of the book provides a title that describes its content, an introduction to the purpose of that phase, an approximation of the time required, materials that will be needed, directions for presenting the activity, and further suggestions. Elements of each activity and the author's comments are highlighted with bold type, and sample handouts that can be duplicated are also provided in each section. A sample flowchart that details each step students will follow in sequence is included.

The phases of research involve the subject teacher along with the school media specialist, and the need for planning together and the roles of each are clearly presented. The phases include presenting the assignment, which is the teacher's task; selecting a topic, which will involve students, teacher, and library media specialist; exploring the information that is available; deciding on a theme or focus; collecting the relevant information and refining and revising the theme, if necessary; preparing the presentation after completing the research, organizing and outlining notes, and preparing bibliography and footnotes; and reexamining the process as a whole, which will include a student-prepared flowchart, conferences, and a summary statement among the concluding activities.

As a result of her previous studies, Kuhlthau has an enlightened awareness of possible student reactions (such as discouragement, frustration, and, in many cases, satisfaction and gratification when the report has been completed), and forewarns the readers of what to expect.

AUTHORITY

Kuhlthau is currently on the faculty of the School of Communication, Information and Library Studies, Rutgers University. She was also a school library media specialist in elementary and secondary schools.

COMMENT

This comprehensive, practical, and informed guide will assist secondary school library media specialists and teachers painlessly through each phase of the research process, one step ahead of the students. It is highly recommended.

Pennsylvania State Library. *Integrating Information-Management Skills: A Process for Incorporating Library Media Skills into Content Areas.* SEE Chapter 13, The Library Media Center and the Curriculum.

Pennsylvania State Library. *Pennsylvania Online: A Curriculum Guide for School Library Media Centers.* **Pennsylvania Department of Education, 1985. 74 pp.**

PURPOSE

To provide students with the skills needed to become lifelong learners includes teaching them to use on-line data bases, to design search strategies, and to understand the role of information in our society. This handbook was prepared as a guide for librarians ready to embark on this new course of instruction.

CONTENTS

Intended for use with high school students, this guide supplies a course framework rather than a ready-to-use set of lessons. Course objectives include understanding the role of information in society, selecting and refining a topic, preparing an annotated bibliography, conducting a manual search, and developing an awareness of on-line searching.

This introductory material is followed by instructional objectives on the various aspects and components of on-line searching. All are presented in chart form, with each objective followed by statements of content, suggested resources, expected levels of achievement, and evaluation procedures. Lesson plans are provided for selected objectives, but the actual methodology is left open to the librarian/ teacher. A second section, on on-line management, offers guidance on such management concerns as budget, vendors, software, security, record keeping, and so forth, as well as references and an annotated bibliography.

Appendixes include a sample budget, record, and search; lists of vendors, networks, and data bases; a glossary; and "quality goals of education."

AUTHORITY

Although no single author has been credited, the list of contributors includes school librarians, library educators, and the director and staff members of the state library's Division of School Library Media Services.

COMMENT

Although the guide promises help for the novice, it would take a very well-informed novice to make proper use of it. Geared primarily for the experienced user of on-line data bases who is committed to teaching youngsters how to search them, this guide provides a logical, sequential, and thorough approach to on-line instruction and management.

Polette, Nancy. *The Research Almanac*, 2nd ed. Book Lures, 1986. 172 pp. ISBN 0-913839-27-2 (pap.).

PURPOSE

Research activities based on world events throughout history are presented for the use of school library media specialists.

CONTENTS

Events from September to May that require the use of reference sources available in most libraries are presented in chronological order. The topics are varied and will appeal to young people.

Each month begins with its special flower and gem, and special events of the month and its weeks are listed, with sources of free information. January, for example, is March of Dimes month, and its special weeks include Nurses' Week and International Printing Week. Users are left to their own devices to create research projects for the weeks. Activities are presented, however, for each day. Examples are January 12, the birthday of Charles Perrault. The activity is a quiz, where the first and last halves of folktale titles are mixed and have to be matched. Children are asked to identify those collected by Perrault. On January 16, National Nothing Day, students are urged to read one of the books with "nothing" in its title and to locate more in the school library. February 1 is the anniversary of the Emancipation Proclamation, and students are asked to find out its causes and effects. March 22 is the anniversary of the first Indian treaty. A brief description of the event is followed by a suggestion for compiling a scrapbook of famous American Indians. The anniversary of the sinking of the *Lusitania* prompts a group of sentences about famous ships, which students are required to identify.

For schools whose programs continue into summer, birthdays are listed for the summer months, and sports topics inspire a variety of research projects. Answer keys are provided for the quizzes, and an index helps to identify the location of all the events.

AUTHORITY

Polette is a professor of education and director of the Laboratory School for Gifted Children at Lindenwood College, Missouri. She is a prolific writer of books for teachers and school librarians.

COMMENT

When inspiration wanes, this is a handy book to turn to for mini research ideas.

Polette, Nancy. *The Research Book for Gifted Programs K–8.* **Book Lures, 1984. 170 pp. ISBN 0-913839-28-0 (pap.).**

PURPOSE

Activities designed for the special characteristics and needs of gifted children have been organized into independent learning and research projects for use in school library media center programs.

CONTENTS

The book is divided into five sections following an introduction, which describes the characteristics of gifted children and relates them to instruction, and then presents a model for curriculum development that incorporates learner characteristics with curriculum imperatives.

Section 1 focuses on thinking skills, defining them and suggesting goals and exercises that will help gifted children to "warm up thinking processes." Among the skills described are productive thinking, critical thinking, critical reading, and communication skills. Components of these are analyzed and simple activities are provided; for example, for judging sources, a critical reading skill, the author lists criteria for determining reliability and suggests that students examine a news report and rate it on a continuum scale. Section 2 presents research skills and activities designed to foster their growth. A taxonomy of skills that covers grades K through 12 is also included. Isolated skills are presented in practice exercises that include dictionary and encyclopedia use, puzzles and games that require the use of reference materials, and other kinds of reference and research activities.

In Section 3 a variety of research activities for primary grades is presented, and Section 4 offers research activities for grades 4 through 6. Handout sheets for preparing bibliographies, note taking, outlining, and interviewing are presented along with an independent study plan sheet. Section 5 presents research activities for grades 6 through 8 including such topics as alcoholism, folk literature, future studies, television shows, and the use and abuse of power. A field investigation of a cemetery provides related research activities, and a unit on local history and related reference works concludes the book.

AUTHORITY

Polette is a professor of education and director of the Laboratory School for Gifted Children at Lindenwood College, Missouri.

COMMENT

Many of the research activities will keep gifted children happily investigating for many days, and the author has successfully related learner characteristics with creative projects. There is no hint, however, of relating activities to the curriculum for these children, which makes the research merely practice for its own sake. The line drawings used for illustration are remarkably unattractive and somewhat distracting.

Van Vliet, Lucille W. *Media Skills for Middle Schools: Strategies for Library Media Specialists and Teachers*. Libraries Unlimited, 1984. 263 pp. ISBN 0-87287-410-9.

PURPOSE

Written for both new and experienced school library media specialists, this book presents ideas and models for integrating library media skills with classroom teaching, and suggests how librarians and teachers can form effective partnerships for instruction.

CONTENTS

The author begins Part I by defining the middle school and its curriculum, and continues with a description of the young adolescents that make up its student body. A middle school curriculum is outlined, and objectives are listed and arranged into a scope and sequence. In a chapter that describes the role of the school library media specialist, Van Vliet emphasizes the importance of leadership and participation in the life of the school by its librarian. As a leader, the library media specialist opens lines of communication with all staff members, participating in school activities, welcoming teachers into the library media center, and seeking their participation in library media center activities. Planning involves meeting with the principal and supervisors, scheduling planning sessions with them, and inviting student participation through class discussions and individual conferences.

Part II presents media skills lessons that exemplify an integrated approach. Each lesson includes an overview, the library and subject area objectives, learning strategies, resources to be used, and the respective roles of teacher, librarian, and student. Criteria for determining the quality of student performance are also provided.

For grade 6, initial lessons provide a general introduction to the media center and follow-up lessons locate various areas and explain some of the library tools: card catalog, reference area, vertical file, and so on. In subsequent lessons a variety of subject areas provide the basis for introducing many skills, and library resources are used to explore various clearly defined subjects. In grades 7 and 8 the foundations that were laid in grade 6 are built on, while students investigate literature, foreign languages, mathematics, social studies, and science through the use of library resources. Along the way, they learn about using computers, explore visual and nonverbal communication, prepare storyboards, practice photography, and participate in independent study projects. In all, 70 lessons are provided, many of them involving more than a single class period.

Lists of resources and vendors conclude the book, and an index is provided.

AUTHORITY

Van Vliet has had over 20 years of experience as a school library media specialist in Ellicott City, Maryland. In 1980 she received the Outstanding Media Program of the Year Award from the Maryland Educational Media Organization.

COMMENT

This convenient handbook suggests many approaches to integrating library skills instruction with various subjects in the curriculum. The lessons are ready-made for use, but can be customized to one's own specifications and student body.

Wehmeyer, Lillian Biermann. *The School Librarian as Educator*, 2nd ed. Libraries Unlimited, 1984. 455 pp. ISBN 0-87287-372-2.

PURPOSE

Wehmeyer explores the educational role of school librarians in its many dimensions, and offers a variety of resources for doing the job effectively. She has applied the results of educational research, theory, and practice to the task of designing a learning program that will lead to the ultimate goal: that young people may become autonomous learners.

CONTENTS

Using small type and many pages (455, including the index), Wehmeyer tells all that librarians need to know about instruction in the school library, and then some. She has cited authorities on learning theory and practice and on bibliographic instruction and observed students at work in the library, then studied the intricacies and ambiguities of subject headings and classification. All of this has enabled her to carry her readers along the road of library instruction and into the byways and side streets along the way.

Proceeding from the premise that the school librarian is an educator not only of children but of teachers as well (and one might as well add administrators and parents also), Wehmeyer presents a carefully reasoned approach to these roles. Educating students begins with an exploration of learners as individuals, including those with special needs. It continues with approaches to first teaching basic skills and then search strategies, and culminates with the skills, materials, and organization needed for independent learning. Moving from cognitive to affective learning, Wehmeyer discusses motivation, and presents games, activities, and other motivational devices that may be used. Instructions for creating these are included in the text and amplified in the appendixes. Thoughtful attention is also given to discipline and techniques of behavior modification.

A brief look at the media center environment and its effect on how well students may proceed toward the goal of becoming independent learners is followed by a consideration of how the library media center enhances teacher effectiveness. Strategies for involving teachers in cooperative planning are described, and methods for developing partnerships in the preparation of lessons and units of study are presented. A final chapter deals with management concerns. Using a systems approach, Wehmeyer demonstrates the steps in the process, emphasizing the importance of setting priorities, establishing goals and objectives, and building in evaluation procedures.

Each chapter is followed by notes and recommendations for further reading. Inserted between chapters are provocative "interludes," scenarios for role playing that are followed by probing questions. Several appendixes conclude the book with how-to suggestions, teaching strategies, outlines and lists of media center skills, diagrams, puzzles, and so on. There is also an index.

AUTHORITY

Wehmeyer is assistant superintendent for instruction and curriculum at Riverside Unified School District, California.

COMMENTS

All school librarians recognize the importance of helping children to become self-directed learners. This is, after all, a principal reason for school library media centers to exist. Although some cling to the outmoded teaching of isolated skills, most librarians continue to seek effective ways of linking library instruction to subject learning. While school library media specialists may recognize the importance of team planning with teachers, some have encountered difficulties in accomplishing this. For all who wish to improve their effectiveness as educators in the library, this book provides a vigorous new look at principles and methods and some ingenious ideas and tools for implementing them.

Zlotnick, Barbara Bradley. *Ready for Reference: Media Skills for Intermediate Students.* **Libraries Unlimited, 1984. 255 pp. ISBN 0-87287-411-7 (pap.).**

PURPOSE

This sourcebook was designed to help teachers and librarians integrate instruction in library and content skills for upper elementary grades.

CONTENTS

Teaching library media skills in a subject area context is the outcome of careful planning by the library media specialist and teacher. A further outcome is improved learning for the students. The beginning steps are discussed in Chapter 1, which describes the preparation of educational objectives, both affective and cognitive, for locating materials, learning about reference materials, and organizing information.

Chapter 2 presents a model of integrated instruction, and Chapter 3 introduces teaching strategies for an integrated curriculum, including the specification of integrated objectives, planning the instructional sequence, and a variety of strategies involving the use of audiovisual materials, brainstorming, and others.

Activities are suggested in Chapter 4 for several content areas, among them careers, computer literacy, mathematics, music, reading and language arts, science, and social studies. Several lessons are provided. Worksheets that may be duplicated are provided in Chapters 2, 3, and 4, along with answer keys at the end of each chapter; pretests and posttests are included.

An annotated bibliography and an index conclude the book.

AUTHORITY

Zlotnick is an elementary school teacher in the Montgomery County public schools, Rockville, Maryland, and a participant in the Reading/Language Arts Project for Montgomery County public schools.

COMMENT

The integrated approach to teaching library and information skills has demonstrated a greater effectiveness than teaching skills in isolation. Worksheets, on the other hand, have far from proven value and tend to dampen student enthusiasm. When children use library materials to solve a problem or fill an information need and then communicate their newly found knowledge in a report or other product, they will develop the requisite skills and understandings. Worksheets are neither necessary nor helpful, nor are they particularly adaptable for meeting curriculum goals other than those for which they have been specifically prepared.

15
Principles of Curriculum Development

It is not a very long step from a curriculum support role to one of curriculum leadership. In working with teachers to demonstrate the connection between the school library media center and the subjects they teach, librarians have an opportunity to become involved as partners with teachers in planning library-based curriculum units. Successful joint planning is enhanced when partners share a background in child development and curriculum planning. The books included here offer a firm grounding in curriculum theory and a basic understanding of the learning process.

Like any other management process, curriculum development requires planning, definition of goals and objectives, and deciding on evaluation methods and procedures before implementation begins. Librarians who are prepared with an understanding of these and other steps in the planning process will be better able to exercise a leadership role, and students need no longer be required to learn library and information skills in a vacuum, devoid of curriculum content.

Brandwein, Paul F. *Memorandum: On Renewing Schooling and Education.* **Harcourt Brace Jovanovich, 1981. 308 pp. ISBN 0-15-158857-0.**

PURPOSE

Brandwein presents a critical view of education in America for the informed reader for the purpose of examining current views of education and suggests new perspectives on educational reform.

338

CONTENTS

Brandwein begins by establishing a distinction between education, which is the result of interaction with the environment, and schooling, which provides predetermined instructional patterns and curriculum in an institutional setting as a means of guiding learners toward self-fulfillment. He analyzes the failure of attempts at curriculum reform, noting the swings of the pendulum between two basic concepts of schooling: that it should emphasize imparting knowledge and that it should focus on children and their needs. Translated into classroom practices, these swings result in either the "telling," or the lecture method, or inquiry/discovery, which encourages children to direct their own learning. External methods, such as educational television or programmed instruction, tend to supersede the teacher, and the justifiable fear that teachers will be replaced by machines has interfered with their effective employment in the schools.

Brandwein studied a number of effective schools, and observed that there was a common factor in all, an "ecology of achievement" (p. 28), in which all elements in the school community—administrators, teachers, students, parents, and community groups—contribute to an effective, continually changing but self-renewing, schooling system. Brandwein notes the following among the specific qualities that were present: Clear teaching objectives, along with administrative devices to achieve them, were in place; principals and supervisors were in the classrooms and otherwise visible in the school, not in their offices; parents, boards of education, and other community groups supported the school's objectives. .

The changes in the structure and content of schooling that are being imposed by the postindustrial economy and its attendant social changes and intellectual requirements will have an unprecedented and still not fully understood impact on schooling. The ability to nurture competence in lifelong learning has become an essential goal of schooling, and this attitude and skill is best developed in an atmosphere that recognizes the individuality of children and encourages inquiry. Essential to the renewal of education is the provision of balance in curriculum, instruction, and evaluation, and before that can be achieved, the society must ask and determine, "What kind of world do we want for our children? What kinds of individuals will secure such a world?" (p. 93).

In an effort to define how schools can effectuate the answers to these questions, Brandwein examines the impact of instruction, curriculum, and evaluation in schools and suggests how differing concepts in these areas affect children's achievement of their learning potential. He stresses the need for developing a national consensus on educational goals and suggests the development of a "Commission on Educational Systems" (p. 264) to assist the states to provide demonstration schools, provide consultants, and develop a system for lifelong education that will continue past the years of schooling.

A superlative bibliography and an inclusive index conclude this book.

AUTHORITY

Brandwein is a teacher, scientist, and conservationist and is currently co-publisher and director of research at Harcourt Brace Jovanovich. He has written more than 30 books, many of which are in current use in the schools.

COMMENT

This author's questions, conclusions, and prescriptions for the future of schooling in America are thoughtful in themselves and provocative of thought in his readers. In school library media specialists' quest to establish the library's primacy as a center for nurturing independent learning, critical thinking, and self-actualization, this book is an invaluable tool.

Brubaker, Dale L. *Curriculum Planning: The Dynamics of Theory and Practice*. Scott, Foresman, 1982. 201 pp. ISBN 0-673-16031-9.

PURPOSE

A textbook for university students of curriculum planning, this book offers management and group theory as a framework for understanding the process of planning, with professional decision making rather than bureaucratic structure as the model.

CONTENTS

Curriculum planning is a people-intensive process, unless the method used is to hand down a curriculum by fiat. Since the school library media specialist who is embarking on a curriculum planning project lacks the organizational authority for defining teachers' roles, the exercise of leadership in planning is a necessary part of the process. This book deals with leadership as a basic part of the planning process.

Brubaker begins by attempting to define the terms that he uses: curriculum, teaching, learning, curriculum planning, and setting. Curriculum is defined as "what persons experience in a setting," a definition so broad that it is not particularly helpful, at least to this reader. Setting means two or more people sharing relationships

340

with the purpose of achieving goals. Combining the two definitions, curriculum planning comes to mean: that which is experienced when two or more people share a relationship to achieve goals.

The reader who can tolerate such hazy definitions, and proceeds through the rest of the book, will find in it much food for thought. Among the topics considered are styles of leadership, networking (in the sense of creating mutually advantageous relationships, rather than in the narrower sense in which librarians now think of networks), developing goals and objectives, and working within the restrictions imposed by limited resources. Of particular interest is the section on evaluation, in which Brubaker considers self-evaluation, presents guidelines for using the evaluation process, and suggests ways of using the resultant data, of motivating others, and of assessing leadership. The chapters on leadership are informative, discussing leadership in formal and informal settings, providing a self-inventory, and presenting effective ways of motivating groups toward accomplishing goals.

Two detailed case studies illustrate the practical results of applying the theoretical material discussed in the book. Appendixes further extend theory with practical applications. They involve interpreting behavior and program effects in a classroom setting, deciding who makes the decisions in a school and who should be doing it, moving to a professional decision-making model from a bureaucratic one, and sparking a discussion of strategies for decision making. An index completes the book.

AUTHORITY
Brubaker teaches curriculum planning at the University of North Carolina, Greensboro.

COMMENT
As school systems and individual schools move toward the goal of providing teachers with decision-making power in curriculum planning, those who are able to exercise leadership in the process will influence the outcome. School library media specialists who accept a role for themselves as instructional leaders will be able to perform more effectively with an understanding of group processes and leadership. This book presents some important theoretical concepts for proactive school librarians.

Bruner, Jerome S. *The Process of Education.* **Harvard Univ. Press, 1960. 97 pp. ISBN 0-674-71001-0 (pap.).**

PURPOSE

This report of a conference designed to improve elementary and secondary education in the sciences had a profound effect on educational thinking in the 1960s. It synthesizes the precepts of curriculum development that so greatly influenced education.

CONTENTS

Thirty years ago America's leading scientists gathered at Woods Hole National Laboratories to explore ways of teaching science that would better prepare American youth for the postindustrial age. The immediate goal was to surpass Russian advances in space exploration, for the advent of *Sputnik* sent shivers of fear into America's intellectual and political leaders that this country was no longer first in scientific achievement and that it might lose the race for primacy in space exploration. At the same time, scholars in mathematics, the social sciences, and the humanities were also examining curriculum in their areas of expertise and working to develop new patterns for teaching their subjects. The results of their efforts were short-lived, and American education has again fallen on hard times.

But out of the Woods Hole conference came Bruner's report, which dealt, as the scientists did, not with the content of education but with the process, and in which Bruner suggested the principle that "the foundations of any subject may be taught to anybody at any age in some form" (p. 12).

The Process of Education considers aspects of this conclusion. How to construct curriculum so that the basic structure of a discipline can be grasped by learners is the first concern, and is discussed in the second chapter. The following chapter considers the child's intellectual development, with frequent references to Piaget, and relates the various stages of readiness for learning to curriculum development. This is followed with an examination of how intuitive thinking and analytic thinking can be balanced, and intuitive thinking encouraged, while at the same time, corrected, if the intuition is wrong.

Motivation for learning is touched on in the next chapter. Bruner expresses the growing concern that students were becoming spectators rather than participants in activities, and the influence of peer groups was becoming pervasive. The need for further research is identified. The role of "teaching aids" in education is briefly discussed in the final chapter with the conclusion that there need be no conflict between teachers and the use of films and other media in the educational process.

AUTHORITY

Bruner is a professor of psychology and director of the Center for Cognitive Studies at Harvard University.

COMMENT

When this book was written it was alarm over Soviet initiatives in space that sparked an impetus toward reform of education. Today the specter of Japanese technological advancement looms; perhaps that will spur educational reform in the 1990s. Meanwhile many of the questions raised here still need answers and new questions have arisen.

Bruner, Jerome S. *Toward a Theory of Instruction*. Harvard Univ. Press, 1966. 176 pp. ISBN 674-89700-5.

PURPOSE

Writing for the informed general reader, Bruner explores various aspects of learning theory in order to arrive at a theory that can be used to help children learn.

CONTENTS

Each of the eight essays in this book is on a different subject, yet all are intertwined in their effects on one another. As Bruner notes in the preface, when he changed one, he had to make changes in one or more of the others as well. What they all add up to is an exploration of the nature of the growth of human intellect.

Bruner has studied Piaget and other theorists of human intellectual development, studied children in laboratory situations, and observed children as they learned concepts in mathematics and social studies, based on innovative learning programs in those subjects. The first was an experimental math curriculum developed by the School Mathematics Study Group (SMSG); the second was "Man: A Course of Study," prepared under the aegis of Educational Services, Inc. Both of these were products of the flurry of new curriculum creation that occurred in the 1960s.

The first essay discusses the phases of growth through which children pass, from action to "summarizers of action" to the "translation of experience into language," eventually applying reasoning and logic in abstract thinking patterns. This leads to the next essay, which deals with the invention of education as a social phenomenon, and some exploration of what curriculum is and does. The third essay describes an experimental situation in which eight-year-old children learn quadratic equations using blocks of different shapes, under the tutelage of several psychologists, leading to Bruner's formulation of his theory of instruction.

Moving to "Man: A Course of Study," Bruner continues his demonstration of how a well-ordered curriculum can amplify learning, even allowing children to sense the power of myth and enabling them to create myths that mimic those of primitive peoples. He describes the course of study and its component parts, and lists its five goals, which go a long way toward explaining why there has been considerable controversy over its use. In the next essay he offers some thoughts on the nature of language and its interaction with thought and some comments about the teaching of English. Motivation to learn, how children sometimes build up defenses against learning, and why, and some final thoughts about curriculum construction, subject disciplines, and evaluation round out the book. An index completes it.

AUTHORITY
Bruner is a professor of psychology and director of the Center for Cognitive Studies at Harvard University.

COMMENT
Bruner's thought has had a great influence on curriculum planning and design. His insights on learning and human growth and development, as well as his overall clarity of thought and language, make this book must reading for all school professionals.

Clendening, Corinne P., and Ruth Ann Davies. *Challenging the Gifted: Curriculum Enrichment and Acceleration Models.* See Chapter 12, Serving Special Learners.

Evans, Richard I. *Jean Piaget: The Man and His Ideas.* **Trans. by Eleanor Duckworth. Dutton, 1973. 189 pp. ISBN 0-525-13660-6.**

PURPOSE
Inevitably, any study of curriculum theory and development has as its starting point an understanding of the theories of Jean Piaget, so pervasive has been the influence of his thought. This book summarizes Piaget's observations of the steps of growth in children's cogni-

344

tive development. It also compares his thought with corresponding theories of Sigmund Freud, B. F. Skinner, and Erik Erikson.

CONTENTS

The structure of the book is that of a dialogue between the author and Piaget, one of a series of filmed dialogues conducted by Evans with leading theorists in the fields of personality development and human behavior. The book is based on transcripts of the Piaget film, which was designed to reflect personality as well as thought. Without the nonverbal clues that are visible in a filmed conversation, however, much of this is lost.

David Elkind, a leading interpreter of Piaget, introduces Piaget to the reader; the author and associates contribute a summary of Piaget's model of child development along with comparisons with the models of Skinner, Freud, and Erikson. An autobiographical sketch by Piaget, a list of his major published works, and a biography conclude the book.

Piaget's theories developed from observation of children and analysis of their behavior rather than from the hypothesis-and-experiment method usually employed by behavioral scientists. His background in epistemology, biology, and mathematics contributed to the development of his ideas. Most notable are his explanations of how children move from sensorimotor to preoperational to operational periods of development, and how inner perception and reordering of experience and outward events and observation of them combine to transform the child's cognitive structure as the child moves from one stage to the next.

Piaget was motivated by a need to know rather than a specific concern for educational practices. He refers to the origins of his work with children as an outgrowth of his epistemological pursuit of the origins of human thought and knowledge. Nevertheless his work's influence on curriculum development is considerable, and most curriculum experts today would quake at the thought of placing an operational activity in an early childhood learning program. Hence, working with objects is a basic part of the learning experiences devised for early childhood education, while abstract thinking is saved for later years.

Piaget's differences with Bruner are touched on in this dialogue, and the later comparison of his conclusions with those of Freud, Skinner, and Erikson are informative.

AUTHORITY

Evans is professor of psychology and coordinator of the graduate social psychology program at the University of Houston, and has published a number of professional articles.

COMMENT

This book provides an introduction to Piaget's thought and its development that is considerably more comprehensible to the layperson than Piaget's writings themselves. It therefore lays a groundwork for the understanding of child development theory that underlies a good part of curriculum development. It is also a great deal more palatable, at least to this reviewer, than Skinner's behaviorism. School librarians, as teachers also, owe themselves some exposure to his work, and this book is a beginning.

Wigginton, Eliot. *Sometimes a Shining Moment: The Foxfire Experience.* **Doubleday, 1985. 438 pp. ISBN 0-385-13358-8.**

PURPOSE

Written for teachers but with important lessons for everyone whose job it is to work with young people, this book attempts to define how teachers can work effectively to enrich their students' lives as well as their own.

CONTENTS

This is a book about being a teacher, about getting the best out of oneself and the youngsters one works with. It is also about the birth of *Foxfire*. A magazine started by the author and his students in a moment of desperation, when nothing Wigginton was doing with his classes seemed to work, *Foxfire* became a solid business—the subject of books and a popular play—and the inspiration for many similar projects. That is all described in the book's first section.

The second section is concerned with the principles and philosophy of education that underlie the author's approach to the young people he works with. Starting with the frustrations he felt at the inadequacy of the preparation for teaching that had been afforded him in college, he continues with a discussion of what he has learned during the 20 years of a teaching career that started with some ninth and tenth grade English classes in Rabun Gap, Georgia.

He discusses power, likening teachers' power over students to that of principals over teachers, reminding readers that just as a potentially fine teacher can be destroyed by an overbearing principal, so can a child's confidence be shattered by a careless teacher. The principles of good teaching are basic human values applied to teaching. Among those discussed are the teacher's view of his or her subject, an understanding of how learning occurs, a familiarity with students and their environments, care in making assumptions about the reasons for students' behavior, a recognition of the importance of self-esteem, and a willingness to be seen as human and fallible.

In a chapter entitled "How Do We Measure Up?" Wigginton discusses self-evaluation, and comments on how communities fail to measure up in their financial and moral support of teachers. In the following chapter he considers basic skills and how they are best taught, and some educational goals and how they may be achieved.

The third section of the book introduces a course in grammar and composition based on the *Foxfire* experience, one of 20 that have been developed by the organization that grew out of *Foxfire*. It is built on the principles described in the previous section and the events that transpired as *Foxfire* blossomed. All of this is presented in a conversational tone, with illustrations and anecdotes from the author's own experiences and those that others have shared.

AUTHORITY

Wigginton has worked with teachers at conferences and workshops and has experience as a teacher and as an editor of *Foxfire*.

COMMENT

Wigginton writes from a love of and a deep commitment to the teaching profession and his students and an understanding of all the woes the profession is heir to, and never fails to engage the reader. School library media specialists, like other teachers, will find inspiration in this book's pages.

The Current Scene

16
Technology and Automation

As computer use has evolved in school libraries, the microcomputer has moved to center stage as a learning and reference tool even more than an administrative one. On-line searching has been facilitated by the appearance of CD-ROM applications in increasing number, simplifying research for students and refining thought processes.

Microcomputers in libraries were first seen as the answer to many of the time-consuming administrative tasks of librarians that distract them from the real focus of school librarianship, the student. Yet, with all their power and speed, microcomputers have not eliminated the real time needed for inputting data, and downtime is still an annoying factor in automated catalogs and circulation systems. But offer students a CD-ROM disk with periodical abstracts and index, or textual data bases such as *Academic American Encyclopedia, World Book,* and *Compton's Encyclopedia,* and they are off and running.

The end user in on-line searching has thus become a center of interest among reference and other librarians; the issues and management concerns that have arisen as a result are the focus of numerous books. One title of particular interest and value is Elizabeth Aversa and Jacqueline Mancall's *Management of Online Services in Schools.* See also Beverly Hunter and Erica Lodish's *Online Searching in the Curriculum,* reviewed in Chapter 14, "Teaching Library and Information Skills." Librarians who have not yet ventured into on-line searching will find a number of how-to books here, some directed specifically at librarians, others aimed at the general, computer-owning public.

Computers have even been drawn into the promotion of the school library media specialist's role as curriculum consultant. Curriculum mapping and collection mapping are the new enthusiasm in some segments of academe, and are cheerfully encouraged in books by David Loertscher and Michael Eisenberg, reviewed in Chapter 13. Books about computer applications in specific aspects of school library service are in Chapters 1, 2, 7, and 10, and they are cross-referenced from this chapter. Those who wish to go beyond the books discussed here will find a wealth of sources for further study in Thomas Kilpatrick's *Microcomputers and Libraries: A Bibliographic Sourcebook,* which is reviewed in this chapter. For convenience in locating data base vendors and library automation products, two supplementary directories have been provided at the end of this chapter.

Aversa, Elizabeth S., and Jacqueline C. Mancall. *Management of Online Search Services in Schools*. ABC-Clio, 1989. 175 pp. ISBN 0-87436-513-9 (pap.).

PURPOSE

A sound, rational plan for introducing and maintaining on-line services in the school library media center is presented here for the use of school media professionals. The book introduces sound management procedures that can be applied to any planning process.

CONTENTS

The book consists of two sections. The first presents the various considerations in developing a program of on-line services. The second is an appendix that supplies the forms and other materials needed to implement the planning process, and each is keyed to the chapter for which it was prepared. A spiral binding facilitates photocopying.

Of the six major aspects of managing an on-line environment, the first is planning for it. After the need for careful planning has been established, the authors discuss the planning steps that should be taken: creating a planning group, establishing goals, objectives, and priorities, planning and putting into action strategies for accomplishing the objectives, and appraising progress. Forms for keeping track of these planning activities are utilized in the text and supplied in Appendix 1. A rationale and discussion accompany each step.

Policies to govern the use of the system once it is in place are the subject of Chapter 2 and the appendix that applies to it. The seven policy elements examined include providing a rationale, determining who may participate in the service and when, who will receive instruction, and who will pay for searches. The skills needed for an on-line search program are not limited to an ability to use data bases.

Chapter 3 provides a checklist of these skills, and raises important issues about selecting data base vendors, familiarity with sources, and knowing how to teach searching, as well as other important concerns.

Chapter 4 discusses the final, major and ongoing commitment that must be made when on-line services are initiated. The decisions about hardware, software, and space allocation are discussed; factors to consider in making these decisions are outlined and a checklist for planning physical facilities is provided.

Marketing the service receives a good deal of attention in Chapter 5, and it is a concept that merits careful thought in terms of its application to other services of the library media center as well. The last chapter deals with financial resources: determining costs, planning a budget, finding outside funding sources, if necessary, and preparing a cost-benefit analysis. Forms and checklists are provided in the corresponding appendixes, with explanations for their use. An index completes the book.

AUTHORITY

Aversa is a faculty member in the University of Maryland's College of Library and Information Services, and author of many articles on on-line searching. Mancall, an associate professor in the Drexel University College of Information Studies, teaches school library media courses. She coauthored *Measuring Student Information Use: A Guide for School Library Media Specialists* (Libraries Unlimited, 1983).

COMMENT

This thorough coverage of a planning process for establishing on-line services is at once commanding and forbidding: commanding because it touches every conceivable base, forbidding because its attention to every detail suggests that an intimidating effort may be in store for the would-be user. Actually, many of the steps described are used in every planning activity, whether for teaching or for administration of the media program. Effective media center managers plan in a similar way without even thinking about each step. What the user of this book may never have had before is step-by-step guidance through every part of the process and the tools for entering an unknown territory. Not every explorer has been that fortunate.

Batt, Fred. *Online Searching for End Users: An Information Sourcebook.* SEE Chapter 10, Reference Services.

Borgman, Christine L., et al. *Effective Online Searching: A Basic Text*. **Marcel Dekker, 1984. 201 pp. ISBN 0-8247-7142-7.**

PURPOSE

This textbook on on-line searching was designed as a self-teaching manual for the use of library school students and practicing librarians who have not yet acquired on-line search skills. It leads users through the entire process, from the initial interview to performing the search.

CONTENTS

Organized around the basic elements of the subject this text begins with an overview (Chapter 1) of data base searching that defines on-line systems and identifies data base producers and vendors and continues with a discussion of telecommunications networks. A historical overview is provided as well. Searchers themselves are discussed in Chapter 2, which offers a historical background and a profile of a good searcher. Chapter 3 describes the initial preparation for searching, including principles of analyzing the information request, determining when to use on-line sources, and planning the search. Constructing the search strategy depends on accurate understanding of the information need, and this is explained in Chapter 4, which also introduces Boolean logic, an essential foundation for on-line searching. The steps in conducting a search are outlined in Chapter 5, which describes log-on procedures, search execution, and printing the relevant portions.

Data bases are the subject of Chapter 6, which considers their origin, types, selection, and structure. Also discussed are the data base industry and the system vendors and their relationship with individual data bases. The chapter provides a comparison of printed indexes with on-line data bases and raises questions about standardization. Chapter 7 examines search vocabulary and standards, provides definitions, discusses the thesaurus, and compares controlled vocabulary with free-text searching.

Advanced searching techniques, measurement and evaluation of searching performance, equipment selection, and sources for further training are considered in the concluding four chapters. Summaries are provided for each chapter, as well as references, exercises, and bibliographies in the appropriate chapters.

AUTHORITY

Borgman is an assistant professor in the Graduate School of Library and Information Science, University of California, Los Angeles, and has written many articles on training for on-line searching. Her co-authors are Dineh Moghdam, assistant professor in computer information systems at Bentley College, Waltham, Massachusetts, and a consultant in library and information sciences; and Patti Corbett, product manager for personal computer education and external data bases, SMS, Inc., Malvern, Pennsylvania, a health care data processing firm.

COMMENT

The theory and practice of executing on-line searching are presented with care and in detail, and opportunities for practice and further study are provided. The advent of microcomputers has made on-line searching a practical reality in school library media centers. Terminals are no longer required for access to commercial data base systems, which is now provided by suitable software, a microcomputer, a modem, and a telephone line. The chapter on equipment is therefore outdated, but little else is. What remains outdated is the reluctance of some school library media specialists to take the first step toward on-line searching competence.

Byers, Robert A. *Everyman's Database Primer: Featuring dBASE III Plus.* **Ashton-Tate, 1986. 250 pp. ISBN 0-912677-85-6 (pap.).**

PURPOSE

Everyman's Database Primer offers guidance in the uses of data base management programs and assistance in using dBASE III Plus.

CONTENTS

Although dBASE IV has recently appeared, this guide to data bases in general, and dBASE III Plus in particular, is a clear and helpful enough introduction to data base management to make it a worthwhile source for anyone interested in the construction and uses of data bases. It guides the user through each step in the planning, creation, use, modification, and maintenance of data bases, starting from a presumption of total ignorance on the part of the user and proceeding to instructions for creating dBASE programs.

The clear and understandable writing and the informative and indispensable illustrations combine to make the book a powerful ally in understanding a formidable but friendly tool.

355

A noted authority on dBASE, Byers was formerly the manager of Mission Control at the Jet Propulsion Laboratory, Pasadena, California. He has written several books about earlier versions of dBASE published by Ashton-Tate.

COMMENT
While dBASE is a powerful data base management system, it is not an easy one to learn. This publication is a considerable source of help for those school librarians still struggling to master it.

Chen, Ching-chih, and Stacey E. Bressler. *Microcomputers in Libraries.* **Neal-Schuman, 1983. 269 pp. ISBN 0-918212-61-8 (pap.).**

PURPOSE
Prepared for librarians and information specialists at all levels, this book describes the fundamentals of computers, their hardware and software, and their present and potential applications in libraries, and offers a glimpse at future directions and trends.

CONTENTS
Books about microcomputers tend to become outdated fairly soon after publication. This book offers a case in point: The capabilities it describes—64K memories, 8-bit CPUs, for example—have been superseded by micros with much greater power at considerably less cost. These words are being processed by a computer with 640K of memory, and a 20-megabyte hard disk is storing them, at a cost of less than $2,000. With *Microcomputers in Libraries,* then, its value is not for the latest information but for the long-range applicability of principles and concepts.

As an introduction to microcomputers, this book has much to offer. It explains the technology and emphasizes the importance of considering what software will be most appropriate for a particular library before hardware decisions are made. It describes applications of microcomputers in school media centers and academic, public, and special libraries. It offers suggestions on staff development programs. It outlines the steps required for careful planning and details the methods of preparing a needs assessment, including cost analysis and presentation of the results.

A concluding section offers some predictions that question the continuing viability of libraries. It warns that while resources for supporting libraries will continue to diminish, the advancement of technology will proceed. Libraries will have to become more concerned with software evaluation and staff training in computer use. Patrons will expect a faster response to their information needs, and librarians had better prepare for the future today.

Appended are a comparison chart of microcomputers with illustrations of computers, now outdated; a bibliography, somewhat outdated; and a glossary. An index is also provided.

AUTHORITY

The book was based on the proceedings of the Institute on Microcomputers in Libraries offered by Simmons College, Graduate School of Library and Information Science. The proceedings were edited by Ching-chih Chen, professor and associate dean of the school, and Stacey E. Bressler, basic skills coordinator of the Massachusetts Department of Education.

COMMENT

This book is recommended primarily for its brevity and clarity. Some of the specifics presented are out of date, but for librarians new to computer technology, it offers a good general introduction, with clear explanations of how computers function and how their power can work for school libraries.

Costa, Betty, and Marie Costa. *A Micro Handbook for Small Libraries and Media Centers*, 2nd ed. Libraries Unlimited, 1986. 325 pp. ISBN 0-87287-525-3.

PURPOSE

This handbook is a comprehensive introduction for librarians unfamiliar with microcomputer technology. Applications of microcomputers in school library media centers are also discussed.

CONTENTS

An overview of computers and their role in contemporary society and a chronology (beginning with prehistoric people who "count on fingers and toes") serve as a good-humored opening to this book. The next two chapters are somewhat less lighthearted as they explore everything one might want to know about microcomputers, their components, and add-ons (peripherals) and the software that provides for the interface of user with computer. Checklists for determining what to look for accompany both of these chapters in which is also an explanation of optical disk technology.

"Applications of Microcomputers in Library Services and Management," Chapter 4, begins with a description of general-purpose software of various kinds (word processing, data base management, spreadsheets, and integrated programs that combine two or more of these functions). The chapter continues with an explanation of the various uses of microcomputers in libraries, from acquisitions to library skills instruction and reference service as well as many other administrative tasks.

In addition to its utility as an instructional and management tool, the microcomputer may be considered a library resource in the same sense as books and audiovisual equipment and materials. Chapter 5 presents this aspect of the microcomputer, discussing the maintenance and circulation of hardware and software, providing evaluation processes of hardware and software for staff members, offering instruction in its use, providing reference materials and other information about computer utilization in the curriculum, and making available special services for handicapped students using computer technology, among other computer-related services.

The computer as a communications device is explored in Chapter 6. Its ability to connect the library to the world outside its walls is explored in discussion of networks and telecommunications services. Its use in providing access to various kinds of data bases, from bibliographic utilities to commercial information services, is described also.

Chapter 7 explains the best ways to choose and develop a microcomputer system, describing how to ascertain the library media program's needs and offering checklists for selecting components and implementing the system design. The importance of careful planning and analysis is stressed, and a log form, sample flowchart, and cost analysis chart help to accomplish these tasks. Perhaps the best advice anywhere on getting started with a computer system is to "take small steps" (p. 166). This is followed by checklists for selection and implementation, which offer useful recommendations. The penultimate chapter deals with the ethics of using computer software and such problems as piracy, and the uses of on-line searches. It emphasizes the need to teach and model ethical behavior.

Three case studies of computer converts are the subject of the concluding chapter. The book ends with Appendix A, a glossary of computer terms; Appendix B, several lists of resources, services, reference, and other works on computers, organizations and user groups, and much more; Appendix C, instructions on caring for the computer; Appendix D, possible funding sources; and Appendix E, charts for comparing and evaluating software and hardware. An index is provided, and bibliographies conclude each chapter.

AUTHORITY

Betty Costa is a library media consultant. Marie Costa is a microcomputer consultant and free-lance writer.

COMMENT

An excellent all-purpose introduction to microcomputers and their uses in school library media centers and other small libraries will be found within the covers of this book. Even the technical portions are easy to read and understand, and this is no small feat to accomplish. Suffused with enthusiasm, sound advice, and a thorough knowledge of its subject, this book is recommended without reservation.

Dewey, Patrick R. *101 Software Packages to Use in Your Library: Descriptions, Evaluations, and Practical Advice.* SEE Chapter 8, Selection Guides and Resources.

Doll, Carol A. *Evaluating Educational Software.* SEE Chapter 7, Nonprint Media and Computer Software.

EPIE Institute. *T.E.S.S.: The Educational Software Selector.* Annual. Teachers College Press, 1986. 948 pp. ISBN 0-916087-00-X.

PURPOSE

Educational software for use with learners, from preschoolers to graduate students, is evaluated in this compendious selection tool for prospective purchasers and users of computer software.

CONTENTS

Composed of five sections, *T.E.S.S.* begins the review process with a description of the steps involved in selecting software. It continues with the software descriptions in Section 2, providing reviews of more than 7,800 software products from over 625 producers and vendors. Based on the Educational Products Information Exchange (EPIE) data base, this section covers over 100 subject areas and includes products compatible with a variety of hardware configurations. Also included are a number of titles for administration, guidance, and other programs.

Each entry provides the title of the program and date of release, the supplier's order number, the use for which it was designed (tutorial, practice of skills, drill, or simulation), grade range, author, and ISBN. Additional information describes how the program can be used (for small group, class, or individuals) and the kind of teaching it supports (remediation, lesson introduction, and so on). A brief annotation offers further description of the software, and final descriptive material indicates copy protection status, components, required hardware, price, vendor, review sources, and contact name and address of product users. Some entries include brief evaluative information, ranging from highly recommended to not recommended.

The entries are arranged alphabetically by subject, grade level, and supplier. Section 3 lists the names of programs that are parts of packages, while Section 4 lists software by type of hardware with which each is compatible. Section 5 is an alphabetical directory of distributors.

The appendixes include a glossary, some sample EPIE evaluations, and evaluation forms and forms for instructional planning utilizing software. A subject index and a product name index complete the book.

AUTHORITY

The EPIE Institute, a nonprofit group, evaluates educational materials.

COMMENT

T.E.S.S. is directly comparable with Bowker's *Software for Schools, 1987–1988* (see the review in Chapter 8, "Selection Guides and Resources"). The Bowker volume offers more reviews (8,800 is the number given), and since it covers software for a narrower age range (K–12), there are still more products covered for elementary and secondary education. Both books offer excellent coverage of individual items and access to reviews by a number of routes. Choice will depend on the importance of evaluations as against comprehensiveness, with *T.E.S.S.* scoring on the former and the Bowker book on the latter.

Epler, Doris M. *Online Searching Goes to School.* SEE Chapter 14, Teaching Library and Information Skills.

Fites, Philip, et al. *The Computer Virus Crisis.* **Van Nostrand Reinhold, 1989. 171 pp. ISBN 0-442-28532-9 (pap.).**

PURPOSE

Having entered the world of automation, librarians now have the task of keeping their microcomputers healthy. One danger that has grown increasingly troublesome is the computer virus. This book, written for those with a reasonable degree of expertise, can help fight off the disease.

CONTENTS

The "virus crisis" that threatens computers and their programs is an increasing threat. Its causes are many, and the infection is spread by contaminated pirated software, interconnections with other computers, downloading, electronic mail and bulletin boards, and even commercial programs.

This book explains how the viruses are transmitted and describes the forms they take and the damage they do. The explanations are left incomplete, however, lest vandals use them to produce a virus. Fites and his co-authors Peter Johnston and Martin Kratz suggest ways of detecting the presence of a virus and describe protective measures, such as write-protecting new software, avoiding pirated programs, exercising extreme care in downloading games and other software from electronic bulletin boards, and testing new programs to ascertain that they are free of infection.

Viruses can destroy data files, erase disks by reformatting them, alter programs, and even render hard disks unusable. The authors describe symptoms to watch for, and provide simple checks for discovering whether an infection has occurred. Among them are checking the directories in DOS computers for unexplained increases in file size or in the number of files, and, in Macs, checking icons and folders for changes. Methods for checking backups and data files and programs are explained as well. Some ways of restoring damaged systems and hard disks are also described.

Examples of virus damage are presented, and the virus protection programs and vaccines that are appearing on the market to combat viruses and undo the damage are also described. The authors predict that as solutions to the virus epidemic are found, so too will new methods of virus attack. Some solutions to this problem are directed at software producers in the final chapter.

An appendix lists virus antidotes and vaccines; a glossary, a list of references, and an index complete the book.

AUTHORITY

Philip Fites is the owner of Fites and Associates Management Consultants, Ltd., and has more than 20 years of experience in data processing. Peter Johnston is a professional engineer and general manager of PSC Consulting, Ltd., and has presented courses and seminars on computer applications. Martin Kratz is an attorney and manager of the Advanced Technology and Intellectual Property Group of Cruikshank Phillips, a law firm.

Apart from the security measures necessary to protect computers from physical damage and theft, it now has become necessary to protect them from damage from within in the form of viruses. While the technical portions of this book may be somewhat difficult to follow, the advice given is not. Apparently, the viruses are spreading, and some simple precautions may help to avoid damage. This book offers guidance for the concerned.

Glossbrenner, Alfred. *Alfred Glossbrenner's Master Guide to Free Software for IBMs and Compatible Computers.* St. Martin's, 1989. 530 pp. ISBN 0-312-02157-7 (pap.).

PURPOSE

Written for owners and users of IBM or compatible microcomputers, this book promises $1,000 in savings for purchasers of public domain software and provides the information needed to obtain it.

CONTENTS

It is not necessary, according to Glossbrenner, to turn to commercial vendors to find software in the most often used categories, such as spreadsheets, word processors, data base management, and communications, and he provides a mini-price comparison chart to illustrate his point. Furthermore, he insists, the commercial product and its equivalent "shareware" are of comparable quality. He answers your next question with a brief explanation of how overhead, marketing and advertising costs, and a hefty profit margin account for the price differences. To market and distribute their software, programmers can turn to user groups, bulletin boards, and mail order, and charge the consumer about what their royalty would have been if they sold their programs to a commercial distributor.

Many kinds of programs are available from the shareware or freeware sources: utilities, games, educational programs, and those that enhance computer and printer performance. Glossbrenner has selected a number of them, which he calls "Glossbrenner's Choice," and provides an order form for readers to use in purchasing some of them from him at the cost of a disk plus mailing charge. The rest of the cost of ownership is a registration fee paid to the originator of the program, which entitles the purchaser to telephone service, printed documentation, and a clear conscience.

The book is divided into three parts, the first consisting of the explanation summarized above and an introduction to the uses of Disk Operating Systems (DOS) and other information basic to understanding computers. The second part describes sources of public domain and shareware programs and provides information about user groups and on-line systems for obtaining programs, such as commercial and other bulletin board systems. The third part offers advice about which programs to buy and runs through a rich array of software, briefly explaining their generic functions and describing what individual products do.

Throughout, Glossbrenner offers "Free Tips," information set in boxes to supplement or explain the text. Products were selected, he notes, after a personal review of close to 1,000 disks. An appendix lists additional software: games, graphics, music, and educational; an order form and a list of "Glossbrenner's Choice" programs are also appended. An index concludes the book.

AUTHORITY
Glossbrenner has written several books about personal computers, among them *The Complete Handbook of Personal Computer Communications* and *How to Look It Up Online,* both reviewed in this chapter.

COMMENT
The author is a consummate salesman, and his style is clear and enthusiastic. Having read Philip Fites, *The Computer Virus Crisis* (reviewed in this chapter), which cautions readers about buying software from the very sources that Glossbrenner extols, this reviewer was somewhat concerned about the dangers described in that book. Glossbrenner, of course, anticipates that concern, and characterizes newspaper accounts of virus-caused computer catastrophes as usually inaccurate and overblown. Both books cite computer programs that will combat viruses, and *The Computer Virus Crisis* describes steps that can be taken to avoid potential damage. In any case, both viewpoints might well be considered before purchases of software are made.

Glossbrenner, Alfred. *The Complete Handbook of Personal Computer Communications: Everything You Need to Go Online with the World.* St. Martin's, 1985. 546 pp. ISBN 0-312-15760-6 (pap.).

PURPOSE
Designed to prepare the reader for utilizing computers to reach into the universe of electronically accessed information, this book is a compendium of ideas, facts, and tips on using the microcomputer as a communications tool: describing what is available and where to

find it, what the cost is, and how to use communications software to get to it.

CONTENTS

That computers can be used to communicate with other computers is no secret. To translate this knowledge into action, however, a sourcebook and users' guide are invaluable tools. *The Complete Handbook of Personal Computer Communications* provides a wealth of sources and guidance in all aspects of the technical background required for their use.

Section 1 provides an overview of what's out there, and helps the reader get started in telecommunications. It describes some of the services available to on-line communicators and provides names, addresses, and phone numbers. It presents and explains terminology, and unravels some of the mysteries of computer technology. Section 2 describes the popular on-line services that provide general information sources and person-to-person communications. An astonishing array of information sources, user groups, bulletin boards, and electronic buying services is presented, along with many pointers on simplifying procedures, saving on on-line costs, downloading, and so on.

Section 3 describes business, financial, and investment services and highlights Newsnet, a service that accesses industry newsletters. A few titles will indicate their potential value for secondary school libraries: "Space Calendar," "Hazardous Waste News," "Air/Water Pollution Report," "Access Reports/Freedom of Information," "Legislative Intelligence Week," "UPI." Section 4 introduces electronic mail services and networks, conferencing, and bulletin boards. Information services such as Dialog and BRS are surveyed in Section 5. For a fuller treatment of this subject, see Glossbrenner's *How to Look It Up Online* (reviewed in this chapter).

Section 6, "On the Home Front," describes on-line shopping, banking, telecommuting and bulletin boards. A concluding chapter lists directories, trade groups, and publishers for the on-line communications industry. A glossary and an index complete the book.

AUTHORITY

Glossbrenner has written extensively on this field. He is president of a company that produces computer documentation and other computer/communications products and services.

COMMENT

While written for the general, computerwise public, this book has much to offer school librarians who seek a handle on this important facet of computer use. The author's enthusiasm is contagious, his writing style is direct and unpretentious, and the book is packed with useful information.

Glossbrenner, Alfred. *How to Look It Up Online: Get the Information Edge with Your Personal Computer.* St. Martin's, 1987. **486 pp. ISBN 0-312-00132-0 (pap.).**

PURPOSE

The essentials for access to on-line information are presented here for all aspiring information hunters. Geared primarily for the businessperson with a basic knowledge of computers and communication technology, this book describes what is available on-line and shows how to get it. Technical explanations are clear and are accessible to those who lack experience or training in data base searching.

CONTENTS

As school librarians add new skills to their already awesome repertoires, one of the most elusive, to many, has been the ability to use on-line data bases. Each service has its own protocols, commands, search terms, cost structure, and collection of data bases and each requires time, patience, and a clear head to use them. How-to books such as this one tend to quell insecurity.

The opening pages outline the contents of the book and the hardware and software needed for on-line searching. Next, some of the major data bases are described and the components of their bibliographic citations are analyzed. Data base systems, their services, peculiarities and methods of conducting business are introduced, followed by explanations of the concepts and commands needed for searching data bases. Information about software packages, other search tools, and software for retrieving downloaded information from hard drives follows.

The second part of the book gets more specific about data base vendors and explains how to access data base systems. Chapters describe the major vendors, providing information on subscribing, billing practices, documentation, and manuals. Directories of on-line data bases are cited also. Help in evaluating data bases in the form of questions begins the third part, which also provides detailed descriptions of indexes to books, magazines, newspapers, wire services, and other news media, including transcripts of "The MacNeill/Lehrer News Hour." According to Glossbrenner, vendors are only too glad to supply requested information about costs, services, data bases available in a particular system, and so on. Also described are biographical indexes and abstracts, indexes to various U.S. government information sources, associations and industry directories, and a variety of data bases of interest to particular commercial enterprises: advertising, sales and marketing, investment, and the like.

Appendix A explains the uses and methods of downloading and "importing" data to such software as Lotus and dBase. Appendix B adds information for further reference and describes additional resources. A copious index concludes the book.

AUTHORITY
Glossbrenner has written extensively on this field. He is president of a company that produces computer documentation and other computer/communications products and services.

COMMENT
It is difficult to conceive of any aspect of on-line data bases that has not been touched on by this book, which is not only comprehensive but also enthusiastic and has the added virtue of a breezy and accessible style. "On-Line Tips," set in boxes, emphasize valuable added information. When Glossbrenner refers to a publication he always provides addresses and telephone numbers. Unfortunately, names and addresses are scattered throughout the pages of the book, rather than in alphabetical directories, which can make locating a particular source somewhat tedious.

Ho, May Lein. *AppleWorks for School Librarians.* SEE Chapter 1, Library Management.

Horenstein, Henry, and Eliot Tarlin. *Computerwise: An Introduction to Understanding, Buying and Using a Personal Computer.* **Vintage, 1983, o.p. 193 pp.**

PURPOSE
The stated purpose is to break down the ignorance and fear of computers that have prevented the inexperienced from enjoying the benefits of the versatile personal computer. Horenstein and Tarlin offer advice on deciding whether a computer will meet one's needs and how to select the best one out of the multitude available.

CONTENTS
Personal computers appeared with much fanfare, a few games, and great anticipation on the part of a trusting public. These expectations were soon dashed, however, when would-be users began to realize that they had to be able to program the thing in order to get

it to work. When programs began to appear, which enabled untrained users to put the computer to work, a whole new vista arose. Many potential users, however, put off by the jargon dear to the hearts of the hackers, still thought of the computer as an impenetrable enigma and wouldn't go near one. The need for a guide was clear, and this one filled a real void.

With the help of clear graphics and precise language, the authors describe the components of a computer system, how they work, and what each part does to accomplish the various tasks of a computer. The emphasis is on software, with clear descriptions of the various types: word processing, spreadsheets, data base management, games, and so on. Terms are defined, and the tasks that can be expected from each kind of software are specified. Various types of operating systems are presented, with emphasis on the importance of compatibility. The descriptions of operating systems' functions provide the understanding that enables readers to go on to the next phase of their education in computers, the chapters on the hardware.

Again, clarity abounds, as the components are described and illustrated and their functions explained. The mysteries of microprocessors and memory are explored and keyboards and cursors are illustrated and explained. Diskettes and disk drives and monitors and printers are also given their share of attention. To complete the picture, catalogs of hardware and software with some specifications, producers' addresses, and list prices are appended. Also provided are a glossary of computer terms, a list of some information services, and a bibliography and periodicals list.

AUTHORITY

Horenstein is a faculty member of the Rhode Island School of Design, who wrote two how-to books on photography. Having been unable to find a book that told him what he needed to know about computers, he decided to write this one. Eliot Tarlin is manager of quality assurance for a software firm. He has previous experience at Wang Laboratories.

COMMENT

The promise that readers will emerge "computerwise" from a reading of this book should be fulfilled. But this is still, basically, an introduction.

Hunter, Beverly, and Erica K. Lodish. *Online Searching in the Curriculum: A Teaching Guide for Library/Media Specialists and Teachers.* SEE Chapter 14, Teaching Library and Information Skills.

Intner, Sheila S. *Access to Media: A Guide to Integrating and Computerizing Catalogs.* SEE Chapter 2, Technical Services.

Intner, Sheila S., and Jane A. Hannigan, eds. *The Library Microcomputer Environment: Management Issues.* SEE Chapter 7, Nonprint Media and Computer Software.

Jones, Maxine Holmes. *See, Hear, Interact: Beginning Developments in Two-Way Television.* Scarecrow, 1985. 155 pp. ISBN 0-8108-1720-9.

PURPOSE

For those interested in the early experimentation with interactive television in schools, colleges, and other settings, the author has described several examples of these adaptations of communications technology.

CONTENTS

Thanks to the communications satellite, large-scale use of interactive television has made it a commonplace event in commercial broadcasting, particularly in network news broadcasting. For example, the on-screen interview, using satellite transmission to connect more than one distant interviewee with the interviewer and permitting the viewer to observe the process, is interactive television on a national, or international, scale. Smaller scale attempts at live simultaneous interaction between students and a distant teacher or between two or more classes using cable or microwave transmission are among the uses that Jones describes.

On the one hand, such uses of video technology have aroused instant uneasiness among many teachers, who have long envisioned their eventual extinction by a broadcast image, especially now that it can interact with students. On the other hand, the advantages of these communications systems are clear: Students may query an expert in a subject they are studying in an almost face-to-face encounter; the distances between schools in rural school districts can be bridged, permitting enrichment of the curriculum; and students develop skills in telecommunications technology. Furthermore, evaluation results indicate that general learning is improved.

Programs for visually and hearing impaired students provide

remediation of shortcomings imposed by their disabilities. Magnification of screen images enables partially sighted students to study facial expressions, a hitherto difficult task. Via the television screen, they are able to see what is being discussed in the classroom at the time of discussion, instead of waiting until the end of a class session to closely examine the chalkboard. Hearing impaired students learn lip reading and other skills through a combined television/computer system of instruction. These and other examples of interactive television and its uses are described by Jones, with much (perhaps too much) attention given to the technical procedures and requirements.

Extensive bibliographies are provided for each chapter and one at the end of the book; a glossary is also appended. Additional sources include names and locations of pilot programs, and a list of directors and coordinators of programs involving the use of this technology. An index concludes the book.

AUTHORITY

Jones has developed her initial interest in the technology and uses of interactive television into a full-scale investigation through conferences and interviews.

COMMENT

Although the glossary helps in understanding the technical terminology, some of the jargon can be frustratingly difficult for the uninitiated and is often downright unintelligible. More discussion of the programs themselves, their impact and ramifications, would have been preferable. Nevertheless, Jones has provided an estimable introduction to a neglected subject.

Kershner, Lois M. *Forms for Automated Library Systems: An Illustrated Guide for Selection, Design & Use.* SEE Chapter 1, Library Management.

Kesselman, Martin, and Sarah B. Watstein, eds. *End-User Searching: Services and Providers.* SEE Chapter 10, Reference Services.

Kilpatrick, Thomas L. *Microcomputers and Libraries: A Bibliographic Sourcebook.* **Scarecrow, 1987. 726 pp. ISBN 0-8108-1977-5.**

PURPOSE

The explosion of microcomputer use in libraries has prompted this index to articles published between 1980 and February 1986.

Although Kilpatrick denies its comprehensiveness, this index to almost 3,700 articles cannot be described in any other way. The entries are numbered consecutively and arranged alphabetically within a number of subject areas. Among those of particular interest to school library media specialists are overviews, planning and management, school libraries and media centers, applications, acquisitions and collection development, audiovisual, cataloging and processing, circulation, interlibrary loan, on-line catalogs, reference and public services, computer-aided instruction, communications and on-line searching, microcomputer operation, software, circulation, directories and information sources, software and systems reviews, hardware reviews, and book reviews.

A combined subject, title, and author index simplifies the location of appropriate entries, and annotations of about 50 words summarize the content of each article.

AUTHORITY

Kilpatrick is director of the Research and Reference/Interlibrary Loan Department at Southern Illinois University, Carbondale.

COMMENT

An indispensable tool for locating articles that describe the many uses and aspects of micros, this book is not necessarily recommended for purchase by individual school libraries. It is, however, a source that school librarians and library school students should use when researching microcomputers and their applications in school libraries.

Langhorne, Mary Jo, et al. *Teaching with Computers: A New Menu for the '90s.* SEE Chapter 13, The Library Media Center and the Curriculum.

Loertscher, David V., and May Lein Ho. *Computerized Collection Development for School Library Media Centers.* SEE Chapter 13, The Library Media Center and the Curriculum.

Miller, Inabeth. *Microcomputers in School Library Media Centers.* **Neal-Schuman, 1984. 165 pp. ISBN 0-918212-51-0 (pap.).**

PURPOSE

This book, a wake-up call to librarians, urges an exploration of the possibilities offered by microcomputers in school library media centers. Directing her arguments also at school administrators, parents, and community leaders, Miller exhorts them to envision the learning opportunities that microcomputers promise.

CONTENTS

Writing at a time when education was in the depths of despondency, underfinanced, overcriticized, and ever-resistant to change, Miller heralded the potent new technology with its promise of revolutionizing learning. Educators who grasped part of the significance of microcomputers have rushed to install them in computer labs, where "computer literacy" is promoted. Like teaching reading skills without providing an abundance of books for the newly literate to enjoy, these labs have neglected the end while concentrating on the means. Library media specialists need to provide the foresight and leadership that will place this new information tool where it belongs, alongside the others that stand on the shelves in school libraries.

While advancing this argument, Miller, in the first three chapters, examines the potential uses of microcomputers in the media center and discusses the selection process and the staff training that should follow. Chapter 4 takes up actual applications of computer technology in schools and cites statistics and projections of current and future use that emerged in a national study. Schoolwide applications include computer literacy programs of instruction, computer-assisted instruction (CAI), computers as management tools, and programs for the gifted and talented. School media center applications, discussed in Chapter 5, encompass technical services, administrative tasks, reference (data base searching), teaching, networking, and recreation.

Chapter 6 describes uses in alternative educational settings: public libraries, learning parks, museums, and computer centers. Software and its evaluation are the subjects of the next two chapters. Also, there are a checklist to consider before purchase, a list of review sources, and recommendations for previewing. Several software programs are described, including games and educational programs. Chapter 9 offers a vision of the future (which, in view of the book's 1984 publication date, is here now). Some of the author's prophecies have not yet come to pass, although several were remarkably foresighted; the growth of telecommunications networks and cable and satellite television broadcasting are some.

The final chapter offers some conclusions and poses some questions for further research. An afterword describes a choice of three scenarios for the year 2000, each of which shows the school library in a different role: as associate to learning, as an anachronism, and as indispensable to the process of learning. The implication is that what school library media specialists do with the technology can determine the direction the future will take.

Appendixes provide sample forms used in the Gutman Library survey of school computer use, software evaluation, and the annual survey of the National Center for Education Statistics. An index is also included.

Miller is former director of the Gutman Library at Harvard University's Graduate School of Education.

Six years have passed since this book was written, and many of the changes foreseen by Miller have indeed come to pass. With a decade to go before a new century begins, there is still time to see which of the scenarios she imagined will take hold. For those school library media specialists who have not yet set forth on the road to automation this book is a persuasive send-off.

Naumer, Janet Noll. *Media Center Management with an Apple II.* SEE Chapter 1, Library Management.

Parisi, Lynn S., and Virginia L. Jones. *Directory of Online Databases and CD-ROM Resources for High Schools.* SEE Chapter 13, The Library Media Center and the Curriculum.

Pennsylvania State Library. *Pennsylvania Online: A Curriculum Guide for School Library Media Centers.* SEE Chapter 14, Teaching Library and Information Skills.

Reynolds, Dennis. *Library Automation: Issues and Applications.* Bowker, 1985. 615 pp. ISBN 0-8352-1489-3.

Although its primary focus is automation in large academic and public libraries, this book offers to school librarians an understanding of terms associated with library automation, steps in planning and budgeting for automation, and familiarity with the variety of configurations an automated system may have.

To understand the possibilities offered by automation in libraries today, Reynolds contends, it is important to begin with a footing in the past. This he provides in the first section of the book, describing the evolution of computer applications in libraries, the growth of bibliographic utilities (for example, OCLC) and the development of on-line information retrieval systems (Dialog, for instance), the automation of public and union catalogs, and the consequent capability for providing efficient interlibrary loan.

With this foundation in place, the second section discusses considerations in planning for automation: deciding whether to automate, selecting hardware and software, selecting system components individually versus choosing an integrated system, providing for retrospective conversion, and the like. While the final say on these issues may not necessarily be in the hands of school librarians, a knowledgeable approach is always an asset when decisions are being made.

The third section provides more information for decision making: the role of bibliographic utilities; the characteristics of automated circulation, cataloging, and acquisitions systems; the options in on-line catalogs, on-line search services, and ways of managing the tasks involved in providing them.

Notes conclude each chapter, and a comprehensive index ends the book.

AUTHORITY

Reynolds is executive director of the CAPCON Library Network in Washington, D.C., and has been manager of bibliographic systems and services at Knox College, Galesburg, Illinois.

COMMENT

While not exactly armchair reading, *Library Automation* merits the serious attention of school librarians who already have automated libraries or who eventually will have them. With the advent of microcomputers powerful enough to accommodate the technical needs of small libraries, and packaged systems specifically designed for them, that doesn't leave too many people out.

Roszak, Theodore. *The Cult of Information*. Pantheon, 1986. 238 pp. ISBN 0-394-54622-9.

PURPOSE

Writing for the general public, Roszak sets out to place in perspective the "information age" and the computer as its auxiliary. While the computer's power to store and process information is acknowledged, its acceptance as the answer to the ills that have befallen American education is questioned, and the responses provided bear consideration.

What is this thing called information, and is it threatening to supplant ideas as the foundation of culture and human knowledge? What is the proper role of the computer in society, in education, and in human thought? What is the relationship between ideas and information, and how can ideas be returned to their rightful place in the hierarchy of knowledge? These are the central questions that Roszak deals with as he examines the history of computers, from Univac and cybernetics to the present day, and describes the political foundations and implications of the computer revolution.

Pointing to the quantities of data stored in government files and their retrievability by public agencies from the network of information that now exists, Roszak cautions that "the violation of privacy is the loss of freedom" (p. 209). Nevertheless, the computer's power to assist, its utility as a tool in the hands of librarians for accessing data bases, for example, is emphasized, as is its ability to connect users to each other through telecommunications networks such as bulletin boards. Roszak also enumerates the dangers of blind acceptance of the computer as a substitute for human thought:

It blurs the distinction between processing information and creating ideas.

It is misused in the education of the young, when misguided educators allow the substitution of computer logic for human creativity.

Its use as a polling tool by politicians encourages political opportunism.

Its use in weapons control threatens to escalate the danger of nuclear war by removing human decision makers from control.

If all of this tempers one's enthusiasm for computers or encourages any resistance to their use, the sections on the library use of computers and the promise of networking provide an antidote.

AUTHORITY
Roszak is a professor of history and chairperson of general studies at California State University, Hayward. He has been nominated twice for the National Book Award.

COMMENT
There can never be too many arguments for the humane uses of the powerful technology offered by computers. The dangers of thoughtlessly embracing the information age and of accepting the notion that artificial intelligence can substitute for human thought are presented with a rationality that emphasizes the supremacy of human intellect, imagination, and ideas. Roszak has punctured the hype that has surrounded information technology and offers a reminder that the computer is just another machine, albeit a most useful one. After all, he

notes, he used word processing to write his book, and explored the information available on data bases with the help of librarians.

Rowley, Jennifer. *The Basics of Information Technology*. Clive Bingley, 1988. 146 pp. ISBN 0-85157-396-7.

PURPOSE

Written primarily for students of information and library science, but also for practicing librarians, this book describes and explains the tools of information technology—computers, software, telecommunications, networks, and the like—as an introduction to the management of information in a library context.

CONTENTS

Written with crispness and brevity, this book manages to cover the basics of information technology (IT) and still touch on a number of issues unmentioned by many of its counterparts. It begins with definitions of information technology and information management and comments on the disagreement that exists about the meanings of the two terms. Techniques that have accomplished information management before and after the advent of computers are discussed and compared. Advantages offered by computers are enumerated and issues posed by IT are examined both here and in later chapters.

The basics of computer hardware, presented in Chapter 2, touch on each of the many components of possible computer configurations. The hardware aspect of telecommunications is discussed in Chapter 3, which includes networks, cable television, videotex, electronic mail, fax, electronic journals, videoconferencing, and other means of telecommunicating.

The coding of data begins with the bit and grows in complexity until it reaches the program and software phase and emerges as files and data bases. These processes are discussed in Chapter 4. The ASCII Code and programming languages are defined, and files and data base structures explained. Systems analysis and design are explained, with tools (flowcharts) and methodologies (decision tables) identified, and the necessity for leadership and decision making emphasized. The final chapter presents information sources. Appendixes and an index complete the book.

AUTHORITY

Rowley is senior lecturer in information technology, Department of Library and Information Studies, Manchester Polytechnic, England.

COMMENT

This compact and well-organized text is an excellent introduction to the technological aspects of information management. Technical terms are carefully explained. Its British orientation is a problem only when resources, acronyms, abbreviations, and organizations are not relevant to American readers. This title is available from ALA.

Rowley, Jennifer. *Computers for Libraries*, **2nd ed. Clive Bingley, 1986. 195 pp. ISBN 0-85157-388-6.**

PURPOSE

Writing for students of librarianship in England, this British author provides a clear and succinct overview of computers and how they operate and their functions in libraries.

CONTENTS

Starting with an introduction that outlines the usefulness of computers in libraries, Rowley discusses computerized library systems and the considerations that go into their planning and design. A flowchart is used to depict the planning process, and elements of the flowchart are defined. Computers and the functions of their component parts are explained in the next chapter, which also characterizes the categories of computers (mainframe, minicomputers, and microcomputers) and provides a comparison chart to summarize the differences. Computer networks and telecommunications are also explained.

The elements of data storage, manipulation of data, software, and operating systems are examined in Chapter 4, which also categorizes library applications software. Data bases are further explored in the next chapter, which provides descriptions of bibliographic data bases and MARC data bases and explains and analyzes the MARC format. A checklist for the evaluation of data bases is also included.

Computer use in information retrieval, storage, and retrospective searching are covered in the next chapters, which describe the major commercial data bases and some major European services. Commands, search terms, support services, Boolean searching, retrieval software, and current awareness services are among the subjects discussed.

Printed indexes made possible by computer capabilities are identified in the following chapter, and their uses and origination explained. Library administrative functions that are performed by computer software are the subject of the concluding chapters, which analyze and explain how computers are used for acquisitions, circulation, cataloging, and other "housekeeping" functions.

Each chapter provides additional references for further information and study, many of them books and articles published in Britain. An index concludes the book.

AUTHORITY
Rowley is senior lecturer in information technology, Department of Library and Information Studies, Manchester Polytechnic, England.

COMMENT
Although this book is decidedly British in tone, language usage, and general orientation, its brevity is a quality to be cherished by those who are merely seeking a quick overview of library applications of computers. It will help readers learn what the jargon means and serve as an introduction to the subject, while at the same time providing a surprising amount of information in a small package. This book is available from ALA.

Schuyler, Michael. *Now What? How to Get Your Computer Up and Keep It Running.* **Neal-Schuman, 1988. 184 pp. ISBN 1-55570-022-5 (pap.).**

PURPOSE
The ultimate in do-it-yourself manuals, this book will save librarians who manage computer services countless maintenance dollars by teaching them how to troubleshoot computer hardware. Although written, the author claims, for the "noncomputer professional," considerable skill is required to apply its instructions.

CONTENTS
Wiring diagrams combine with carefully worded instructions to explain the inner secrets of wires inside the computer and its peripherals and how they are connected with the outside world. School library media specialists who can understand all of this, and who have the patience, time, and tenacity to string cables, run wires, and connect terminals, will be able to solve wiring problems in computers with the help of this book. Those who do not may want to keep a copy handy for a friendly custodian or electric shop teacher who is willing to lend a hand.

The technical side of telecommunications and networks is explained, which should make simple location of problems easier, that is, a wrong button has been pushed, a cable connection has slipped out of place, or the like. Being able to determine whether a telecommunications problem is caused by a faulty modem, an internal wiring failure, or a deteriorating telephone cable can save time and expense, and the author provides some convincing examples.

Beyond that, a considerable amount of space and much good advice are devoted to supplies and suppliers and the tools needed for proper maintenance. The importance of backing up files is emphasized, and Schuyler produces a simple program for making labels for backup tapes or disks and provides some examples of backup logs. Other types of logs and recording are also recommended, including a running record of problems for the field engineer responsible for maintaining an applications program. He also recommends preparing documentation for programs in use, and offers the excellent suggestion of a table or flip chart that provides ready reference on the use of control keys and how to perform various functions.

An annotated list of suppliers is included with the chapter on that subject, and an index concludes the book.

AUTHORITY
Schuyler has been in charge of an automated library system run by a minicomputer (Kitsap Regional Library, Washington). He is also editor of *The Systems Librarian and Automation Review.*

COMMENT
A breezy writing style and clear competence in handling an automated library system are combined in this book to assist librarians in the management and cost control of a computer facility.

Tenopir, Carol, and Gerald Lundeen. *Managing Your Information: How to Design and Create a Textual Database on Your Microcomputer.* Neal-Schuman, 1988. 226 pp. ISBN 1-55570-023-3 (pap.).

PURPOSE
With an appropriate software package, an understanding of how to construct a bibliographic data base, and sufficient time, school library media specialists can design data bases for the school library media center. This book provides general guidelines and advice on how to do it.

CONTENTS
Developing an on-line catalog can be a daunting prospect, even for the most computer-adept school library media specialist. For those

brave enough to try it, Tenopir and Lundeen offer guidance in the process. Those ready to tackle simpler data base building projects, such as community resource files, subject bibliographies, audiovisual inventories, periodicals lists, and the like, will also find the requisite how-to information in this book.

Chapter 1 gives a definition of textual data bases, describing the different types, touching on hardware and software, and illustrating examples of record structure. Chapter 2 describes the various elements of hardware design, including the central processing unit (CPU); devices for inputting, outputting, and storing information; printers; modems; and backup and security devices. The unique qualities of textual data bases are explored in Chapter 3, along with their implications for data base design. Search features such as Boolean logic, field specification, truncation, and indexes are considered here, and the needs of potential users for clarity in operating instructions and search methods are discussed.

Perhaps the most important part of designing a data base and the concomitant user interface is the planning phase that precedes it. After a preliminary needs assessment, a feasibility study is prepared. Among its components are defining the scope of the project, analyzing user needs, estimating financial and time costs and constraints, and identifying potential advantages of the project. A sample table of contents illustrates the information to be included, and the chapter describes how to gather the information required by the study. Decisions on data base content and structure flow from the planning instruments, and the authors delineate what these decisions involve in Chapters 5 and 6. They also describe the importance of documenting the reasons for the decisions. In Chapter 7 the choice of software is examined, and various types are enumerated. An appendix gives producer information. Chapter 8 discusses problems and processes of evaluating data base software, suggests criteria, and provides forms that may be used.

Various considerations in building and maintaining the data base are examined in Chapter 9. Inputting and revising data, retrospective conversion of printed files, the use of on-line data sources, and backup of the data are among the subjects discussed here. Documentation is discussed in Chapter 10. Based on previously described studies and the requirements for use and maintenance of the data base, printed manuals are provided for end users and those who will maintain the data base, and on-line help features are provided for searchers. The final chapter projects current trends into the future in the areas of hardware, software, data storage, and communications.

Appendix A presents a case study in designing a data base that exemplifies the total process described in the book. Appendixes B, C, and D identify software packages, list software directories, and provide review sources, respectively. A glossary and a subject index are provided; an author index locates the bibliographic citations that are appended to each chapter.

AUTHORITY
The authors teach in the School of Library and Information Studies at the University of Hawaii, Manoa, and have written articles on data base design.

COMMENT
The principles and practices of preparing for any major project are applied specifically to data base design, and the result is a manual that offers invaluable assistance to librarians who are planning to provide a data base for the use of patrons. To design a data base of more limited scope, this rational approach may still be used. The steps may be simplified, but can still be followed in the suggested sequence, with careful planning occurring before rather than during data base construction, as so often happens in the rush to get started.

Thomason, Nevada Wallis, ed. *Microcomputer Information for School Media Centers.* **Scarecrow, 1985. 316 pp. ISBN 0-8108-1769-1.**

PURPOSE
To provide a starting point in the understanding of microcomputers and their administrative uses in school library media centers, Thomason has brought together 25 articles that have appeared in the professional literature for librarians and in computer magazines. Preservice students in library schools and librarians without microcomputer experience will find this compilation supportive and informative.

CONTENTS
Whether computers are "just another piece of audiovisual equipment" or a technological marvel without precedent in anything librarians have known before, there is one conclusion about which all the authors represented in this book agree: Computers have arrived in school media centers and they are here to stay. The reason is simply the efficiency and dispatch with which they perform a multitude of tasks and the consequent improvement in library service that they promise.

The first steps in confronting any unknown technology are to learn the insiders' vocabulary and to understand what the technology can do and cannot do and how it works. This done, the tasks become more complicated. How to finance, select, purchase, and maintain it; how to plan for its use; where to put it; how to protect it from damage or theft—these are all considerations, whatever the "it" may happen to be. The complexities of dealing with a computer "it" are the substance of this book.

The principles that underlie the selection and use of computers are presented in clearly written and informative articles. Also included are selections that debunk some common myths about micros, define policy decisions that must be made for its use, and describe the many applications of computers in school libraries. A principal's article describes his view of computer use in schools, and concludes with the reminder to his colleagues, "Computers *belong* in the Media Center!" Some practical articles describe the selection and maintenance of disks, monitors, operating system, and printers, and discuss the rationale and software for computer networks. Appendixes provide criteria and checklists for hardware and software selection, a list of periodicals that deal with microcomputers, and a list of software suppliers and hardware manufacturers. A glossary, a bibliography, and an index end the book.

AUTHORITY
Thomason is an associate professor of library media education in the Educational Foundations Department, College of Education, University of New Mexico, Albuquerque, and author of *The Library Media Specialist in Curriculum Development* (Scarecrow, 1981).

COMMENT
Advances in computer technology come so swiftly that any book about the subject is outdated before it is printed. This one is no exception, especially since most of its articles were published in 1982 and 1983. While improvements in hardware and software have made some of the discussion obsolescent, the principles of selection and utilization, the terminology, the applications, and the administrative considerations remain current. This book will ease the inexperienced would-be user into greater confidence by providing a firm grounding in many aspects of computer use, but it should be supplemented by reading current periodicals.

Waite, Mitchell, et al. *DOS Primer for the IBM PC and XT: Complete Guide to the IBM PC Operating System.* NAL, 1984. 208 pp. ISBN 0-452-25494-9 (pap.).

THE CURRENT SCENE

PURPOSE

The complexities of disk operating systems (DOS) are simplified here for novice users of the IBM PC and compatible microcomputers.

CONTENTS

DOS is the operating system that allows the user to run programs on the IBM PC. While many users go happily right to the applications programs after booting DOS, those who know how to use DOS will have greater power. This instruction guide provides directions, self-tests, and the basic concepts underlying DOS. Some of the advanced concepts may be somewhat impenetrable for the novice, but most inexperienced users will find the book easy to follow, to learn from, and to use.

The version that Waite and his co-authors John Angermeyer and Mark Noble discuss is PC DOS 2, but the basic concepts remain the same even with the more advanced versions of DOS. DOS enables users to create, change, and remove directories, to copy and back up files, to display and print text files, to change from one drive to another, and to use applications or programs. It provides users with error messages so that keying mistakes or other problems can be corrected. These functions, and the meaning and use of DOS commands, are explained and defined.

The creation and use of subdirectories, and such concepts as redirection, piping, and filters are among the more advanced concepts that are simplified and clarified here. All explanations show examples of what appears on the computer screen in response to the various commands and each chapter ends with a summary and a quiz. An appendix lists and explains error messages and an index concludes the book.

AUTHORITY

Waite is president and founder of the Waite Group, a publisher of books on personal computing based in San Rafael, California. Angermeyer is a software engineer and documentation specialist in the telecommunications industry and a consultant on MS-DOS, IBM PC-DOS, and commercial software. Noble is a communications engineer, training director, technical writer, and telecommunications consultant in the San Francisco Bay Area, with over 30 years of experience.

COMMENT

Those who master DOS will enhance their versatility in using the IBM PC and compatible computers. The documentation that accompanies DOS is, unfortunately, so turgid that many novices have found it impossible to use. Waite and his co-authors have come to the rescue with a book that is understandable and easy to use.

°

Walter, Russ. *The Secret Guide to Computers*, 13th ed. Russ Walter, 1988. 843 pp. ISBN 0-939151-13-8 (pap.).

PURPOSE
This introduction to the use of computers and to programming languages and programming is designed to turn the computer novice into a computer expert.

CONTENTS
As the *School Librarian's Sourcebook* goes to press, so too does Walter's latest edition of his computer guide. The 1990 publication is not available for review at this time, obviously, but the enthusiasm for the 1988 edition was so great that a review of it is included here as a preview of what is to come. By the time you read this, chances are that the 1990 edition will be in print. The author has described it in a telephone conversation as follows:

The three separate volumes, *Secret Skills*, *Secret Thrills*, and *Secret Chills* will be combined into one volume with a larger, two-column page format, different type, and fewer pages. The writing style and amount of information presented will be the same, or possibly more information will be included in the new format, but the organization will change. The price is set at $15 for the new edition, as opposed to $24 for the three volumes of the 1988 edition. Walter said that he would much rather sell the improved new edition than the older one, so please wait for it.

Although a serious computer expert and writer, Walter refuses to adopt a serious tone while getting at the essentials of computers with directness and clarity. He can enjoy himself and amuse his readers because he publishes his own books. Some quotes from the book will illustrate his brand of humor. His opening comments include an "Apology: Any original ideas in this book are errors," and a "Disclaimer: The author denies any knowledge of the scintillating illegal activities he depicts."

Volume 1 consists of nine chapters, the first of which introduces the computer industry, types of computers, and the four major houses that produce them: "the house that Jack built, Steve's, trash from Texas, IBM," and notes that IBM could also stand for "Incredibly Boring Machines," "Imperialism By Marketing," "Intolerant of Beards & Moustaches," and others. Chapter 2 describes all the parts of computers and what they do, and the next chapter, a buyer's guide, discusses periodicals about computers, discounters, and the computer models on the market. Chapters 4 and 5 "turn you into an amazing programmer who can use the BASIC language as a sword to cut through all of life's problems—while you giggle." Chapter 6 discusses how to get into DOS, describing its external and internal commands and advanced features. The last three chapters examine the major software types, offering some quick tricks, buying recommendations, and instructions for use of word processing, spreadsheets, and data management software. Appendixes offer versions of BASIC for major and other less commonly known computers, lists of themes, commands, error messages, and BASIC examples.

In Volume 2, "Chapters 1–5 shower you with novel ways to use the computer: you'll see *Amazing Applications,* enjoy *Electronic Pleasures,* create the *Literary Computer* and *Artificial Intelligence,* and learn the best way of *Computerizing Your Business.* Chapter 6 reveals the tricks of *Advanced Programming using BASIC.* Chapters 7–9 take you beyond BASIC by making you fluent in three other popular languages: *LOGO, PASCAL, AND DBASE.*"

Volume 3 "chronicles the ridiculous rise" of IBM, Apple, Commodore, and others, and instructs the reader in FORTRAN, COBOL, C, and other languages. It offers advice about the future after analyzing the past.

AUTHORITY

Walter has haunted the Ivy League as student and teacher, holding degrees from Dartmouth and Harvard and teaching at Northeastern, Wesleyan, and Wellesley. A founding editor of *Personal Computing* magazine, he has been seen dressed up as a witch on roller skates at computer shows.

COMMENT

Having illustrated his personal integrity by warning about his forthcoming book so that no one will buy an edition that is reaching obsolescence, Russ Walter has further proved his mettle by joking about his subject with utmost seriousness, that is, in order to teach. He has succeeded in his efforts.

Walton, Robert A., and Nancy Taylor. *Directory of Microcomputer Software for Libraries.* Oryx, 1986. 564 pp. ISBN 0-89774-342-3 (pap.).

This compilation of software profiles was written to assist librarians in search of microcomputer software tailored for library applications.

CONTENTS
An introductory overview provides 31 important considerations in deciding which software to purchase. These range from hardware compatibility to quality and management criteria to provision of references by the vendor, with the admonition *"no references, no sale, no exceptions!"* Each of the approximately 250 entries includes the following information: an abstract of about 100 words describing what the product was designed to do; a profile, which indicates release number, number of copies sold, costs, training offered by the vendor, and maintenance policy; vendor information; software requirements—operating system(s), programming language(s), other software required or recommended; hardware requirements—which microcomputers it can be used with, minimum internal memory required, peripherals required; and added notes.

There are indexes by title, subject, and vendor. A software citation index lists reviews and their sources, and an index of software not profiled explains why a particular title could not be found.

AUTHORITY
The authors are automation consultants. Robert Walton is a consultant at the Texas State Library and for his own firm, R. Walton & Associates. He has also written *Microcomputers: A Planning and Implementation Guide for Librarians and Information Professionals* (Oryx, 1983). Nancy Taylor is a technical writer for R. Walton & Associates.

COMMENT
The difficult task of comparison shopping for library-oriented computer software has been eased considerably by this directory. Unfortunately, the time that has passed since its publication has brought new software to be considered. Thus, current journals should be consulted for the latest products. Most of the programs profiled here are still available, however, and some will have been updated.

Williams, Kim, ed. *The Equipment Directory of Audio-Visual, Computer, and Video Products,* **34th ed. International Communications Industries Association, 1989. 550 pp. ISBN 0-03078-09-3 (pap.).**

PURPOSE

A directory of equipment and sources, this publication provides ordering information for potential purchasers of equipment and related supplies and furnishings.

CONTENTS

This equipment guide to products available in North America includes items in the following categories: audiovisual equipment for viewing, listening, and production; furniture for storing and housing audiovisual equipment, video products, and computers; learning systems; video projectors, receivers, cameras, and monitors; computer graphics equipment and supplies; and related equipment and accessories. Criteria for inclusion were that listings must have been submitted by the manufacturer or a firm authorized by the manufacturer, and the product must be currently on the market and accepted by the communications industry. Entries include a photograph of the product, the model, price, dimensions and weight, and a description that includes technical information and specifications.

COMMENT

This directory provides complete ordering and bidding information, but no evaluations on which to base purchasing decisions.

Woolls, E. Blanche, and David V. Loertscher, eds. *The Microcomputer Facility and the School Library Media Specialist.* **ALA, 1986. 204 pp. ISBN 0-8389-3325-4 (pap.).**

PURPOSE

Providing services and programs that make use of computer capabilities is becoming another responsibility of school library media specialists. This book was created to help them and other school personnel by providing expertise in starting, maintaining, and expanding the effective use of microcomputers in schools.

CONTENTS

The book is divided into four sections, each of which considers a major aspect of managing a microcomputer facility. The first of these is planning. In his introduction to this section, Loertscher provides a convincing rationale for keeping computers in the school library media center, under the supervision of the media specialist.

Substituting a rational plan of action for the happenstance that has dominated the acquisition of computers, the first article prescribes the planning procedures that should precede purchasing decisions. Selecting software and hardware is discussed in the next chapters, as are factors to be considered in providing a microcomputer classroom or laboratory. Installation, operation, and maintenance are among the considerations examined, along with such problems as compatibility, wiring, and supplies. The last article in this section describes the steps taken to provide and manage microcomputers in an elementary school.

The administrative uses of microcomputers are discussed in the second section, whose first article lists functions for which computers have been used successfully. Criteria for determining whether a particular operation should be done by the microcomputer are also provided. Decisions about what kinds of software should be selected for various tasks are based on the different types that are available, including targeted and generic software, single function programs, integrated ones, and the home-grown variety. Methods of cataloging software and uses of electronic mail, discussed in separate chapters, complete this section.

Services that a microcomputer facility can provide are discussed in the third section, including access to on-line data bases, library networks, on-line utilities, newspapers, and encyclopedias; and the items required for offering these services are described. An article on interactive videodisks explains the technology, still in its infancy, and predicts a promising future. A computer literacy program for secondary schools that includes modules on computer history, hardware, programming, and applications is presented in the final chapter.

The last section explores the school library media specialist's role with the school faculty in managing the computer facility. It offers a review of research on computer-assisted instruction (CAI), the involvement in instruction of the computer coordinator, whether it is the school library media specialist or a computer specialist, and staff development and training of teachers. The design of a plan for providing a microcomputer facility in a middle-sized school district, and computer applications in several curriculum areas, continue this section, and a brief description of the challenges and uses of a microcomputer program in a single high school concludes it.

AUTHORITY

The articles were written by school and district library and media directors, computer teachers, and college and university faculty members. Woolls is chair, Department of Library Science, University of Pittsburgh, Pennsylvania, a member of the ALA Council, and past president of the Pennsylvania School Library Association. Loertscher is senior acquisitions editor for Libraries Unlimited, and is a former professor at the University of Oklahoma Graduate

School of Library and Information Studies, Norman, as well as at the University of Arkansas, Fayetteville, and Purdue University, West Lafayette, Indiana.

This account of the principles, practices, and pitfalls of introducing microcomputers in schools combines technical information with practical guidelines. A book of this kind presents inevitable problems in organization, and one might question the placement of some of the articles. But taken together, they add up to an effective introduction to a vital subject, and considered individually, the articles provide an understanding of some of the problems and insight into some of the solutions. Surprisingly, there is no index, making the locating of specific information a matter of serendipity. A case in point: Some helpful advice about proper storage of software is tucked away in an article about cataloging, not too likely a place to look, but searchers will find it on page 98.

SELECTED DATA BASE VENDORS

BIOSIS
Biosciences Information Service
2100 Arch St.
Philadelphia, PA 19103
800-523-4806

Books in Print *Plus* (CD-ROM)
Bowker Electronic Publishing
R. R. Bowker Co.
245 West 17 St.
New York, NY 10011
800-323-3288

BRS
BRS Information Technologies
1200 Route 7
Latham, NY 12110
800-235-1209

CompuServe
CompuServe, Inc.
5000 Arlington Centre Blvd.
Box 20212
Columbus, OH 43220
800-848-8199

Data Base Informer
Information USA
4701 Willard Ave.
Suite 1707
Chevy Chase, MD 20815

DataTimes
Datatek Corp.
818 N.W. 63 St.
Oklahoma City, OK 73116
(405) 843-7323

DELPHI
General Videotex Corp.
3 Blackstone St.
Cambridge, MA 02139
800-544-4005

DIALOG
DIALOG Information Services, Inc.
3460 Hillview Ave.
Palo Alto, CA 94304
800-334-2564

Dow Jones News/Retrieval
Dow Jones & Co., Inc.
Box 300
Princeton, NJ 08543
800-257-5114

GEnie
General Electric Information Services Co.
401 North Washington St.
Rockville, MD 20850
800-638-9636

InfoTrac
Information Access Co.
11 Davis Dr.
Belmont, CA 94002
800-227-8431

OCLC
OCLC Online Computer Library
Center, Inc.
6565 Frantz Rd.
Dublin, OH 43017
800-848-5878

Resource/One
University Microfilms International

Bell & Howell Information Co.
300 North Zeeb Rd.
Ann Arbor, MI 48106
800-521-3044

SilverPlatter
SilverPlatter Information
37 Walnut St.
Wellesley Hills, MA 02181
(617) 239-0306

The SOURCE
Source Telecomputing Corp.
1616 Anderson Rd.
McClean, VA 22102
800-336-3366

Wilsearch
H. W. Wilson Co.
950 University Ave.
Bronx, NY 10452
800-462-6060

Wilsondisc
H. W. Wilson Co.
950 University Ave.
Bronx, NY 10452
800-462-6060

SELECTED LIBRARY AUTOMATION
PRODUCT SOURCES

ABALL Software
2268 Osler St.
Regina, Saskatchewan, Canada
S4P 1W8
(306) 569-2180
Online catalog, circulation, acquisition.

Alpine Data Services
635 Main St.
Montrose, CO 81401
800-525-1040
Scheduling system for audiovisual media; interlibrary loan management system.

Baker & Taylor
6 Kirby Ave.
Somerville, NJ 08876
800-526-3811
Ordering system for their custom-
ers.

Brodart Co.
Library Automation Division
500 Arch St.
Williamsport, PA 17705
800-233-8467
Public access catalog on CD-
ROM; ordering system for cus-
tomers.

CALICO
Computer Assisted Library Infor-
mation Co., Inc.
Box 15916
St. Louis, MO 63114
800-367-0416
On-line catalog, circulation, over-
dues, retrospective conversion.

Charles Clark Co., Inc.
168 Express Dr.
Brentwood, NY 11717
800-247-7009
Integrated library system for catalog, circulation, and acquisitions.

Dalton Computer Services, Inc.
Box 2469
Dalton, GA 30720
(404) 259-3327
Cataloging, circulation control.

Datatrek, Inc.
621 Second St.
Encinitas, CA 92024
Bibliographic control, circulation, audiovisual management.

Follett Software Co.
4506 Northwest Highway
Crystal Lake, IL 60014
800-435-6170
Cataloging, circulation, overdues,
skills.

Foundation for Library Research
505 McNeill Ave.
Point Pleasant, WV 25550
(304) 675-4350
Bibliographic control, circulation, overdues.

Gaylord Brothers, Inc.
Box 4901
Syracuse, NY 13221
800-634-6304
Circulation control via Gaylord
mainframe computer.

Information Transform, Inc.
502 Leonard St.
Madison, WI 53711
(608) 255-4800
Current and retrospective cataloging.

Library Automation Products, Inc.
875 Ave. of the Americas
New York, NY 10001
(212) 967-7440
Cataloging, circulation, serials
control, acquisitions, and accounting in an integrated system.

Project Simu-School
8160 San Cristobal
Dallas, TX 75218
(214) 327-6914
Circulation and reference.

Richmond Software Corp.
Box 5587
San Mateo, CA 94402
800-222-6063
Cataloging, acquisition, circula-
tion, periodicals control.

Right On Programs
755 New York Ave.
Huntington, NY 11743
(516) 424-7777
Cataloging, acquisitions, circulation, overdues.

Scholar Chips Software, Inc.
#308 2030 Powers Ferry Rd.
Atlanta, GA 30339
(404) 952-8250
Catalog, acquisitions, circulation
inventory budgeting, scheduling.

Scientific Software Products, Inc.
5720 West 71 St.
Indianapolis, IN 46278
(317) 293-9270
Bibliographies.

Scribe Software, Inc.
4435 North Saddlebag Trail
Scottsdale, AZ 85251
(602) 990-3384
  Cataloging, acquisitions, circulation, overdues, bibliography.

Winnebago Software Co.
115 West Main St.
Caledonia, MN 55921
800-533-5430
  On-line catalog, circulation.

17
Issues in School Library Media Services

There are issues involved in every aspect of the school library media specialist's job. Everyday decisions are made based on a professional appraisal of these issues, and eventually their disposal becomes second nature. But some issues defy these easy, habitual responses; they transcend the commonplace, and require the application of introspection and reason. Some of these issues are raised in this chapter. The books that are cited here may not end the controversies but they certainly raise questions that librarians ought to consider.

Intellectual freedom and censorship are opposite poles of an issue that has concerned librarians and educators for many years and continues to polarize parent groups and entire communities. ALA's *Intellectual Freedom Manual* offers practical guidance in preventing or deflecting censorship attempts. Jana Varlejs's *Freedom of Information and Youth* examines some of the subtleties of the debate, while Frank Hoffmann's *Intellectual Freedom and Censorship* provides a wealth of sources for further study. The other books cited here also offer much food for thought.

School reform is another current concern that has raised considerable debate. Both John Goodlad, *A Place Called School,* and Ernest Boyer, *High School,* discuss problems in education that have been addressed nationally, but remain unresolved. While illiteracy plagues the education system, an answer may be at hand in the whole language approach to teaching reading. Why school librarians have not become completely involved in this approach is one of the issues explored in *School Library Media Annual,* edited by Jane Bandy Smith. A supplementary list of briefly annotated sources appears at the end of this chapter.

Copyright regulations continue to frustrate the efforts of educators in libraries and classrooms to reproduce documents and tapes for use in education. Also, the desires of authors and producers to protect their intellectual properties come under the heading of copyright issues. Copyright law and regulations are explored and explained in Mary Hutchings Reed's *The Copyright Primer for Librarians and Educators* and R. S. Talab's *Commonsense Copyright.*

Among other current concerns that are highlighted here are AIDS, child abuse and neglect, teenage suicide, and substance abuse. As many school systems address these nationwide problems, their school libraries have an important role in providing needed resources. The books discussed here provide background information on these subjects. Two areas of study that are only now making an appearance in some schools' curriculum are the Holocaust and ethnic studies. One of the best works in the growing literature on the Holocaust is Martin Gilbert's *The Holocaust: A History of the Jews of Europe During the Second World War.* Oscar Handlin's classic *The Uprooted* and Mary Dearborn's *Pocahontas's Daughters* provide an introduction to the sweeping influences of immigration in the United States. For guidance in curriculum planning see in Chapter 13 James Banks's *Teaching Strategies for Ethnic Studies* and Karen Shawn's *The End of Innocence.*

ALA, Office for Intellectual Freedom. *Intellectual Freedom Manual,* **3rd ed. ALA, 1989. 230 pp. ISBN 0-8389-3368-8 (pap.).**

PURPOSE
To set forth its tenets and policies concerning intellectual freedom and the right to read, and to provide practical advice concerning the implementation of these policies, ALA's Office of Intellectual Freedom prepared this manual for the use of all librarians.

CONTENTS
Although some stirrings by ALA in response to censorship were noted in the 1920s and early 1930s, it was not until the publication of John Steinbeck's *The Grapes of Wrath* and subsequent attempts to censor it that the first Library Bill of Rights was adopted. Through the ensuing years, the statement has been reconsidered and revised to meet emerging needs and challenges. A description of ALA's responses to the various threats to intellectual freedom that have occurred during the organization's existence is given in an opening section of the manual.

The manual is divided into seven parts. Part 1 focuses on the

Library Bill of Rights, a discussion of which precedes its presentation. Further interpretations include statements on free access to libraries for minors, administrative policies and procedures that can affect access, a statement on labeling, circulation of motion pictures and videos, expurgation of library materials, diversity in collection development, evaluating library collections, challenged materials and restricted access, access to resources and services in the school library media program, and more. Each of the policy statements is preceded by discussion of the issues.

Part 2 deals with the freedom to read, and includes discussion of various issues and statements of policies and procedures. Among the issues addressed are confidentiality of library records, governmental intimidation, and access to libraries and information by physically and mentally disabled users. Concepts of intellectual freedom are the subject of Part 3, which includes discussion of the issues with respect to public and academic libraries, school library media centers, federal libraries, and state library agencies. Legal issues, the courts, and legislators and their relationship to intellectual freedom concerns are considered in Part 4, which is largely devoted to discussion of school library censorship and the courts.

Effective resistance to censorship attempts is most readily achieved in situations where preparations have already been made. What to do before the censor comes is the subject of Part 5, which discusses the development of a materials selection program, having ready procedures for handling complaints, and an active communications program to keep the public informed. Also discussed are motives and tactics of censors. Part 6 details ALA assistance, and what it can do to help libraries faced with censorship attempts. Part 7 urges librarians to work toward promoting intellectual freedom, building coalitions among like-minded groups and organizations, and lobbying on intellectual freedom issues. A bibliography of selected readings concludes the book.

AUTHORITY

The Office for Intellectual Freedom of ALA has long been a defender against censorship attempts, and its policy statements have been applauded by librarians.

COMMENT

However fervent librarians are in resisting censorship, the attacks keep coming. This manual serves not only to set up some important lines of defense but also to remind librarians who they are and what they must defend, and why.

American Foundation for AIDS Research (AmFAR). *Learning AIDS: An Information Resource Directory,* **2nd ed.** SEE Chapter 8, Selection Guides and Resources.

Berman, Sanford, and James P. Danky, eds. *Alternative Library Literature, 1986/1987: A Biennial Anthology.* **McFarland, 1988. 285 pp. ISBN 0-89950-336-5 (pap.).**

PURPOSE

The third in a biennial series, this anthology includes articles on various subjects of interest to librarians from a diversity of sources. They offer ideas, provocation, and a few laughs.

CONTENTS

Divided into sections of varying length, this compilation of articles and a few cartoons presents some alternative thoughts on a variety of issues. They range in subject from work, women, and children to censorship, peace, and Nicaragua, and include a "Dewey's Believe It or Not," and a "Librarian's Songbook," among other items just for fun.

In a touching salute to the burned-out Los Angeles Central Library, Glen Creason recalls what working there had meant to him, and mourns its passing. An article about the role of women's associations in the establishment of public libraries urges those interested in the history of libraries to investigate this aspect further. A bibliography on the peace movement includes books about children and peace, curriculum guides, reference books, and computer networks, and a very brief bibliography lists books for children that promote peace.

Of particular interest is Neil Postman's article on freedom of information, which argues that opposing book banning is irrelevant in a time when watching television has largely supplanted the reading of books. "Disinformation," seeing for a few seconds some moving visual images on the screen and taking that for information and/or reasoned thought, is the real danger, he asserts, and refers the reader to Aldous Huxley's *Brave New World* as the metaphor for understanding the problem. It is not the banning of books (as in George Orwell's *1984*) that we should be fearing, but rather Huxley's prophesy of a world where nobody wants to read any books because of their fascination with those technologies that make thinking, and therefore books, unnecessary.

The articles in the "Kids" section are also challenging, including such varied subjects as Dr. Seuss, Uncle Remus, small press books, the Gypsy image in children's books, reluctant adolescent readers, and writing for teenagers, among others. A section called "A/V" includes a discussion of music videos by Marilyn Kaye and Kay Vandergrift's thoughtful examination of the implications for teaching critical thinking prompted by young students' and library school students' responses to the film *The Shooting Gallery.* How students derive meaning from a work of art such as this film, or from reading literature, is a matter of concern when the thought processes they use lead them astray. Teaching critical thinking skills as part of literature-based programs is as important as teaching research skills and will help students interpret and evaluate the literary and other material they will encounter throughout their lives.

A total of 64 articles will entertain, interest, or annoy, but few will bore the reader. A detailed index is provided.

AUTHORITY

Berman is a librarian in the Cataloging Section/TSD, Hennepin County Library, Minnetonka, Minnesota. Danky is librarian for the State Historical Society of Wisconsin in Madison. Contributors include librarians, teachers, and authors.

COMMENT

A sense of humor, curiosity, and a taste for the offbeat should accompany an adventure through the pages of this book, enabling the possessor of these gifts to encounter some treasures along the way. Readers are invited to submit their recommendations for articles to be included in the next issue.

Boyer, Ernest L. *High School: A Report on Secondary Education in America.* Harper & Row, 1983. 363 pp. ISBN 0-06-015193-5.

PURPOSE

The virtues and shortcomings of American public high schools are examined in this report of the Carnegie Foundation for the Advancement of Teaching. Written for concerned parents, citizens, and educators, this book has made some important recommendations about improving education in high schools.

CONTENTS

This comprehensive study considers the present condition of the American high school. Schools throughout the United States were studied in depth to identify the factors that lead to lack of success and those that can produce a degree of success in spite of generally unfavorable circumstances.

In great detail the reader is introduced to classroom situations where failure is inevitable: poor physical conditions, lack of supplies, overcrowded classes, overworked teachers with too much paperwork and nonclassroom assignments, lack of community support, low pay, and more. Students are not learning how to think; teachers lose hope and give up on the students and their profession.

Out of this dismal picture, a number of recommendations emerge. The importance of clarifying state education laws and of schools' examining and stating their mission and goals is emphasized. Issues in teacher training are addressed, and the idea that recruitment of teachers might be boosted with higher pay and more reasonable working conditions is advanced. Better utilization of technology is urged; service opportunities should be provided for students within and outside schools; a core curriculum needs to be established; the principal's role clarified, and so on. Most important, a public commitment to education is called for, along with a recognition of the need for reform.

AUTHORITY

Boyer is president of the Carnegie Foundation for the Advancement of Teaching, a former U.S. Commissioner of Education, and a former chancellor of the State University of New York.

COMMENT

These recommendations are neither unfamiliar nor lacking in value. Had similar recommendations been followed sooner, the schools would have been in better condition when these observers went to study them. What is needed is a reordering of America's priorities. Until that millennium arrives, though, schools will struggle as they have done before, and education will decline a bit further, while new commissions study them to determine how to correct the flaws they find, and suggest once more the need for schools to define their mission and set some goals.

Burress, Lee. *Battle of the Books: Literary Censorship in the Public Schools, 1950–1985*. **Scarecrow, 1989. 385 pp. ISBN 0-8108-2151-6.**

PURPOSE

This comprehensive study of censorship in the schools defines the nature of censorship pressures, describes who the censors are, and underscores the imperative for maintaining intellectual freedom. It is a book for all school library media specialists.

CONTENTS

Burress takes the reader back to his early acquaintance with censorship during the McCarthy era and his subsequent involvement with the National Council of Teachers of English (NCTE) censorship committee, whose name was swiftly changed to Committee Against Censorship after a would-be censor called to ask for help in his effort to remove a book from a school.

A case study of censorship in Montello, Wisconsin, reveals some of the ugliness that surrounds censorship attempts, including an anti-Semitic attack on the author of the censored book (*The Magician*, by Sol Stein), a physical attack on members of the school district administration, lack of any support for the book's advocates from its publisher, Dell, or its owner, Doubleday, and the attempted removal of 33 books from the school library. As Burress notes, while a nationally publicized controversy such as this rages infrequently, its wake is filled with soft-spoken requests for removal of an offending book, and equally quiet compliance. He goes on to discuss various surveys and studies of censorship, undertaken by himself, doctoral candidates, and others; lists books that have been attacked; and provides a 147-page chart in the appendix that lists censorship targets, objectors and their objections, results, place, and legal case, if any.

Among the subjects considered in the book, chapter by chapter, are regional differences in approaches to censorship; reasons for its increase; the Bowdlerization of textbooks and other publishing appeasements of censors; censorship from the left, whose zeal to protect women's and minorities' rights results in attempts to deny access to a number of books; and secular humanism and the attacks on it by religious fundamentalists. In his concluding chapter, Burress suggests positive ways of avoiding censorship conflicts and of dealing with them when they do arise. He offers some eloquent arguments in favor of intellectual freedom, bolstered by persuasive passages from John Milton's *Areopagitica*.

In addition to the appendix, the book includes an extensive bibliography that represents a variety of opinion, including those the author disagrees with. An index concludes the book.

AUTHORITY

Burress is a professor of English at the University of Wisconsin–Stevens Point. Since 1963 he has conducted six state or national surveys of censorship problems in the public schools, and has been active in various organizations that oppose censorship.

COMMENT

This thoughtful report provides an overview of censorship in schools and its causes and effects, and never ceases to defend people's right to read and to know. It is an important book for all librarians and library school students.

Dearborn, Mary V. *Pocahontas's Daughters: Gender and Ethnicity in American Culture*. Oxford Univ. Press, 1986. 266 pp. ISBN 0-19-503632-8.

PURPOSE

This ultimate minority book, *Pocahontas's Daughters* examines the acculturation of ethnic groups in America as filtered through the perceptions of ethnic women writers. It offers school library media specialists who are involved in implementing ethnic studies programs a female view of the immigrant experience.

CONTENTS

Pocahontas is Dearborn's prototype because she represents, in a mythical sense, the perennial outsider, the exotic woman who adapts to the majority culture by marrying into it. It is an ironic choice of progenitor, Pocahontas being a native American in a land of the foreign-born who left no written words for the literary critic to examine. She does, however, symbolize the dominant themes that the book takes up: the conflict between the generations, the renunciation of the writer's ethnic heritage, the search for cultural identity, and intermarriage, which promises a resolution of the conflicts but only extends them to the next generation.

Dearborn begins with a discussion of the meanings of ethnicity and gender in American culture, then proceeds to examine the writings of ethnic women, primarily Indian, black, and Jewish Americans, although Martha Ostenso (Norwegian American) and Maxine Hong Kingston (Chinese American) are also discussed. The consideration of education as a process of Americanization is of particular interest, for in it are the seeds of the intergenerational conflict that is such an important theme in the works considered, and that still resounds.

The book concludes with a lengthy examination of Gertrude Stein's *The Making of Americans,* among the first of the "generational sagas," which were to become so popular in the 1970s and 1980s, and a "monumental" work in spite of the difficulties presented by its length and language. An extensive bibliography and scholarly notes complete the work, which also includes an index.

COMMENT

Although it lacks the cohesiveness and historical definition of Oscar Handlin's *The Uprooted* (see the review in this chapter), *Pocahontas's Daughters* has a different intent, to explore ethnicity in American culture from the unique viewpoint of the women who experienced it and were moved to write about it. As such, it adds new insight to an attempt to understand America from the standpoint of its ethnic diversity.

Demac, Donna A. *Liberty Denied: The Current Rise of Censorship in America.* **PEN American Center, 1988. 177 pp. ISBN 0-934638-09-8.**

PURPOSE

Trying to restrain the right to know is not a new phenomenon, and public vigilance remains the only antidote. *Liberty Denied* places current threats to free expression in a historical context, and expands the concepts of the meaning and scope of censorship activities in America today.

CONTENTS

School librarians have a dual responsibility to the populations they serve: As librarians they are committed to providing free access to ideas and information, and as teachers they have the obligation to promote free inquiry in the marketplace of ideas. The challenges to these freedoms are not only those posed by book banning and burning, sinister though they may be. While they have been librarians' primary concern, various public and governmental denials of access to information, expressed in various forms, have posed equivalent threats. These are detailed in the book and are summarized below.

Libel suits and their costs in time and money have inhibited the free flow of information in the news media. Two noteworthy examples are the Westmoreland and Sharon suits against CBS and *Time* magazine, respectively. Other examples are cited as well, and Demac charges that libel suits have been used aggressively by some individuals and organizations to discourage press coverage of their activities. The pornography debate has widened as sexual explicitness has increased. Complicating the issue has been the move toward censorship by those feminists who view pornography as a contributory factor in the oppression of women. The campaign against pornography has been escalated not only by private groups but by governmental action as well. The resultant censorship activities are described in Chapter 4.

Corporate control of free speech is described in the next chapter, which deals with employee rights to engage in private political activities, and to "blow the whistle" on corporate misdeeds. Succeeding chapters describe the potential for abuse in the government's use of surveillance in the name of security and protection against terrorism, along with the rise of computerized networks of information and the propensity for secrecy in governmental activities. Deceit in the use of executive power was exemplified by the Iran-Contra affair, an exercise in "shadow government" that was by no means limited to the Reagan administration. The author charges, however, that the "momentum of the move toward closed government has increased dramatically during the Reagan years" (p. 91). By such steps as privatizing federal agency libraries, eliminating thousands of government publications, reducing data collection by government agencies, and interfering with access to the documents of regulatory agencies, the government has succeeded in restricting the public's access to information, the author asserts. This trend is the subject of another chapter.

Demac also turns her attention to attempts at suppressing the media, restricting travel, and influencing and constricting scientific and academic research, all in the name of national security. Her final chapter, subtitled "The Future of Free Expression in America," discusses the ominous implications of censorship and secrecy in government, and the portents for future problems of access posed by information and communications technologies.

AUTHORITY

Demac, a lawyer, writer, and educator, has written about public access to information; she is also a board member of the National Coalition Against Censorship.

COMMENT

This book builds a strong case for concern about where the United States is headed in the areas of free inquiry and access to information. Whether fears of terrorism, subversion, foreign spies, and sexual promiscuity justify the curtailment of intellectual freedoms is an issue about which many opinions exist. Demac provides material that will ensure a lively debate, one that demands the participation of all.

Felsted, Carla Martindell, ed. *Youth and Alcohol Abuse: Readings and Resources.* SEE Chapter 13, The Library Media Center and the Curriculum.

Gilbert, Martin. *The Holocaust: A History of the Jews of Europe During the Second World War.* **Holt, 1985. 959 pp. ISBN 0-03-062416-9.**

PURPOSE

The culmination of anti-Semitism occurred in this century on the European continent where so many American families originated. A new wave of anti-Semitic incidents and attacks against ethnic and other minority groups appears to be breaking in America. At the same time, school systems are acknowledging that the Holocaust was a unique event in world history and are including courses about it in their curricula. This book, written for the general reader, has been acclaimed as a definitive account of the Holocaust. It is included here to provide a historical background for those who may need it.

CONTENTS

Gilbert places the events of the Holocaust in a historical context, touching on the early roots of anti-Semitism in Europe and describing its increasingly violent character in twentieth-century Germany, Poland, and Russia. As the persecutions of Jews increased in cruelty under the Nazis, the rest of the world closed their doors to Jewish emigration from Nazi Germany. At the international Evian Conference in 1938 their fate was sealed as government after government placed severe limits on the number of Jews who would be permitted to enter their countries. *Kristallnacht* signaled the beginning of the end of European Jewry, as new immigration restrictions were enforced in every country to which they might have fled. As a result of British diplomatic pressure, Jews were not even allowed to pass through the countries that were on the route to Palestine, where Arabs in this British protectorate were already rioting against Jewish immigration.

As the Nazi war machine surged through Europe, the atrocities against the peoples in their path reached an unequaled level of ferocity, while the Jews, targeted now for extinction, were rounded up and shipped to concentration camps to be tortured and murdered. The evidence supplied in this book came from accounts of survivors and from the diaries of Jews who were imprisoned in the many ghettos that held them until the time arrived for shipping them to a concentration camp for gasing and cremation. Also included are the accounts of Jewish resistance in the Warsaw ghetto, in concentration camps, and in forests and villages and cities, as well as accounts of the aftermath of these attempts, the torture and killing of hundreds of Jews for each person who attempted to resist.

The destruction of Jewish life in Europe was the inevitable result of this calculated onslaught against them, which continued even as the Nazi attempt at world domination was being turned back in the waning days of the war. An estimated 6 million Jews, of the 8 million who had lived in Europe, were slaughtered, and the story of their destruction is told in this book. Lengthy documentation and a detailed index conclude the book.

AUTHORITY

Martin Gilbert, a fellow of Merton College at Oxford University, is the official biographer of Winston Churchill, and has published more than 30 books and atlases.

COMMENT

In writings, interviews, and speeches, Holocaust survivor Elie Wiesel has commented repeatedly on the inadequacy of words to convey the realities of the Holocaust. Another survivor, Alexander Donat, called his book, based on his own experiences, *The Holocaust Kingdom* (1965), a title that suggests that the Holocaust existed on a plane apart from the world known to most people. For obvious reasons, great care must be used in selecting books and nonprint materials about this subject.

A conflict rages as to whether the Holocaust was a unique occurrence in human history or but another particularly vicious and successful manifestation of humanity's dark side. Survivors of the Armenian massacre, the Cambodian tragedy, slavery in America, and the wars against native Americans will have their own views. Perhaps it can be agreed, at least, that a knowledge and understanding of these events will help to avoid future genocides and that to deny them their place in history will ensure their repetition. A catalog of books and nonprint media suitable for children and young adults may be obtained from the Anti-Defamation League of B'nai B'rith in New York City.

Gong, Victor, and Norman Rudnick, eds. *AIDS: Facts and Issues,* rev. and updated ed. Rutgers Univ. Press, 1986. 388 pp. ISBN 0-8135-1201-G (pap.).

PURPOSE

This overview of AIDS and the issues surrounding it provides information about the disease and its impact. Written for the general reader, it offers the informational background necessary to enable school librarians to participate professionally in AIDS education programs.

CONTENTS

It was in the summer of 1981 that AIDS was first identified and its main characteristics began to be understood. Since then, the spread of the disease has caused it to be recognized as a major health problem. Its epidemic proportions have raised fear among the public, while medical researchers have not yet achieved success in treating or curing it or in preventing its spread.

What medical science has learned is summarized in this book, which is divided into seven sections. The first section begins with an overview of the problem and a discussion of some of the facts and fallacies in public awareness of it. Its causes and epidemiology are the subjects of the next two chapters. Section 2 presents a clinical overview, describing the effects of AIDS on the immune system and the signs and symptoms of the disease. It is the failure of the immune system that allows infectious diseases to attack the AIDS patient, and these deadly infections are identified and explained, along with the cancers and blood disorders that also bring death.

Section 3 discusses the at-risk groups and risk factors such as the blood supply, and their threats to the general public, real and imagined, is examined. Included in this coverage are childen with AIDS, the Haitian population, and prisons. Later attention in this book is given to intravenous drug users. How the public has responded to the AIDS crisis is the subject of Section 4, which begins with an examination of the ethical issues, and considers the moral responsibilities of health professionals, researchers, AIDS patients, and society. Economic costs, the gay perspective and public health issues, and legal aspects of AIDS are also discussed. Section 5 deals with AIDS research. The slow progress toward finding a preventive vaccine, restoring damaged immune systems, attacking the AIDS virus itself, and treating the infectious diseases it causes are all discussed.

Ways of avoiding or coping with the disease are the subject of Section 6, which describes care of the AIDS patient and considers psychological, social, spiritual, and religious issues. AIDS prevention and mental health are also discussed. The concluding section presents information sources, health resources, hot lines, and referral centers. A glossary, a list of references and sources, an index, and a list of contributors complete the book.

AUTHORITY

Victor Gong, a physician in private practice, was formerly with the Department of Emergency Medicine at Johns Hopkins Hospital.

Norman Rudnick is a science editor with a background in physics and biomedical sciences.

COMMENT

Public health officials are agreed that the only effective measure against the spread of the AIDS epidemic is prevention through education. While some school systems and parent and religious groups are loath to introduce AIDS education programs in their schools, others have added it to the health or sex education curriculum. Certainly curiosity and fear induce young people to seek information about it. After an examination of several books about this disease, this one was selected for inclusion here because of its comprehensive treatment of the subject, providing librarians with a factual basis and understanding of the issues needed for selecting materials for the school library media center. For further help in locating AIDS information sources, see Malinowsky and Perry, *AIDS Information Sourcebook,* and American Foundation for AIDS Research (AmFAR), *Learning AIDS,* both in Chapter 8, "Selection Guides and Resources."

Goodlad, John I. *A Place Called School: Prospects for the Future.* **McGraw-Hill, 1984. 396 pp. ISBN 0-07-0223626-7.**

PURPOSE

Writing for educators and informed citizens, Goodlad has examined some typical schools and surveyed their students, parents, and teachers in an effort to determine the causes of the malaise that permeates American education, and what solutions might be proposed to existent problems.

CONTENTS

Following a decade of nationwide dissatisfaction with its schools, Goodlad, funded by a number of sources, embarked on an intensive study of a relatively small number of schools representing different regions and types of communities. His expectation was that the data he gathered would reflect the condition of schools nationally, and enable him to determine the actual state of the schools and what might be done to reevaluate the nation's perception of them and their actual performance.

The data were based on students', teachers', and parents' perceptions of what the problems were in teaching, curriculum, student behavior, and a number of other factors. Although there were wide variations in some of the characteristics, the problems that emerged were to some degree reflected in all the schools that were studied. High on the list of problems in junior and senior high schools were drug and alcohol use, student misbehavior, and lack of student and parent interest. In elementary schools, where student opinion was not sought, the problems were student misbehavior, lack of parent interest, and school and class size.

That the education students are receiving does not come from school alone was suggested by the percentage of time spent in school as compared with the percentage of time watching television. About 8.5 percent of total hours lived are given to school by the age of 18, while the average American child will have spent 9 to 10 percent of his or her lifetime in front of a television set.

Nevertheless, Goodlad believes, considerable improvement in education can be achieved by significant changes. Among those he suggests are organizing curriculum research and development centers similar to those that led to curriculum reform in the 1950s and 1960s. In these centers K through 12 curricula in the various disciplines can be studied and redesigned and the accompanying pedagogy altered to suit the results. Smaller schools and classes, or, where this is not possible, schools within schools and elimination of tracking are other recommendations.

Linking schools to universities where exemplary practices presumably would originate and be replicated was another recommendation, as were changes in teacher training, in the teacher-principal relationship, and differentiated staffing. Changes in the way staff is selected, particularly in elementary schools, where no concern is given to balancing teachers' expertise in academic subjects, were also suggested. Perhaps most startling is the advocacy of a new age range for schooling, which would begin at the age of 4 and conclude at 16. After that, patterns of additional schooling in community colleges, work-study programs, and community service would occupy the 16-year-old graduates.

References for each of the chapters appear at the end of the book, followed by appendixes that identify source materials and the author's staff. An index concludes the book.

AUTHORITY

Goodlad is professor of education, and was dean of the Graduate School of Education, University of California, Los Angeles. He has written extensively on education.

COMMENT

This compilation and interpretation of data resulting from an indepth study of schools has produced an interesting array of insights. Goodlad's recommendations are thoughtful and innovative in some respects and reminiscent of the past in others. Although this reader could not find a single reference to school libraries, nor an index entry on that topic, nor were they reported as objects of field study when schools were visited, school library media specialists will find an important role for their centers in fulfilling many of the educational goals identified in the book. It merits attention.

Handlin, Oscar. *The Uprooted: The Epic Story of the Great Migrations That Made the American People*, 2nd ed., enlarged. Little, Brown, 1973. 333 pp. ISBN 0-316-34301-3.

PURPOSE

Written for the general public, this book is a classic study of the immigrant experience. It is included here because it provides an invaluable background for those who may be involved in developing or implementing an ethnic studies curriculum.

CONTENTS

What happens to a young nation when 35 million people seek refuge within its borders over the space of a few decades? What happens to these immigrant peoples themselves? Handlin seeks to understand and to transmit this understanding to his readers.

This is the story of the massive immigrations of the nineteenth and early twentieth centuries, from the often unendurable journey across the sea to the landing on a strange and unwelcoming shore, and the years of striving that followed. The often poetic narration depicts the effects of this huge migration, both on the immigrants themselves and on their new land. An understanding of the peasant origins of the emigrants is an important factor in perceiving their difficulties, as they strove to adapt to a strange environment, without the support of the communal culture they had left behind. Handlin details the adjustments they had to make, in occupation, in religion, in family life, in living conditions, and in countless other aspects of their existence. Often he uses the words of the immigrants themselves as they describe their plight in letters and newspaper articles. The story is dramatic and touching, and will leave the reader with new insights into the hazards of immigrant existence in America.

AUTHORITY

A noted historian, Oscar Handlin was a professor of history at Harvard University when this book, winner of the Pulitzer Prize for history, was published.

COMMENT

A landmark in the attempt to describe and define the immigrant experience, *The Uprooted* remains the classic source even now, almost 40 years after its publication, for those who would understand the significance of the immigrant experience in American history. As Handlin points out, immigration is not just a thread in the story of America; it is the very fabric of its economic growth and the dye of its national character, and remains so today. While they may come from different shores and nations, today's immigrants face the same perils, the same privations, and the same potential. This book is a powerful teacher to all who work with immigrant populations, and a moving human story for those who don't.

Hoffmann, Frank. *Intellectual Freedom and Censorship: An Annotated Bibliography.* **Scarecrow, 1989. 254 pp. ISBN 0-8108-2145-1.**

PURPOSE

This guide to the literature on censorship was prepared primarily for the use of students as a research tool. It also can be used as a resource and to some extent as a purchasing guide for high school and academic libraries.

CONTENTS

Each of the book's five parts provides a different perspective on the subject, and each is introduced by Hoffmann's comments on the content of that part and its relevance to the overall issue. The first part is concerned with the historical development and theories of intellectual freedom and censorship. A chronological table of events in the history of censorship begins with John Peter Zenger and ends with the 1986 report of the Meese Commission. The bibliography for Part 1 is divided into subtopics that include readings on the First Amendment (again with topical subdivisions), censorship, obscenity, and pornography. Part 2 provides citations of court cases that have dealt with various issues on censorship and intellectual freedom, and these are subdivided by subtopic. Hoffmann's introduction to this part explains how to interpret the citations and comments on its overall content.

Part 3 is composed of materials about the professions most closely involved in censorship issues: education, library service, journalism, and politics and government. The introduction provides a justification for limiting the discussion to those four and explores the relationship of each to the censorship issue. Subdivisions identify each aspect of a profession's relationship to the issues.

In Part 4 a number of procensorship and anticensorship groups are identified; and their publications, as well as those by individuals of various persuasions, are listed. Part 5 discusses censorship cases in the media and indicates sources for further exploration. Books, films, magazines, songs, and other forms of expression that have been subject to censorship are listed in a table that, Hoffmann acknowledges, is not complete. The bibliography continues with citations that comment on this aspect of the subject.

Indexes of personal names and subjects complete the book.

AUTHORITY

Hoffmann is an associate professor at the School of Library Science, Sam Houston State University, Huntsville, Texas, where he teaches library collection development and conducts a seminar on intellectual freedom.

COMMENT

While far from exhaustive, this bibliography provides excellent coverage of key issues in censorship, intellectual freedom, and the schools. Included in the recommended sources are a broad spectrum of viewpoints, encouraging access to a variety of opinions, which, after all, is what intellectual freedom is all about. Students, teachers, and librarians will find it an abundant source for pursuing further study.

Jay, Margaret, and Sally Doganis. *Battered: The Abuse of Children.* **St. Martin's, 1987. 211 pp. ISBN 0-312-01625-5.**

PURPOSE

Writing for the general reader, from the premise that exposing a problem is a first step toward finding some possible solutions, Jay and Doganis describe cases of child abuse. They comment on futile attempts at intervention by social service agencies, and reveal confusion on the part of authorities about how to deal with child abuse.

CONTENTS

Judging from the contents of this book, written by two English journalists about notorious cases in their country, the increase in child abuse is not limited to the United States but is as serious a problem in Great Britain. The authors present graphic descriptions of physical abuse, neglect, and sexual abuse and demonstrate how the lasting effects of the abuse twist adult lives and affect their children as well.

Social work theory seems to work against the best interests of abused children, by seeking to keep the family together in spite of every indication that the factors that led to abuse or neglect are still not under control. As a result, children are often removed from foster care situations where their condition improves and returned to the biological family for further abuse, and sometimes death.

According to the authors, cases of sexual abuse are overwhelmingly incestuous, with fathers, grandfathers, and brothers often victimizing young female children. The family characteristics that are likely to result in this abuse are explored, and lists of warning signs, including physical and behavioral indicators, that can alert those who work with the children are presented.

The histories of the cases discussed emphasize the importance of early intervention to try to break the cyclical pattern of abuse. The legal system, however, often fails to protect the abused child, frequently because the child's testimony is not believed. As a partial answer to the problem, school authorities are now taking the lead in informing pupils about aspects of sexual abuse and in providing situations where abused children may feel able to disclose what has happened to them. The authors also recommend that courses be provided where secondary school students may learn about child care and other practical topics that will help them organize their households and families so that their own approaching parenthood can be met with knowledge instead of ignorance.

AUTHORITY
Jay and Doganis are television journalists. They have spoken with pediatricians, social workers, lawyers, and others involved in child abuse cases, and have studied research on the subject in the United States as well as Great Britain and Canada.

COMMENT
The dilemmas posed by child abuse and family dysfunction will not be readily solved until the social causes are better understood. Nor is it clear what school librarians can do in their professional capacity, beyond providing the information resources that will foster greater awareness on the part of teachers and students. Understanding the dimensions of the problem is, at least, a first step.

Jenkinson, Edward B. *Censors in the Classroom: The Mind Benders*. Avon, 1982. 184 pp. ISBN 0-380-59790-X (pap.).

Jenkinson juxtaposes the rights to know, to read, and to teach against the right, sought and exercised by many organizations, to abrogate those rights through censorship. By understanding the motives and methods of such groups, he contends, those who are concerned about intellectual freedom are better able to protect it.

CONTENTS

Few would argue against the idea that intellectual freedom is a basic cornerstone of American democracy. But where their children and beliefs are concerned, some parents, and the groups they turn to, insist on controlling the content of the curriculum, textbooks, and library books that not only their children but all children in the schools are exposed to. This is the crux of the censorship controversy: Who shall control the intellectual content of what is taught in schools? Does any self-appointed group have the right to determine what books or what subjects shall be studied, or even just what books shall be allowed to stand on library shelves?

In their conviction that they alone possess knowledge of absolute truths, censorship groups have mounted serious and sometimes violent attacks against those who would foster a spirit of inquiry and openness to ideas in classrooms and libraries. Jenkinson describes these censorship campaigns, the organizations behind them (over 200 such groups by his count), and the results of their efforts, in the schools and in court rulings. He presents these crusaders temperately, never denying their right to their thoughts, only opposing their insistence on forcing their thoughts on others.

He is concerned, however, with who the censors are and what their targets are, so that open inquiry, student rights, and teacher rights may be protected. He advocates the preparation of selection policies for books and other materials and the development of procedures for handling complaints. He urges the use of publicity as a means of exposing attempts at censorship, rather than giving way to the temptation to avoid controversy, and concludes that citizens who are concerned about what children read should band together to preserve freedom of choice rather than joining together to censor books.

AUTHORITY

Jenkinson is a professor of English education at Indiana University. He is also chairman of the NCTE's Committee Against Censorship.

COMMENT

"We can never be sure that the opinion we are endeavoring to stifle is a false opinion; and if we were sure, stifling it would be an evil still."
—John Stuart Mill, in *Liberty*.

There is too much diversity of thought in the United States for any group to be allowed to decide what others should read or think, even if that group constitutes a majority. This is a basic tenet of U.S. society and its educational system. Yet, in the name of protecting the young, and by virtue of their persistence and zeal, groups that claim to be in possession of some absolute and incontrovertible truth are being allowed to decide what should be removed from school libraries and what should be in the textbooks the schools use. Jenkinson reveals who these groups are and how they operate, and suggests ways of frustrating their efforts at censorship.

Johnston, Jerry. *Why Suicide? What Parents and Teachers Must Know to Save Our Kids.* **Oliver-Nelson, 1987. 190 pp. ISBN 0-8407-9089-9.**

PURPOSE

Writing for teenagers, parents, and educators, Johnston attempts to answer his title's question and suggests ways of helping to prevent the tragedy of teenage suicide that includes a Christian fundamentalist solution.

CONTENTS

In the last ten years over 50,000 American teenagers have taken their own lives, according to Johnston. Between 1950 and 1980, suicide had risen from fifth to second place as a cause of death among adolescents. American teenagers are the only group whose mortality rate has gone up during the past two decades. The number of unsuccessful suicide attempts among this group has also increased tremendously. Johnston states these facts and describes the incidents of suicide and failed attempts that give them even greater poignancy.

Implicit in the stories Johnston relates are the influences of drugs, sex, alcohol, family problems, and pressures from parents to excel and from peers to share their confused values. A near-suicide himself, Johnston shares his own story as an example of how it is possible to turn from despair to hope, in his case as a result of religious conversion. He describes the warning signs of unbearable depression, suggests what parents and friends can do, and devotes a chapter to the role that teachers can play in identifying at-risk students and ways in which they can help students cope with their problems, among them making referrals to professional counselors. When left alone, he notes, a teenager who is moderately or severely suicidal will usually get worse, rarely get better. Most young people exhibiting warning signs of suicide desperately want to be helped. Therefore, it is important for school personnel to be able to recognize some of the behavior characteristics that warn of impending trouble and to respond to the warning.

Johnston concludes with an open letter to teenagers, telling them why suicide is the wrong answer to their problems and persuading them of its ultimate futility.

AUTHORITY

Jerry Johnston has been carrying his message to over 2 million youths in 2,200 public schools throughout the country and has appeared on television and radio talk shows.

COMMENT

There can be no doubt of the urgency of the problem of teenage suicide, particularly as the statistical evidence demonstrates its rising incidence. While this book offers neither professional detachment nor sober analysis, it does offer a graphic reminder of the dimensions of the tragedy and some clear advice on how to detect warning signs and help the potential suicide victim.

Malinowsky, H. Robert, and Gerald J. Perry, eds. *AIDS Information Sourcebook,* **2nd ed.** SEE Chapter 8, Selection Guides and Resources.

Merritt, Le Roy Charles. *Book Selection and Intellectual Freedom.* **Wilson, 1970. 100 pp. ISBN 0-8242-0420-4.**

PURPOSE

An exploration of issues in the selection of library materials as they relate to intellectual freedom, this book was written for all librarians and emphasizes the importance of preparing a selection policy with input from the community.

CONTENTS

Merritt describes the selection process as it relates to intellectual freedom and sets forth a compromise between the value theory and the demand theory of selection: Give the patrons what you think they should have versus give them what you think they want. The essential criterion, he asserts, is to select books that make a positive

413

contribution to the collection and that are of some benefit to the library's clientele. Although what is useful to some may be objectionable to others, a positive choice has been established.

Support for selection decisions can be provided by a statement of the library's selection policy. By involving members of the library's community in determining the policies, and by obtaining the approval of those governing authorities who may be called on to defend the policy, the librarian will have ensured support should the need arise. Beyond this, a selection policy provides day-to-day guidance in defining the scope of the collection and in selecting materials.

The book offers a detailed sample selection policy. An appendix presents the ALA documents in support of intellectual freedom and the Right to Read. A bibliography and an index are also provided.

AUTHORITY

Merritt was dean of the School of Librarianship at the University of Oregon, and a former editor of ALA's *Newsletter on Intellectual Freedom.*

COMMENT

This brief monograph makes some valid distinctions between selection and self-censorship, always a source of controversy when book selection is discussed. The sample selection policy is a good model for adaptation, although school librarians may opt for a more general statement.

Reed, Mary Hutchings. *The Copyright Primer for Librarians and Educators.* ALA and NEA, 1987. 60 pp. ISBN 0-8389-0472-6 (pap.).

PURPOSE

Working with the advice of a copyright attorney to interpret the copyright law for librarians and educators, Reed has presented the basic provisions of the law and how they affect various activities.

CONTENTS

Moving from the general to the specific, Reed uses a question-and-answer format as well as exposition to present information about the copyright law, its ramifications in libraries, schools, and higher education, and specific applications in photocopying and off-air taping and with music, videotapes, and computer software. Infringements, their remedies, and obtaining permissions are also discussed.

The tension that exists between the need to protect authors' rights to their work and the educational uses and scrutiny to which these works can be put with the use of copying devices is touched on but left to a treatment of wider scope. Reed notes that while some of the potential hindrances to libraries' ability to deliver information have been removed as a result of compromises that were made before and after the law was enacted, advances in technology are creating new problems. As court decisions and the fair use rights evolve, it is to be hoped that the spirit of compromise will prevail. The booklet concludes with lists of information sources on legislative materials and case law. An index is also provided.

AUTHORITY

Reed is the legal counsel to the American Library Association and a partner in the law firm of Sidley and Austin in Chicago. She has published articles on copyright and other legal issues related to libraries.

COMMENT

Briefer, and less inclusive, than R. S. Talab's *Commonsense Copyright* (reviewed in this chapter), this booklet provides a more library-oriented perspective and considers a few questions not covered by Talab. Together the two will probably answer most of the commonly asked questions.

Reichman, Henry F. *Censorship and Selection: Issues and Answers for Schools.* **ALA and AASA, 1988. 141 pp. ISBN 0-8389-3350-5 (pap.).**

PURPOSE

This information manual was prepared to help school personnel and the general public understand the issues that are raised when books and other materials for learning are challenged by interest groups or individuals, and to recommend effective procedures for dealing with these challenges.

CONTENTS

Censorship continues to stimulate controversy, and defending the concept of classroom and library as "free marketplaces of ideas" remains an important preoccupation of educators and librarians. Consensus may not even exist as to whether or not censorship efforts have increased substantially in recent years.

The three basic areas in which challenges to the free and open pursuit of knowledge have been made are the selection and retention of school library materials, the selection and use of curricular materials, and students' rights to free expression of thought. Attention is given to each of these concerns, with the major focus on providing free access to a diversity of information and ideas. In its eight chapters, the book sums up the crux of each issue, the substance of conflicting opinions, and the necessity of previously approved policies and procedures for resolving disputes peacefully and rationally.

The first two chapters define censorship, placing it in the context of the library and education worlds, emphasizing the necessity of academic freedom in a democratic society, exploring the differences between censorship and selection, and identifying who the censors are. That the desire to avoid controversy can readily lead to censorship from within is also a point to ponder. The issues that lead to occurrences of censorship are discussed in Chapter 3. They range across the political spectrum from right to left, and include political issues, offensive language, sexuality, secular humanism, sexism, racism, and witchcraft. Issues may be intertwined when censors step forward, and objections may be expressed on one issue when another is really the point.

Success in resisting censorship lies in being ready for it, and the next three chapters outline preparedness measures: a rational, evenhanded, confident, and calm approach, supported by a selection policy that is already in place, with procedures for dealing with complaints, including complaint forms conveniently at hand. The importance of not deviating from the established procedures is emphasized. The general rules for handling complaints begin "DO NOT PANIC," and proceed with further sound advice. Supreme Court and applicable lower court rulings are discussed in detail, and a checklist for school systems is also supplied. A brief concluding chapter suggests that conflict may often be avoided by more open communication between school and parents.

Several appendixes provide interpretations of the School Library Bill of Rights, tips of various kinds, sample documents to be used or adapted by schools and districts, summaries of court cases, a list of concerned organizations, an annotated bibliography, and footnotes.

AUTHORITY

Henry F. Reichman taught at the University of California and Northwestern University; he is currently a member of the history department at Memphis State University. He has written for and been associate editor of ALA's *Newsletter on Intellectual Freedom* and has written many articles and publications on the subject.

Although by no means insignificant, its currency is not the only reason for recommending this book. It is also clear, concise, thorough, and practical.

Shawn, Karen. *The End of Innocence: Anne Frank and the Holocaust.*
See Chapter 13, The Library Media Center and the Curriculum.

Smith, Jane Bandy, ed. *School Library Media Annual,* **Vol. 6. Libraries Unlimited, 1988. 297 pp. ISBN 0-87287-635-7.**

PURPOSE
Events of major importance to school library media specialists are the focus of this annual publication. The 1988 volume looks at the whole language approach to reading and writing instruction from several different perspectives, and presents an inside view of a censorship case in Georgia. Other yearly features are included as well.

CONTENT
While alert school library specialists can see a role for their programs in almost any curriculum, the whole language approach to reading seems particularly apt to lend itself to integration with school library programs. After all, if children are to be engaged in reading actual children's literature as they develop reading skills, then the school library with its collection of the best books for children and a librarian with an intimate knowledge of these books and skills in presenting them to children would seem to be the ideal place and person for helping to move such a program forward. Whether such a partnership will emerge from the theoretical discussions about whole language and the practical realities of classroom, library, and school is another matter. In the final analysis, the ultimate decision will rest in how school systems and their individual schools approach whole language teaching and how effective school library media specialists are in uniting with reading teachers to provide literature, and foster that engagement with reading that will lead toward successful implementation of the whole language approach.

Eleanor Kulleseid, editor of the section devoted to the whole language approach and the library media center's potential role, raises some significant questions, and offers some titles for further reading on whole language theory and practice. Some distinguished contributors present their views from the varying perspectives of teacher educator, school district administrator, curriculum leader, library science educator, textbook writer, and school principal.

Section 2 of the *Annual* presents a case study of censorship based on an incident that occurred in the Gwinnett County, Georgia, public schools. The increase in censorship incidents is noted, and citizen and press responses to the challenges are described as well. Appendixes to this section present a censorship survival kit, the Gwinnett County selection policy, appeal procedures, and a form for filing an appeal. Section 3 is devoted to research, and includes brief notes on research in progress, ERIC reports, and completed research related to school library media programs. Section 4 updates information about automation, and includes articles on CD-ROM, on-line searching, and on-line catalogs.

The second part of the publication offers current information on events of the year, which includes a statement of the goals and objectives developed by the National Association of State Educational Media Professionals (NASTEMP). Among the goals are the establishment of a national office for school library media programs and provisions for adequate personnel, materials, and financial resources. An "Almanac of Information" includes notable people, statistical information on school libraries, and notable publications on children's literature, professional concerns, and ERIC resources. An index completes the book.

AUTHORITY

Smith is an education specialist in the State Department of Education, Montgomery, Alabama.

COMMENT

The discussion of the whole language approach offers thoughtful commentary on this recent development in reading instruction, particularly in its examination of the school library media program's role. Equally valuable are the other sections. This annual publication provides summaries of the year's events and trends in readable and stimulating articles. It should be on every school library's professional shelf, budget permitting.

Talab, R. S. *Commonsense Copyright: A Guide to the New Technologies*. McFarland, 1986. 162 pp. ISBN 0-89950-224-5 (pap.).

PURPOSE

Written to clarify those aspects of the Copyright Law of 1976 (P.L. 94-553) that affect policies of acquisition and use in libraries and classrooms, this book describes the law itself and the opinions and case law that have emerged as a result of its application.

CONTENTS

"A Copyright Primer," Part I, describes the effects of modern technology on the use of copyrighted materials, and the remedies that have been prescribed by the law to protect authors and producers of original, copyrighted works. Included here are an explanation of copyright, its subject matter and duration, the copyright owner's rights, and the law's infringement provisions. Part II, "Uses of Copyrighted Materials," explains first the doctrine of fair use and then presents criteria for determining whether use falls within this provision. This is followed by chapters that describe both acceptable and unacceptable uses of print materials, music, audiovisual materials, and computer software. Guidelines and examples are used to clarify the law's provisions regarding such use of copyrighted materials as the reproduction of articles, poems, and parts of books, off-air taping, making videotapes of films and filmstrips, downloading from data bases, and other uses of computer software. Permission policies and how to secure permissions are also described.

The use of photocopying equipment by librarians and patrons and problems arising from interlibrary loan systems and library networks are the principal subjects of Part III, which also discusses the use of copyrighted materials in libraries. Various aspects of film, video, and software use are considered, and examples of permitted and nonpermitted usage are provided. The book also offers details about the Library of Congress Copyright Office Information hot line, the Television Licensing Center, and the Copyright Clearance Center. Part IV provides a bibliography that includes resources on copyright, video and computer copyright, information on Library of Congress and other resources pertaining to copyright in libraries, notes on all the chapters, and charts that present guidelines in simplified form for print materials, computer software, films, and television. The appendixes in Part V include reprints of significant portions of the copyright law (both P.L. 94-553 and the more recent P.L. 96-517, the Computer Amendment) and guidelines and policies set forth by ALA and the International Council for Computers in Education (ICCE).

AUTHORITY

Talab is an assistant professor of educational technology and media at Kansas State University. She has had experience with various types of libraries, and is also a business consultant.

419

COMMENT

Ignoring the copyright law with regard to uses of copyrighted material may be tempting when trying to stretch the shrinking dollars available for library and other educational purchasing. However, excusing transgressions by claiming ignorance of the law, it is clear, provides no valid excuse for breaking it. Many of the ambiguities of the copyright law have been resolved as a result of court cases, and the examples in this book will clarify many doubts about what librarians can and cannot do with copyrighted materials of all kinds. It is *must* reading for all school library media specialists.

Tower, Cynthia Crosson. *Understanding Child Abuse and Neglect*. Allyn & Bacon, 1989. 402 pp. ISBN 0-205-11767-8 (pap.).

PURPOSE

Primarily a text for social workers and other family service professionals, this book presents an overview of aspects of a problem that all who work with children and young adults, particularly in schools, need to understand.

CONTENTS

Neglected and abused children often become abusive adults. They bear the scars of their mistreatment in their bones and bodies and in their hearts and minds. Some of the worst cases have been sensationalized in the press, and then are quickly and conveniently forgotten. The questions posed by this book are: How can this growing trend be reversed? And, ultimately, how can children be protected from those who would abuse them? While Tower addresses social service workers, one of her chapters is also concerned with the role that schools can play. A first step, however, is understanding the nature of the problem.

The author begins with a historical approach, tracing maltreatment of children from early recorded history to the present. She then proceeds to a discussion of the family, defining and describing its functions, problems, and dysfunctions, and continues with a discussion of the effects of abuse and neglect on children's accomplishment of developmental tasks. The next several chapters deal with each of several categories of abuse: physical abuse and its causes and effects; child neglect and its results; sexual abuse, its types and incidence and the resultant trauma; incest and its varying manifestations; and sexual abuse and exploitation outside the family. These chapters discuss the abused child and the perpetrator, using anecdotal descriptions as illustrations.

Succeeding chapters deal with the subject from a social service, legal, and therapeutic perspective. Considered here are assessment, intervention, and case management by social work professionals; the role of family and criminal courts; and treatment of children, parents, family groups, and other individuals within the family. Foster care and alternative solutions are explored, along with the role and rights of the natural parents. The social work system and the roles of workers within it are explored in a chapter that describes a protective worker's typical day, presents some comments of social workers on their ability to be effective within the bureaucratic and other constraints in which they function, and concludes that the system does work and suggests ways for these professionals to avoid burnout.

Concluding chapters discuss effects of child abuse on adults who had been abused and their therapeutic treatment, recommendations for prevention efforts in schools and communities, necessary changes in the social system and in the system that provides help, and the need for further research.

Each chapter concludes with questions to explore, activities for applying what has been learned, and suggested reading and references. An index completes the book.

AUTHORITY
Tower is associate professor of human services at Fitchburg State College, has worked in protective services and as a trainer of others working with child abuse victims, and is a consultant and private therapist specializing in the treatment of survivors of child abuse.

COMMENT
Abused children and the causes and effects of abuse are the concerns of every professional who works with children. This book provides a background for understanding an increasingly pervasive problem. It is recommended for inclusion in the professional collection.

Varlejs, Jana, ed. *Freedom of Information and Youth*. McFarland, 1986. 92 pp. ISBN 0-89950-189-3 (pap.).

PURPOSE
The proceedings of a symposium conducted by Rutgers University's School of Communication, Information, and Library Studies, this book examines the constraints on intellectual freedom that are imposed by censorship of books in school libraries.

THE CURRENT SCENE

Librarians tend to think of censorship only as misdirected attacks against sexual explicitness, offensive language, or liberal thought by "narrow minded fundamentalists." The territory, however, is much wider than that. Some of it has been explored by the participants in the symposium recorded in this book.

In her foreword, Varlejs comments on the continual appearance of new groups that would censor, taking aim at new targets. Guidelines simply do not exist for many school librarians, as school boards, acting as parents' representatives, prefer to accede to parents' wishes rather than to consider students' First Amendment rights. Where, then, is the right, the responsibility, to select materials in accordance with one's best professional judgment? How can school librarians answer those vociferous parents who are able to persuade a school board that a book is objectionable because it is racist, or sexist, or offensive to a religious group?

But that is far from being the only impediment to freedom of information. Mary K. Chelton, a participant in the symposium, not so gently takes note of the ease with which librarians ignore the demands of intellectual freedom when selecting books, while espousing its principles, and then describes several instances that prove her point. And beyond her accusation of hypocrisy are the honest questions about the freedom to encounter ideas that we are willing to allow young people, ideas that librarians may have rejected themselves, such as creationism, or the denial of Nazi Germany's deliberate murder of 6 million Jews. Among other concerns expressed during this symposium are those raised by the Reagan administration's attempts at imposing prior censorship on government employees and its general cutback in responding to requests for information from government agencies. Another concern was whether the *Pico* vs. *Island Trees* Supreme Court decision was a victory for freedom of information or a defeat, evoking considerable disagreement. Questions raised by the views of the Moral Majority and other fundamentalist groups may seem somewhat less clear-cut after reading this discussion.

For further study of the issues, an annotated bibliography is provided. Appendixes include a directory of national organizations concerned with intellectual freedom, ALA's Library Bill of Rights and statement on Free Access to Libraries for Minors, the Freedom to Read Committee's "Books and the Young Reader," and AASL's "What Can a School Library Media Specialist Do to Preserve Intellectual Freedom?"

422

AUTHORITY

Jana Varlejs is director of the Library and Information Studies Professional Development program, Rutgers, The State University of New Jersey, School of Communication, Information and Library Studies; and also faculty liaison to the Alumni Association. Contributors include Kenneth Carlson, associate dean of Rutgers University, Graduate School of Education; Mary K. Chelton, graduate library educator at Rutgers and former young adult librarian; John Hurley, assistant library director of Westfield Memorial Library in New Jersey; Leanne Katz, executive director of the National Coalition Against Censorship; and Betty Turock, faculty member at Rutgers, School of Communication, Information and Library Studies.

COMMENT

In dealing with questions of censorship and intellectual freedom there are few quick and easy answers. One group's claims are another group's anathemas, and court decisions, being made by human beings, only interpret law and do not always establish justice. The complexities can only be touched on by these discussions, while the issues raised often remain ambiguous. Yet the subject is one of such import in school libraries that it must continue to be reexamined, and this book continues the discussion on a high level.

West, Mark I. *Trust Your Children: Voices Against Censorship in Children's Literature*. Neal-Schuman, 1988. 176 pp. ISBN 1-5570-021-7 (pap.).

PURPOSE

Interviews of authors and publishers whose books have been attacked and of other advocates of intellectual freedom reveal their views on the merits of preserving children's freedom of choice in the books they read. Those in a position to act against censorship, librarians, teachers, and school board members, are the audiences addressed.

CONTENTS

In his thoughtful foreword, Anthony Podesta, founding president of People for the American Way, establishes the educational philosophy that underlies the book's contents, that our future rests on our children and will be determined by how successfully they learn how to think. The discipline of thinking can only be learned when conflicting ideas are understood and examined. Censorship impedes critical thinking by denying access to diverse points of view.

The interviews explore many facets of censorship and its effects:

Authors note the subtleties of self-censorship, publishers describe the censors' effects on the books they publish, activists consider how censorship has affected what subjects are being taught and how they are approached. When science teachers have to tiptoe around the theory of evolution, and history teachers avoid discussions of Watergate, the Vietnam War, and the Holocaust, our young people are denied the right to the information on which thought processes are built.

But what has this to do with the books of Judy Blume, Norma Klein, Maurice Sendak, Robert Cormier, Betty Miles, Harry Mazer, Nat Hentoff, Roald Dahl, Daniel Keyes, and John Steptoe, the authors who were interviewed because their books have been consistently among those that provoke censorship attempts? Taking the responses together, one must conclude that what many parents fear is the books' very success in depicting the realities of children's and young adults' lives, which are often in conflict with the adult view of their world. What the organized censors fear is that their view of morality may be undermined when children are exposed to ideas that differ from their own. The easiest tack to take is to attack frank language, or honest writing about sexuality.

The publishers (Richard Jackson, Phyllis Fogelman, and Stephen Roxburgh) and anticensorship activists (Judith Krug, Leanne Katz, Barbara Parker, and Amy A. McClure) discuss the broader implications of censorship attempts. Among the questions they consider are the reasons for the increase in censorship of children's books in recent years, publishers' responses to censorship issues, and the reasons people feel threatened by the books they seek to censor. Perhaps most alarming is the interview of Timothy B. Dyk, a specialist in First Amendment law. His comments on the *Mozert* vs. *Public Schools* case indicate how a U.S. district court ruling might have had national effects on American education had it not been overruled by the Circuit Court of Appeals. The final outcome, however, is still to be determined by the Supreme Court's decision on the anticipated appeal.

AUTHORITY

West is a member of the English Department faculty, University of North Carolina at Charlotte. The authors, publishers, and anticensorship activists he interviewed are leaders in their fields and in the struggle to protect intellectual freedom.

COMMENT

No single book can adequately explore all aspects and issues of the censorship controversy. This one builds a strong case for the necessity of protecting children from encroachments on their right to read and continuing to allow them to read books that explore the real worlds of childhood and adolescence. Its title sums up the argument.

ADDITIONAL READINGS

Adler, Mortimer J. *The Paideia Program: An Educational Syllabus.* Macmillan, 1984. 238 pp. ISBN 0-02-500300-3. Essays by scholars in the Paideia Group follow an introduction by Adler with discussions of teaching methods, the content of instruction, and the concept of the Paideia school and how it should be structured and organized.

Berman, Sanford. *Worth Noting: Editorials, Letters, Essays, an Interview and Bibliography.* Foreword by Bill Katz. McFarland, 1988. 176 pp. ISBN 0-89950-304-7. Witty and thoughtful selections from Berman's writings will provoke the reader to reexamine such diverse subjects as cataloging, creationism, censorship, and intellectual freedom.

Oboler, Eli M. *Defending Intellectual Freedom: The Library and the Censor.* Greenwood, 1980. 245 pp. ISBN 0-313-21472-7. Librarians should be leaders in defending intellectual freedom and the freedom to read. Evidence indicates that these freedoms are in danger of extinction.

Powell, Arthur G., Eleanor Farrar, and David K. Cohen. *The Shopping Mall High School: Winners and Losers in the Educational Marketplace.* Boston: Houghton Mifflin, 1986. 360 pp. ISBN 0-395-42638-3 (pap.). Based on a study of 15 diverse high schools, the authors found that schools are trying to meet varied student needs by providing something for everyone, thus diluting standards and discouraging serious academic work. The title metaphor suggests the need for reexamining the curriculum focus of high schools.

Ravitch, Diane. *The Schools We Deserve: Reflections on the Educational Crises of Our Time.* Basic Books, 1985. 337 pp. ISBN 0-465-07236-4. These reprints of Ravitch's articles from education journals reflect her critical approach to education practices as well as her view of the distortion of statistics in many recent reports urging education reform.

Schexnaydre, Linda, and Nancy Burns. *Censorship: A Guide for Successful Workshop Planning.* Oryx, 1984. 114 pp. ISBN 0-89774-093-9. Techniques and outlines, publicity ideas and sample materials, and model policies and case studies are among the offerings of this practical manual for planning and implementing workshops on censorship.

Sinofsky, Esther R. *Off-Air Videotaping in Education: Copyright Issues, Decisions, Implications.* Bowker, 1984. 163 pp. ISBN 0-8352-1755-8. Legislation and case law and their effects on educational use of off-air taping are explained. Which practices constitute fair use and which are infringements are discussed, and guidelines and policies are presented.

U.S. Department of Education. *What Works: Schools Without Drugs,* 1986. This handbook recommends approaches for stopping drug use in schools. It includes drug abuse prevention programs and discusses how parents and teachers can recognize students who are using drugs. Includes a list of resources and organizations. Call 1-800-624-0100 for a free copy, or write Schools Without Drugs, Pueblo, CO 81009.

Professional Periodicals

AAAS Science Books and Films. American Association for the Advancement of Science, 1333 H St., NW, Washington, DC 20005. Reviews books, films, and filmstrips on life sciences, physical sciences, social sciences, and mathematics.

ALAN Review. National Council of Teachers of English, 1111 Kenyon Rd., Urbana, IL 61801. Reviews trade and paperback books for young adults.

Appraisal: Children's Science Books. Boston: Children's Science Book Review Committee, Boston Univ. School of Education, 606 Commonwealth Ave., Boston, MA 02215. Reviews trade books in science and mathematics for children from preschool to high school.

The Book Report: The Journal for Junior and Senior High School Libraries, Carolyn Hamilton, ed. Linworth Publishing, Inc., 2950 N. High St., Box 14466, Columbus, OH 43214. Each issue offers practical articles focused on a particular theme. Evaluative reviews written by school librarians and educators cover books and audiovisual and computer software.

Booklist. American Association of School Librarians, 50 E. Huron St., Chicago, IL 60611. Evaluative reviews of books, media, reference works, computer software, and U.S. government publications for public libraries and school media centers.

Bulletin of the Center for Children's Books. Center for Children's Books, Univ. of Chicago, Box 37005, Chicago, IL 60637. Reviews books for children from pre-K to middle school; lists recently published books for parents; includes award winners, journal articles, and other material about children's books.

Censorship News. National Coalition Against Censorship, 132 W. 43 St., New York, NY 10109. News about book banning and censorship in schools.

Children's Magazine Guide. R. R. Bowker Co., 245 W. 17 St., New York, NY 10011. Elementary school library media specialists may find the professional index in *Children's Magazine Guide* helpful in locating articles by subject. However, the publication primarily indexes popular children's magazines.

Choice. Association of College and Research Libraries, 100 Riverview Center, Middletown, CT 06457. Reviews of print and nonprint media for high schools and colleges.

Classroom Computer Learning. Pitman Learning, Belmont, CA. Subscription address: Peter Li, Inc., 2451 E. River Rd., Dayton, OH 45439. Articles about using computers in classrooms; educational computer software, new textbooks, catalogs, and periodicals about computers are reviewed.

The Computing Teacher. International Council for Computers in Education, 1787 Agate, Univ. of Oregon, Eugene, OR 97403. Information for teachers using or teaching about computers; articles about applications in the curriculum, and reviews of books, software, and films.

Educational Leadership. Association for Supervision and Curriculum Development, 225 N. Washington St., Alexandria, VA 22314. Articles about curriculum development and school administration; reviews of professional books.

EFLA Evaluations. Educational Film Library Association, 45 John St., Suite 301, New York, NY 10038. Reviews of educational films.

Electronic Learning. Scholastic, 900 Sylvan Ave., Englewood Cliffs, NJ 07632. Articles for teachers who are not necessarily computer specialists, including instruction for classroom use of software and managing class records.

The Elementary School Journal. Univ. of Chicago Press, Box 37005, Chicago, IL 60637. Articles about current practices and trends in elementary education.

Emergency Librarian. Dyad Services, Box 46258, Station G, Vancouver, BC V6R 4G6, Canada. Feature articles about services for young people in public and school libraries; reviews magazines and paperbacks for young adults and children; includes records for children and professional books.

English Journal. National Council of Teachers of English, 1111 Kenyon Rd., Urbana, IL 61801. Issues, trends, and practices of teaching the communication arts in secondary schools. Reviews of professional books, media, and computer software for young adults.

Film Library Quarterly. Film Library Information Council, Box 348, Radio City Station, New York, NY 10019. Reviews films, videos, and books about films and reports current happenings in the film world.

High Fidelity. High Fidelity, 825 Seventh Ave., New York, NY 10019. Reviews of equipment and recordings.

Horn Book Magazine. Horn Book, Inc., Park Square Bldg., 31 James Ave., Boston, MA 02116. Reviews hardcover and paperback books for children from preschool to high school. Provides articles about authors, illustrators, and the publishing of children's books.

Interracial Books for Children Bulletin. Council on Interracial Books for Children, Inc., 1841 Broadway, New York, NY 10023. Reviews books about various cultures, minorities, and related issues.

Journal of Learning Disabilities. Professional Press, 633 Third Ave., New York, NY 10017. Articles about various aspects of learning disabilities and reviews of professional publications.

Journal of Youth Services in Libraries. Formerly *Top of the News.* Association for Library Service to Children and Young Adult Services Division, American Library Association, 50 E. Huron St., Chicago, IL 60611. Articles about library services to children and young adults and reviews of professional literature.

Language Arts. National Council of Teachers of English, 1111 Kenyon Rd., Urbana, IL 61801. Articles about teaching, writing, speaking, and reading for elementary school teachers; reviews of children's literature and professional materials.

Media and Methods. American Society of Educators, 1511 Walnut St., Philadelphia, PA 19102. Articles about media projects and their management in the classroom and library. Includes reviews of audiovisual media, AV equipment, and computer software. Columns mention new books and AV media events.

Newsletter on Intellectual Freedom. American Library Association, Committee on Intellectual Freedom, 50 E. Huron St., Chicago, IL 60611. News and information on censorship and issues bearing on intellectual freedom.

The Reading Teacher. International Reading Association, Box 8137, Newark, DE 19714. Articles on trends and issues affecting the teaching of reading.

School Library Journal. Bowker Magazine Group, Cahners Magazine Division, 249 W. 17 St., New York, NY 10011. Articles about current news, trends, and issues in school library media programs, and reviews of books, media, and computer software for children and young adults.

School Library Media Quarterly. American Association of School Librarians, American Library Association, 50 E. Huron St., Chicago, IL 60611. Current research about school library media service and general articles for the school library media specialist, with reviews of professional literature and software.

Science and Children. National Science Teachers Association, 1742 Connecticut Ave., NW, Washington, DC 20009. Articles about teaching science in elementary schools, and reviews of curriculum materials, books, and software.

The Science Teacher. National Science Teachers Association, 1742 Connecticut Ave., NW, Washington, DC 20009. Articles about teaching science in secondary schools, and reviews of professional and young adult books and software.

VOYA: Voice of Youth Advocates. Scarecrow Press, 52 Liberty St., Metuchen, NJ 08840. Current news and articles for public and school librarians who serve young adults, with reviews of books and audiovisual media and professional publications.

Wilson Library Bulletin. H. W. Wilson Co., 950 University Ave., Bronx, NY 10452. Articles on subjects of current interest to librarians, with reviews of reference and trade books and media for adults, young adults, and children; monthly columns on young adult and professional books.

Wired Librarian's Newsletter. c/o Eric Anderson, ed., 393 E. Huron, Jackson, OH 45640. Reviews and discussions about computer hardware and software, offering frank and perceptive comments.

Directory of Publishers

AAAS
American Association for the Advancement of Science
1333 H St., NW
Washington, DC 20005
(202) 326-6459

AASA
American Association of School Administrators
1801 North Moore St.
Arlington, VA 22209
(703) 528-0700

AASL
American Association of School Librarians
50 E. Huron St.
Chicago, IL 60611
(312) 944-6780

ABC-Clio
ABC-Clio
2040 A.P.S. Box 4397
Santa Barbara, CA 93140-4397
1-800-422-2546
(from CA 1-800-824-2103)

AECT
Association for Educational Communications and Technology

1126 16 St., NW
Washington, DC 20036
(202) 466-4780

ALA
American Library Association
50 East Huron St.
Chicago, IL 60611
(312) 944-6780

Ablex
Ablex Publishing Co.
355 Chestnut St.
Norwood, NJ 07648
(201) 767-8450

Academic
Academic Press, Inc.
Subsidiary of Harcourt Brace Jovanovich, Inc.
1250 Sixth Ave.
San Diego, CA 92101
1-800-321-5068

Addison-Wesley
Addison-Wesley Publishing Co., Inc.
Route 128
Reading, MA 01867
(617) 944-3700

Allyn & Bacon
Allyn & Bacon, Inc.
160 Gould St.
Needham Heights, MA 02194
1-800-852-8024

American Association for the Advancement of Science. *See*
AAAS

American Association of School Administrators. *See* AASA

American Association of School Librarians. *See* AASL

American Council on Education
One Dupont Circle
Washington, DC 20036
1-800-257-5755

American Guidance Service
American Guidance Service, Inc.
Publishers' Bldg.
Circle Pines, MN 55014
1-800-328-2560

American Library Association. *See*
ALA

Anti-Defamation League of B'nai
Brith. *See* International Center
for Holocaust Studies

Ashton-Tate
Ashton-Tate Publishing Group
20101 Hamilton Ave.
Torrance, CA 90502
1-800-437-4329

Association for Educational Communications and Technology.
See AECT

Avon
Avon Books
Div. of Hearst Corp.
105 Madison Ave.
New York, NY 10016
1-800-238-0658

Basic Books
Basic Books, Inc.

10 E. 53 St.
New York, NY 10022
1-800-242-7737

Clive Bingley
Clive Bingley Ltd.
7 Ridgmount St.
London WC1E 7AE, England

Book Lures
Box 9450
O'Fallon, MO 63366

Bowker
R. R. Bowker Co.
245 West 17 St.
New York, NY 10011
1-800-521-8110

Brodart
Brodart Co.
500 Arch St.
Williamsport, PA 17705
1-800-233-8467

CIBC. *See* Council on Interracial
Books for Children

Center for Applied Research in
Education
The Center for Applied Research in Education, Inc.
Subs. of Prentice-Hall/Simon &
Schuster
Englewood Cliffs, NJ 07632
(201) 592-2481

Consumer Information Center
Pueblo, CO 81009
1-800-624-0100

Council on Interracial Books for
Children
1841 Broadway
New York, NY 10023
(212) 757-5339

Marcel Dekker
Marcel Dekker, Inc.
270 Madison Ave.
New York, NY 10016
1-800-228-1160

432

Delacorte
  Delacorte Press
  Dell Publishing Co.
  666 Fifth Ave.
  New York, NY 10103
  (212) 765-6500

Doubleday
  666 Fifth Ave.
  New York, NY 10103
  1-800-323-9872

Dover
  Dover Publications, Inc.
  31 East Second St.
  Mineola, NY 11501
  (516) 742-5049

Dutton
  E. P. Dutton
  Division of New American Library
  2 Park Ave.
  New York, NY 10016
  1-800-526-0275

Educational Facilities Laboratories
  c/o Academy for Educational Development
  680 Fifth Ave.
  New York, NY 10019
  (212) 397-0040

Foundation Center
  The Foundation Center
  79 Fifth Ave.
  New York, NY 10003
  (212) 620-4230

Franklin Watts. *See* Watts

Freline
  Freline, Inc.
  Box 889, 32 East Ave.
  Hagerstown, MD 21740
  (301) 797-9689

Gale
  Gale Research, Inc.
  Book Tower, Dept. 77748
  Detroit, MI 48276
  1-800-223-GALE

Garland
  Garland Publishing, Inc.
  136 Madison Ave.
  New York, NY 10016
  (212) 686-7492

Greenwood
  Greenwood Press, Inc.
  Box 5007
  88 Post Rd. West
  Westport, CT 06881
  (203) 226-3571

Harcourt Brace Jovanovich
  Harcourt Brace Jovanovich, Inc.
  6277 Sea Harbor Dr.
  Orlando, FL 32821
  (407) 345-2000

Harper & Row
  Harper & Row, Publishers, Inc.
  10 East 53 St.
  New York, NY 10022
  1-800-242-7737

Harvard Univ. Press
  Harvard University Press
  79 Garden St.
  Cambridge, MA 02138
  (617) 495-2600

Hastings House
  Hastings House Publishers
  9 East 40 St.
  New York, NY 10016
  1-800-526-7626

Haworth Press
  The Haworth Press, Inc.
  12 West 32 St.
  New York, NY 10001
  1-800-342-6978

Heinemann Educational Books
  Heinemann Educational Books, Inc.
  Subs. of Octopus Publishing Group PLC
  70 Court St.
  Portsmouth, NH 03801
  (603) 431-7894

433

Hi Willow Research
Hi Willow Research and Publishing
Box 266
Littleton, CO 80160
(303) 770-1220

H. Holt
Henry Holt & Co.
115 W. 18 St.
New York, NY 10011
1-800-247-3912

Holt
Holt, Rinehart & Winston, Inc.
111 Fifth Ave.
New York, NY 10003
1-800-782-4479

Horn Book
Horn Book, Inc.
31 St. James Ave.
Park Square Bldg.
Boston, MA 02116
1-800-325-1170

Houghton Mifflin
Houghton Mifflin Co.
One Beacon St.
Boston, MA 02138
(617) 725-5000

Indiana Univ. Press
Indiana University Press
Tenth & Morton Sts.
Bloomington, IN 47405
(812) 335-4203

International Center for Holocaust
Studies
Anti-Defamation League of B'nai
B'rith
823 United Nations Plaza
New York, NY 10017
(212) 490-2525

International Communications Industries Association
3150 Spring St.
Fairfax, VA 22031
(703) 273-7200

Knopf
Alfred A. Knopf, Inc.
201 E. 50 St.
New York, NY 10022
(212) 751-2600

Libraries Unlimited
Libraries Unlimited, Inc.
Dept. 47, Box 3988
Englewood, CO 80155-3988
1-800-237-6124

Library of Congress
Div. of U.S. Government
Washington, DC 20540
(202) 287-5000

Library Professional
Library Professional Publications
The Shoe String Press, Inc.
925 Sherman Ave.
Box 4327
Hamden, CT 06514
(203) 248-6307

Lippincott
J. B. Lippincott Co.
East Washington Square
Philadelphia, PA 19105
(215) 238-4200

Little, Brown
Little, Brown & Co., Inc.
34 Beacon St.
Boston, MA 02108
1-800-343-9204

Longman
Longman, Inc.
Longman Bldg.
95 Church St.
White Plains, NY 10601
(914) 993-5000

McFarland
McFarland & Company, Inc.
Box 611
Jefferson, NC 28640
(919) 246-4460

McGraw-Hill
 McGraw-Hill, Inc.
 1221 Ave. of the Americas
 New York, NY 10020
 1-800-262-4729

Macmillan
 Macmillan Publishing Co.
 866 Third Ave.
 New York, NY 10022
 (212) 702-2000

Merrill Publishing
 Merrill Publishing Co.
 1300 Alum Creek Dr.
 Columbus, OH 43216
 1-800-848-1567

NAL
 New American Library
 1633 Broadway
 New York, NY 10019
 (212) 397-8000

NCTE
 National Council of Teachers of
 English
 111 Kenyon Rd.
 Urbana, IL 61801
 (217) 328-3870

NEA
 National Education Association
 1201 16 St., NW
 Washington, DC 20036
 (202) 822-7250

NYPL
 New York Public Library
 Committee on Books for Young
 Adults
 455 Fifth Ave.
 New York, NY 10016
 (212) 340-0833

National Council of Teachers of English. *See* NCTE

National Education Association. *See*
 NEA

Neal-Schuman
 Neal-Schuman Publishers, Inc.
 23 Leonard St.
 New York, NY 10013
 (212) 925-8650

New American Library. *See* NAL

New York Public Library. *See* NYPL

Oliver-Nelson
 Oliver-Nelson Books
 Div. of Thomas Nelson, Inc.
 Nelson Place at Elm Hill Pike
 Nashville, TN 37214
 1-800-251-4000

Oryx
 The Oryx Press
 2214 North Central at Encanto
 Suite 103
 Phoenix, AZ 85004
 1-800-457-ORYX

Oxford Univ. Press
 Oxford University Press
 200 Madison Ave.
 New York, NY 10016
 1-800-451-7556

Pantheon
 Pantheon Books, Inc.
 201 E. 50 St.
 New York, NY 10022
 (212) 751-2600

PEN American Center
 568 Broadway
 New York, NY 10012
 (212) 334-1660

Penguin
 Penguin Books, Inc.
 40 W. 23 St.
 New York, NY 10010
 1-800-631-3577

Pennsylvania Department of Education
Bureau of State Library
Div. of School Library Media Services
333 Market St.
Harrisburg, PA 17126-0333
(717) 787-1953

Prentice-Hall
Prentice-Hall, Inc.
Div. of Simon & Schuster
Route 9W
Englewood Cliffs, NJ 07632
1-800-634-2863

Princeton Univ. Press
Princeton University Press
Princeton, NJ 08540
(609) 452-4900

Professional Press
Professional Press Books
Div. of Fairchild Books & Visuals
7 E. 12 St.
New York, NY 10003
(212) 741-6640

Rand McNally
Rand McNally & Co.
Box 7600
Chicago, IL 60680
1-800-323-4070

Rutgers Univ. Press
Rutgers University Press
109 Church St.
New Brunswick, NJ 08901
(201) 932-7764

St. Martin's
St. Martin's Press, Inc.
175 Fifth Ave.
New York, NY 10010
1-800-221-7945

Scarecrow
Scarecrow Press
52 Liberty St.
Box 4167
Metuchen, NJ 08840
1-800-537-7107

Scott, Foresman
Scott, Foresman and Co.
1900 East Lake Ave.
Glenview, IL 60025
(312) 729-3000

Southern Illinois Univ. Press
Southern Illinois University Press
Box 3697
Carbondale, IL 62901
(618) 453-2281

Syracuse Univ. Press
Syracuse University Press
1600 Jamesville Ave.
Syracuse, NY 13244
(315) 443-2597

Teachers College Press
Teachers College
Columbia University
1234 Amsterdam Ave.
New York, NY 10027
1-800-356-0409

U.S. Department of Education
400 Maryland Ave., SW
Washington, DC 20202
(202) 245-3192

U.S. Government Printing Office
Publication Order Branch
Stop SSOP
Washington, DC 20402

Univ. of Chicago Press
University of Chicago Press
5801 Ellis Ave.
Chicago, IL 60637
1-800-621-2736

Van Nostrand Reinhold
Div. of International Thomson
Publishing Corp.
115 Fifth Ave.
New York, NY 10003
(212) 254-3232

Viking
Viking Press
40 West 23 St.
New York, NY 10010
1-800-631-3577

Vintage
  Vintage Press/Random House
  201 East 50 St.
  New York, NY 10022
  1-800-638-6460

Russ Walter
  Russ Walter Publishers
  22 Ashland St.
  Somerville, MA 02144
  (617) 666-2666

Watts
  Franklin Watts, Inc.
  Subs. of Grolier, Inc.
  387 Park Ave. S.
  New York, NY 10016
  1-800-672-6672

Wiley
  John Wiley & Sons, Inc.
  605 Third Ave.
  New York, NY 10158
  (212) 850-6000

Wilson
  H. W. Wilson Co.
  950 University Ave.
  Bronx, NY 10452
  1-800-367-6770
  NY 1-800-462-6060

Author Index

Title Index

Subject Index

461

467

Ho, May Lein. *AppleWorks for School Librarians,* 17

Curriculum planning
Bradley, Leo H. *Curriculum Leadership and Development Handbook,* 290
Brubaker, Dale L. *Curriculum Planning: The Dynamics of Theory and Practice,* 340
Bruner, Jerome S. *The Process of Education,* 342
Clendening, Corinne P., and Ruth Ann Davies. *Challenging the Gifted: Curriculum Enrichment and Acceleration Models,* 265
Loertscher, David V. *Taxonomies of the School Library Media Program,* 307

Curriculum reform
Brandwein, Paul F. *Memorandum: On Renewing Schooling and Education,* 338

Curriculum support role
Davies, Ruth Ann. *The School Library Media Program: Instructional Force for Excellence,* 293
Eisenberg, Michael B., and Robert E. Berkowitz. *Curriculum Initiative: An Agenda and Strategy for Library Media Programs,* 297
Loertscher, David V., and May Lein Ho. *Computerized Collection Development for School Library Media Centers,* 309
Pennsylvania State Library. *Integrating Information-Management Skills: A Process for Incorporating Library Media Skills into Content Areas,* 312

Cybernetics
Roszak, Theodore. *The Cult of Information,* 373

Data base management systems
Byers, Robert A. *Everyman's Database Primer: Featuring dBASE III Plus,* 355

Costa, Betty, and Marie Costa. *A Micro Handbook for Small Libraries and Media Centers,* 357
Horenstein, Henry, and Eliot Tarlin. *Computerwise: An Introduction to Understanding, Buying and Using a Personal Computer,* 366

Data base vendors
Aversa, Elizabeth S., and Jacqueline C. Mancall. *Management of Online Search Services in Schools,* 352
Borgman, Christine L. *Effective Online Searching: A Basic Text,* 354
Glossbrenner, Alfred. *How to Look It Up Online: Get the Information Edge with Your Personal Computer,* 365
Parisi, Lynn S., and Virginia L. Jones. *Directory of Online Databases and CD-ROM Resources for High Schools,* 311

Data bases
Rowley, Jennifer. *Computers for Libraries,* 376

Data gathering
Schmid, William T. *Media Center Management: A Practical Guide,* 31

dBase III
Byers, Robert A. *Everyman's Database Primer: Featuring dBASE III Plus,* 355

Demonstration schools
Brandwein, Paul F. *Memorandum: On Renewing Schooling and Education,* 338

Depression in teenagers
Johnston, Jerry. *Why Suicide? What Parents and Teachers Must Know to Save Our Kids,* 412

Descriptive cataloging
Scham, Alan M. *Managing Special Collections,* 88

471